NINTH JUSTICE

NINTH JUSTICE
The Fight for Bork

Patrick B. McGuigan
and
Dawn M. Weyrich

*with an analysis of media coverage by
R. H. Bork, Jr.,
and the Judicial Notice interview with
Judge Robert H. Bork*

Free Congress Research and Education Foundation
Washington, D.C.

Distributed by arrangement with
University Press of America
4720 Boston Way
Lanham, Maryland 20706

Library of Congress Cataloging-in-Publication Data

McGuigan, Patrick B.
Ninth justice: the fight for Bork.
Includes bibliographical references and index.
1. United States. Supreme Court—Officials and employees—
Selection and appointment.   2. Judges—United States—Selection
and appointment.   3. Bork, Robert H.   4. Political questions and
judicial power—United States.   I. Weyrich, Dawn M.
II. Bork, R.H. (Robert Heron).   III. Title.
KF8742.M33   ✓1990   347.73'26'092   89–23661
347.3072609

ISBN 0–942522–17–6 (pbk. : alk. paper)

 The paper used in this publication meets the minimum requirements of
American National Standard for Information Sciences—Permanence
of Paper for Printed Library Materials, ANSI Z39.48–1984.

for Pam
and for the 42 who voted yes

"[I]f a king is about to march
against another king to do battle with him,
will he not sit down first
and consider whether,
with ten thousand men,
he can withstand an enemy coming against him
with twenty thousand?"

—Jesus (Luke 14:31)
New American Bible

Contents

Preface   ix

Foreword: The Story After the Story   xiii
  Winter 1987–88
  Late Fall 1987
  August 1988

Chapter One: The Chance of a Presidency   1
  June 26–July 1, 1987

Chapter Two: The War Begins   11
  July 1987

Chapter Three: A Steamy Month—And a Steamier Battle   53
  August 1987

Chapter Four: Smears, Distortions and Lies   73
  September 1–14, 1987

Chapter Five: "His Own Best Witness"   105
  September 15–19, 1987

Chapter Six: The Tide Shifts   135
  September 20–October 4, 1987

Chapter Seven: Liberal Victory   171
  October 4–23, 1987

Afterword: One Year Later   207

References   227

Essay: "The Media, Special Interests, and the Bork
   Nomination," by R. H. Bork, Jr.   245

Appendices   279
   Appendix A: "Mendacity is No Defense: An Analysis of
     Larry Tribe's testimony," by Patrick B. McGuigan   279
   Appendix B: The *Conservative Digest/Judicial Notice*
     interview with Judge Robert H. Bork   285
   Appendix C: Larry Tribe's America   305

Biographical Notes   307

Index   309

Preface

This book was conceived a few weeks after the defeat of Judge Robert Bork's nomination to the Supreme Court. Besides providing what I hope is a useful chronological narration of the confirmation battle, my purpose in writing this is to provide journalists, historians and fellow conservatives with an "inside" look at how I and, to some extent, Dan Casey—the other principal leader of the "outside" conservative groups supporting the distinguished jurist—approached the problems and opportunities the Bork nomination afforded. Further, I offer in some detail the lessons I believe conservatives and other supporters of limited constitutional government should draw from the confrontation. Finally, I offer many personal recollections from what thus far is easily the most significant four months of my life.

Writing this was not easy. The Bork battle itself began just as I was finishing the editing of a lengthy book, *The Judges War*. The entire purpose of that endeavor was to help sustain an intellectual and political atmosphere of fair play on judicial nominations. I had hoped to prevent, with that book, the emergence of exactly that state of affairs which the Bork battle brought to fruition.

By the time *The Judges War* was released in September 1987, it was clear to me one objective of the book was already trending toward failure: Adherence or perceived acquiescence to the liberal judicial agenda had replaced faithfulness to the Constitution as the standard by which judicial nominees would be judged. By the end of October, devastating failure for me came again with the defeat of the good Judge Bork.

In the hopes this new book might succeed, let me state at the outset that my goals are the modest ones indicated in the opening paragraph of this preface. The idea is merely to offer an accurate narration and supply fresh information on what motivated the outside groups at various points in the struggle.

This book is *not* intended to serve as the final word on a political confrontation which, I suspect, will provide virtually limitless opportunities for the explorations of journalists, political scientists and legal analysts. I do hope this book offers a starting point for at least those who suspect Judge Bork was mistreated, and that his supporters were insufficiently prepared for the most important domestic policy confrontation of President Reagan's second term.

Not quite everything is here. Even in a story where I consciously decided to pass on a good deal of my recollections and contemporaneous materials, there are some matters I have chosen not to reveal.

A brief word about organization. Except for the foreword and afterword, the treatment is chronological, beginning with Justice Powell's retirement and concluding with Judge Bork's defeat. This straight narration of events, set in regular type, is largely the work of my co-author, although I assisted in the compilation of voluminous data from my files, and offered help in giving the reader context and trends. My personal reflections and recollections of events as they unfolded, and the narration of events as they transpired at Coalitions for America— in fact, all of the first person writing save for this preface (and the appendix on Larry Tribe's testimony)—are in italics.

I am extremely grateful to Dawn Weyrich, my co-author. She is an excellent reporter and a gifted writer. It was my good fortune to assign her the task of telling the tale, from A to Z, based on the existing, published data. We are particularly grateful to John Stuart, Cleatis Moore and Paul Gannon, the Free Congress computer gurus who guided our efforts to produce this lengthy document on the in-house computer.

I am also appreciative of the excellent work of Harold Rymer, my intern in the summer of 1988, who helped reconstruct the data on activities undertaken at Coalitions for America, the conservative organization that worked with the American Conservative Union in coordinating pro-Bork activity. Bill Myers of the Free Congress Center for State Policy kindly read the manuscript and offered helpful suggestions which improved the text.

Whatever merit this book has is due in part to the willingness of several friends, including Dan Casey, to read the entire manuscript. Their honest comments helped improve this work, though of course I am solely responsible for any remaining weaknesses.

Special gratitude goes to my colleagues at the Free Congress Foun-

dation, in particular Paul Weyrich and Jeffery Troutt, the President of
the Foundation and former Director of the Center for Law and Democracy, respectively.

Finally, my deepest gratitude goes to my family. My son Stefan
misses the beard (see Chapters 2 and 7), but his twin sister Erin likes
the smooth face better than that "itchy thing". Josef, the oldest,
understands and regrets the fact that the judge didn't make it, while
Andrew, the youngest, is just glad to have me around a lot more than I
was during the months of July–October 1987.

My wife Pamela has for these many years endured hours, days and
weeks of separation to support my work, but never so intense a time
of tension and sadness in our life as the final weeks of Bork's struggle,
when it gradually became clear to me he would not prevail. It is with
abiding love that this book is dedicated to Pam. She, in turn, asked me
to extend the dedication to the 42 Senators who voted yes.

The campaign of lies and vilification, unhappily, succeeded in securing a majority of the votes cast in the Senate. The Big Lie technique,
incredibly but effectively, intruded itself into the process of legislative
deliberation over the custodians of our sacred liberties. The brilliant
constitutional separation of powers was, for a time, undermined via
the mechanisms of high dollar political advertising and deliberately
distortive innuendo.

The liars got their way on this one.

They got their way because those who knew what Judge Bork stood
for were not really ready to fight for his confirmation. Including me.
Among those of us who failed to get ready for the most important
political confrontation of the Reagan presidency, a sense of shame and
outrage over what was done to a good man—and, more ominously, to
the institution which helps to guard our freedom—should be the basis
for continued committment and principled action.

The defeat of Bork cannot be the end, any more than—in presidential politics—the defeat of Barry Goldwater was the end. As Goldwater
led to 1980, so Bork's defeat can lead to restoration of principled
jurisprudence—if not in 1989, then perhaps in 1993 or even some
further year. The American structure does not guarantee anyone
victories, even restorative victories. It does, still, guarantee us a
structure within which to try.

Ironically, the Senate—at least in this case—seemed to say it does
not want to re-establish its role, with the House of Representatives, as
the prime legislators in the American system of government. The

senators may, indeed, have made such a choice. But that is not the *constitutional* choice.

Nor, I believe, will it be the ultimate verdict of the American people. It is upon the wish, the hope, the belief in a final victory for democratic governance that I leave this fight behind, confident in the ultimate restoration of principled jurisprudence. It was Abraham Lincoln (but some southerners insist it was Woodrow Wilson) who said it well: "I would rather fail in a cause that I know will some day triumph than to triumph in a cause I know some day will fail."

I am mindful that, as my childhood political hero John Fitzgerald Kennedy put it more than a quarter century ago: "Here on earth, God's work must truly be our own."

> pbm
> Washington, D.C.
> December 1988

Foreword:
The Story After the Story

Winter 1987–88: Another Kennedy Comes to Washington

The months between Robert Bork's defeat and the eventual Senate confirmation of Anthony Kennedy as a justice of the U.S. Supreme Court were a time of incredible frustration for conservatives. Since the 1986 elections, political insiders had recognized that the reality of Democrat control of the U.S. Senate—after six years of Republican domination of the upper chamber—severely crimped President Reagan's ability to move forward with any serious domestic or international initiatives—let alone continue aggressive efforts to reestablish the abiding concepts of the rule of law, separated powers and restrained jurisprudence.

But understandable frustration is one thing, outright despair is another. An intensive degree of cynicism settled in among the conservative grass roots, coinciding with the Administration's increasing drift toward accommodation of the permanent power structure in the nation's capital. Cynicism and despair are all too understandable, but nonetheless must be combatted, even given the shocking spectre of a "conservative" administration in the process of surrendering in Central America, accommodating our Soviet enemies in Europe and around the world, acquiescing in the tax increase policies of Democrats, and pursuing a non-confrontational policy on the most important domestic issue of this era: restoration of the rule of law through the elevation of a principled majority to the Supreme Court.

(Later, the sense of conservative drift and despair dissipated somewhat as the 1988 presidential campaign progressed with George

Bush's nomination, his selection of Dan Quayle as a running mate, and the immediate emergence of an aggressive Bush campaign style. For some, memories of the Bork battle eased even more when the jurist became an issue after the second presidential debate, and appeared to contribute to Bush's ultimate victory. In a way, the Bush-Quayle campaign may have paid a modest first installment on what is owed the Left for the attacks on Bork.)

But the despair that permeated conservative ranks from late 1987 through the summer of 1988 was palpable and real. No one can fault Ronald Reagan for his selection pattern when it comes to Supreme Court justices—it was his post–1986 follow up that could rightly be questioned.

Nonetheless, when the President picked Ninth U.S. Circuit Court of Appeals Judge Anthony Kennedy as his nominee to the Supreme Court late in 1987, I thought to myself: "Well, here we go again." I fully expected a knock down drag out full scale fight from the beginning.

But those who so successfully thwarted Reagan's early efforts to replace Justice Powell surprised me once again by constraining their initial comments. On reflection, I realized once again that they've been at this inside Washington game a lot longer than conservatives, and in point of fact they were reacting in just the proper modulated tone, holding their fire while aggressively researching his past decisions for every distortable nuance.

Despite his clearly conservative record, Anthony Kennedy on the Circuit bench was never an aggressive, articulate advocate of judicial restraint. Thus, the best efforts of the anti-Bork forces never found materials for distortion comparable to Judge Bork's incisive, penetrating assertions for the judicial philosophy of the Founding Fathers.

I waited throughout the weeks before the Kennedy hearings, believing the Left would probably follow the sort of strategy they employed in opposing the confirmation of William Rehnquist as Chief Justice, waiting to turn up the heat until the hearings began. Or, perhaps, they would even pursue the low key (until the end) strategy they employed in opposing the elevation of Alex Kozinski to the Ninth U.S. Circuit Court of Appeals, actually waiting until after the Judiciary Committee hearings in 1985 to make opposition to Kozinski a party line issue. With Democrats pressured to oppose Kozinski, he only secured confirmation by ten votes. Rehnquist, of course, won somewhat more easily—but after watching the other side "practice" on Manion, Kozinski, Rehnquist, Bork and other good men, I was scarcely com-

fortable about the Kennedy confirmation's chances as I pondered the Senate Judiciary Committee.

After Judge Kennedy's confirmation, I found myself talking to reporters from all over the country who were calling me to express disappointment at the lack of a fight. "Pat, isn't this a victory for the moderates?" they asked.

The moderates? Professor Laurence Tribe of Harvard called Judge Kennedy "refreshingly moderate." But Tribe, one of Robert Bork's chief executioners, apparently made a decision. Larry, you see, argues several cases before the High Court every year, for handsome legal fees (this is a capitalist system, you know). As long as Judge Kennedy was going to make it, there was no need to antagonize him, was there? Larry probably figured he might as well try to be on Judge Kennedy's "right" side.

After you go through a few of these things, you learn to recognize the honest souls among your opponents, men like Professor Alan Dershowitz, Tribe's colleague at Harvard Law School. During the height of the judges war of 1985–88, I was shocked by occasionally being on the same side of a question as Dershowitz. When it came to Judge Kennedy he was apparently reading the same cases I was, and concluded, "What President Reagan seems to have in Anthony Kennedy is an agreeable judge who votes like Judge Robert Bork and writes like Lewis F. Powell, Jr."

Credit Dershowitz, surely, for prescience. Tony Mauro of USA Today/Legal Times *quoted Herman Schwartz (February 17, 1989) to good effect concerning Kennedy: "Reagan lost the [Bork] battle and won the war." In his "Courtside" analysis, Mauro observed of Anthony Kennedy's first year: "[I]t seems he is following Scalia's pattern, though more slowly and subtly."*

In truth, Judge Kennedy's nomination stood four square in the tradition of Ronald Reagan's previous Supreme Court choices. There was some sniping going on in the winter of 1987–88 about the purity of this cautious conservative nominee, including some from brethren who got spoiled by the aggressive articulation of strict constructionist jurisprudence which flowed from the writings of many of Ronald Reagan's nominees. While that articulation is something I wholeheartedly endorsed, it is always a mistake to let the perfect be the enemy of the good. If Robert Bork was the perfect, Anthony Kennedy was the good. If Robert Bork was this generation's nearest equivalent to James Madison, the father of the Constitution, Anthony Kennedy is a reasonable approximation of Daniel Carroll of Maryland—a distinguished

*patriot who assured ratification of the Constitution in his home state
(and one of only two Catholics to sign the document).*

*Anthony Kennedy's nomination must have caused furrowed brows
of worry at the American Civil Liberties Union. Judge Kennedy had
participated in a staggering 400 cases involving crime (1,000 dealing
with other issues) during his eleven years as a circuit judge. He had
actually written in more than 100 of those criminal cases. He dissented
from the majority in an important Arizona case, saying that the death
penalty should be upheld for the murderer of a reporter. Although the
majority successfully thwarted justice in that instance, it was Judge
Kennedy who wanted to allow evidence against a defendant gained
from what his Ninth Circuit colleagues regarded as an invalid search
warrant. The Supreme Court later used the case,* U.S. v. Leon, *to
adopt a "good faith" exception to the controversial exclusionary rule.*

*As long ago as 1976, Judge Kennedy held (before the good guys
started winning cases like this) that pornographic materials seized by
federal officers were admissible against a defendant in an obscenity
prosecution. He voted in 1985 to allow into evidence the videotaped
testimony of a dying member of the notorious Hell's Angels. The
admitted evidence was against other members of the motorcycle
"club" who had committed several brutal murders.*

In the Beller v. Middendorf *case, Judge Kennedy wrote a unanimous
opinion upholding the constitutionality of U.S. Navy regulations which
provided for the discharge of those who participate in homosexual
activities.*

*As for fans of forced busing, how could they be pleased with the
good judge's principled ruling in a 1977 case, in which he found there
is no constitutional obligation to maintain a certain racial mix in the
schools, only a requirement to refrain from forced segregation by race
(sounds as if he believes in the Fourteenth Amendment)?*

Then there's the famous comparable worth case—yes, it's the comparable worth case, AFSCME v. Washington. *Feminists had hoped to
force the state of Washington to adopt the comparable worth scheme
for public employees, an idea the late Clarence Pendleton described
as "the looniest idea since Looney Tunes." Judge Kennedy found that
we do not have to pretend that janitors and librarians perform "comparable" economic activities, thus sensibly leaving to the marketplace
the determination of pay levels for differing job categories in the public
sector.*

*What must have made the liberals more nervous than anything else,
and what should have given at least some comfort to conservatives, is*

that Anthony Kennedy looks *an awful lot like a conservative, a family man whose life exudes traditional American values. A practicing and devout Catholic, Judge Kennedy has been married for some 25 years to Mary Davis. They have three outstanding children, Justin, Gregory and Kristin. When you look at them, you probably say, "Reminds me of Mr. Jones, that pillar of the community down the street." One friend of mine at the time of Kennedy's nomination remarked: "My God, their house looked like Beaver Cleaver's."*

A young woman close to the (Anthony) Kennedy family told me that winter, "I've always been amazed that they could raise three such wonderful kids in this day and age." Yes, there's a lot of love in Anthony Kennedy's family; a sincere kind of love that pours out into the lives of all those with whom they are close. One such man, who had known Kennedy for more than a decade, told me, "His gentle demeanor can fool people. Everyone who [knew] him at the Ninth Circuit thinks of him as a strong conservative. He's not flamboyant, but he's also not mushy. Sometimes he [used] soft, persuasive language, but [he was] a leader of the conservative wing on the court."

Which reminds me of a story. It was Thursday, February 18, 1988. I was at the White House enjoying the hors d'oeuvres. *Only the day before I'd returned from a stint as Pete du Pont's Deputy Political Director in Iowa and New Hampshire. I was ready to get back to the reporting I love, and the writing on legal questions that engages much of my energy, but the truth is I'd never quite gotten over the heart break and disappointment resulting from the Bork defeat.*

All my instincts told me Kennedy would be a good justice, but the non-stop questions from friends had fed some lingering doubts, despite all the evidence that his judicial philosophy was rock solid interpretivist.

Perhaps the Lord chose that moment to grant me some peace. My doubts went away as the swearing-in ceremony progressed. I sat with Dan Casey of the American Conservative Union and Elizabeth Kepley of Concerned Women for America, the finest advocates Bob Bork could have had during his months in the Washington meat grinder, even though he did not know either of them. We were all a bit transfixed, even after several years in national politics, by the simple decency of Tony Kennedy and his family.

As we joined in a glass of champagne after sharing the privilege of shaking the new justice's hand, Don Baldwin of the National Law Enforcement Council joined us. Then, another soldier from the war walked over, Congressman Hamilton Fish of New York, who was one

*of the four distinguished politicians to introduce Bork at his confirma-
tion hearings. I told him, "There weren't enough guys like you in the
other chamber to get Bork in there."*

*As the five of us chatted, Elizabeth asked me, "Pat, how do you
think Justice Kennedy will do?" I replied, "Justice Kennedy. Sounds
nice. How will he do? I think he'll do just fine." I raised my glass in a
toast and said, "We can't start gloating, 'til he starts voting, but
here's to Anthony Kennedy and the Supreme Court." We all drained
our glasses, but I am pleased to report I refrained from smashing mine
in the nearby fireplace.*

Late Fall 1987:
Ginsburg's Youthful Folly Ends Chance for Supreme Contribution

*The tragic and untimely demise of the nomination of Douglas
Ginsburg underscores pitfalls facing most of a generation of Americans, including many conservatives. Doug Ginsburg's mature philosophy of the law—his approach to legal questions—stands square in the
tradition of all of Ronald Reagan's nominations to the Supreme Court.*

*His personal life of some years back, however, became the target of
opportunity for elements of a media establishment determined to
prevent Ronald Reagan, in the wake of the Bork defeat, from elevating
a 41 year old non-smoker to the High Court. And conservatives
themselves helped push Ginsburg out of the picture. Incredibly, a
series of previous FBI checks had never revealed Ginsburg's occasional use of marijuana many years ago.*

*The first time the matter arose, like a scene out of a bad political
novel, was when he was asked about it during one of his meetings with
a conservative member of the Senate. As this was happening, energetic reporters were on the trail of the long dissipated marijuana
smoke. The first journalist to break the story gave it priority treatment.
Thus, the beginning of the end had begun.*

*When Ken Cribb called me from the White House with the news on
Thursday, November 5, 1987, forty-five minutes before Judge Ginsburg's statement acknowledged past marijuana use, I immediately
asked, "A key thing is, I assume he told the truth on his government
employment form and in the interviews with the FBI?" It turned out
that Ginsburg did tell the truth on all his forms, but he'd never been
asked a question about past marijuana use. To me the significant thing
was his ready admission of a long-past illegal activity, but I guess I
need to "grow up."*

Virtually the only light moment in those couple of days, for me, came when Pete du Pont was ambushed by reporters with the information about Ginsburg. Pete supports (and I back him on this) a program for drug testing of young people who, if they test positive for drug abuse, will lose their driver's licenses for a year (or not get it in the first place). Asked what should be done about Ginsburg, du Pont replied, "I think the Senate ought to confirm him—and take away his driver's license."

To many conservatives it seemed obvious that marijuana use—even if many years ago—constituted sufficient justification to abandon Judge Ginsburg. And so, most conservative leaders cooperated fully with the killing of the nomination. Secretary of Education Bill Bennett became the guy who delivered the message that Ginsburg ought to withdraw for the sake of the President. I admire Bill Bennett immensely, and I've been active in anti-drug efforts since my days as a teacher in the late 1970s, but I agree with my colleague Paul Weyrich, National Chairman of Coalitions for America: the President should have delivered his own message.

Further, an effort to put Ginsburg's errors in context—not to explain them away, but to acknowledge them as mistakes and use the controversy as an opportunity to discuss his enlightened judicial philosophy— might have borne fruit. Dan Casey of the American Conservative Union suggested a national speaking tour by the nominee himself to focus the debate aggressively on judicial philosophy, but this was apparently just not in the picture.

No, in Washington, conservatives who get in trouble are frequently expected quietly to slip out of the picture. That's not what Bob Bork did, praise God, and it's not what we wanted him to do. Given the very different nature of his problems, most conservatives wanted Doug Ginsburg to just go away, but I did not. (Orrin Hatch was also among those who continued to back Ginsburg as his support evaporated among conservatives.)

I was obviously in the minority, working in dozens of frenzied conversations with friends all over the country, trying to convince them of all the reasons we could and should stick with the nominee. In brotherly ways, the message was the same over and over: "It just can't be, Pat, he's got to go."

Within 48 hours of the news about marijuana, he did. In doing so he praised President and Mrs. Reagan for "leading the fight" against drug abuse and said, "I hope that the young people of this country, including my own daughters, will learn from my mistake and heed the

Reagans' message." He expressed regret that he would not get to share "with the American people my views about justice and the role of courts in our society." It just wasn't meant to be.

I realize, in a way my comrade conservatives cannot, what was lost in the collapse of the Ginsburg nomination. Certainly, I much prefer to live in a country where citizens oppose drug abuse and work steadily for the eradication of both supply and demand. As a former teacher who occasionally saw stoned students in class, I long ago left behind any libertarian leanings on drug issues. But I also recognize the irony in the truth that an unwillingness among conservatives to grant absolution for long gone mistakes kept a young, vibrant conservative version of William O. Douglas off the bench.

My perspective on Doug Ginsburg is "skewed", I suppose, from having observed him in action for five years. I met him in 1983 and took him as I found him: One of the brightest, ablest, and most principled conservatives in the Reagan Administration. In one internal confrontation in the Department of Justice after another, he was on the right side, working to advance conservative values within the halls of power, while serving all the people of the country through reasoned enforcement of the anti-trust provisions.

In June of 1988, I had the great honor to introduce Doug Ginsburg to my father and mother, at a reception I sponsored in honor of my folks during a visit they made to the nation's capital. When I introduced Doug to Daddy, I kept it simple: "This is Doug Ginsburg, one of the finest men I know."

Unhappily, my countrymen were deprived, at least for a time, of the chance to know the witty and capable conservative it is my honor to call a friend, the dedicated public servant and restrained jurist who has stood with Ronald Reagan's principles throughout his time in government service.

August 1988: Grin, Don't Gloat

For the third time in as many years, I was addressing a meeting of the Heritage Foundation's gathering of the Third Generation. A regular presentation and discussion, the Third Generation meetings bring together conservatives born since 1953 (I just make the cut). Tonight my purpose was to summarize the 1987–88 term of the U.S. Supreme Court.

Somewhat tongue-in-cheek, Ben Hart, moderator of these sessions, and I had crafted three questions for me to answer in my conclusions.

After presenting some of the nuances of the 1987–88 term of the Court, I submitted to the group the questions and my answers:

1. Is Chief Justice Rehnquist moving to the center? No.

2. Is Antonin Scalia the greatest justice since John Marshall? Probably.

3. Can Anthony Kennedy be the answer to conservatives' prayers? Maybe. All the early evidence is good.

My message to Kepley, Casey and Baldwin—and Congressman Fish if he is interested—is this: Grin, Don't Gloat.

Chapter One

The Chance of a Presidency

Despite the approach of his eightieth birthday and an exhausting battle with prostate cancer that involved major surgery in 1985, Supreme Court Justice Lewis F. Powell Jr. seemed determined to cling to the bench until Ronald Reagan's term in the White House expired. But as 1987 in Washington, D.C. matured into another sticky summer, the Justice's son, Lewis F. Powell III, himself a lawyer, gently reminded his dad, "It's a whole lot better to go out when some people may be sorry than it is to wait until, when you decide to go . . . people say, 'Thank God, we got rid of that old gent.' "[1] So the ailing Powell took his cue and resigned from the nation's highest court on June 26. "For me, age 80 suggests retirement," he said in parting.[2] Later that day, the remaining eight Justices adjourned for their summer recess.

I was sitting at my desk engaged in yet another morning of trying to clear it of the seemingly never-ending stacks of paper which come in the door every day. I figured I must be doing something right—the sheer volume of work was sure better than the alternative.

At the far left corner of my desk, about nine inches thick, was the nearly-completed manuscript for The Judges War, *the Free Congress Foundation's effort to reframe the debate in the accelerating "war" surrounding the President's judicial nominees. Horrified at the ordeal men like Dan Manion and Chief Justice Rehnquist had faced on their paths to confirmation, I had designed the book in the fall of 1986 after conversations with my colleague Paul Weyrich and allies in judicial reform circles. I was looking forward to just another few days of work,*

1

hoping to close the compilation of essays before the Fourth of July holiday.

A time of transition was upon our organization. Only yesterday Connie Marshner had chaired her last meeting of the Library Court coalition. The woman who hired me to work for Paul Weyrich was leaving to concentrate on being a mother for a few years, and I was losing daily contact with the closest friend I had in the organization. I was, as a result, a bit pensive as the news came.

My summer intern, Les Syren from Notre Dame University Law School, peeked in the door and asked me, "Did you hear about Powell?"

My heart skipped a beat. "What about him?"

"He's having a press conference in 10 minutes to announce his resignation."

"Oh—!" I said.

I immediately called John Richardson, the Attorney General's Chief of Staff. John's receptionist told me he was in a meeting. For the only time in the several instances I called him over the years, I told her, "I don't care if he's in with the AG, tell him I need him immediately."

John came on the line. "Pat, what's goin' on?", he said, with his distinct Richmond accent.

"John, tell the Attorney General, Brad, Chuck and everyone else I called. Tell them I said, 'If you guys don't do Bork this time, I'm gonna slash my wrists.'"

He roared with laughter. "Now, don't do anything crazy. I think there's a pretty good chance of that. Just keep cool."

I told him, "John, I'm serious about this much: We should have done him last time. It's gonna be a war, but I won't have any trouble explaining to our people that he's worth fighting for. Please do Bork."

I ended my conversation with Richardson this way: "If you need me to call anyone, just say so. We've got to do it right this time."

Then, I called Peter Keisler at the White House Counsel's office. "Peter, tell the big boys if they don't do Bork I'm gonna slash my wrists."

He, too, laughed and replied, "Now, now. Don't do that. We're going to need you, I think. I'll pass your sentiments along."

Briefly, I remembered my book. I called Bruce Fein of the Heritage Foundation, one of the authors.

I got right to the point. "Bruce, we're gonna need a new introduction for the judges book. Could you write it?" He allowed as how he could. I got back to the war.

*I called Dan Casey of the American Conservative Union. He'd
already heard. He always hears stuff before me. Bastard. I volunteered, "I'll call all of the people in the 721 Group [the anti-crime/pro-
judicial reform coalition of some 15—sometimes more—conservative
and law enforcement organizations meeting every two weeks, which
I'd chaired since 1983] and get them to inundate the White House and
the Hill, demanding that it be Bork."*

*Casey replied, "That ought to be a pretty easy sell, don't you
think?" I countered, "I don't trust the jerks to do the right thing, do
you?"*

"Not really."

*So the conservatives spent the first days concentrating on seeing
that Bork was selected. Meanwhile, the liberals began to plan based
on their greater certainty the White House would do the "right" thing.*

Justice Powell, the "swing" vote on the nine-member court, was a
Southern-bred gentleman who rarely worked less than a 70–hour week.
He prided himself on what court observers believed was a case-by-
case approach that belied any judicial philosophy. A conservative
Democrat appointed by President Richard M. Nixon, Powell's votes—
usually favoring the rights of victims over those of criminals, and
easing some government restrictions on business—pleased conservatives. But the Justice often pivoted to the judicial left on social justice
and moral issues, making him the champion of liberals on cases
involving abortion, affirmative action, and school prayer. Conservatives had become less and less enamored with Powell during the last
few terms of his 15 years spent on the high court, prompting Patrick
McGuigan to observe, "This term [1986–87] he essentially picked
sides, and the side he picked was [liberal Justice William J.] Brennan's."[3]

In the flurry surrounding Powell's decision, political liberals began
to fear for the future of their agenda, which had been championed by
an activist-dominated court since Earl Warren rose to Chief Justice on
October 5, 1953. "Oh my God," cried Marsha Levick, executive
director of the National Organization for Women's Legal Defense
Fund, when she heard the news. "I'm appalled. This means a lot of
bad things for the civil rights community."[4]

On the other hand, strict constructionists—those who believe that
judges should interpret the Constitution and not usurp legislative
authority to make law—were ecstatic. "This is the last chance Ronald
Reagan has to leave his mark on the Supreme Court," said Daniel J.

Popeo of the Washington Legal Foundation. Reagan "will have a tremendous opportunity that few presidents have" to influence the Court after the close of his term.[5]

Weeks before, Judge Bork and I had scheduled a lunch with one another for the first time in years. I called his secretary, Judy Carper.
"Is it crazy over there?"
She replied, "It's getting that way."
"Let him know I called. If he wants to cancel I'll understand."
A few minutes later, Bork called me.
"I don't want to get out of the office, to tell you the truth, Pat," he told me.
I reminded him that I had always been sensitive to the possibility that our friendship could become an issue in a confirmation.
He replied, "Don't be silly. If they want to get me, they've got other things they'll go after." We agreed to do the lunch later.
It was just as well we did not try to meet. At my office, the day got progressively crazier. Before the end of the day, our office left at the front desk of our building (this was in the days before we acquired a fax machine) 20 copies of a press packet that included the full text of an interview I'd done with Bork in 1985 for Conservative Digest *and* Judicial Notice, *copies of two of Judge Bork's speeches, including one he had given in 1982 at the Free Congress Foundation's Conference on Judicial Reform, and copies of news articles in which Senator Joe Biden and Tony Podesta of People for the American Way had indicated they could support Bork. My colleague Jeffery Troutt and I had the pleasure of informing the vast majority of the reporters we spoke with in the first two days about Biden's and Podesta's surprising past indications of support.*
We mailed the same material to our judicial media list of 70 other journalists. Troutt also "pre-"prepared statements for both of us based on the assumption the President's choice would be Bork, or perhaps Orrin Hatch or J. Clifford Wallace, the Ninth Circuit Court of Appeals judge.
The Coalitions for America staff called everyone in the 721 Group, triggering them to inundate the White House with demands that Bork be the nominee—or Hatch. Paul Weyrich, who happened to be going to a farewell reception for a White House staffer, hammered the appropriate parties on behalf of Bork. It was a thoroughly exhausting and exhilarating start to a few days that could be characterized the same way.

Powell's unexpected resignation gave Ronald Reagan his last chance to fill a Supreme Court vacancy, and perhaps undo the judicial activism that had plagued its chambers for more than three decades. Reagan successfully placed Justices Sandra Day O'Connor and Antonin Scalia on the High Court in 1981 and 1986, respectively, and elevated Justice William Rehnquist to Chief Justice in 1986. The Reagan appointees, when teamed with Justice Byron White (who usually voted with the conservative bloc in the sharply-divided court) might tip the vote 5 to 4 in favor of strict interpretation, and could provide "the opportunity . . . to roll back 30 years of social and political activism by the Supreme Court," Popeo said. "The activists who have used the Supreme Court as a vehicle for political and social change instead of the ballot box are in big trouble."[6]

President Reagan's successful placement of justices on the Supreme Court had occurred while Republicans were in control of the Senate and the Senate Judiciary Committee was under the chairmanship of Senator Strom Thurmond (R-SC), a close ally to the President. White House officials realized that Powell's replacement would face a hostile Senate, now dominated by Democrats who had seized control of the upper chamber following the 1986 election cycle. Further, the crucial Senate Judiciary Committee of eight Democrats and six Republicans was now chaired by liberal Senator Joseph R. Biden Jr. (D-DE)—also a candidate for his party's presidential nomination.

Biden, anticipating such a fight, realized that his actions as chairman of the Judiciary Committee could determine the future of his bid for the White House. He had placed near the bottom of the field in early national presidential polls. "Like most major political developments in the midst of a campaign, it's an opportunity and a potential problem," said Greg Schneiders, a political consultant for former Arizona Governor Bruce Babbitt, one of Biden's six rivals. "If he handles it well, it's a great opportunity."[7]

Capitalizing on his position, Biden thrust himself into the media spotlight by threatening that a conservative nominee would be in for "big trouble."[8] This was one of the first publicly recorded hints of what President Reagan's choice might face.

I was lonely as I finished The Judges War *book manuscript that weekend. As much as Bork's potenial nomination was on my mind, I was missing Pam and the kids, who were visiting the family in Oklahoma. After a morning of editorial work at the desk, I drove to the National Shrine of the Immaculate Conception, where the Latin Lit-*

urgy Association was holding a convention. I attended the noon service in the crypt church and saw Paul Weyrich. In a brief discussion I described the activity underway to support Bork as the nominee. Paul concurred with everything we were up to, and whispered to me as we parted, "They should have done him the last time."

Biden won media attention when he quickly reversed a number of stands on the judicial confirmation process and the Senate's role in it. In 1979 when liberal Congressman Abner Mikva (D-IL) was nominated to the Court of Appeals Biden declared on the floor of the Senate that the Senators' role in judicial nominations is limited to a probe of a candidate's qualifications.[9] Eight years later, speaking on CBS's "Face the Nation," Biden maintained that he and his colleagues retained the right to reject or accept a nominee on the basis of ideology, or how that person will affect the "balance" of the court. "The Constitution says the president has the right to choose whomever he wished," Biden said. "Conversely, it also indicates that the Senate has equally as much right to insist on ideological purity as the president does."[10]

The Senate's conduct during most judicial nominations in this century conflicted with Biden's claims. Most recently, during the nomination of Justice Rehnquist to chief justice, liberal Democrats attempting to squash his elevation "went through contortions to deflect any appearance that they were opposing Justice Rehnquist because they didn't like his views," New York *Times* reporter Linda Greenhouse noted.[11] An outraged Congressman Robert Walker (R-PA) demanded that Biden be ousted from his position on the Senate Judiciary Committee. "Biden is saying an ideological test should be imposed by the Senate on presidential nominations to the high court, and that is nothing less than a complete misreading of the US Constitution," he said.[12]

In 1968, however, conservative Senator Strom Thurmond (R-SC) had succeeded—largely with the help of Democrats—in killing President Lyndon B. Johnson's nomination of Justice Abe Fortas to the position of Chief Justice through the use of the filibuster. The Senator said at the time that he opposed Fortas' liberal views on such issues as obscenity and crime, noting that he "has shown, by his record on the Supreme Court, that he is not only content with the Court's trend in these cases, but also that he is willing to take these trends to further extremes. By refusing to confirm this nomination, we can reassure a concerned America that standards do exist, and that action will be taken to preserve them."[13]

This whole argument was relatively new in our history, according to liberal University of Michigan Law School Professor Yale Kamisar:

> The modern view is that a president should get his pick once you satisfy considerations of ability, integrity and competence. People only recently have made a contrary argument. But it never came to a test before because presidents really never gave that much weight to ideology. With all respect, a Supreme Court appointment was not considered that important until 20 years ago.[14]

Editorial writers and academics championed both sides of the debate with relish. The Richmond (VA) *Times-Dispatch* argued that the liberal interpretation of "advise and consent" was merely a cover for rejecting a nominee with views unsavory to them:

> Liberal Democrats on the Senate Judiciary Committee, including Chairman Joe Biden and Ted Kennedy, have said they wanted Mr. Reagan to send them a nominee very much like Lewis F. Powell Jr., not someone (in Sen. Biden's words) with "ideologically honed points of view." What they really mean is that because Mr. Powell took the liberal side in a number of celebrated 5–4 decisions, notably on abortion, affirmative action and church-state separation, they want someone who can pass the liberals' own little litmus test and preserve the ideological status quo.[15]

Arguing for the liberal side in a commentary featured by the New York *Times,* Herman Schwartz, professor of constitutional law at the American University, asserted:

> If a Senator thinks a nominee will undermine his conception of the Constitution, the Senator has exactly the same right and duty as the President to protect his conception. It is not just a question of whether the candidate had high grades in law school or is a good and honorable lawyer.[16]

Senator Paul Simon of Illinois, another Judiciary Committee Democrat and presidential hopeful, fanned the fire by telling ABC News that the committee would "proceed with some prudence" unless its members believe the nominee has "balance, is open-minded, is fair, is sensitive to civil rights and civil liberties."[17] Democratic Whip Alan Cranston (D-CA) asked his Democratic colleagues in a letter to build a "solid phalanx" of opposition if the nominee was an "ideological extremist."[18]

But black civil rights leader Roy Innis, who runs the Congress of Racial Equality, argued that such thinking was out of bounds because the Senate's roll is to "deal with the technical competence of a nominee and any question of moral turpitude. Once a person is deemed competent, decent, and law-abiding, there is no other role for the Senate." Innis added, "Joe Biden is one of the brightest members of the Senate, but in this case he is mistaken. It was the intent of the framers [of the Constitution] that the president will decide what balance, if any, the court should have."[19]

Senator Howell Heflin (D-AL), a Judiciary Committee member who often cast the "swing vote" on judicial nominations, seemed to agree. "My general philosophy is that the president has the right to make appointments unless there is an overriding reason why the nominee should not be confirmed," he said. "We ought to look, number one, to qualifications."

But conservative Judiciary Committee member Gordon J. Humphrey (R-NH) seemed to understand something others were missing—that the nomination process this time would be "all about philosophy, and everyone knows it."[20] Nan Aron of the liberal Alliance for Justice proved Humphrey right: "This battle won't involve smoking guns or skeletons," she said. "It's going to come down to philosophy."[21]

Senate Majority Leader Robert C. Byrd (D-WV), also a Judiciary Committee member, threw another wrench in the path of the future Supreme Court nominee by promising that he would "slow down" confirmation unless Republicans abandoned their filibusters on various Democratic bills, including efforts to restrict campaign spending and delay or ban testing of President Reagan's Strategic Defense Initiative. "It might not be a bad idea to say there are equally important matters facing the Senate," he said. "If we're going to have all this stalling by the Republicans, then let's just slow down and take a closer look at this nomination."[22]

In the midst of this brouhaha, the White House was assembling the list of possible replacements for Justice Powell. The top three names leaked to the press were Judge Robert H. Bork of the U.S. Circuit Court of Appeals for the District of Columbia; Senator Orrin G. Hatch (R-UT); and Judge J. Clifford Wallace of the U.S. Court of Appeals in California.

In light of the Democratic Senate majority, White House officials hinted that "confirmability" would be one of the main factors in choosing a nominee. "It's imperative that the Senate begin hearings on that nomination before the August recess so they can have a justice in place through the whole process in time for the October session of the Court," said Attorney General Edwin Meese III.[23]

As the Reagan years had waned, conservatives—the president's main constituency—grew less and less enchanted with the decisions of their hero in the Oval Office. Recent disappointments, such as the appointments of Frank Carlucci as Secretary of Defense and Melissa Wells as Ambassador to Mozambique, had made conservatives wary of trusting their "Gipper." Conservatives who had worked on legal issues for years dreamed that Judge Bork, high on the list of nominees, would be the choice. With Bork the first choice of the entire leadership of the groups most interested in legal questions, there was nonetheless substantial support for Senator Hatch, the Utah Republican, and Judge Wallace of California, who had carried the judicial restraint banner for 15 years. Fearing that their top choice, Bork, would be scrapped for a judge with more "centrist" tendencies, conservatives lobbied the White House heavily in support of the bearded jurist.

The liberals, on the other hand, exhibited more faith in President Reagan's conservatism, and began acting as though their worst fear— a Bork nomination—was reality. Not two days after Justice Powell's announcement, feminist Eleanor Smeal released this missive to the subscribers of her report:

> Women's groups and civil rights groups have pledged to fight a Right Wing ideological take-over of the Supreme Court with the nomination of U.S. Appeals Court Judge Robert Bork—or for that matter any nominee who will shift the majority of the Court to oppose legalized abortion and birth control, to abolish the right to privacy, to destroy affirmative action, or to roll back 30 years of civil rights and women's rights progress. Group leaders who attended an emergency meeting of the Leadership Conference on Civil Rights made it clear they would fight one-two-or-more nominees who would give reactionaries the coveted 5th vote on the Court. Women's, civil rights, labor, senior citizen, and disabled groups see a possible Bork appointment enabling the Right Wing to amend the Constitution with just one vote.[24]

One umbrella group, Leadership Conference on Civil Rights, gathered representatives from some of its 190 organizations for an emergency meeting on June 30—two days *before* the White House would announce its decision. Plans for a major Bork offensive were drawn up.

Meanwhile, groups representing feminists, abortionists, blacks, "gays", and other traditional liberals jammed the phone lines at the offices of the 14 Senate Judiciary Committee members, warning them that a thumbs-up for Bork would mean nothing less than war. "We're going to wage an all-out frontal assault like you've never seen before on this nominee, assuming it's Bork," threatened Kate Michelman of the National Abortion Rights Action League. Ralph Neas of the Leadership Conference underscored the urgency by warning, "There's no question that a Bork nomination or the nomination of anyone who would put in jeopardy the court's achievements of the past three decades would trigger the most controversial and confrontational legislative battle of the Reagan years."[25] A few days later, in words that resonated even with conservatives, Neas told one reporter: "This is about what people have worked their whole lives for."[26]

Opponents began to pull from Bork's massive paper trail of academic writing dating to the early 1970s, as well as the opinions he had written during his five years on the appeals court. Hastily-commissioned mailings were sent out to members across the country, potential contributors, and Senate offices. Their message: Bork is a dangerous man. His nomination must be aborted. Send money. Phone your Senator.

The attack had begun.

Chapter Two:

The War Begins

The weekend following Justice Powell's Friday announcement, President Reagan and Attorney General Edwin Meese III met to discuss possible replacements. The President held another meeting to discuss potential nominees that Monday, June 29, with Meese and White House Chief of Staff Howard Baker. Anonymous White House sources said Baker, a moderate, was ambivalent at that point about the reported first choice, U.S. Court of Appeals Judge Robert H. Bork, fearing that the Democratic-controlled Senate would reject him. Joe Biden praised Baker for his hesitation, saying he "understands the reality of this place."[27] (Whether or not Baker at first hesitated on Bork, by the time of the announcement, he was behind the President's decision.[28])

The following day, Meese and Baker handed Senate leaders a list of about ten possible replacements for Justice Powell. Reviewing the list were Senators Strom Thurmond (R-SC), the ranking Republican on the Judiciary Committee, Minority Leader Robert Dole (R-KS), Majority Leader Robert Byrd (D-WV), and Judiciary Committee Chairman Joseph Biden (D-DE).[29] Biden again hinted at the battle a Reagan nominee might face by noting that the list had "some very good people . . . and some, I bluntly told them, would cause a contentious fight if they came up."[30] Bork remained the Administration's top candidate.

The morning of July 1, 1987, White House Counsel Arthur B. Culvahouse and Judge Bork met at a hotel in Washington, D.C. to chat over coffee. Culvahouse grilled the Judge about his past, but could find no evidence of skeletons or personal problems in his background that might ruin his chances of confirmation later on.[31]

President Reagan then called Bork into the Oval Office for a "chat." Some of his colleagues maintained Bork had been prepping himself for a Supreme Court nomination since Reagan entered office in 1981, but Bork himself had his doubts his day would ever come. As he told Pat McGuigan's conservative legal policy newsletter *Judicial Notice* during an interview published in June 1986: "I know no more than what the newspapers say, so I have no idea whether it might be in the cards. And, it has been going on for a number of years now, so it really doesn't make me feel any particular way. I have gotten inured to it." Judge Bork, who had been overlooked in favor of Justice O'Connor in 1981, was passed over again in favor of Scalia only a short time after that interview was published.

So when the President asked that day if he would be the nominee, Bork answered with a typical quip: "I've thought about it for at least ten or twelve seconds, and I would be highly honored." Reagan rejoined, "Does that mean yes?"[32]

Soon after their meeting, the two entered the White House briefing room for the announcement. "Judge Bork, widely regarded as the most prominent and intellectually powerful advocate of judicial restraint, shares my view that judges' personal preferences and values should not be part of their constitutional interpretations," President Reagan began. "The guiding principle of judicial restraint recognizes that under the Constitution, it is the exclusive province of the legislatures to enact laws and the role of the court to interpret them." As Judge Bork stood quietly beside the President, Reagan introduced him on national television as "a premier constitutional authority," and reminded the audience that "when confirmed by the Senate as an appellate judge in 1982, the American Bar Association gave him its highest rating—exceptionally well-qualified." The President continued, "On the bench he has been well-prepared, even-handed and open-minded. I urge the Senate to expedite its consideration of Judge Bork so the court will have nine justices."[33]

After President Reagan and Judge Bork left the briefing room, White House spokesman Marlin Fitzwater told members of the press, "We recognize that any conservative would receive some opposition, but we believe that Mr. Bork will be confirmed." He said despite the expected opposition, "there doesn't appear to be any deep-seated animosity."[34] Another senior White House official predicted a "tough and lengthy" fight[35] while yet another said the President would actively campaign to secure Bork's confirmation.[36]

Senator Howell Heflin of Alabama, the Judiciary Committee's most conservative Democrat, foreshadowed Bork's confirmation process by predicting, "I think he will have the most complete and exhaustive investigation of any nominee to the Supreme Court in history."[37]

Robert Heron Bork, 60, was the only son of a Pittsburgh steel company purchasing agent. Following two separate stints with the Marine Corps, he received both his undergraduate and law degrees from the University of Chicago. He established himself as an anti-trust specialist at the prestigious Chicago firm of Kirkland & Ellis, but left in 1962 to join the faculty of Yale Law School because, he said, "I wanted a more interesting life than this, something more intellectually challenging in the sense of large ideas."

During his tenure at Yale, Bork's views evolved from a strong belief in libertarianism to a philosophy of strict adherence to the Constitution. An eloquent writer, he issued erudite academic studies, expressing his interpretation of various legal issues (many of which would be used against him later).

Bork left teaching to serve the country from 1973 to 1977 as U.S. solicitor general in the Nixon Administration. Within the first months on the job, he fired Watergate Special Prosecutor Archibald Cox on orders from President Nixon.

Following his job with the government, Bork returned to Yale, but left in 1981 following the death of his first wife, Claire Davidson. He returned to Kirkland & Ellis in their Washington, D.C. branch, but left in 1982 when President Reagan appointed him to the U.S. Circuit Court of Appeals for the District of Columbia.[38]

With such an extensive background, Judge Bork's record and name were well-known in both legal and political circles. The reaction to his nomination was instantaneous and immense. "Our phones have been ringing off the hook," said a Senate Judiciary Committee aide the day after the President's announcement. By mid-afternoon of July 1, the Committee had received "several hundred" calls that were "overwhelmingly liberal, overwhelmingly against" confirmation, according to the aide.[39]

His opponents had focused against Bork days even before the announcement, and skipped nary a beat. Perhaps the most frequently quoted statement was made on the Senate floor by Edward Kennedy (D-MA), one of the Judiciary Committee's most liberal members:

Robert Bork's America is a land in which women would be forced into back-alley abortions, blacks would sit at segregated lunch counters, rogue police could break down citizens' doors in midnight raids, schoolchildren could not be taught about evolution, writers and artists would be censored at the whim of government, and the doors of the Federal courts would be shut on the fingers of millions of citizens for whom the judiciary is often the only protector of the individual rights that are the heart of our democracy.[40]

(This was the same senator who had asserted during the nomination of Congressman Mikva to the Court of Appeals: "The question is whether he is willing and able to interpret the law as we and those before us have written it. The answer does not turn on politics; it turns on ability, sensitivity, and perhaps most importantly, integrity."[41])

Kennedy's statement angered conservative Congressman Newt Gingrich (R-GA) so much that he sent the Senator a note requesting that they meet to debate "the proper ethical standards for government figures." Kennedy flippantly replied, "Keep up the good work. Your support for Bork is making my case—and making my day."[42]

The Senator's assault on Bork prompted Ray Kerrison, in a New York *Post* commentary, to remind readers:

[Kennedy] was once asked by Thomas Dennelly, of Baldwin, N.Y., for his sentiments on abortion. In a letter dated August 3, 1971, Kennedy wrote Dennelly as follows: "While the deep concern of a woman bearing an unwanted child merits consideration and sympathy, it is my personal feeling that the legalization of abortion on demand is not in accordance with the value which our civilization places on human life. Wanted or unwanted, I believe that human life, even at its earliest stages, has certain rights which must be recognized—the right to be born, the right to love, the right to grow old. On the question of the individual's freedom of choice, there are easily available birth control methods and information which women may employ to prevent or postpone pregnancy. But once life has begun, no matter at what stage of growth, it is my belief that termination should not be decided merely by desire."[43]

Benjamin Hooks, executive director of the National Association for the Advancement of Colored People, and Ralph Neas from the Leadership Conference on Civil Rights, issued a joint statement warning that:

A very substantial majority of the civil-rights community will strongly oppose the nomination of Robert Bork [whose confirmation would] jeopardize the civil rights achievements of the past 30 years. Well-established law on affirmative action, on privacy, on women's rights and on school desegregation could overnight be substantially eroded or overturned.[44]

Arthur Kropp, President of People for the American Way, a 270,000–member liberal group founded by television producer Norman Lear, announced, "Whatever we have to do to defeat his nomination, we'll do it."[45] Kropp's organization delivered this release to the media within two hours of Bork's announcement:

> . . . [T]he Senate is constitutionally obligated to make its own judgment about whether confirmation of a Supreme Court nominee would be in the best interest of the country. . . . One of the Senate's fundamental functions in confirming judicial nominees is to prevent partisan, ideological court packing by a President determined to remake the Supreme Court to mirror his views. . . . Judge Bork's record on constitutional and civil liberties suggests that he would move us into the next century by repealing many of the gains in rights and liberties won in this century. In rights of citizens to keep government out of their private lives, to exercise their rights to free speech, and even to look to the courts to uphold their rights, Judge Bork's views and rulings are a radical departure from the mainstream position upheld by the Courts and exemplified by Justice Powell.[46]

(People for the American Way's Anthony Podesta, speaking to attendees at a Federalist Society luncheon in 1986, had said he would oppose placing a conservative *ideologue*—but not a conservative—on the high court. When asked by someone in the crowd if he believed conservatives belonged in the federal courts, Podesta answered yes. Asked to name a few, he initially blanched, but sources at the luncheon said Podesta finally admitted he could support conservatives such as Robert Bork and Antonin Scalia.[47])

Ralph Neas, executive director of the Leadership Conference on Civil Rights, held an emergency meeting on July 2 with representatives of some 200 liberal groups determined to derail the Bork nomination.

Even the seven Democratic presidential hopefuls got in on the initial Bork bashing by holding hurried press conferences to assert their positions. Senator Albert Gore (D-TN) was the only Democratic candidate who said he would not take a stand until after the hearings.

July 2, 1987 special action memo
"That for which we exist is upon us." That opening sentence described my feelings about the fight ahead.

This nomination was the one. It was time to go to work.

For two years Dan Casey had tracked the voting patterns of the Senate on judicial nominees. Working with ten roll call votes from recent years, Dan divided the Senate into four basic groups. Group 1 was titled "99% definite votes for Reagan nominee." These were Senators whose votes should be solid. However, we noted "caveats" even on these Senators. Group 2 was listed as "usually supports Reagan nominee." The Senators in here had voting records that indicated they should be helpful, but we just couldn't be sure at this early stage.

Group 3 consisted of "can sometimes be counted on to support Reagan nominee." This group of senators had mixed records. They had normally voted against the President's nominees, but did on occasion back some. And Group 4 became the "almost never votes right—can probably be written-off" group. Obviously, the Senators making up this group had always voted wrong in the votes we had targeted. However, there were a handful of even these Senators that were worth our attention if the time and resources could be spared. They were Baucus (D-MT), Byrd (D-WV), Daschle (D-SD), Exon (D-NE), Fowler (D-GA), Gore (D-TN), Moynihan (D-NY), Reid (D-NV), and Sasser (D-TN).

All in all we calculated 43 votes in Group 1, 13 in Group 2, 10 in Group 3 and 34 in Group 4. After Dan assigned freshman Senators to one category or another based on our best "guesstimates", our initial breakdown looked like this:

	Group 1	Group 2	Group 3	Group 4
	Armstrong	Bentsen	Bingaman	Adams*
	Bond*	Boren	Bumpers	Baucus†
	Boschwitz	Breaux*	Chiles	Biden
†	Chafee	DeConcini	Dixon	Bradley
	Cochran	Ford	Graham*	Burdick
†	Cohen	Heflin	Nunn	Byrd†
	D'Amato	Hollings	Pell	Conrad*
	Danforth	Johnston	Proxmire	Cranston
	Dole	Kassebaum	Sanford*	Daschle*†
	Domenici	Pryor	Weicker	Dodd
	Durenberger	Shelby*		Exon†
†	Evans	Specter		Fowler*†
	Garn	Stennis		Glenn

Gramm

Grassley

Hatch

† Hatfield

Hecht

† Heinz

Helms

Humphrey

Karnes

Kasten

Lugar

McCain

McClure

McConnell

Murkowski

Nickles

† Packwood

Pressler

Quayle

Roth

† Rudman

Simpson

Stafford

Stevens

Symms

Thurmond

Trible

Wallop

Warner

Wilson

Gore

Harkin

Inouye

Kennedy

Kerry

Lautenberg

Leahy

Levin

Matsunaga

Melcher

Metzenbaum

Mikulski

Mitchell

Moynihan†

Reid*†

Riegle

Rockefeller

Sarbanes

Sasser†

Simon

Wirth*

*represents arbitrary assignment of freshmen
†indicates a normally predictable Senator who, for various reasons, should be considered a possible switch on the Bork vote.

(This initial analysis of the Senate was very close to the ultimate vote—with Bork's supporters losing nearly everyone in categories 2, 3 and 4).

By the morning of July 2 our 300 or so leaders and activists in past judicial confirmation battles were delivered or mailed the Senate breakdown and given suggested themes to present to senators. The themes were straightforward: "1. The President has nominated an *exceptionally well qualified man. 2. We hope you will encourage your colleagues on the Judiciary Committee to hold speedy hearings on this excellent nominee. There can be no justification for delay because the Supreme Court begins its work in October and needs the new justice. 3. We hope you will not support delaying tactics, but will vote to invoke cloture . . . on any obstructionist filibuster. 4. We are counting on you to support this outstanding nominee when the final vote is taken on his confirmation."*

Members of the Senate Judiciary Committee were immediately targeted for priority phone calls and letters. The effort was beginning in earnest.

In what was a fairly civil debate, Nan Aron of the Alliance for Justice and I went head to head for 45 minutes on C-SPAN's call-in show July 2, 1987. Nan said she believed that the Committee would conduct a "more thorough kind of investigation" than in the past. I commented that, in truth, the Committee strategy on Bork would be what it had been for some time on all of Reagan's nominees, "the old four corners offense." In the 1940s and 1950s, Oklahoma State University's basketball team had developed a "stall" offense to hold on to small leads. They would position players in each corner of the half-court and simply pass the basketball around. In short, I said, "The Committee's gonna be tough for Judge Bork."

Nan insisted Bork believed "there is no right to privacy. He has come out opposed to contraception, [and] probably abortion, and he has written that the gay man had no right to privacy to remain employed in the Navy . . ."

I countered, "I'm not aware that Judge Bork has ever commented on the substance of the issues of either abortion, contraception, or homosexuality. He has commented on their standing under the law. What Judge Bork questions is making it up as you go along."

Perhaps making my most effective counter of the show, I continued:

The 1973 decision in Roe . . . invented a right to abortion on demand, which had not existed in the Constitution prior to that . . . Even the most liberal states, prior to Roe . . . had provisions more restrictive of abortion than what the court invented that day . . . If Roe . . . was reversed . . . what would happen is that these questions would return to the states. Now I think you would see more regulation of abortion, but I don't think you would see more regulation of contraceptive materials. I don't see state legislatures or legislators out there clamoring to restrict people's access to condoms.

Nan asserted that this battle was "not just looking at Judge Bork alone and what his views are or aren't, but . . . the impact that he will have on the future direction, the future role of the Supreme Court. . . . That Court . . . will undergo a major reversal, a major transformation, where it begins to turn its back on women, on the rights of individuals." Simply, Nan asserted that the battle would be "deciding upon the future of the Supreme Court as an institution."

I countered that her assertion about the Court turning its back on anyone was an example of the "very unfortunate rhetoric" Nan and her allies were using to raise the temperatures of their constituents.

At the conclusion of the exchange, Nan asserted her belief that the debate "will be elevated" in comparison to the debate in 1968 over Abe Fortas's nomination for chief justice.

That was too much for me. I countered sarcastically, "I watched some of the commentary from some of your colleagues yesterday and I felt real elevated." On that somewhat bitter note the show ended.

As we and the moderator, Carrie Collins, sat together with the cameras still on but with the sound off, I asked Nan, "Aren't you afraid you people will go too far?"

She shot back, "Are you threatening me?"

In shock, I replied, "Threatening you? My God, I'm talking about the country—you could go too far for the sake of the country! My people could get so bitter they could do the same thing to you some day."

Nan, with the disbelief of an elder, answered, "Oh please. Grow up."

At that, I grasped the C-SPAN cup wrapped in blue in my right hand, stood up, walked out of the studios onto North Capitol Street, feeling very depressed as I faced the walk back to my office before the drive home. I looked at the Capitol dome only a few blocks away.

"Grow up," she said. If that kind of cynicism is what it takes to be effective in public life, I guess I'll never grow up.

The quick and furious liberal offensive put Senate Judiciary Committee Chairman Joseph Biden in a precarious situation. Judge Bork, who during the 1982 confirmation hearings to the U.S. District Court of Appeals had received high praise from his colleagues and Senators on both sides of the aisle, had been at the top of the list of those being considered to replace Justice Rehnquist when Rehnquist replaced Chief Justice Warren Burger in 1986. It was shortly after Rehnquist's elevation that Senator Biden had conceded, "If Judge Bork were to replace Judge Rehnquist or to replace Judge Scalia, I would have no problem. I'd have to vote for him, and if the [liberal special-interest] groups tear me apart, that's the medicine I'll have to take."[48]

But Biden, who feared that the powerful liberal interests could wreck his fledgling presidential bid, backed away from his statement when Judge Bork's nomination overnight became the focus of massive liberal outcry. Indeed, on the evening of July 1, Biden said: "I continue to have grave doubts about the nomination and expect it to cause a difficult and potentially contentious struggle in the Senate."[49] Biden also promised at that time, "I will not take a formal position on the Bork nomination before [the] hearings begin."[50]

Eager to explain his 1986 statement, Biden claimed the next day that his meaning had been misconstrued. What he had really meant to say, said the Senator, was that he could support a Bork nomination to the High Court only if the Judge were to replace another conservative. "I would attempt to have diversity on the bench," Biden said. "I would see to it that there was a Scalia on the bench and a [liberal Justice William J.] Brennan on the bench. . . . It is wrong to send someone to tip the balance."[51]

The Senator's flip-flop did not go unnoticed by the members of the press, who noted that such an obvious reversal might harm his presidential interests. Outraged editorials such as this one from the Baltimore *Sun*, appeared in newspapers across the country:

> Senator Biden's explanation of his switch was intriguing: Before, he had been speaking "in the context of replacing a conservative with a conservative." Really? In the context of a year ago, most speculation focused on whether Mr. Bork would be named to replace Justice Thurgood Marshall or Justice William Brennan, the oldest and most liberal members of the Supreme Court.[52]

One week after the nomination, on Wednesday, July 8, Biden held virtually back-to-back meetings, with decidedly different purposes. At 10 a.m., he regaled the nominee himself for an hour with stories about his campaign for the presidency. He concluded the meeting by asking the jurist if he had any questions, to which Bork replied, "I thought you might have some for me, Senator." Biden replied, "No, I haven't read your opinions yet."

The Senator then met with lobbyists from the left-wing Leadership Conference on Civil Rights, NAACP Legal Defense Fund and the Women's Legal Defense Fund. He vowed to them that the anti-Bork effort would be his number one priority. Emerging from the private pow-wow, Biden admitted to reporters, "I haven't been able to do anything but have a cursory look at Judge Bork's record," but added, "It's highly unlikely I'll be able to vote for Judge Bork." He said he would not announce his actual decision "probably for 10 more days."[53] But one of the representatives who attended the session later said that Biden had "made it very clear to us that he knows what he's going to do, and that he considers the confirmation fight so important that he's willing to work on this, and not on the presidential campaign."[54] By mid-July, some 75 liberal groups would be in constant contact with Biden's staff.[55]

Even columnists employed at some liberal newspapers expressed disgust as the battle unfolded. Michael Barone's scorching depiction of Biden appeared in the Washington *Post* the day following the meeting: "It was the pro-choice groups which first loudly attacked Bork and whipped the Democrats into line: the National Abortion Rights Action League snapped its fingers and Joe Biden, doing what he said he'd never do, jumped."[56]

Biden's "jump" had actually occurred at least as early as a July 7 meeting at his Wilmington, Delaware home with crucial members of his campaign and judiciary committee staffs, during which he decided to head up the anti-Bork campaign. To aid him in that effort, these staff members began gathering volunteers from Washington, D.C. law firms to provide an analysis of Bork's scholarly writings and legal opinions.[57]

Biden also gathered a small army of prominent academics and lawyers, including Democratic elder Clark Clifford of the Washington, D.C. firm of Clifford & Warnke; Duke University law professor Walter Dellinger III; University of Chicago law professor Philip Kurland; Susan Prager, dean of the University of California at Los Angeles' law school; Floyd Abrams, a First Amendment specialist and a partner at New York's Cahill, Gordon & Reindel; and Kenneth Bass III, former Justice Department official under the Carter Administration and a current partner in Venable, Baetjer, Howard & Civiletti in Washington, D.C.[58]

The same day he met with the liberal interest groups, Biden held a two-hour conference with his platoon of advisors. "Our role is to provide Senator Biden and the other Democratic members of the committee with advice on the constitutional issues that are raised by this nomination," said Bass, who (with Kurland and Dellinger), had helped Biden plot ways to slow Rehnquist's confirmation to chief justice.[59]

Dellinger said the group would help Biden write speeches that argued for the Senate's authority to include ideological considerations in its "advise and consent" role. "Whether a Senator will take philosophy into account should depend to a large degree upon whether the president has done so in making the nomination," Dellinger said. Bass added: "It isn't the Senate that's taking an ideological position on this, it's the president that did."[60]

(Biden had learned this argument from Kurland and liberal Harvard Law Professor Laurence Tribe during their June 1986 meetings to discuss the nomination of Daniel Manion to the U.S. Circuit Court. The nation "has a right to insist that the Senate . . . recall the Framer's vision of its solemn duty to provide advice and consent, rather than perfunctory obeisance, to the will of the President," wrote Tribe and Kurland in their summary for the Judiciary Committee, assertions Biden used during the Manion confirmation battle.[61] In their work for Biden, Tribe and Kurland complained that numerous typographical errors were contained in the briefs Manion had submitted to the Court. However, as *Judicial Notice* pointed out, the law professors' own report to the Committee contained the word "ingelligently"—an obvious mistake for the word "intelligently."[62])

Biden's group didn't plan to limit themselves to consulting—they hoped to bombard major media outlets with anti-Bork columns, and jockey for a chance to testify before the Senate Judiciary Committee.[63]

Conservatives attacked when the members of Biden's group of advisors became known. "These are people who believe that the Constitution is a nice amorphous thing that you bend and shape to advance your views, and the American people just don't agree with that," said Patrick McGuigan.[64]

In the days following the Bork nomination, the storm of protest escalated as the opponents vowed to plow all available resources into stopping confirmation of the man they believed might ruin the advancement of their agenda. Ralph Neas of the Leadership Conference on Civil Rights, the Left's capable point man on the nomination, estimated that "probably 300 organizations" would join in Bork bashing activities, and predicted a "grass-roots effort in all 50 states."[65]

"As a political organization we are contacting senators to urge them to consider Bork's ideology," said Irene Natividad of the National Women's Political Caucus. "As a grass-roots organization of 77,000 members we are galvanizing our membership nationwide to work against this nomination." People for the American Way's executive director, Arthur Kropp, was the first to mention money—big money. "People are really upset," he said. "Everyone wants to go to the mat on this one. We expect to spend as much as $1 million on this."[66]

Kropp later explained: "We're talking about a heavy newspaper print-ad strategy and radio strategy, hoping to reach saturation in some of the markets," especially in the "opinion-making markets" of Chicago, Los Angeles, Washington, New York, and Atlanta. "We want the American public to be speaking with anyone who might be wavering. We view it as being probably the most important thing we do this year."[67]

Conservatives had reasons for concern—PAW boasted a $10 million annual budget. Within a week, PAW's 250,000 members received an "alert mailing" to "get them prepared" for the anti-Bork blitz by advising them to call key senators during the week of the Senate Judiciary Committee hearings. PAW also teamed with the liberal Alliance for Justice and distributed a joint mailing to 1,700 editorial writers across the country, hoping to influence their opinions on the Senate's use of ideology as a reason to reject Bork.[68]

Richard Mintz, spokesman for the National Abortion Rights Action League, said its 42 nationwide affiliates planned to "operate phone banks [and] distribute literature."[69] Meanwhile, the 150,000 members of the National Organization for Women were busy organizing anti-Bork protests and preparing mailings to send to key senators, according to President Eleanor Smeal. NOW also hoped to erect a computerized bulletin board that would provide its members with up-to-date information on the progress of the nomination.[70]

AFL-CIO officials shied away from such active Bork bashing, but President Lane Kirkland urged affiliated unions and state federations to pressure senators to "not make any early commitment" on Judge Bork. Clayton Roberts, vice president of the National Right to Work Committee, charged that Kirkland's hands-off attitude was merely a shrewd political game featuring Senator Biden as chief pawn. "Biden . . . sees the Bork confirmation hearings as his personal key to organized labor's coffers," Roberts said.[71]

Meanwhile, delegates for the National Association for the Advancement of Colored People (NAACP) gathered in New York for their 78th annual conference. Opening the six-day meeting on the first weekend in July, NAACP Executive Director Benjamin L. Hooks promised, "We will go all out in seeing that Bork is not appointed to the Supreme Court."[72] NAACP officials said their more prominent members, who were busy researching Bork's legal past, planned to schedule meetings with all senators individually before the hearings.

The second day of the NAACP convention, several hundred delegates approved a resolution attacking Bork for his advocacy of the death penalty, and what they believed was his political opposition to public accommodations laws and affirmative action. "We must let our senators know that a vote against Mr. Bork is a prerequisite for our vote in the next election," said Coretta Scott King, widow of the Reverend Martin Luther King Jr. The convention hall erupted in cheers and thunderous clapping.[73]

Passage of the anti-Bork resolution allowed Althea Simmons, the NAACP's top Washington lobbyist, to begin organizing members to write letters and lobby their Senators. "We've got some people reading his law articles and going through his past rulings with a fine tooth comb," Simmons said. "We are setting up an operational network for letter-writing and telephoning. I can assure you we are pulling out all the stops."[74]

Several politicians speaking at the convention, including Democratic presidential candidates, promised to fight against the Bork nomination. New York Governor Mario Cuomo told the delegates he opposed Bork for his "racist" leanings and said the nomination shows the American people "how far we still have to go" to insure black-white equality. "Today we are confronted by the possibility that the Supreme Court, which in recent decades has insisted on the social progress that has been denied us by the legislative branch and executive branch, may be about to turn back the clock," he claimed.[75]

Democratic Presidential hopeful Congressman Richard Gephardt of Missouri told convention attendees: "I say that if Robert Bork refuses to find room at the inn for the black citizens of this nation, then the citizens of this nation should refuse to find room for him at the Supreme Court."[76] His rival, former Arizona Governor Bruce Babbitt also pledged to NAACP members that he would fight the nomination adding, Bork "has a right to those opinions. The president has a right to admire them. And the Senate has the right to reject them. In the fullness of time, every Democrat will see that there can be no two ways about this vote."[77] Senator Albert Gore, however, remained publicly uncommitted. "I will render my verdict in the Senate," he told the delegates. "But only after hearing all the evidence."[78]

White House Chief of Staff Howard H. Baker Jr. appealed to NAACP members to give the President's nominee a fair chance. In a speech to the convention on July 9, Baker said:

I ask you today not to judge Robert Bork upon a fragmented record, reflected in newspaper clippings. I ask you to consider the full record and Judge Bork's views as they emerge during the confirmation process. As an organization that prides itself on fairness, as individuals who have been victims of prejudice based upon race, I am sure that you understand the importance of allowing all the facts to be put forward in a nonheated or emotional fashion, particularly as the Senate . . . affords Justice Bork an opportunity to be heard, examined and confirmed.[79]

The National Education Association, the nation's largest teachers union with 1.86 million members, held its 125th annual convention on the same weekend. "Judge Bork is a compulsory pregnancy man . . . too conservative on race, women's rights and reproductive freedom," teacher Jane Stern of Rockville, Maryland complained, prompting the 8,000 NEA delegates to vote overwhelmingly in favor of blocking the nomination.[80] "We intend to work to defeat this nomination through our normal congressional and legislative procedures," said Michael Edwards, manager of congressional relations for the NEA. "We have already in place methods to communicate with our members and members of Congress, so it's just a matter of activating members, not a question of adding new dollars."[81]

Editorials on Judge Bork and the potential "effect" his influence would have on the court ran day after day throughout the battle. The arguments frequently sounded echoed this piece, which appeared in the St. Petersburg *Times*:

Bork is more extreme in his views than the other ideologue on the court, Chief Justice William Rehnquist. Bork claims falsely to practice judicial restraint; he is a judicial activist for a backward-looking ideology. If he replaces the moderate Lewis Powell, shock waves ultimately will be sent throughout American society.[82]

or this one, which was featured in the Raleigh *News & Observer*:

Just like the President, Bork is a radical masquerading as a conservative. Reagan praises the nominee's advocacy of judicial restraint, the doctrine emphasizing that judges are to interpret the laws, not to establish new law through their rulings. But as Bork has conceived it, "restraint" conveys upon a judge the right to ignore the principles laid down in past decisions simply because he dislikes their consequences. . . . The ramifications of that view are enormous—and frightening. It would threaten to undermine whole bodies of opinion by which the court has secured the nation's progress in civil and individual rights. Any judge who would embrace such a radical departure from the consensus of constitutional law is more accurately described as an activist—one who would roll back the clock to a time of legal racial discrimination and individual powerlessness at the hands of the state.[83]

Senate Majority Leader Robert Byrd (D-WV) reiterated his warning of the week before that if Republicans failed to end "this binge of stalling and delay" on Democratic initiatives "I'll play a little of this hardball in calling up the nomination."[84] Byrd also claimed that it would be the Reagan Administration's fault if the confirmation hearings digressed into a political battle. The Senate Judiciary Committee has "no intention of doing that," he said. "I just hope the White House doesn't try to politicize this. But that is not only possible, it's probable."[85] Byrd, however, shifted ground in his statement when he declared that the Bork nomination "would be inviting problems" because of his involvement with the Watergate scandal.[86] And freshman Senator Kent Conrad (D-ND) announced he would have a "very difficult time voting for Mr. Bork" because of the Judge's involvement with the "Saturday Night Massacre" during Watergate.[87]

Former U.S. Solicitor General Rex Lee was among those who jumped to Bork's defense: "Bob Bork is probably the most qualified person to be a Supreme Court Justice from the standpoint of intellect, temperament and training."[88]

The opponents, in the early going, tried to capitalize on Judge Bork's role as Solicitor General during the Watergate era. "It would be the ultimate chutzpah to appoint the same guy who fired Archie Cox at the same time the Justice Department is attacking the special prosecutor statute and the country is embroiled in Irangate," said People for the American Way's Arthur Kropp.[89] Some editorialists tried to stimulate public outrage against Bork by magnifying the Cox firing, but supporters countered that Bork had testified extensively about his involvement in the Cox firing during his 1982 confirmation hearings for the appeals court, and had never been accused of any wrong doing in relation to the scandal. (The initial furor over the incident eventually faded, to reappear briefly during the hearings.)

Meanwhile, pro-Bork conservatives, already days behind in strategy, did not react to Bork's nomination with the same panache the liberals had. An early setback occurred when Senate Minority Leader Robert Dole (R-KS) openly worried about Judge Bork's chances of confirmation. "If you look at the numbers, you look at confirmability, then you've got a tough fight on your hands. I think he's a little better than 50–50." Dole said it was "speculative" whether he would have chosen Bork had he been president.[90]

But conservative leaders who had long supported Bork, such as Patrick McGuigan and Dan Casey of the "721 Group," worked round-the-clock to make up for lost time. Through their coalition, they hoped to employ the same muscle the liberals had threatened to use against them—the grass-roots, including some 110 "various right-to-life groups, law enforcement agencies and various . . . religious groups," such as the National Association of Evangelicals, Casey said.[91]

"We're doing what we did in the [Daniel] Manion and the [William] Rehnquist battles by umpty-umpty-umpt millions more," McGuigan said. The "bottom line is the vote count. There are probably 46 solid votes for, probably 30, maybe a little more, against. The balance is the swing votes, and that's what everyone is going to be targeting."[92] McGuigan added that efforts for Bork had begun "immediately. The first meeting of conservative leaders to brainstorm and begin to start action were the very next morning" following the nomination.[93]

Out of that meeting came the following strategy: "First, we will try to alert and influence opinion makers, editorial boards, church leaders, and others with the ear of a senator in order to urge them to weigh nominations on the merits, resist pressures from liberal special-interest groups and exercise good judgment in confirming Judge Bork," Casey explained. "The second track is helping funnel information to grass-roots organizations, so that they in turn can feed it to their active members to energize . . . efforts."[94]

An invaluable ally in this respect was Beverly LaHaye, president of Concerned Women for America, who promised to help by pledging that her 500,000 members would do "everything in our power to help secure Judge Bork's confirmation."[95] CWA began its efforts by mailing letters to some 50 "area leaders" across the country requesting that they call members and urge them to flood Senate offices with pro-Bork letters. "We're alerting our membership," said spokeswoman Rebecca Hagelin. "We're very thrilled about the Bork nomination."[96]

Phyllis Schlafly, president of the Eagle Forum, said, "We're just writing to our senators and asking them to support Bork. We're essentially relying on our 80,000 members." The 1.7 million-member National Right To Work Committee launched a direct-mail effort for Bork, "and we're looking at strategy from here," said NRWC Vice President Clayton Roberts. "We operate on a shoestring budget here, but we'll do anything we can."[97]

At the 721 Group meeting I chaired on June 23, 1987—one week before Justice Powell announced his retirement and the President nominated Judge Bork—we had focused on the judicial confirmation process, Senator Biden's masterful "stall" of the President's lower court nominees in the Senate Judiciary Committee, and Biden's presidential campaign.

We had several special, short meetings immediately after the nomination involving myself, Dan Casey, Elizabeth Kepley of Concerned Women for America, Don Baldwin of the National Law Enforcement Council and other leaders, including folks from the National Right to Work Committee and the National Right to Life Committee. None of us had ever been through anything like this, but we were fairly certain speed was important. We made plans for regular communications with media around the country, and scheduled regular mailings to the compilation of several hundred leaders and activists around the country I'd built through several judicial-linked confrontations beginning in 1983–84. (The admiration members of the group felt for embattled former Attorney General Ed Meese was shown in what we called the compilation for short-hand purposes: the "pro-Meese" list.)

On July 6, a Time *magazine reporter speculated about Bork's personal religious beliefs, describing him as an "agnostic". When this incident occured, we had no idea the grief this particular report would later cause us, although Dan Casey set his southern network to work immediately to counter the distortion. Although Bork was quoted only two days after the first report as specifically denying the characterization, it would prove an effective mischaracterization in softening support for the jurist in the south.*

By the time the next regular meeting had rolled around on July 21, status reports on the Judiciary Committee and on the full Senate were given. Elizabeth Kepley of Concerned Women for America began to form lobbying teams drawn from the various groups to focus on both Senate staff and the Senators themselves, while Don Baldwin of the National Law Enforcement Council focused on who, from the outside groups, should testify, and who should merely submit statements. The push was on.

July 6, 1987 media packet

It had only been a few days since Judge Bork's nomination, but a compilation of surprisingly positive editorials and articles from "establishment" media had emerged. American Conservative Union and

Coalitions for America paid for a mailing pulling the "greatest hits" together, which Dan's operation then sent to editors across the country. This was "their" stuff, not ours. As the Left made its voice heard, the idea was to get a good word in for the Judge, even as all the attacks began. Their current thrust, headed by Senator Biden, was to change the standards for selecting judges. If editors read articles from their establishment "brethren" about this preeminent conservative legal scholar, they might consider his qualifications on the merits. Then attacks against him, particularly from Senator Biden, could be blunted—or so we hoped.

I learned later that in those early days we at Coalitions for America and the American Conservative Union were not the only ones providing a massive supportive education on Bork's background to swamped reporters who were at least trying to get the full picture. When the White House proved not helpful to the press, they were able to secure lengthy biographical information and copies of many of his scholarly articles (only a few of which we had at hand in our shop) from Terry Eastland, Director of the Office of Public Affairs at the Department of Justice.

And, veteran conservative activist Howie Phillips made plans to alert as many as 500,000 conservatives through the mail on the importance of the Bork confirmation. He traveled to Oregon at mid-month to work with his people on how to reverse Packwood's clear inclination to go against the jurist.

McGuigan and Casey drew some media attention by calling a mid-July press conference to denounce Senator Biden for taking a lead in the anti-Bork effort before the jurist had a chance to testify in front of the Senate Judiciary Committee.

Some 1,000 American Conservative Union contributors received a "here-we-go-again" mailing, which solicited financial support for the Bork battle. ACU Executive Director Casey said 40,000 to 60,000 more letters would be sent to contributors by July 31. "We're going to go all out," he said. "This is an issue that will fund itself because it's what they would say in the direct-mail world is a 'hot-button' issue. Frankly, the liberals have made this a hot-button issue for conservatives . . . with the absolute incredible reaction," he added. "Every dollar that Norman Lear spends is probably more support for Judge Bork."[98] But McGuigan was forced to concede that Coalitions for America, with a total annual budget of only $150,000, would have a tough time outgunning People for the American Way, which had pledged to spend at least $1 million to defeat Bork's nomination. "We haven't yet budgeted any money," said McGuigan. "Our budget may be low-tech, but it's high-brain."[99]

Conservatives hoped their big money for paid media would come from the California-based Dolphin Group, which was best known for its role in the recall of three ultra-liberal justices on the California Supreme Court. In its early efforts on behalf of Judge Bork, the Dolphin Group gathered support from such luminaries as former President Gerald Ford, California Governor George Deukmejian and members of President Reagan's informal "Kitchen Cabinet," including former Ambassador William Wilson and businessman Holmes Tuttle. "We hope to raise and spend $2 million to $2.5 million in about 10 targeted states, including California, probably Alabama and Arizona," said Dolphin spokeswoman Karen King, referring to the home states of two of the Senate Judiciary Committee's key votes, Democrats Howell Heflin and Dennis DeConcini.[100]

With the Bork nomination only six days old, the National Conservative Political Action Committee and the Conservative Caucus also began to organize what they hoped would be extensive fundraising drives in support of the nomination.[101]

Bork supporters were suprised when Harvard Law School Professor Alan Dershowitz said he supported their argument against rejection of judicial nominees for political reasons, while the Center for Judicial Studies worked to produce a briefing book in response to liberal attacks on Bork's views and opinions. "We are not going to sit back and let the other side beat up on this guy," said James McClellan, the Center's president.[102]

A central argument the right used to support Bork was his unanimous confirmation to the U.S Court of Appeals in 1982. During those Judiciary Committee hearings Senator Max Baucus (D-MT) had declared: "I want to congratulate the president on his confirmation of you. I think there is no doubt that you are eminently qualified to serve in the position to which you have been nominated." This time around, Baucus seemed ambivalent about the man he had praised so highly. Baucus aide Scott Williams explained, "In the circuit court, [Bork's] views on constitutional issues were important, but not so much because he's bound by judgments of the Supreme Court." Even Bork's most outspoken Senate opponent, Edward Kennedy, had made no noise against him during the 1982 hearings. Questioned about this Kennedy said, "The Supreme Court is ten times more important, and Bork can do ten times more damage with his anti-civil rights and anti-civil liberties ideology. When he was a circuit court judge there was always a Supreme Court to keep him in line." Senator Howard Metzenbaum (D-OH), also an avid Bork opponent, had in 1982 merely asked the nominee about his views on anti-trust law. "My concerns are not that your views might differ from mine, but whether you would interpret the law on the basis of heretofore decided Supreme Court opinions," Metzenbaum had said then.[103]

Despite the fact that more and more Senators and liberal groups had been capturing the headlines by coming out against Bork, conservatives felt they at least had one major thing going for them—support from one of the century's most popular presidents. During a radio address that first weekend in July, President Reagan asked that the Senate "keep politics out of the confirmation process . . . Judge Bork is recognized by his colleagues and peers as a brilliant legal scholar and a fair-minded jurist who believes his role is to interpret the law, not make it."[104]

One of the lightest moments of those four months occurred in early July. Steven Roberts of the New York Times *called. He described to me the incredible volume of activity he was perceiving on the liberal side, conveying his belief they were outdoing us in the early going. I told him Bork's supporters on the outside were doing their best and working hard and fast and would catch up.*

He pursued the point, reasonably asking me for specifics. I described the last several days of activity and pointed him to American Conservative Union, Concerned Women for America, National Right to Work, National Right to Life and other allies for further examples of how we were trying to trigger the grass roots.

Jokingly, I concluded: "Listen, Steve. I'll tell you what this is really about. It's about the first man on the Supreme Court in fifty years with a beard. First one since Charles Evans Hughes. We're talking about the restoration of principled jurisprudence here. I'll tell you what I'm gonna do. I'm not gonna shave 'til Bork is confirmed. It's Beards for Bork."

Laughing, he asked if he could send a photographer to catch the beard and told me, "This is the first light moment in this whole thing."

I replied, "Everybody's so somber on both sides. It's just the most serious Supreme Court nomination in fifty years. Lighten up."

He loved it. He sent a photographer. The story was carried coast to coast. Out in Oklahoma, my wife heard about the beard. She was not happy, having encouraged removal, in 1980, of the beard I sported at our marriage in 1976.

Seven years of serious work in journalism, legal research and other writing. One book of my own. Editor of five more books. And the most coverage I've ever received in my career was for that damn beard. Pam was one of the first to ask me: "What if he loses?"
I told her, "Don't worry. He's not gonna lose."

The confirmation fight took on an interesting twist that added some punch to the conservative argument when several self-described liberals went public in defense of Bork. Perhaps the greatest coup in this regard was a pro-Bork commentary that eventually appeared in the July 16 issue of the New York *Times*. The author was Lloyd Cutler, former counsel to President Jimmy Carter and founder of the notoriously liberal Lawyers Committee for Civil Rights Under Law. Cutler wrote:

> In my view, Judge Bork is neither an ideologue nor an extreme right-winger, either in his judicial philosophy or in his personal position on current social issues. I base this assessment on a post-nomination review of Judge Bork's published articles and opinion, and on 20 years of personal association as a professional colleague or adversary. I make it as a liberal Democrat and as an advocate of civil rights before the Supreme Court. . . . Every new appointment creates some change in the "balance" of the Court, but of those on the list the President reportedly considered, Judge Bork is one of the least to create a decisive one.[105]

Cutler's public defense of Bork created friction within his liberal Washington, D.C. law firm, Wilmer, Cutler & Pickering, where about a dozen lawyers were busy preparing an analysis for the Lawyers Committee attacking Bork. Also angered were officials at the American Civil Liberties Union and Common Cause, organizations he had worked closely with in the past, and other liberals, such as Ralph Nader. Cutler's editorial "was very insincere," Nader charged. "Cutler is trying to come on as a civil-rights leader and a liberal Democrat—neither which he is. He's a Washington corporate lawyer." Public Citizen President Joan Claybrook sent the New York *Times* a letter to protest what she believed was Culter's hidden agenda. "There is probably no jurist before whom a corporate lawyer would rather plead in Washington, D.C. than Judge Bork,"[106] she wrote. The *Times* declined to publish her remarks. But Nan Aron at the liberal Alliance for Justice noted that Cutler's endorsement "was a setback," adding, "Lloyd Cutler is such a respected luminary of the bar here that it demanded a response, and a response by someone of equal stature."[107]

Cutler was surprised at the agitation from the Left. "I think it's overblown. I don't like the notion that opposition to Bork [results in] his supporters having their motivations attacked," he said. "If the litmus test of being a liberal is opposing Judge Bork, then I'm no liberal." Cutler also noted that there had been no personal gain from his endorsement: "Whatever the firm gets . . . means nothing to me financially. I'm looking at the Bork nomination from the point of view of a constitutional lawyer, not from whether the nomination is pro-business."[108]

July 10, 1987 LIFELETTER #7, Ad Hoc Committee in Defense of Life
The Ad Hoc Committee in Defense of Life (AHCDL) thought that the Bork nomination could wind up being the decisive battle in "the Abortion War." (Robert M. Patrick, " 'Party of Abortion' Digs in to Defeat Bork's Nomination," Lifeletter #7, Ad Hoc Committee in Defense of Life, Inc., 1987) Abortion was making the headlines with the Bork nomination announcement. Roe v. Wade *and Bork were suddenly synonymous with each other. After Biden had pulled his switcheroo under pressure from the pro-abortion people and Ted Kennedy made his "extremist" remarks, "the Abortion War" intensified.*

Ted Kennedy and Joe Biden really got jumped on in the AHCDL "Lifeletter #7." They were characterized as members of the "Party of Abortion," and scathed for their highly visible support of the "Dem's special-interest groups . . . led by the entire pro-abort apparat. . . ." For the AHCDL, abortion was the issue.

I recognized there was some irony in all of this, though. As the Lifeletter *piece admitted, "nobody knows whether Bork himself is for or against abortion."*

As the battle raged on, Raoul Berger, a former professor at Harvard and a self-described liberal, confessed:

What it boils down to is if you're a liberal—and I am a liberal—it's my ideology against yours and I don't like yours . . . There are areas where I haven't agreed with Bork, but on whole he will make a fine judge. I'm for abortion . . . my sympathies are with [Senate Judiciary Committee Chairman Joseph] Biden and [Judiciary Committee member Paul] Simon rather than with [abortion foe Senator] Jesse Helms, but along with almost all academics, I don't think the Constitution guarantees it. So we hear talk about ideologues. The Supreme Court decision on abortion was the work of ideologues.[109]

Though he was wary of Judge Bork's judicial philosophy, Geoffrey Stone, dean at the University of Chicago Law School, said he would also support the nominee:

> If it were a person of lesser ability, I would vote against the confirmation, but my own view is that Bork's capabilities are so unquestionable that he would make significant contributions even though I think his views are out of sync [with the establishment legal community].[110]

Prominent conservatives wrote in eloquent defense of Bork as well, attacking the accusations that Bork was an extremist who would force women to perform wretched coathanger abortions on themselves and send minorities back into slavery. The black nationally syndicated columnist Lawrence Wade wrote:

> For 200 years of racist sins, they want Robert Bork's blood.
> It's all so hypocritical. With the civil rights struggle two decades behind us, many Americans smugly forget how far we've come since Martin Luther King's dream. If Robert Bork is forever guilty of bigotry, then so, too, is most of white America. . . . Must all whites suffer for age-old racist sins? By 1967, the cities were burning and many young blacks are angry. I'd hate to pay today for what I said and thought of whites back then. Raymond A. Randolph, a lawyer and former associate of Judge Bork, recalls working with him: "I never saw him flinch from what he considered to be his duty to support the rights of minority groups, to support the laws as Congress had written them."[111]

Remaining true to the flashy fashion that had made it famous, the New York *Post* printed a furious attack on the motives for bashing Bork:

> Anti-administration liberals seem intent on provoking a gunfight at the O.K. Corral over President Reagan's nomination of Robert Bork for the Supreme Court. Or maybe it's Custer's Last Stand they want to emulate. Seldom has a nomination to high office produced a reaction so strident in tone and so vicious in content. In near-desperation over the popular rejection of their entire political philosophy, liberals seem to have abandoned rational argument in favor of hysteria and character assassination. . . . But liberals have long relied on interventionist judges to implement the policies that liberals themselves advocate—policies that have been rejected by the American people in the voting booth again and again.[112]

The immediate volume of response on both sides led Washington *Post* editorial writers to note that they "hoped" the confirmation proceedings wouldn't degenerate into a "a mud-pie contest. That kind of approach to the nomination would be wrong, wrong, *wrong.*"[113]

Liberals and conservatives embroiled in the confirmation battle worked furiously to activate the grass-roots members of their organizations. But in the arena of the actual fight—the nation's capital—the four Senate Judiciary Committee members who had remained uncommitted became the focus of the intense lobbying efforts: Senators Howell Heflin (D-AL), Dennis DeConcini (D-AZ), Arlen Specter (R-PA), and Patrick Leahy (D-VT). Conservatives predicted they would win the votes of Heflin and DeConcini, as both had indicated they would generally support a president's judicial nominee. DeConcini explained, "I look at Judge Bork as I do any nomination by any president, and the presumption is with the nominee."[114]

Heflin said that political considerations would not determine his vote. "I do not believe the confirmation will be based solely on ideology, certainly not with me,"[115] he said. "I think we'll eventually get his vote," said Patrick McGuigan, noting that the Senator's career on the Alabama Supreme Court indicated that he "believes in principled judicial restraint."[116]

Armed with a statement by Heflin asserting his belief in "a right of implied privacy in the Constitution," Estelle Rogers, director of the liberal Federation of Women Lawyers, said she was "optimistic" that Heflin would vote with her side.[117]

Clearly, Heflin was a toss-up. But both sides were acutely aware of the importance his support would carry. "A lot of the Southern Democratic senators look to Heflin on nominations," said a former Heflin Judiciary Committee aide. "They don't necessarily follow him, but they look to him, like people look to [Senator] Sam Nunn [D-GA] on defense."[118]

Opponents believed they would draw Leahy's support because the Senator had expressed concern that Bork might vote to overturn *Roe*. Specter was unreadable, saying simply, "I shall participate fully in the judicial hearings with an open mind."[119] All four of the "swing-vote" Senators backed Scalia's nomination to the Supreme Court in 1986, but Leahy had rejected the elevation of Justice William Rehnquist to Chief Justice.

The five Senators who had united early behind the Bork nomination were Republicans Orrin Hatch (UT), Alan Simpson (WY), Gordon Humphrey (NH), Charles Grassley (IA), and Strom Thurmond (SC).

The five committee Democrats whose initial statements were interpreted as immediate opposition were chairman Joseph Biden (DE), Edward Kennedy (MA), Howard Metzenbaum (OH), Paul Simon (IL), and Robert Byrd (WV).[120]

Meanwhile, Chairman Biden had yet to set a date for the hearings. The Democrats, hoping to buy the special-interest groups enough time to penetrate the average household with anti-Bork ads, said the Judge would not receive his hearings fast enough to put him on the high court before the opening of its new term on October 5. Pressed for action, Biden finally announced on July 8 that the Senate Judiciary Committee hearings had been scheduled for September 15, and would run at least two weeks. "My first job is to get this nomination up before the committee and voted on," said Biden. "Everything else is secondary now. This is probably the most significant Supreme Court nomination in the last several decades and arguably in this century."[121]

At a meeting of the Senate Judiciary Committee earlier that day, Senator Gordon Humphrey (R-NH) had challenged Biden's decision. "I would just like to suggest that the date cited for the commencement of the hearings, September 15th, is not consistent with the primary purpose of the matter and I would urge the chairman to reconsider that date; indeed, to move that up to something in July," Humphrey said. Biden replied, "I would remind the Senator on average from the time the nominee has been sent to this committee to the time hearings have begun it has been somewhere between 45 and 60 days. . . . I have no intention nor do I know of anyone on the committee who has the intention to keep this nomination in committee. We will move expeditiously in the committee."[122]

This delay of nearly 10 weeks infuriated most Republican Senators and the Reagan Administration. "The most important consideration is that we need to fill that vacancy by the start of the new term," Senator Humphrey said. "If that seat is empty, many cases will end in deadlock. What we're talking about is justice, not politics, and justice delayed is justice denied."[123] Senator Hatch agreed: "Unless a time agreement can be worked out so that Judge Bork can sit on the Supreme Court for the first Monday in October [traditional first day of its session] I think the stalls and delays are politically outrageous and should not be tolerated by the people of this country." White House spokesman Marlin Fitzwater agreed: "It is regrettable that [Biden] has chosen to politicize the hearings in this kind of partisan fashion and further regrettable that we won't be able to have a full court when the term starts. We are hopeful that they will reconsider." Senate Minority

Leader Robert Dole pledged that Judiciary Committee Republicans would be "willing to stay here during the August recess if necessary" to speed up the process.[124]

Biden's decision sparked a new round of editorials, such as this one appearing in the Detroit *News*:

> Joseph Biden, chairman of the Senate Judiciary Committee, wants to delay hearings on Judge Robert Bork's nomination to the Supreme Court until September so that committee members will have plenty of time to prepare. But Sen. Biden appears to need no time to prepare himself for his advise-and-consent role. He has already decided, he says, that Judge Bork is unfit for the high court.[125]

. . . or this one from the San Gabriel *Valley Tribune*:

> The reason for Sen. Biden's craven dilatory maneuver is twofold: To preclude Judge Bork from being available when the other eight justices begin the court's new term on the first Monday of October; and to allow liberal opponents time to mount an impassioned lobbying campaign among senators to defeat President Reagan's conservative nominee. The lengthy delay engineered by Sen. Biden is especially inexcusable when one considers that the Senate studied Judge Bork's record in exacting detail only five years ago and overwhelmingly confirmed him to the federal appellate court.[126]

Everyone who had ever had a connection with Bork wanted a piece of the action and the media attention that would follow. Michael Milone, the city controller for New Haven, Connecticut, where Bork had lived while teaching at Yale Law School, told the press that the Judge owed the city $1,009.72 in back taxes and interest for a 1972 Buick station wagon and a 1968 Volvo listed on the tax records for 1972 and 1973. City officials said they had sent Bork as many as 25 reminders of his failure to pay, and when the story hit, Bork's accountant told city officials their money was in the mail.[127]

The story flared again a week later when Controller Milone alerted the media that his office had indeed received Bork's personal check totaling $1,316.09. "Judge Bork's account with the city is now current," he said. On top of the $1,009.72 Bork supposedly owed for his two cars, he paid $306.37 for his son's auto taxes from 1977. Bork said he was "never informed of a tax liability remotely resembling the size of the one now assessed."[128]

Daniel Sheehan, co-founder and general counsel of the radical

Christic Institute made headlines when he accused Judge Bork of an ethics violation for his participation in a case the institute had argued before Bork in 1984.[129]

By mid-July, with so many interest groups taking an active part in the anti-Bork effort and even more preparing to do so in the weeks before the hearings, officials at the American Civil Liberties Union and Common Cause faced a dilemma. They laid claim to a non-partisan reputation, and traditionally both groups strove to maintain their apolitical status in the public eye by, among other things, usually withholding comment on judicial nominees.

The ACLU had made only one exception in 50 years when, in 1971, it fought the Supreme Court nomination of William Rehnquist. The 17-year-old Common Cause broke its rule only in 1984–85, when it opposed the nomination of Edwin Meese III to the position of attorney general, and in 1986 when it launched an offensive against Daniel Manion for a position on the Seventh U.S. Circuit Court of Appeals.[130]

Despite the "rule" and the consequences of breaking it, ACLU activists were straining to untie their hands. "The Bork nomination is an extraordinary event in terms of civil liberties," said Paul Hoffman of the ACLU Los Angeles chapter. "There is a feeling by a lot of people within the ACLU that this is too important for us not to take a position."[131] Their stake in Bork's downfall was clear. The Supreme Court had agreed to hear six cases involving the ACLU when it returned for its fall session. In five of those cases, the lower court had issued rulings favorable to the ACLU. In the event of a tied vote on an eight-member court with one vacancy, the decision of the lower court would stand. "The balance of voting power is unpredictable," said ACLU Associate Legal Director Helen Hirshkoff. "One could certainly wager" that some of their cases might end in split decisions.[132]

Pending a decision from the board to oppose the nomination, the 250,000–member group would target key Senators and file for permission to testify before the Senate Judiciary Committee hearings.

David Cohen, co-director of Advocacy Institute, a lobbying group, and a member of the Common Cause board, said his group was also thinking of violating its precedent. "This straightforward an issue is not something you ignore," he said. But such a move by Common Cause could be costly, as its chairman, Archibald Cox, had been the man fired by Judge Bork during the "Saturday Night Massacre."

If it decided to make Bork an exception, Common Cause planned to work exclusively on the grass-roots level, activating its 275,000 members to lobby their senators against Bork.

Groups already in the throes of the Bork war were hoping the ACLU and Common Cause would choose to join them. "From both organizations, it would be a significant boost," said Nan Aron of the Alliance for Justice. "They are both well-respected by the public and they've got a vast network of citizens, lawyers, and interested people, who, if mobilized, would add a significant voice to the battle."[133]

While the ACLU and Common Cause were deliberating, members of the National Abortion Rights Action League gathered in Washington, D.C. for their annual three-day convention, which was spent creating anti-Bork strategy. Sporting "Borkbuster" buttons, NARAL activists drew up a target list of certain senators they hoped to win to their side. The Democrats on the list included undecided Senate Judiciary Committee members Howell Heflin (AL) and Dennis DeConcini (AZ). Many of the Republican targets were friendly to abortion advocates but had voted for the confirmation of William Rehnquist as Chief Justice in 1986. They included Senators Bob Packwood (OR), Lowell P. Weicker Jr. (CT), Daniel J. Evans (WA), and Arlen Specter (PA).

"We'll try to stop this nomination in the committee," Bob Bingaman, the NARAL Washington lobbyist, said. "But I think at this point a best-case scenario would be that the committee will send the nomination to the full Senate without any recommendation." Kate Michelman, executive director of the 250,000-member league, said her group would also hold several anti-Bork demonstrations and lobby Senators while they were home during Congress' August break. Arlene Swartz of New York NARAL said members in that state had already begun phoning senate offices and flooding the mails with postcards and telegrams. According to Swartz, her group could activate the mailing campaign almost instantaneously because it had access to a high-tech computer system allowing NARAL members to authorize use of their names on lobbying correspondence without specific authorization in advance of each mailing.[134]

July 17, 1987 media packet
In less than two weeks, another packet was sent to the news editors' list. It was filled with columns, articles, and quotes from academics, editorialists and court observers describing a consensus that recognized Judge Bork as the preeminent conservative legal scholar and jurist of our time. Because the battle over his nomination was becoming so fierce, we hoped, perhaps naively, that this material would help the editors see for themselves the qualifications and merits of the nominee. With Teddy Kennedy interjecting the term "extremist" into

the picture so decisively with his powerful floor speech, Dan and I believed it was imperative to convince such opinion leaders that Bork's opposition was willing to put politics ahead of the national interest.

By mid-July, Biden was focusing on the Bork battle on the campaign trail. During an appearance at Scott Community College in Davenport, Iowa, Biden expanded on his initial expressions of opposition, making perhaps his clearest public declaration since his comments on July 8:

> I see no way in which I can support Judge Bork. I feel President Reagan made a mistake in offering Judge Bork as a nominee for the court. [Bork] is very bright and a very decent man, but he has sharp-edged views. He is a product of the Reagan-Meese agenda. I believe it was a very straight-forward political appointment. Everybody [sic]—the left, the right and the middle, senators and press alike—say this has the potential of turning the clock back 30 years. [I could support him] if it was a matter of Judge Bork having an open mind on a whole lot of issues.

Biden said that he was worried about Bork's outspoken views on "fundamental questions such as is there a right of privacy," adding, "When the president makes what appears to be a pure political judgment to forward his political agenda . . . it's totally appropriate for the U.S. Senate to challenge that."[135]

The following day, Senate Minority Leader Robert Dole (R-KS) and Senator Gordon Humphrey (R-NH) asked Chairman Biden to set a "date certain" for the Judiciary Committee to cast its vote on Bork. Biden, asserting that "we have no intention to hold up this nomination," turned down the request, but promised to send the nomination to the full Senate by October 1.[136]

An infuriated Humphrey said the 70-day delay between Bork's nomination and the scheduled September 15 hearings was "unprecedented and outrageous," and part of a political game Biden was playing with the American people. Humphrey charged there was "a strong circumstantial case" that Biden delayed the nomination hearings to further his presidential bid and give Bork bashers "more time to conduct a witch hunt." Humphrey cited a Congressional Research analysis written by Denis Steven Rutkus indicating the average time between Supreme Court nominations and hearings had been only 17.5 days in the past quarter century. Humphrey declared, "the study shows just how unprecedented and outrageous is the plan of the chairman of the Judiciary Committee to delay" the hearings. Biden spokesman Peter Smith countered, "Senator Humphrey is not a member of the Republican leadership in the Senate and is a freshman on the [Judiciary] committee who as far as I know has played no role whatsoever in any decisions of the process."[137]

For the first time in its history, the National Hispanic Bar Association announced that it would oppose a Supreme Court nominee. Judge Bork was not the Hispanic they had hoped would be nominated, and they believed his judicial philosophy was insensitive to their concerns. "He's a bad choice," said Mike Mendez, president of the 3,000-member bar association, which had announced its decision July 18. "Mr. Bork is an intellectual and he is respected within certain communities. But he is predisposed, he already has a set opinion on a number of issues which would impact heavily on our community." Mendez continued, "The administration has consistently failed to get our input. The Hispanic community is a nonentity when it comes to this sort of thing." Washington, D.C. lawyer and Hispanic activist Maria Carmen Aponte said young Hispanics were in desperate need of a respectable hero. "We can't look to anybody. We do not have a role model. We don't have an idea if something like that is possible. Having an Hispanic on the court would tell us the American dream is alive. It would say that if you train well and do the right thing and work hard you can become a policy maker in this country."[138]

Not all Hispanic groups and leaders were opposing Judge Bork, however. Among those in the Hispanic community who announced public support of the nominee were the Hispanic Economic Council; Dr. Hernan Padilla, director of the Presidential Scholars Commission; Dr. Luis Queral, director of the Maryland Hispanic Chamber of Commerce; Jose Manuel Casanova, U.S. director for the Inter-American Bank; Dr. Tirso del Junco, director of the Presidential Commission on Broadcasting to Cuba; Carlos Perez, director of Concerned Citizens for Democracy; and Dr. Alba Moesser, chair of the National Center for Hispanic Women.[139]

Joe Biden made headlines that same day, claiming he had "made a mistake" by failing thoroughly to explain why he would oppose Bork when he had indicated his position on the nomination. But in a speech to the Association of State Democratic Chairs in Cleveland, Biden said he would stand firm by his new position on Bork. "It was more of a public-relations mistake than a substantive mistake," he explained.[140]

A few weeks into the battle, Weyrich came to see me in my office one afternoon. On July 14, he had reflected on the meaning of the

Bork nomination at a joint Coalitions for America/Moral Majority press conference actually called on another topic. He told reporters Bork was "one of the most scholarly and thoughtful" jurists of this Century but confessed "I didn't like Judge Bork before he was Judge Bork, in a lot of things that he did in the Nixon administration . . . Judge Bork has not been some long creature of the conservative movement who all of a sudden has been rewarded because of his faithfulness to conservative views . . . I fear for the day that we say scholarship and judicial temperament don't matter, what matters is a position on a particular issue that must be decided in advance in the absence of a particular case . . . Anybody who thinks this guy is a doctrinaire conservative has another thought coming."

When he came to my office around that same time, Paul expressed concern for my well being. Rather than the stern look that conveys urgency or intensity, I saw in his eyes the concern that occasionally moves him to slow his amazingly frenetic pace, to offer counsel to a friend.

He got right to the point.

"Pat, you are as uptight now, only a couple of weeks after this started, as you were at the end of the Manion fight. You've got to step back, ease up, keep things in perspective."

"You're probably right. It's just this simple: They [the liberal opponents of Bork] are doing so much, so fast, so thoroughly and so effectively. Do you think we can win?" I asked.

"We have a chance because it's Bork. But the other side has the Senate, and some of our normal champions aren't exactly pulling out all the stops for this guy. We can win, but we might lose," he answered.

He told me to pray, to stay focused, to work hard and do my best— and to go home early that one day and spend time with my kids and Pam. So I did.

For a time it seemed that every major liberal group was holding national meetings and discussing Judge Bork. The weekend of July 19, newly-elected National Organization for Women (NOW) President Molly Yard presided over their convention in Philadelphia. "Our first action will be to stop the confirmation of the Bork nomination," she cried to the crowd. "He is a Neanderthal. I don't quite know why he is still around. For the women of America we are not going to take someone on the court who is going to reverse [legal abortions]. It's our lives. We are going to fight every inch of the way to keep him from being confirmed."[141]

Some elements of the Reagan Administration, meanwhile, began to express outrage at the way Senate Democrats had pandered to the liberal special interests. President Reagan's chief domestic policy advisor, Gary Bauer, told reporters for the Washington *Times* at a July 19 luncheon: "The Bork nomination is an opportunity for the Democratic party to show that they are not in the hip pocket of special interests and leftist ideologues, who are insisting on a litmus test for the confirmation process." Bauer added that "the early signs" were "not good" for confirmation, especially considering that Senator Kennedy's outrageous attack against Bork on the Senate floor went unchallenged among his Democratic colleagues. This "seems to me a sign of the incredible power of ideologues in that party to cower otherwise principled men into silence." Bauer continued: "There was a time when the Democratic party was . . . the kind of party that could have George Wallace and Martin Luther King Jr. under the same tent, with all the ferment that meant." But, he cautioned, the liberals should be wary of the potential fall-out of their attacks. "To the extent they try to picture this man as some kind of Neanderthal who gets up every morning trying to figure out how he can strip the American people of their rights, that will not be what the American people see when they watch the hearings," he said.[142]

Senator Biden was also sensitive to the fact that if the voters discovered how the special interests had dictated opposition to Bork, they might leave the Democratic party. If Democrats don't focus on Bork's lack of fitness for the bench, they could be seen as "a special-interest, single-interest vehicle," Biden said, adding, "I don't have an open mind. The reason I don't have an open mind is because I know this man. . . . I see no way, based on my knowledge of Bork's record, that I could vote for Bork." Biden also asserted that he would "strongly recommend" that the nomination be withdrawn if the Judiciary Committee vote went against Bork.[143]

Joe Biden was not the only presidential candidate using Bork on the stump. Vice President George Bush told voters:

> Judge Bork has been universally acclaimed as a brilliant jurist and scholar of the constitution. But Senator Kennedy has already gone after Bork, before the hearings, before giving the man a chance. Never mind that the American Bar Association has given Bork its highest—its very highest rating. Others said Judge Bork would upset the "balance" on the court. You know, when liberals talk about "balance," I'm reminded of the line from *Animal Farm*: "All animals are equal, but some animals are more

equal than others.'' When close votes go their way, liberals say the court is balanced; when close votes go against them, it's the end of the world. I recall that three years ago, Walter Mondale, in an effort to scare the voters, warned that President Reagan might get the chance to reshape the Supreme Court. The voters considered that possibility and pulled the Reagan-Bush lever.[144]

As Patrick McGuigan had indicated when the battle first began, the bottom line was votes. According to Senate Majority Whip Alan Cranston (D-CA), the mid-July Senate vote was split 45–45, with 10 uncommitted.[145]

July 23, 1987   American Conservative Union/Coalitions for America joint press conference
Almost a month into the confirmation battle. Dan and I held a joint press conference presenting the two sides of Senator Joe Biden. As we had been noting since the start of the battle, the Delaware Senator had really flip-flopped in his views on selecting judges. Up until 1986 he said things like this: courts create problems when they involve themselves in non-judicial functions; Judge Bork was one of the finest solicitors to hold that office; and if someone like Judge Bork was nominated he would have to support him regardless of how the liberal interest groups felt.

Now, the man who would be president was saying that the founding fathers meant for the Senate to be very broad and political in its votes on judges. Senate confirmation, he said, wasn't guaranteed just because a nominee was moral, competent and qualified. If a nominee was philosophically unfit, the president must choose someone else.

I asked the assembled reporters to find who the real Joe Biden was. Using the Delaware Senator's own words about Bork's view of the Constitution, Dan said that Joe Biden was "insignicant and pliant" and wanted a Supreme Court that doesn't adhere to the doctrine of original intent.

In this press conference Dan and I called on Biden to recuse himself and step down from the chairmanship of the Senate Judiciary Committee. More exasperated than I with the progress of the battle thus far, Dan said Biden should "stick to the pursuit of his own personal ambition and let the country's business be taken care of by men with more integrity."

At least one of us was beginning to pay attention to the Left's modes of operation.

working the Hill: Rudman

On July 27, Casey and I met with Senator Warren Rudman. The meeting resulted from a chance encounter a few days before between Paul Weyrich and Rudman at a restaurant in the nation's capital.

Given Rudman's conduct in the recent Iran-Contra hearings, Weyrich was a bit cool to the New Hampshire Republican, who without waiting for an invitation sat next to him.

Rudman leaned over to Weyrich and declared intently, "Paul, you and I may disagree on some things, but we ought to be able to agree on the most important battle either of us has been involved in in recent years."

Weyrich responded. "Oh. Really. What's that?"

"Bork, of course!" Rudman responded.

Back at he office, Paul told me, "The jerk wants to make up for playing ball with the Democrats in the hearings. He's catching hell from the [Manchester, N.H.] Union Leader. Fine. Let's make him deliver." Paul suggested Casey and I seek a meeting with Rudman.

The session was amicable and productive, or so we thought at the time, but I could not help conveying some of the skepticism I felt about his asserted intensity on judicial questions. Picking up on my skepticism about his committment to conservative jurisprudence, Rudman lobbied me, "Listen, in some respects I'm more conservative than Bork. I have my doubts about the doctrine of incorporation [of the Fourteenth Amendment] that Bork seems to accept."

I drily responded, "Well, I have my doubts about incorporation, too."

Casey pulled out a four pager on Bork's judicial views he had prepared overnight. "Senator, why don't you take this with you on your vacation in New Hampshire during the break? Perhaps you could use it."

"Absolutely, I want to do whatever I can for Bork. I'll read it back in the state and prepare something for later."

"So we can count on you to do something substantive to help on this—an op-ed for the Post or one of the other papers?" Dan pressed respectfully.

"You bet," came the reply. We shook hands and left.

Dan and I walked out into the Hart Building atrium.

I felt uneasy about Rudman. As we parted to walk back to our offices in the Washington heat, I asked Casey, "Why do I feel like I need to wash my hands?"

Bork foes in the Senate tried to sway their undecided colleagues by emphasizing their interpretation of "advise and consent." On July 23, Senator Joe Biden delivered the first in a planned series of speeches on the Senate floor—written by his cabinet of advisors—purporting to outline historical examples of when Supreme Court nominees had been rejected for their personal views. Biden, who spoke for an hour, asserted that "history, precedent and common sense" explain why the Senate has "not only the right but the duty" to subject Judge Bork's views to close examination, adding, "Political or philosophical issues have played a role, sometimes a dominant one, in the outcome of all but one of the 26 Supreme Court nominations rejected or withdrawn since 1789."

Senate Republicans were furious. Even Minority Leader Robert Dole (R-KS), disappointing to Bork supporters at times, responded aggressively to Biden's assertions, saying, "We could all conjure up an imaginary nominee whose ideology was so bizarre, whose thought processes were so alien, that we would feel obliged to vote against him or her." But such an "imaginary candidate" could not have served in the many prestigious positions Bork had, including U.S. Solicitor General, federal judge, and Yale Law School professor. "Our inquiry should focus on the nominee's ability and integrity, and upon whether the nominee would faithfully and neutrally apply the Constitution in a manner that upholds the prerogatives of the three coordinate branches. If we go beyond this and require that judicial candidates pledge allegiance to the political and ideological views of particular senators or interest groups, we will do grave and irreparable violence to basic separation of powers principles that act as the ultimate safeguard against the tyranny of the majority," Dole said.[146]

Senator Alan Simpson (R-WY) agreed. "If we're going to oppose the Bork nomination simply because Judge Bork has been nominated by a conservative Republican President, why don't we just come out and say so. Let's admit we don't like Judge Bork."[147]

The issue of ideology continued to be a topic of debate outside the Senate floor as well. Senator Paul Simon (D-IL), another candidate for his party's presidential nomination, told the Washington Council of Lawyers: "The Senate is broadly representative of the country's political diversity. It does not defer to the president when it thinks his proposed budget or legislation will harm the country, and the same should be true with respect to his judicial nominees." Simon added that although he did not plan to announce his vote until after the hearings, he had "serious reservations on the balance and sensitivity issues. The law shouldn't be a pendulum that swings back and forth according to who is president."[148]

The debate even inspired a New York *Times* poll. In phone interviews conducted July 21 and 22, 745 people were asked: "When senators decided how to vote on confirming a president's nominee for the Supreme Court, after satisfying themselves about the nominee's legal experience and background, how much importance should a senator attach to the nominee's positions on major constitutional issues?" A full 62 percent answered, "a lot"; 25 percent, a little"; 7 percent, "no answer"; and 6 percent, "none at all." Asked for an opinion on recent Supreme Court decisions, 36 percent said they considered the court too liberal, 38 percent said it was too conservative, 43 percent said it had been too soft on criminals, and 41 percent said it had acted properly in protecting criminals' rights. The most interesting statistic the poll found was that although the Bork battle had been raging for more than a month and a half, not many people outside of Washington even knew what was going on. Only 23 percent of the respondents were educated enough to give an opinion on Judge Bork: 11 percent said they had a favorable opinion of him, while 12 percent had an unfavorable opinion.[149]

The third week in July, conservative leaders engaged in the Bork battle held a clandestine strategy meeting in Washington, D.C. to discuss their outrage over White House lack of action on behalf of their nominee. They believed that Chief of Staff Howard Baker and White House lobbyist William Ball were too weak to battle hostile Senate Democrats. Conservatives also expressed concern that their closest ally in this fight, Attorney General Edwin Meese III, was being denied his part in helping the confirmation. And pro-Bork leaders were outraged that conservatives who did take a strong pro-Bork stand, namely Education Secretary William Bennett and Gary Bauer, White House domestic policy advisor, received no support from their own administration. Bennett had only angered the Bakers and the Balls when he demanded that Biden remove himself from his post on the Judiciary Committee. Bauer too, had encountered cold shoulders within the Administration for chastising Democratic Senators who refused to challenge outrageous anti-Bork statements made by Edward Kennedy (D-MA) on the Senate floor.[150]

As July came to an end, Christian broadcaster Pat Robertson, a Republican presidential candidate, predicted that Biden's presidential hopes would be ruined by the fight over Bork, mainly because Americans knew Biden had "flip-flopped four times on the issue" of Judge Bork's confirmation.[151]

Revising some of his early, if not explicit, indications of opposition (in remarks before the NAACP convention), New York Governor Mario Cuomo, a Democrat who was rumored to be considering a bid for the White House, infuriated members of his party by saying he would "not be distressed" with the Bork nomination, as long as he were satisfied that Bork's opinions "would leave intact the workings of the political branches of government, the presidency and the Congress." Cuomo added: "If he is the kind of conservative who leaves in place wherever possible the acts of the president and Congress then, convinced as I am that the Democrats are going to have the presidency and hold Congress, I need not be concerned about a Judge who will leave our political acts intact." Cuomo, who stressed that he would not make a judgment until after the hearings, said he was concerned whether Bork would "strike down statutes he believes have gone too far." Cuomo also criticized Joe Biden and other Senate Democrats for condemning Bork before the nominee had his chance before the Judiciary Committee. "It is the worst kind of irony to condemn Bork on the grounds that he's not open minded about the law when you yourself haven't waited for the hearings to take place," said Cuomo, who once taught law at St. John's. "Certainly you ought not make a judgment until Judge Bork has had the benefit of a hearing."[152]

As the battle dragged into its second month, Senate Minority Leader Robert Dole (R-KS) noted that President Reagan had the authority to give Bork a short-term position on the Supreme Court during the congressional recess, scheduled for August 10 through September 9, on the grounds the Senate had gone too far in delaying the nomination. Dole noted that if the full Senate did not overturn such action by the President, Bork could serve as a Justice until three weeks before the end of the Reagan presidency. Dole told the National Conference of State Legislatures in Indianapolis that the "Constitution allows the President to fill any vacancy on the Supreme Court while Congress is in recess, and provides that the person filling that vacancy shall serve until the end of the congressional session." Dole, who said he was not pressing Reagan into taking such action, said Biden was responsible for "the kind of stall being tried now." Dole offered the replacement scheme as "food for thought" for Biden.[153]

During the week of of July 27–July 31, when the White House finally issued its "blue book" on Bork—four weeks after the nomination—an aide to a conservative Republican Senator had a screaming match with Tom Korologos, the private lobbyist working with the White House to support Bork, in the hallway of a Senate office building. The unpleasant scene underscored growing perceptions on the Hill and in the conservative movement that the administration was not doing enough, and certainly not moving quickly enough, to promote Bork's prospects. The incident was eventually even reported in the New York Times *(July 30).*

By July 29 it appeared that President Reagan had finally recognized the urgency of the Bork battle and decided to do something about it. In remarks to members of the National Law Enforcement Council, President Reagan asked them to lobby the Senate on behalf of Bork, telling them:

> I believe Judge Bork will be an extraordinary addition to the Supreme Court. No man in America, and few in history, have been as qualified to sit on the Supreme Court as Robert Bork. Judge Bork deserves to be evaluated on his merits and he deserves to be considered promptly before the court goes into its session in October. [During his] remarkable legal career, [Bork] was recognized as among the best in his field . . . one of the preeminent legal scholars of our time, [who] has been widely acclaimed for his intellectual power and his fairness. . . . The Supreme Court has shown its own esteem for Robert Bork. Judge Bork has written more than 100 majority opinions and joined in another 300 majority opinions. The Supreme Court has never reversed a single one of these more than 400 opinions. That's a vote of confidence any judge in America would envy. And what's more, nine of the ten times the Supreme Court reviewed a case that Judge Bork had ruled on, Justice Powell agreed with Bork. It's hard for a fair-minded person to escape the conclusion that, if you want someone with Justice Powell's detachment and statesmanship, you can't do better than Judge Bork.[154]

Conservatives were cheered by several other developments as well. Judiciary Committee swing vote Dennis DeConcini (D-AZ) told his colleagues they should follow his example and allow Bork to testify before making a decision. And Senator Byrd (D-WV) followed suit, seeming to back off what had appeared to be firm initial opposition, admonishing fellow Democrats who viewed Supreme Court nominations as a "litmus test of party affiliation and loyalty."[155]

A big boost for Bork's supporters came when Supreme Court Justice John Paul Stevens, a centrist who often voted with the liberal justices on social issues, told attendees at the Eighth Circuit Judicial Conference in Colorado: "I personally regard him as a very well-qualified candidate and one who will be a very welcome addition to the court. There are many, many reasons that lead me to that conclusion."[156]

A poll commissioned by the *National Law Journal* became good ammunition for Bork supporters: a full 50 percent of the 348 state and 57 federal judges interviewed said they would vote for Bork if given the chance. Only 24 percent said they would not, while the remainder reserved opinion. The judges were split on interpretation of the Senate's "advice and consent" role, as 48 percent said a nominee's philosophy should not be considered during confirmation, while 46 percent said it should. Of the group interviewed, 47 percent described themselves as moderate-to-conservative, 31 percent as liberal-to-moderate, 6 percent as liberal, and 9 percent as conservative.[157]

It was early August, more than four weeks after the nomination. Key conservative leaders had been working nearly around the clock to get millions of pieces of mail out to grass roots activists. The typical such letter made a simple pitch for letters to members of the Senate (this part of the operation was wildly successful) and asked for contributions so that the fight could be sustained (the mailings were typically only moderately successful in this respect).

The 721 Group, our coalition of conservative and law enforcement groups, was meeting regularly. Informal communication with key players in the Department of Justice was frequent then and throughout the confirmation battle.

Around the country, hundreds of conservative organizations large and small—including Free the Court!, a coalition based in Illinois— were regularly communicating with conservative leaders in the nation's capital. In short, the conservative movement was a beehive of activity for Bork. While nowhere near as well funded as the aggressive leftist coalition opposing Bork, this broad pro-judicial reform coalition was without precedent in the annals of judicial confirmation battles in this decade.

But there was no coordination or consultation between the White House legislative operation and the outside groups supporting Judge Bork. It should be understood that not all of Howard Baker's people were incompetent. Some of them were both competent and conservative. The White House public liaison staff under the able leadership of Rebecca Range, for example, coordinated regular communication between the outside groups and the Chief of Staff. However, the public

*liaison staff is limited in what it can do, and it cannot cross over into
the legislative shop's turf. Until late in the Bork fight, conservative
leaders kept quiet about the utter lack of communication and coordination between the White House legislative people and the outside
groups. Requests for consultation were rebuffed, and feelings grew
increasingly bitter.*

*At that point, the President of a prominent Washington policy
organization suggested a peace parley on (his) neutral territory. Invited to the meeting were key players from the White House as well as
representatives from the two key outside groups working for the
nomination, Coalitions for America and the American Conservative
Union. As sketched above, these organizations had developed a target
list of swing vote Senators within hours after the President's nomination in early July. The meeting was amicable enough, but the White
House types would offer no specifics as to strategy, tactics or target
lists.*

*Finally, one of the conservatives in attendance had had enough. He
asked, "Can't we at least share target lists and consult on who the
key votes are going to be?"*

*The incredible reply was, "It's too early for that, that's not really
necessary."*

*Either Will Ball and company did not have a target list of Senators
or they were so secretive about it that high powered attention was
never focused on those Senators. What's the use of a target list unless
you target the Senators on it? Whereas conservatives had such lists
within hours of the nomination, I can only conclude that the White
House legislative people did not have one four weeks after the nomination.*

Will someone, some day, explain this to me?

Chapter Three

A Steamy Month—A Steamier Battle

The heat over the Bork battle increased as July ended and August—Washington's hottest and most oppressive month—began. On August 1, the governing board of Common Cause voted to become an active participant in anti-Bork efforts, noting, "The record of Robert Bork convinces us that he cannot judge fairly, constitutional claims to liberty and equality."[158]

Judiciary Committee "undecided" Senators Dennis DeConcini (D-AZ) and Howell Heflin (D-AL), said on the August 2 edition of the ABC News program "This Week" that their constituent mail was already running approximately 7 to 1 in favor of Bork's confirmation. And Attorney General Edwin Meese III, speaking on the same program, said he believed Judge Bork's wit and intelligence at the hearings would win enough votes to stave off a Democratic filibuster and put the Judge on the court. "By the time they see Judge Bork in person, by the time they examine his history and background, and by the time they evaluate his capabilities, his philosophy, his approach to the judiciary, I think they're going to vote for him and I think they're going to vote against the filibuster," Meese predicted.[159]

Trying to make up for weeks of apathy and inaction in the Administration, The Justice Department, White House counsel Arthur B. Culvahouse Jr., and several of Bork's colleagues produced a 77–page briefing book outlining arguments in defense of their nominee. Critics who accused Judge Bork of right-wing extremism were greeted with a

53

list of his opinions favoring minorities, women, unions, and even homosexuals, as well as a two-and-a-half page defense of his role in the "Saturday Night Massacre." The report also highlighted Bork's criticisms, on process grounds, of some tenets of the conservative agenda, including his assertion that a constitutional amendment mandating a balanced budget could provoke "nightmare litigation" that would threaten to bring about "judicial dominance in the budget process." The book pointed to Bork's stated opposition to proposed legislation that would deny federal courts jurisdiction over such sensitive social issues as school prayer and abortion. Arguably painting Bork as a moderate in the vein of Justice Powell, the briefing book asserted:

> Judge Bork's appointment would not change the balance of the Supreme Court. In every instance, Judge Bork's decisions are based on his reading of the statutes, constitutional provisions and case law before him. A justice who brings that approach to the Supreme Court will not alter the present balance in any way. Judge Bork's legal philosophy follows directly in the mainstream tradition exemplified by jurists such as Frankfurter, Harlan and Black rather than the "activist" trend which resulted in the invalidation of major New Deal legislation in the 1930s and has recently reemerged in some quarters . . . Judge Bork is an open-minded judge who is well within the mainstream of contemporary jurisprudence . . . Statistics prove that Judge Bork voted with the majority in over 94 percent of those cases. Judge Bork's record on appeal is impeccable. The Supreme Court has never reversed any of the majority opinions written by Judge Bork, which total over 100. Indeed, the Supreme Court has never reversed any of the over 400 majority opinions in which Judge Bork has joined in one way or another.

Answering critics who charged Judge Bork with racism and sexism, the book noted:

> Judge Bork has never wavered in his consistent and principled protection of civil rights, civil liberties and other values that can actually be derived from the Constitution and federal law. . . . Since being elevated to the District of Columbia Circuit Court of Appeals, Judge Bork has participated in a number of important opinions upholding the rights of minorities. In the extended voting rights litigation in *Sumter County v. United States*, he joined an opinion refusing to allow a county to implement an at-large election system because the county failed to show that the voting system had "neither the purpose nor effect of denying or abridging the right of black South Carolinians to vote.". . . . Judge Bork has joined in

several far-reaching decisions that expand the force of laws prohibiting discrimination based on sex. He agreed, for example, that the Foreign Service was subject to the Equal Pay Act, and reversed a district court that had adopted the contrary view. . . . Bork has always emphasized his "abhorrence of racial discrimination."

Responding to the belief of Senator Kennedy and others that Bork would deny women the "right" to abortion, the briefing book stated:

[Regarding abortion] Judge Bork has never stated whether he would vote to overrule *Roe v. Wade*. . . . [He] has in the past questioned only whether there is a right to abortion in the Constitution.

And attempting to eradicate the liberal assertion that the nominee would vote against constitutional protection for every form of speech but political, the briefing book asserted:

During his five years on the bench, Judge Bork has been one of the judiciary's most vigorous defenders of First Amendment values. . . . In *Ollman v. Evans and Novak*, Judge Bork greatly expanded the constitutional protections courts had been according journalists facing libel suits for political commentary. . . . In a letter published in the ABA Journal in 1984, [Bork wrote], "I do not think . . . that First Amendment protection should apply only to speech that is explicitly political. . . . I have long since concluded that many other forms of discourse, such as moral and scientific debate, are central to democratic government and deserve protection."[160]

Explaining why the book was produced, one senior White House official said, "Bork is going to be interrogated on every aspect. You've tempered a little of the argument by saying, 'On this issue, here he is.' " Another White House official added, "Simply put, when you have a man who has written and said as much as he has, we felt that we ought to fairly present the record in terms of what he has said. The document is in our mind a very scrubbed one—[we] tried to make it fair."

Bork bashers, such as Ralph G. Neas of the Leadership Conference on Civil Rights, accused the White House of engaging in a "campaign of disinformation," and charged, "They're attempting to repackage Judge Bork but they can't change the contents." Melanne Verveer of People for the American Way agreed: "It's part of an orchestrated effort, being played out very much in the last week or so to make Bork over in the cloth of Justice Powell, to say he's centrist, to say he's flexible. Obviously their rhetoric is a lot more toned down than what we would have expected and what we heard the first 24 hours after the nomination was made."[161]

Some Bork supporters said that the Bork that they had labeled as "conservative" was no different from the White House depiction of the Judge as a centrist. "Some of us emphasize the judicial philosophy and the possible ramifications of it more than, say, the White House. Comparing him in 90 percent of the cases to Powell, well, it's the other 10 percent that's a step in our direction," said Dan Casey of the American Conservative Union. "We're not talking about a different Bork. [Reagan] is talking about the most qualified nominee in the country and answering the charges that he's a radical. I'm saying . . . by the way, also he's going to begin turning the court back [to the rule of law]." But University of Chicago Law School professor Philip B. Kurland, an advisor to Senator Biden, said "to repaint Robert Bork as a closet liberal [is an] assault on Bork's integrity." In a letter he distributed to the media, Kurland said, "To make Bork over in the image of a Lewis Powell, a Robert Jackson or a Felix Frankfurter, as they would seek to do . . . is to give the lie to Bork's public extrajudicial professions of his beliefs."[162]

Although, unlike Kurland, Bruce Fein of the Heritage Foundation supported Bork, he too believed the report was misleading. "They chose Bob Bork because they wanted him to make changes in the law," Fein said, adding that Reagan should admit "these are the major areas where he believes the court has erred in the past and where he believes Justice Powell perhaps cast an errant vote and he would hope that Judge Bork would correct these."[163]

(Eventually the context of the briefing book's release was forgotten—even balanced elements in the media forgot that the "he's not so extreme" tone of the booklet came in the wake of the massive assaults on Bork released immediately after his nomination. As a result, the White House booklet came to be viewed as a duplicitous effort to refashion Bork's record—rather than as a detailed reply to the key points of the initial assault on his record.)

The same week the White House defense of Bork was released, Ralph Nader's Public Citizen Litigation Group distributed its own briefing book accusing Judge Bork of carrying judicial extremism to unethical lengths. The report asserted, "When a private corporation or business group . . . sued the government, he was a judicial activist."[164]

The week of August 4, People for the American Way began a two-week media blitz in the major U.S. cities of Washington, New York, Chicago and Los Angeles. Its full-page newspaper ad, featuring a magnifying glass trained on the words "advice and consent," was headlined in huge, bold letters: "Why the U.S. Senate should take a very close look at Robert Bork." The advertisement's text zeroed in on the "Saturday Night Massacre," and raised concerns about Bork's opinions on minorities, privacy, and freedom of speech, while avoiding a statement of its actual opposition to the nominee. "In the end, a Supreme Court justice is not supposed to be a White House 'team player,'" the ad declared.[165] The week before Congress recessed for their summer break, PAW also ran radio ads in Washington, D.C., urging Senators to consider Bork's "philosophy, his record, and his sense of judgment," and declaring, "an active Senate role in the confirmation process is the American way."[166]

Dan Casey of the American Conservative Union said the ads showed that the liberals realized they would not win the Bork game without shifting the focus from simply attacking Bork to emphasizing the Senate's duty to closely examine his views. "They realized that their raw political power was not sufficient to deliver a knock-out blow early on, and so they decided to move the argument into changing the rules of the game in order to give themselves time to regroup. They thought they had the groundwork laid, and they quickly realized they didn't. So they've had to sort of step back and start with new building blocks," Casey said.[167]

Mindful of the importance of winning the Southern Democrats—who had a prior history of voting for Reagan nominees—to the anti-Bork side, PAW's Arthur Kropp said his group had also launched plans to reorganize parent-teacher groups in the South into anti-Bork units.[168]

As a counter to the PAW ads, Coalitions for America began running "fairness time" radio spots on two Washington, D.C. stations the same week. "Listen to the reasonable things being said about Judge Bork," the ad said, reading quotes from editorials that had run in the *Wall Street Journal*, the Washington *Post*, and the Baltimore *Sun*, as well as from other sources, including New York's Democratic Governor Mario Cuomo.[169] "The concern of the Senate in the confirmation process should be focused on the proper role of the courts," the ad continued. "Judge Bork believes that judges should not overturn laws passed by our elected officials merely because they personally disagree with them. This judicial philosophy will restore government by the people."[170]

Concerned Women for America also placed pro-Bork advertisements in Alabama and Pennsylvania newspapers asking readers to lobby swing-votes Howell Heflin and Arlen Specter for Bork's confirmation, but these and similar support media efforts were like trying to put out a fire with a garden hose.[171]

On August 5 Committee Chairman Joe Biden finally made the announcement on the Senate floor that his Judiciary Committee would pass the nomination to the full Senate for a vote by October 1—four days before the High Court was scheduled to begin its fall term. "We're concerned the Supreme Court may be starting with only eight members," said Walt Riker, press secretary to Senate Minority Leader Robert Dole.[172]

That same day, also on the Senate floor, freshman Senators Terry Sanford (D-NC) and Wyche Fowler Jr. (D-GA) joined Biden and others in asserting that Bork's ideology should be a main consideration in the confirmation process. "I join with those who argue that it is entirely proper, indeed incumbent upon the Senate, to examine carefully all aspects of a nominee's background and qualifications, including his or her political views and judicial and philosophical inclinations," Sanford declared, adding that he believed Bork's "ideology to be the essential element of his qualifications for this lifetime appointment, and the president has been fairly explicit in saying ideology was a factor with him." Fowler agreed, noting the men and women sitting on the Court should not be "political ideologues—to the left or right—with predetermined agendas. Constitutional adjudication does not, or should not, stem from the theories concocted by the justices. Any discernible pattern of writing decisions to conform to such an ideology must be carefully scrutinized."[173]

Again that same day, the United Church of Christ, which usually reserved public judgment of judicial nominees, announced that it would urge its 1.7 million members to lobby their Senators against Bork because he "seeks to minimize the Bill of Rights."[174]

Meanwhile, Judge Bork was touring Capitol Hill in an attempt to meet with the Judiciary Committee members and other Senators before Congress adjourned for its summer break. During his session with Dennis DeConcini (D-AZ), the Senator pushed for an assurance from Bork that he would comment on his legal theories during the hearings. This prompted DeConcini to write 53 of his Democratic colleagues asking them not to make a decision until the hearings. Bork's session with Ted Kennedy (D-MA), perhaps his most vocal opponent in the Senate, was a token gesture. "Basically, they just shook hands; they didn't have much to say to each other,'' noted one person who had sat in on the meeting.[175]

On August 7, a Friday, an ABC News/Washington *Post* poll claimed 55 percent of all Americans were unaware of who Judge Bork was. Of those who did know, 45 percent approved of him, 40 percent disapproved. On the questions of qualifications, 48 percent considered him qualified while only 12 percent did not.

Most Capitol Hill offices, with the exception of the Senate Judiciary Committee, curtailed activity as Congress ground to a halt for its summer recess on August 10. As Judge Bork continued to hear cases on the court of appeals bench not three blocks away, the Judiciary Committee staff combed through an FBI background check on the nominee, an American Bar Association evaluation of Bork's professional abilities, a 24-page questionnaire completed by the Judge himself, as well as his extensive resume as lawyer, judge, and scholar.[176] "The Democrats are looking for places to attack Judge Bork's record and the Republicans are trying to anticipate where the Democrats will attack and prepare a defense,'' a committee aide explained.[177]

The politically "sexier'' parts of the questionnaire were made public prior to the hearings, including Bork's disclosure that he had quit his membership in a New York City males-only club after signing an unsuccessful petition to eliminate the sex discrimination and allow females to join. "I resigned in October 1985 when I became aware that there was a dispute as to whether a club with an all-male membership was engaged in invidious discrimination,'' Bork wrote.[178]

The Judge disputed critics who had charged that President Reagan only nominated people for judicial seats who passed a "litmus test'' on issues such as abortion and school prayer. "No one involved . . . has discussed any case, legal issue or question in any way that could be interpreted as seeking any express or implied assurances concerning my position on such matters,'' Bork wrote.

Bork, who had been accused of sexism and racism by women and minority groups opposing his nomination, also noted in the wide-ranging questionnaire that he had employed two female lawyers and a black female deputy solicitor during his term as U.S. Solicitor General between 1973 and 1977. Of the 18 law clerks who had worked for him since he became a federal judge in 1982, Bork said that two had been women, while another woman was scheduled to begin working for him later in August.[179]

Meanwhile, a nervous Senator Biden told a reporter in San Diego that Judge Bork had "a slightly better-than-even chance of being confirmed," adding, "I don't know whether or not the nomination can be stopped."[180]

As Senators scattered to their home states, ostensibly to review piles of material on Judge Bork before the full floor vote, the American Bar Association opened its annual convention in San Francisco. It was here that former Chief Justice Warren E. Burger announced, "I don't think in more than 50 years since I was in law school there has ever been a nomination of a man or woman any better qualified than Judge Bork. He has the experience and training. He has got it all. I don't really know what the problem is."[181] Burger added, "No judge up for nomination under any circumstances should ever be asked to commit himself on how he's going to vote on a case that's coming before the court at some future date."[182]

Joe Biden showed up at the conference as well to hold a news conference announcing that he would send Bork's nomination to the full Senate "even if we have enough votes in the committee to say we don't want him to be Justice."[183]

Hoping to influence the ABA's decision on how to rate Bork's fitness for the court, Bork opponents worked the convention with fervor. The liberal Alliance for Justice teamed with the Federation of Women Lawyers to produce a seminar for convention attendees that offered free food and drink along with a panel of speakers that decried the Bork nomination. "I think I've talked to every lawyer here," said Nan Aron of the Alliance.[184]

While the liberal activists continued their campaign, not all jurists were listening. Judge Ralph Adam Fine of Wisconsin, author of *Escape of the Guilty*, defended Bork's "neutral principled" philosophy of the law and said his confirmation "would help restore a proper constitutional balance."

On August 11, Majority Whip Senator Alan Cranston (D-CA) issued another report on the status of Judge Bork's nomination, asserting that 46 senators had chosen to oppose it, 44 had said they would support it, and 10 remained uncommitted. But Bork supporters charged that Cranston's office was manufacturing the figures to influence the vote. "In too many cases, he assumes how Republican and Democratic members will vote," said one senior Republican aide. "I don't know anybody who really takes those as firm figures."[185]

The following day, President Reagan delivered a nationally televised address from the Oval Office, urging Senators to hasten Judge Bork's confirmation . Joe Biden commented that Reagan's appeal would make it harder for him and fellow Democrats to squash the nomination. "I think it's always a boost to a candidate when a president comes to his defense," Biden said.[186]

Reagan delivered occasional defenses of his nominee through the hot month of August, explaining to an audience in North Platte, Nebraska: "The American people want to see a full complement of nine justices on the bench when the Supreme Court reconvenes" October 5. "No other issue [before Congress] could be more pressing."[187]

The reason the President was engaged in such a campaign for his nominee, Joe Biden told an audience on the stump in Iowa, is that Reagan "sees the opportunity to achieve an agenda he's been unable to achieve in Congress. It reinforces my point. [Bork] is not a moderate fellow."[188]

I had called Mary Ellen Bork for a luncheon date. We met at the Monocle on Capitol Hill on August 13.

The conversation was mostly about my wife and four children, and the impact of the ongoing battle on private time.

I did tell her, "I don't think we can match what the other side is doing—and I cannot guarantee we will win. I can say there are a number of us who are doing nothing other than this battle. Some people told me I shouldn't poormouth our chances, but I won't lie to you. We can win, but we might lose. Anyone who tells you differently is lying or is unrealistic."

The one comment I remember most distinctly from Mary Ellen, a lovely woman of intense religious conviction and of devotion to her family, was this: "The hardest thing of all if not being able to answer all of the lies about the kind of man Bob is. He's so rare. Completely devoted to the process of the law, and not concerned with whose ox gets gored, as long as the law prevails."

Knowing my own anguish about the course of the battle could only be a shadow of what she felt, I told her, "He's the greatest man I know. I'm gonna do everything I can for him. Know that."

In an August 13 speech to the Fraternal Order of Police convention in Mobile, Alabama, Senate Minority Leader Robert Dole hit Biden and his liberal colleagues, saying they "wouldn't know a judicial moderate from an Iranian moderate. [Bork's] opponents want a nominee that they feel will decide particular issues in their favor, judicial restraint and legal analysis be damned." Following Dole's remarks, probably the strongest and most effective presentation he made for

Bork during the battle, the FOP voted to support Bork for the bench, another one of the scattered "firsts" in this battle.[189]

U.S. Communist Party chief Gus Hall, not to be out done in the liberal/conservative sparring over Bork, accused President Reagan of forcing Justices Warren Burger and Lewis Powell to resign so the President could staff the court with right-wing ideologues. In words no less defamatory than those uttered by many of the other Bork foes, Hall declared, "The pieces fit too well into the Reagan plan of leaving the nation an ultra-reactionary federal court system. I would bet they either got big money under the table or were threatened with some skeleton found in their closets, or both."[190]

As the battle progressed there were increasing signs we were going to have trouble holding the Republican base in the Senate, let alone securing the swing votes necessary for victory. The clips coming to my in box reflected that reality.

Charles Bakst reported in the Providence (RI) Evening Bulletin *(August 6, 1987), that Senator John Chafee was urging the Senate Judiciary Committee to "probe Bork's views on abortion, civil rights and free speech."*

Gerry Baum, writing in the San Diego Union *(August 15, 1987) later brought better news: "Wilson is likely to back Bork". Although critical of Judge Bork's position on* Roe v. Wade, *Senator Wilson said he would probably support the Judge's confirmation. Although Wilson is pro-abortion, his overall judicial philosophy of restraint was confirming our initial instincts in placing him in the likely "yes" vote category.*

The picture was muddled in the Seattle Times *and Post-Intelligencer (August 16, 1987). An analysis from Linda Keene of States News Service found that Senators Evans, Hatfield and Packwood proclaimed they would remain uncommitted on Bork until after the hearings. But staff aides were giving clues as to how the senators might vote.*

An Evans aide said that the senator was "inclined" to support Judge Bork as he would other executive appointments.

A Hatfield aide said that if you took a look at the senator's record, "he has generally supported the president's nominees, provided they're qualified."

Packwood, because of his staunch pro-abortion views, was making it clearer and clearer he would not support Bork if "there's any possibility that he'll overturn Roe vs Wade."

Bork supporters lost the grass roots battle in the early weeks. By mid-August, the Senate Judiciary Committee office had received hun-

dreds of telephone calls on the Bork nomination, which ran an estimated 3–to–1 against the Judge. Since July 1, the committee had
received 18,000 letters and postcards tallying an even 50–50 for and
against the nomination.[191]

The National Women's Law Center on August 18 released a 39–page
study of Bork's record as a judge and scholar, and announced they
would join groups opposing the nomination because his record was
"unparalleled in its hostility to women's rights." Bork "would leave
women defenseless against governmental sex discrimination," declared Suzanne E. Meeker, the report's co-author, who based her
statement on Bork's reasoning that under the Fourteenth Amendment
the government is barred only from racial, and not sex-based discrimination. Meeker also said her group opposed Bork because he could
find no right to privacy, and therefore no right to legal abortion, in the
Constitution.

Concerned Women for America lawyer Rebecca Hagelin said the
study was a gross misinterpretation of Bork's record. "This report
was written by women who are angry that Judge Bork won't expand
affirmative action to include their feminist agenda," she said. "The
report completely ignores the many wonderful opinions Judge Bork
has written in defense of women's rights," including a ruling that
charged the State Department's foreign service with discriminating
against women.[192]

*On my thirty-third birthday (August 18), the 721 Group shared
impressions and information on the status of the confirmation battle
as the senators broke for the Labor Day holiday. Then talk shifted to
the obvious effectiveness of the anti-Bork crowd.*

*The Group reviewed Elizabeth Kepley's coordination of direct lob-
bying efforts in the fight, focused on both Senate staffers and direct
lobbying of the senators themselves. The importance of singling out
particular senatorial targets was emphasized. The teams Elizabeth
had formed from the 721 Group were regularly carrying the pro-Bork
message up the Hill. It was difficult to fault the efforts of any of our
regulars, or of the recent recruits to the effort—but the sheer volume
on the Left gave them the edge as the Senators broke for the recess.*

Four days later, some 1,000 women gathered in Portland, Oregon for
the National Women's Political Caucus convention. Five Democratic
Presidential hopefuls courted the group, including Congressman Richard Gephardt of Missouri, who drew an enthusiastic response when he

declared: "Ronald Reagan has stepped out of the mire of the Iran-Contra affair to nominate one of the villains of the Watergate scandal to the highest court of the land."[193]

But another presidential candidate had bought a piece of the action, using not only stump speeches, but his own campaign funds. A flood of postcards found in Senator Biden's overflowing mail box had been inspired by this message from Congressman Jack Kemp (R-NY): "The liberal establishment is pounding out the drumbeat of all-out war against President Reagan's Supreme Court nominee. . . . The single most important thing you can do right now to help President Reagan's Supreme Court nominee be confirmed . . . [is] sign and mail the enclosed postcard to Sen. Joseph Biden."[194]

For a time it looked as if Joe Biden and his allies had more to fear than a few thousand postcards from pro-Bork constituents. Three of the four most activist Supreme Court justices—the youngest was 78—had checked into the hospital for various ailments in mid-August and early September. Thurgood Marshall, 79, received treatment for a blood clot in his right foot; 81–year-old William Brennan checked in for a prostate examination, which showed no trace of cancer; and Harry Blackmun, 78, was treated for prostate cancer.[195]

By late August, groups that had otherwise stayed out of Supreme Court confirmation battles were still marshalling their forces in support of or against the nomination. In a letter dated August 24, United Auto Workers national director Joe Mangone and legislative director Dick Warden urged their membership to lobby against Bork, declaring: "The UAW strongly opposes the Bork nomination on the basis of a record which we believe has been contrary to the interest of workers, minorities, women and, in fact, contrary to the interest of the great majority of Americans."[196]

Meanwhile, Peter Waldron's Contact America, A Christian radio show, set up a toll-free "Bork hotline". Those in the predominantly conservative audience of Waldron's show could ask for an information packet about the nominee. Not merely a support piece for the nominee, however, the material explained the judicial process, and identified groups who had taken a stand for or against the nomination.[197]

The last week in August, Bill Roberts, who had headed Ronald Reagan's gubernatorial campaigns in California, and other member's of the President's informal group of advisors announced plans to spend $2.5 million on a media blitz dubbed "We the People." The purported aim was to influence senators in 12 states who remained uncommitted on the nomination.[198]

Gossip around Washington, D.C. that last week in August centered around American University Law School Professor Herman Schwartz, who, according to several former Yale law school students of Bork's, had been calling them in an attempt to "dig up dirt on Judge Bork." A member of the Judicial Selection Project steering committee, Schwartz had reportedly admitted to conducting his interviews on behalf of the Senate Judiciary Committee. His committee, Bork's former students noted, believed "Judge Bork's philosophy is one which would reverse over 50 years of progress in civil rights and individual liberties."[199]

President Reagan, on vacation in California, engaged in modest lobbying on behalf of Judge Bork. At a strategy meeting in Los Angeles with several law enforcement officers, White House officials, and Illinois Governor Jim Thompson, once a state attorney general, it was decided that the "campaign for Judge Bork will be on positive lines," explained one senior White House official, who added, "We are going to emphasize his record of fairness and of never putting his own opinions ahead of the law. We don't think his nomination will alter the balance of the court at all."[200]

Also at the meeting with President Reagan were representatives from a pro-Bork coalition of law enforcement groups, including the National Law Enforcement Council; the 200,000–member Fraternal Order of Police; the National Sheriffs Association, with 25,000 members; the International Association of Chiefs of Police, with 25,000 members; the 15,000–member National District Attorneys Association; the National Troopers Coalition, with 50,000 members; and the International Narcotics Enforcement Association, with 10,000 members.[201] Illinois Governor Jim Thompson explained to the attendees: "Nearly one-third of the Supreme Court's time is taken up with criminal justice, yet there has been little focus . . . on Judge Bork's views in this area." Reagan declared that Bork could have "impact on law enforcement and criminal justice long after my administration leaves office" if he were to be placed on the Supreme Court.[202] The President continued:

That's why when it comes to crime and safety of our citizens, it's so important for our courts to take a tough, clear-eyed look at the Constitution's purpose to establish justice and insure domestic tranquility. Judge Bork, whom I nominated nearly eight weeks ago, would be just such a Justice. His guiding principle is one of judicial restraint. And Judge Bork believes that judges should not make the laws; their function is to interpret the laws based on the Constitution and precedent. It's time we reassert the fundamental principle of the purpose of criminal justice is to find the truth, not to coddle criminals.[203]

Following his remarks, officials of the law enforcement contingents told the President they had formed a coalition to support his nominee. "The predominant view among law enforcement officials is that criminals now are protected more than the victim," explained Tom Finn, assistant director of the National Sheriffs Association. "The courts have made it difficult for an officer stopping a vehicle to know what he can search for and how to search for it. He's at a loss as to how to proceed because he can't tell what evidence a judge will accept or throw out." Jerald Vaughan, executive director of the International Association of Chiefs of Police, added, "I think traditionally the police have felt that judges and lawyers tend to look down on them with little understanding of the day-to-day pressure a law officer must face. A policemen has a few split seconds on the street to make a decision that judges will be able to study for months and then conclude that the officer acted illegally. It appears to us that Judge Bork applies a more straight-forward, common sense approach."[204]

Access to Justice, a group of California lawyers against Bork's nomination, held a press conference at the same hotel where Reagan's meeting with the pro-Bork law enforcement coalition was scheduled. The liberal lawyers declared that "there is simply insufficient evidence to allow anyone to ascertain how Judge Bork would resolve issues involving the exclusionary rule, Miranda rights, and other basic criminal procedure questions."

Despite this, the President emerged from his gathering optimistic that his nominee could pass the scrutiny of an increasingly hostile Senate. "We think support for Judge Bork is growing, that his outstanding record and credentials are being discussed and examined with a great deal of approval by all aspects of the legal community," said White House spokesman Marlin Fitzwater.[205]

Hoping that the strength of their membership might help push undecided senators toward support of Bork, the Public Affairs Committee of the Southern Baptist Convention, representing 14.6 million members, moved to counteract liberal religious opposition to the jurist. The Committee endorsed Bork in a resolution that urged Southern Baptists to "prayerfully consider writing letters to their United States Senators to support the Bork nomination." Resolution author Les Csorba of the First Baptist Church in Alexandria, Virginia, said:

Judge Bork has stood firmly for the traditional Baptist position respecting the First Amendment guarantee of the free exercise of religion while opposing the establishment of a state religion. Judge Bork's opinions that the Constitution does not protect pornography, that homosexual activity is not a Constitutional right, that some public recognition of the role of religion in our history should appear in textbooks, and his respect for the establishment clause, are consistent with the sentiments of the Southern Baptist Convention. By all judicial standards, he is extremely qualified to serve on the Supreme Court: we think the Judge should be confirmed.[206]

The historic resolution prevailed 7–5, and although organizational divisions prevented the expenditure of substantial sums in support of Bork, the vote itself was a watershed in the history of the Convention. For the first time, the Southern Baptists were moving to counter the powerful influence of lobbyists from the United Church of Christ and the United Methodist Church, which were working aggressively against the nominee.

The American Legislative Exchange Council, representing a membership of over 1,900 of America's Democratic and Republican state legislators, also wrote a resolution supporting the nomination.[207]

release of The Judges War

On August 26, I joined three of the co-authors—Paul Kamenar, Dan Peterson and Bruce Fein—for a press conference at the National Press Club releasing the book conceived only 10 months before. Even though it came during the normal "dead time" in Washington, the intensity of the Bork battle was perhaps represented in the fact that some 30 journalists joined us to ask about the book.

For most of the recent weeks, I had engaged largely in Coalitions work, having no choice but to shift from the Foundation to the lobbying hat. However, I had edited the manuscript with Jeffrey O'Connell's help (he was now back at CBN University) and the assistance of friends like Kristin Blair, Jeffery Troutt, and my wife. We had taken the book from manuscript to published books in seven weeks—from late June through a few days before the press conference.

Hoping I might spark discussion in the press as a means of framing the issue, I sat at the typewriter late at night, after the crisis phone calls died down, playing with ideas O'Connell had left and trying to craft words that would be persuasive on the need for at least some degree of restraint in senatorial consideration of Supreme Court nominees. With memories of the struggles for Alex Kozinski, Sidney

Fitzwater, Dan Manion and William Rehnquist surging through my brain, here's some of what I spoke that day:

"Temperament," "sensitivity," "fairness," "ethics"—these words and concepts have been used over the last three years in attempts to defeat judicial, as well as Justice Department, nominees. In two cases, these attacks proved successful. But even unsuccessful, it is clear that liberal opponents of judicial restraint were learning important political lessons and carefully honing their arguments.

Gaffes of opponents to judicial nominees—gaffes revealing their intentions—are forgotten eventually. But remaining in the minds of many analysts I have talked with over the last two years is the incorrect impression that President Reagan has been nominating unqualified, undistinguished and intemperate men and women to the federal bench. . . .

We've tried to offer a chronology of events with an explicit effort to reach for underlying themes and methods of operation steadily perfected by opponents of the "interpretivist" nominees. In sum, this is a story of a steady escalation of judicial politics into what one reporter for the Washington Post *has described accurately as "flat-out fight over ideology."*

Anti-conservative activists have engaged in a travesty of postured philosophical neutrality throughout the years covered in The Judges War. *But their posture has not held up to scrutiny. It has become clearer and clearer that the overriding concern of many senators and interest groups opposing Reagan's judges is whether or not a particular judge will carry out the social agenda of these senators and interest groups. . . .*

We hope for honesty and fairness from all our public officials, including those who oppose this nomination. If they really believe judges should make up the law as they go along, then they should vote against Robert Bork. On the other hand, if they believe in the rule of law, they should vote for Robert Bork. . .

Eventually, 71 days will have elapsed between the nomination of Bork and the opening of his hearings. This is. . . the longest gap in decades, but it is really quite in keeping wilth the evidence compiled for this book. The Democrats have resorted to the political equivalent of the old-fashioned "four corners offense" in college basketball. If you have a small lead, send a man to each corner of the court and just pass the ball around the eat up time on the scoreboard clock. In other words: stall, stall, stall.

The analogy is not all that mixed. Under Sen. Edward Kennedy's chairmanship in the late 1970s, the average elapsed time between a judicial nomination and a hearing on that nomination was six and a half weeks. Under Republican Strom Thurmond, the average time between nomination and hearing was three weeks. But under Joe Biden in this current Congress, the average time has stretched to nine weeks. One respected nominee, Bernard Siegan, was nominated in early February and finally had a hearing slated for July only to see it canceled by Joe Biden...

... Fair play for Reagan's judicial nominees may require the senatorial equivalent of the 30-second shot clock introduced in basketball when the four corners offense was judged an abuse of the rules.

Everyone needs to understand something. Republicans and conservatives are not dumb. They are watching very carefully what is happening in these battles. In politics, what goes around, comes around—all too often. Is this really what Americans want for present, and future, judicial nominees? ...

That night, speaking on a panel at the Heritage Foundation's Third Generation meeting, I predicted victory for Bork—but only after a bitter and contentious fight in the coming month.

On the same day, August 26, Paul Weyrich sent to Bill Proxmire one of the several letters they exchanged during the course of the fight. Weyrich argued to the veteran Democrat:

You know I am committed to achievement of the conservative political agenda. But this nomination is about much more than a notch on my—or anyone else's—political agenda. Ultimately, this confrontation is about something you and I share, whatever our differences. It is about democracy, representative (republican) government, and the rule of law.

Do either one of us want a country where you can predict the outcome of the next Supreme Court term on the morning after an election? Of course not. But that seems to be what the more radical opponents are pushing for... [T]his is a guy I criticized at times when he was Solicitor. In fact, I probably criticized him for some briefs you would have liked in the area of civil rights!

Weyrich noted areas of disagreement with Bork and defended the incisiveness of some of the jurist's writings, saying, "It is the job of a legal scholar to criticize, to question, to cajole. Bill, as you and I well know the actual fact of public service can serve as a dramatic check on one's theoretical disposition. In the real world, theories are honed by reality and by the actual impact of one's actions." On a question where they agreed, Weyrich argued to Proxmire, "Justice Bork will at least allow the states and communities to grapple with the issue [of abortion] substantively... [H]e is an ardent defender of the Constitution's appropriate separations of power."

August 28, 1987 Public Policy Education Fund letter

Typical of the hundreds of letters that gave me hope as the battle progressed was a note in late August from John Sparks of the Public Policy Education Fund in Pennsylvania. He appreciated the regular updates and let me know he and his people supported Bork intensely. He included a copy of a letter that he sent to all the members on the Senate Judiciary Committee, and indicated his supporters were concentrating on Specter and other key votes.

Free The Court Campaign Intensifies

One of the bright spots of the Bork confirmation struggle were the efforts of Free The Court!—a coalition formed in several mid-American states under the leadership of Steve Baer of United Republicans of Illinois. Baer's hard work began to result in both positive press coverage and good "street theatre" as August ended.

In Chicago, members of Free the Court! debated Bork opponents on television affiliates of CBS, PBS and on Christian networks, as well as on radio stations WBBM, WBEZ, WJJD, WFYR and WLS. Downstate, Baer's activists took to the air on radio stations in Peoria, Rock Island, East Moline and Galesburg.

Even in far-away Oregon, 200 demonstrators gathered to support Bork on August 22, simultaneously attacking Senators Biden, Simon and Packwood for catering to members of the Women's Political Caucus.

Back in Chicago, on August 24, 25 demonstrators greeted Simon as he arrived at a B'nai B'rith appearance. The modest number of bodies nonetheless garnered heavy media coverage—as did a bipartisan Free The Court! press conference two days later, at which the Chicago Fraternal Order of Police (the nation's largest local police union) announced its support for the jurist.

Pro-life and Free The Court demonstrators began to dog Senator Biden as he ended the month campaigning in the Iowa communities of Mason City and Dubuque.

The American Civil Liberties Union leadership voted 47–16 on August 29 to take a position on the Bork nomination. The board of directors then voted 61 to 3 to lobby the Senate against the jurist. At a news conference to announce their decision, ACLU President Norman Dorsen declared, "Judge Bork, is in fact, more radical than conservative. He is certainly well outside the mainstream of conservative judicial philosophy." ACLU Executive Director Ira Glasser asserted that Bork was "unfit" for the Supreme Court because "he believes the highest right in the society is for the majority to impose its moral views on the minority. Had he been around in the 18th century, he would have been against adding the Bill of Rights to the Constitution."[208]

(Glasser's comments were especially noteworthy in light of a letter he had once written to the *Wall Street Journal*:

> The ACLU is non-partisan . . . we do not support or oppose particular candidates . . . We prefer to argue each issue on the merits rather than attempting to characterize particular judicial candidates as "for" or "against" civil liberties when in fact most are likely to reflect a wide range of views. Moreover, were we to engage in such prognostication, we would likely live to regret it. Might we have opposed Hugo Black because of his early membership in the Ku Klux Klan?[209])

Even with all the bad news for Bork supporters, there was increasing evidence that the conservative direct mail and "telephone tree" mechanism around the country was turning the tide in terms of the raw volume of communications to Senators. By August 31, the office of Judiciary Committee swing-vote Senator Arlen Specter (R-PA) had received some 12,000 letters from constituents on the Bork nomination. A full 60 percent were in favor, 40 percent opposed.[210] Conservatives were beginning to win at the grass roots—just as the tide (with the benefit of hindsight) was turning against Bork inside the beltway.

Late August saw conservative supporters of Bork agreeing with elements of the news media that Bork would secure eventual approval. Analyses of the Senate prepared by Coalitions for America/ACU, on the one hand, and CBS News, on the other hand, predicted that Judge Bork would probably capture the 10 swing votes he needed to win confirmation. The studies argued that Bork had already gained 40 of the 51 votes needed to confirm. A maximum of 34 senators strongly opposed the nomination, both studies showed, while about 25 from both parties expressed no opinion. "These figures don't assume a filibuster by the Democrats—but if that did happen, Bork would need to pick up most of those swing votes in order to secure passage," McGuigan said. "When it comes down to the hearings, the Democrats will try to pretend they have some shocking revelation about Judge Bork because they'll realize they don't have enough votes to win. But I don't think it will work."[211]

August 31, 1987 media packet

Concerned Women for America teamed up with the Coalitions for America, which was running tight on money as the confrontation dragged on, to send out another media packet. Because the CWA was paying for it, I suggested the cover letter be on CWA stationery, with Dan Casey, myself and Bev LaHaye signing.

A lot was going on at this juncture. The Senate was in recess for the Labor Day break and The Judges War was scheduled for release tomorrow. More articles and editorials were going to the editors' list in hopes of preparing them for the anticipated personal smear campaign that opponents of Judge Bork would wage. It was hoped that these packets, along with the senatorial letter campaign and the lobbying efforts, would get the word out that Judge Bork was both a qualified man and a good man.

Chapter Four

Smears, Distortions, and Lies

As September dawned, the flood of groups speaking out on the nomination of Judge Bork touched so many communities that even the most disinterested citizens were being affected in some way. Some of the news was even good for Judge Bork.

The 24 board members of the American Farm Bureau Federation, representing 3.5 million rural families across the U.S., made a first-ever decision to take action on a judicial nomination by voting to support Bork. AFBF President Dean Kleckner explained, "Farmers are as much affected by judicial decisions as any other citizens. As farmers, we see the need to stand up and be counted this time."[212]

Knights of Columbus officials urged members through their newsletter to lobby for Bork with this in mind: "Not since the infamous *Roe vs. Wade* pro-abortion decision in 1973 has the pro-life movement in the United States had such a golden opportunity as now to bring an end to the slaughter of the innocent unborn."[213]

September 1, 1987

The Bork battle was in its sixty-second day. At times it struck me that our discussions in the 721 Group resembled those you might hear in a briefing room full of guerilla field commanders who were doing their best but getting steadily surrounded.

Today we were discussing the news from the law enforcement "front." It was good for Judge Bork. Whatever the other failures, we had had good success in obtaining support from key leaders within

73

law enforcement circles. Even the White House had been active, and the President inspirational, on this front.

Elizabeth Kepley of CWA reviewed the lobbying efforts she was coordinating on the Hill with the Senators and their staffers treated as distinct categories for separate treatment.

Given the centrality of the media treatment in the closing weeks of the battle, of equal importance to the direct lobbying were the themes we had decided to push during the final weeks. These themes came to permeate all of our speeches, interviews and the like until the Senate voted on the Judge. We were surprised to find it took only a little time to develop these ideas, with the result a cluster of ten positive themes and nine negative ones. The positive themes we agreed to concentrate on at this juncture of the fight, as drawn from my minutes of the meeting, were:

1. *"Spin Control" for the hearings: Content vs. Style (getting ready in case Bork is a "cool" personality in the TV medium).*
2. *Their surprises vs. our surprises—*

Common Cause	*Southern Baptist Convention, Public Affairs Committee*
AFL-CIO	*Knights of Columbus*
ACLU	*Law Enforcement*

3. *Call attention to CBS News' accurate vote count (38 yes, 30 no, 22 undecided) in contrast to Cranston's disinformation (45–45)*
4. *Qualifications*
5. *The rule of law*
6. *Federalism*
7. *Mainstream*
8. *This nomination takes court out of politics*
9. *Specific mandate for President*
10. *First Amendment—free press*

On the negative side the members were agreed on themes such as:

1. *Radical left vs. America*
2. *Predict to reporters and our people the assaults on Bork's ethics and character*
3. *Crime/Death Penalty/Victims Rights*
4. *Why are the liberals imposing litmus tests?*
5. *Joe Biden is engaging in prez politics*
6. *This is raw politics from the left*

7. *Their idea of a "balanced" court is nothing but a super legislature*
8. *Other specific issues: homosexuality, etc. (depends on audience)*
9. *If Bork can be rejected, anyone can be.*

We didn't do everything right, but in using these themes we were finally crafting words to influence the ways both our own troops and the press looked at the nominee. In the closing weeks, this modest compilation of words and ideas made the circuit of all the regular Coalitions meetings and was distributed to our national outreach of leaders. The eventual feedback was that it helped everyone in sustaining easy to grasp, pointed discussions with reporters and fellow conservatives.

So, we found that it was possible to craft such themes and effectively to share talking points across institutional divisions. Unfortunately, the other side was in the process of doing a better job of communicating the raw political power necessary to their success.

On September 2, the National Legal Aid & Defender Association came out against Bork on the premise that his voluminous academic and legal career reflected an insensitivity toward the common man. A letter to supporters warned:

> In [Bork's] record we find a pattern of deference to government prerogatives over individual rights, a preference for powerful economic interests at the expense of ordinary citizens and government and a cynical disdain for civil rights and liberties. When we translate this pattern into the everyday world of the indigent and the politically disadvantaged, whom NLADA members most often represent, we are left with clients without access to the courts, without standing to challenge or constitutional protection in challenging governmental abuse in the civil and criminal defense areas, and minorities and women without legal protection in matters of manifest discrimination.[214]

Norman Dorsen, president of the American Civil Liberties Union, held a news conference that same day to bash the White House for its efforts on the Bork nomination. Bork's extensive legal writings have Reaganites "plainly afraid," he charged, asserting that the Administration had "made a strategic judgment they can't sustain the nomination based on [Bork's complete] record."[215]

That record was the subject of a 72–page document written for

Senator Biden's office by Duke University law professor Christopher Schroeder and Washington attorney Jeffrey Peck. The document attacked the White House analysis of Bork's legal career, charging that it "seriously distorts" the Judge's record with "major inaccuracies. . . . as it stretches to find moderate allies." The rebuttal continued: "The picture painted by the White House is inaccurate and incomplete. Among the omissions are clear examples of Judge Bork's advocacy and implementation of conservative activism, which demonstrate that he is not the apostle of judicial restraint and moderation described in the White House position paper." Schroeder and Peck wrote that placing Bork on the Supreme Court "would cement a five-vote majority for undoing much of the social progress of the last three decades." Their thesis attacked Bork, among other things, for his opposition to "every major civil rights advance on which he has taken a position," and his method of judging that "would narrow many well-established First Amendment protections." The report went on to assert:

> Judge Bork has repeatedly and consistently rejected the right to be free from governmental interference [in] one's private life. . . . The nominee has repeatedly rejected the decision upholding the right of married couples to use contraceptives. . . . Judge Bork described as "unconstitutional" the decision upholding the right of a woman to decide with her doctor the question of abortion. . . . Judge Bork's writings show that he would protect only speech that is tied to the political process, and that he would not protect artistic and literary expression such as Shakespeare's plays, Rubens' paintings and Baryshnikov's ballet.[216]

Administration officials brushed off the accusations contained in Biden's report. "It's nonsense to say that he's a judicial activist," said Justice Department spokesman Terry H. Eastland. "His career as a judge has been spent in the service of defining and applying neutral principles of law, whatever the political outcome might be."[217] But Dan Casey of the American Conservative Union called the document a "desperate" smear: "Biden has been reduced to quibbling over semantics with the White House because he knows he's no match for Judge Bork." Peck and Schroeder refused to talk about the matter, asserting Biden's senatorial immunity. Schroeder told one reporter, "I'm consulting for the Senator and his opinion is the one that counts, not mine."[218]

The weekend of September 4, President Reagan told *USA Today* he was "confident that any concerns raised by political opponents will be answered during a fair and thorough review of Judge Bork's record during confirmation hearings." Reagan defended his nominee as "a mainstream jurist who never had a ruling reversed by the Supreme Court and has been widely praised for his intellect and his impressive legal background."[219]

On September 4, the National Forum Foundation (the conservative public policy organization started by former Senator Jeremiah Denton and directed by his son James), included my name in a mailing to 259 radio stations around the country. Deborah P. Fritts of the Foundation had recruited me, asking if I would be willing to be part of their "Radio Forum". As a result of their alert to the media, the volume of calls from radio talk show hosts, both on secular and religious stations, steadily escalated for me in the weeks that followed.

"Evangelical friends" were getting the message on the Bork nomination in the September Insight, *the monthly newsletter of the National Association of Evangelicals (NAE). The message was clear—Judge Bork's confirmation would be a "polarizing political battle, with the media in a major role." The folks in the NAE believed that if evangelicals read the newspapers and watched television, they would quickly and "overwhelmingly" support the Judge. But reading and watching TV would not be enough—*"evangelicals must speak up," *the* Insight *piece underscored. For the NAE's largely non-politicized base, the* Insight *crafted specific suggestions. "Face-to-face conversation, letters and telephone calls to staff are excellent ways to let your state's two Senators know your wishes."*

The bottom line in the instructions to this crucial, traditionally reserved constituency was this: "do something. All the marbles are up for grabs with this nomination."

Meanwhile, the earlier work of Les Csorba, securing the Southern Baptist Convention Public Affairs Committee's endorsement of Judge Bork, was being undermined by liberal Baptist lobbyist James Dunn, who runs the Baptist Joint Committee on Public Affairs, an increasingly controversial umbrella group for Baptists. A week after the Southern Baptist Convention's Public Affairs Committee (PAC) registered its historic vote for Bork, Dunn wrote to all the members of the Senate, saying:

Please don't be misled. While some groups have deliberately attempted to make the 7–5 vote of the [PAC] appear to be an official action of the Convention and your office has received notification to this effect, you

*need to be fully informed . . . The Baptist Joint Committee . . . serves
nine Baptist conventions and conferences . . . and we have taken no
action regarding Judge Bork's nomination.*

As Dr. James Carl Hefley later noted in his book, The Truth in Crisis:

*The PAC majority was infuriated. They had been told that "you have no
staff but the [BJC] staff." Dunn's name was listed directly below the
Public Affairs Committee in the SBC annual. They, not Dunn, had been
elected by the convention.*

*The SBC provided over 90 percent of the BJC budget and did not
control how the money was spent. Now it appeared Dunn (supported
largely by SBC money) was trying to sabotage the majority endorsement
from the only public affairs commitee which the SBC had.*

In a September 6 interview with the New York *Daily News*, Bork
offered a reaction to the storm of controversy steadily escalating
around him. Aware of the divergent views of some of his supporters,
he reflected: "Anybody who thinks I am going to be an activist is in
for some surprises. . . . One group [of backers] is painting me as a
judge who tries to interpret the law, and the other group is painting me
as a judge who will do conservative things for them. I would disapprove
of conservative activism as much as I would of liberal activism."[220]

Conservative and liberal activists were flooding Capitol Hill with
hundreds of thousands of cards and letters for and against the nomination. As the battle wore on, the anti-Bork side was forced to admit
that correspondence supporting the Judge far outnumbered mail from
the Left in nearly all Senate offices. Staffers working overtime to
handle bag upon bag of constituent mail delivered to Senator Howell
Heflin's (D-AL) office—one of three undecided votes on the Judiciary
Committee—had a good chuckle when letters urging Heflin to "Vote
for Bark" began trickling in. Apparently, grass roots activists belong-
ing to a pro-Bork group in Montgomery had distributed a form letter
containing the humorous typographical error.[221]

*There was clear evidence we were turning the tide at the grass roots,
even as the prospects in Washington worsened. One reason we were
not stronger as the Committee deliberations approached was that the
powerful National Rifle Association had decided to sit this one out.*

*When Richard Gardiner and Dave Connover, the NRA staffers who
used to attend the 721 Group meetings, told me their leadership was*

not inclined to take a supportive position, I personally researched Bork's judicial record on Second Amendment questions. I found decisions in which Bork had ruled in favor of reasonable interpretations of gun ownership regulations, and in favor of the rights of gun owners. In fact, in one case Judge Bork had ruled in favor of the NRA itself, as the object of a suit brought for use of a gun stolen from the NRA's national headquarters in Washington, D.C. But of course I'd not found—nor could I—any evidence of an overly broad reading of the Second Amendment on the part of the jurist.

We received multiple indications that the gun lobby found troubling Bork's expressed concerns about the excessive reach of the judicially created exclusionary rule, because it indicated an unwillingness to suppress evidence gained during investigations and searches of, among others, the owners of firearms stores.

On September 8, after Casey and I determined our own efforts to bring the NRA back into the judicial reform coalition had failed, Paul Weyrich asked Senator James McClure, a favorite of the NRA, to intervene.

With assistance from volunteers in our network on the Hill, McClure personally communicated with every member of the NRA Board of Directors, which was slated to meet in Washington during the Bork hearings.

As my friends in the media would put it, "sources close to the NRA" say a major confrontation ensued. Wayne LaPierre and those who wanted the organization to stay out of the battle prevailed, and the Bork support coalition remained without one of its most powerful potential allies.

(In fairness to the NRA, LaPierre later claimed the fault for the NRA's inaction lay with the Reagan Administration. In response to a question I posed to him when he spoke at a "Monday Club" gathering in the spring of 1989, LaPierre said

If there was a mistake made on Bork, it was the Administration's mistake, because they continually told us that they did not want us in that battle until the very end. They started out saying 'We don't need you guys, You will only make it tougher. You guys are gonna polarize this issue.' That was the signal we got from the very top people at the White House all the way through on that . . .

LaPierre's explanation could be true. Indeed, plenty of conservative groups got subtle and not-too-subtle hints from the misguided forces of the Reagan White House to keep silent. But the other most powerful units in the pro-Bork effort—the National Right to Work Committee and the National Right to Life Committee [both had their own reasons for believing Bork's jurisprudence might make him, in terms of their issue, an "80 percenter", and not a purist]—understood the importance of that battle to the coalition they are part of, and devoted substantial resources to the confrontation.)

With a week to go before the hearings, strategists on both sides of the battle were feverishly speculating on who would capture the votes of Heflin and his undecided committee colleagues, Senators Arlen Specter (R-PA) and Dennis DeConcini (D-AZ). Strategists noted that Heflin would be the most crucial vote to either side, because Southern Democrats—considered to be one of the main forces that could make or break the nomination—usually looked to him for guidance on controversial votes.[222]

Ralph Neas of the Leadership Conference on Civil Rights expressed confidence that his side would win Specter: "Senator Specter is and has been a very articulate advocate of civil rights. I do not believe that Senator Specter would vote for anyone who would turn back the clock on civil rights and civil liberties."

But McGuigan, who had retained a civil relationship with Specter despite the Pennsylvanian's vote against William Bradford Reynolds in 1985, hoped conservatives might win over the Senator. He noted that although "Arlen Specter is as consistent a vote against the President's nominees as any Republican in the Senate, if the answers to the questions seem reasonable and within the rule of the law, then he'll probably go with Bork."[223] A pro-Bork vote from Specter would send "a strong signal that [Bork is] nearly unbeatable" in the Senate, said the ACU's Dan Casey, adding that to lose him would mean "we're in for a tough fight." The Pennsylvania Republican's office had received some 15,000 letters by early September, which Specter aide Neal Manne said were running "about 2-to-1 pro-Bork."[224]

Specter, who had been the subject of an intense lobbying campaign from such diverse sources as White House Chief of Staff Howard Baker, New Right guru Paul Weyrich, Dan Casey, and NOW President Molly Yard, seemed to be struggling with the decision: "I don't know whether to put the Constitution first or the country first. It's important to the country in terms of a lot of cases which are coming up, where he's going to be the critical vote, and I'm concerned about where we're heading on constitutional interpretations. There's been a lot of talk about original intent, and you don't know exactly where that doctrine is heading."[225] Bork's views on the so-called "right to privacy," which liberal judicial activists argued could be found in the Constitution, apparently bothered him the most:

> You take the abortion case. If you want to pick a single issue, that would be, of course, the issue that most people are concerned about. My concern is that the Court should have the power to decide the question. Here you have a conflict between the constitutional right of the fetus to live and the constitutional right of a woman to choose what's going to happen to her own body. On a matter where there are so many reasons to have a unified national policy, so that you don't have people crossing state lines for abortions, for example . . . I believe that the court has to decide these questions. And Judge Bork suggests that the court does not have the jurisdiction to decide that question. That's what I want to pursue with him.[226]

Strategists speculated that DeConcini began showing signs of sympathy for the opposing camp when he told the *Arizona Republic* that the hearings would, incredibly, probably address "the amount of alcohol [Bork] drinks" as well as "his capability of carrying a full [case] load."[227]

This and similar comments were indicative of a shift in the opposition strategy, McGuigan said. "Every tactic you're seeing now has been tested out in the past," said McGuigan. "The only way they're going to get 50 votes in the Senate is with these personal smears."[228] As Bork's prospects worsened, Ralph Neas noted: "When Bork was first named, most everyone in Washington thought [his confirmation] would be a fairly certain thing. Obviously the nomination is no longer a certain thing. I'd like to think we're somewhat responsible. We have tried to educate people about Bob Bork."[229]

Further dampening conservative hopes for his vote, it was noted that DeConcini's wife, Susan, was an active member of the liberal wing of the Arizona Democratic Party. "Suzie is very progressive and has been very active in the past," said one family friend. "Sometimes peace at home is the most important factor in these things." To top this off, "all the major DeConcini supporters I know are against Bork," noted another friend of the Senator's, John Frank of Phoenix's Lewis & Rocca.[230]

Nonetheless, McGuigan doggedly hoped that Bork would win DeConcini's approval. "DeConcini is being pressured to find a reason other than judicial philosophy to vote against Bork, and thus responds to leftist assaults on his integrity," he said. "But I think we can manage to show him that Bork's integrity is intact."[231]

Meanwhile, Bork, though still a judge on the U.S. Court of Appeals, was spending countless hours meeting with senators to address their concerns about his record. He also attended a "murder board" session in which administration officials acting as hostile Senators grilled him extensively on his academic writings and opinions on the court to give him a taste of what his opponents might use against him at the hearings.

On September 9, Pete du Pont gave a speech at the National Press Club, and asked me to join him at the head table. Parting company with the majority of close friends who were backing other candidates, I'd crossed the Rubicon a few weeks earlier, and written an essay for Conservative Digest *endorsing the former Delaware governor. Pete warmly endorsed Bork's confirmation in his remarks and privately mentioned in passing, "We might need you to come up to New England and let our fellow conservatives know you're backing me."*

A few weeks later I made my first trip to New Hampshire.

In the meantime, that evening I prepared to fly to Grand Rapids, Michigan, for the meeting of the Council for National Policy, a conservative leadership organization which had asked me to brief its members on the confirmation struggle.

Senator Specter's office had called and indicated the Pennsylvanian, responding to a letter I wrote him on August 24, wanted to meet with us before *the hearings, as we had requested. Remembering our direct conversations during the battle for Brad Reynolds two years before, I decided to write Specter a long note, as the Michigan trip was taking me out of town on the only day he could see us. Don Baldwin delivered the note for me, in which I told Specter:*

> We need your leadership for Judge Bork and are likely to fail without your help. It's that simple. I will do anything I can to help you if you can see your way clear to join us in this battle. Many of your concerns will be addressed, I believe, in the excellent analysis of Bork's record coming out in Benchmark. It will be delivered to you on Monday. . . I hope you will listen to my friends.

When we talked later, everyone thought the meeting had gone well, but they were haunted by Specter's increasing refrain that the Supreme Court must remain the place where difficult issues are resolved, even (our interpretation) when the Court has no warrant in law to act.

Based on recent confirmation battles, supporters of the nominee knew that he might face questions about his integrity. The liberals received a boost during the second week in September when the Judiciary Committee released to the press a five-page letter written on August 23 by retired U.S. District Court Judge James F. Gordon of Kentucky. In the letter, Gordon accused Bork of being unethical, charging that in 1983 Bork had demonstrated "serious flaws in his character" when the two jurists disagreed on a controversial case.

Gordon, who had sat on the case with Judge Bork and the late Judge Roger Robb, said that he and Robb had decided the court should not hear the case. Gordon claimed that they "took immediate vigorous exception" when Bork had said he thought the case should be heard. The Kentucky judge then claimed in his letter that he was "shocked" upon receiving the majority opinion, crafted by Bork, which said the case should have been decided. "There is no way Judge Bork could have misunderstood Robb's and my position," Gordon wrote. Gordon said he had "grave reason to suspect that perhaps Judge Bork intended to have his narrow 'no standing' view become the majority opinion of the court and the law of the circuit when, in fact, it was the minority opinion . . . I do not believe one who would resort to the actions toward his own colleagues and the majesty of the law as did Judge Bork in this instance possesses those qualities of character, forthrightness and truthfulness necessary for those who would grace our highest court."[232]

In answer to Gordon's attack, Bork made public a letter he had written to the Judge at the time. "It occurs to me too late that I should have notified you in advance that I had changed the rationale . . . to one of lack of standing," the letter said. Gordon claimed he never saw that letter. But Paul J. Larkin, Bork's clerk in the case, noted that his boss had gone back to talk the case over with Judge Robb.[233] "I remember when he [Bork] came back and said Robb had agreed to change the focus of the opinion," Larkin said. "There was no attempt to pull a fast one." Gordon's charges were "all a misunderstanding," he added, because the Kentucky judge did not attend discussions on the case between Bork and Robb.

Presidential spokesman Marlin Fitzwater issued this response to Gordon's charges: "In the judicial process, there are always disagreements. This sort of thing is very normal." Fitzwater also noted that Gordon "has long had disagreements with Bork."[234]

Although the issue steadily faded from view, it added to the collection of smears tarring Bork as not only controversial, but possibly unethical. A political pattern of "throw it all up there and see what sticks"—standardized in the judicial confirmation confrontations of 1985–86 and documented in *The Judges War*—was repeating itself.

Both liberals and conservatives were agreeing that the Bork battle was a crucial test of strength. But by early September it was becoming evident who was winning the tug-of-war and why. "Liberals are going to spend over $3 million," McGuigan said, while "conservatives just don't have that kind of money." Ralph Neas of the Leadership Conference agreed: "The intensity on this one is probably unprecedented. We are creating a coalition bigger than ever before because the Bork nomination is certainly the most historic moment of the Reagan presidency." Indeed, National Abortion Rights Action League spokesman Richard Mintz said his group was submitting a written request urging each member and five friends to pressure Senators for a negative vote; organizing public rallies against the nominee; speaking to college students, women's groups and public health groups; and contributing to a media advertising blitz. The pro-abortion group also took the fight to the streets and shopping malls, handing out anti-Bork literature to passersby.[235]

Meanwhile, People for the American Way feverishly researched Bork's writings and decisions to gather ammunition for use in the anti-Bork effort. By September, PAW had already sent lobbyists to the Senate, distributed an op-ed piece to the press (which appeared in the New York *Times*), and gathered funds for a multi-million dollar media campaign.[236]

Organized homosexuals and lesbians joined the fight as well, raising hundreds of thousands of dollars for the National Gay Task Force's efforts to oppose the nominee, and supplying anti-Bork intelligence to Senators. As Lisa Keen of the *Washington Blade* later explained:

> One ["gay"] group was able to provide an early dramatic assist to opponents of Bork on the Senate Judiciary Committee. Officials of the Human Rights Campaign Fund revealed this week that it was one of their lobbyists who supplied Senator Edward Kennedy with a tape recording of a 1985 Bork lecture . . . which demonstrated Bork emphasizing his opinion two years ago that "precedent isn't all that important."[237]

By its sheer size, conservatives worried that the 1.86 million members of the National Education Association could have a staggering impact on the anti-Bork effort. Chief NEA lobbyist Mike Edwards said that although the union had budgeted no extra money to help block the nomination, the NEA used its many periodicals, state and local affiliates, and a congressional contact team to lobby the Senate and "educate" its members on Bork's record. NEA members were asked to contact their Senators directly, and to use their local affiliates to set up anti-Bork coalitions.[238]

The September issue of *NEA Today* warned teachers:

> The opposition to his nomination [is] based on the fact that Bork is a foe of individual liberties—including the constitutional right of public employees—and an unabashed opponent of judicially enforced equality for women and minorities. . . . But public employees enjoy fundamental constitutional rights—the right to due process, free speech, privacy, and equal protection of the laws—*not* because the framers of the Constitution specifically intended to establish such rights, but because, over the last 20 years, an activist Supreme Court has applied the Constitution's general principles of fairness and equality to complex issues not anticipated by the framers. Bork's theory, if adopted by the Court, would have devastating repercussion for the rights of NEA members. . . . in considering a teacher's free speech claim, Bork would ask simply whether the framers of the First Amendment intended to prohibit school boards from firing employees who publicly criticize them. Bork's answer . . . is a painfully clear *no*.[239]

With 100,000 volunteer members nationwide, the National Council of Jewish Women used "women power," instead of the check book, to attack Robert Bork. Working with other groups from the mega-coalition, the NCJW was busy conducting "a big push against the nomination" by "educating" its members and inundating Senate offices with anti-Bork literature from groups such as People for the American Way, according to NCJW's Sammie Moshenberg. On the state level, members visited their senators during the congressional recess, wrote letters, and lobbied other groups that had remained neutral on the nomination. "We have a lot of very active women across the country who are very savvy when it comes to public affairs, and are teaching them to organize and make their voices heard," Moshenberg said.[240]

The National Association for the Advancement of Colored People was also busy campaigning to defeat Bork. According to its chief lobbyist, Althea Simmons, members from the NAACP's chapters in 21,000 communities nationwide were donating their time to prepare fact sheets and lobby Senators with personal visits and letters.[241]

Money was pouring into the various group coffers for use in the fight against the nominee. As GOP consultant Eddie Mahe Jr. explained the phenomenon: "It's a fund-raising bonanza. There's been nobody to beat up: No Goldwater, no Nixon. Ted Kennedy has become irrelevant—you can't beat him up. Bork does represent the prospective swing vote. Either side can make the case that if they fail, there's a clear and present danger." Direct-mail specialist Roger Craver, who helped several anti-Bork organizations fatten their war chests, said liberal groups had netted some $6 million in funds through early September. Craver speculated that the figure would double by the full Senate vote on the nomination. People for the American Way's Art Kropp, perhaps the biggest winner in the Bork sweepstakes, conceded that "the response has been much stronger than anything we've ever had." The July test-mailing his group sent to 541,000 potential contributors exploded, Kropp said, prompting PAW to mail out 3.8 million more pleas for money. "We wanted to raise $1 million but now it looks like closer to $2 million."[242]

Though they had less to work with than their opposition, Bork advocates fought back, and fought hard. Christian Voice distributed buttons to its grassroots that read "Love Liberty, Support Bork."

Eventually millions of concerned citizens across the country sent cards, letters and telegrams, and phoned their Senators, urging them to support the nomination. As McGuigan later observed, "The grassroots of America has been delivered to the in-box of the United States Senate."[243]

Some of the conservative activity was not linked to any particular group. With logistical support from Coalitions for America, three Bork supporters focused a letter on attorneys and law students throughout the country. Lee S. Liberman, a professor at the George Mason University School of Law; former Justice Department official Frederick D. Nelson; and E. Spence Abraham, president of the Harvard Journal of Law and Public Policy sent some 4,500 letters asking recipients to send pro-Bork correspondence to the Judiciary Committee.

The letter noted: "It is precisely for his faith in and obedience to our constitutional system that Judge Bork has come under such heavy attack by special interest groups. The independence of the Supreme Court is at risk of being subverted by political gamesmanship." Liberman said they sent the mailing because "there seemed to be a lot of people on the other side who were writing against Judge Bork."[244]

The integrity of the pro-abortion forces—one of the most militant interests rallying against Bork—came under further review after release of syndicated columnist Carl Rowan's startling interview with

Norma McCorvey, the "Jane Roe" from the 1973 *Roe v. Wade* legalized abortion decision. Eighteen years after her suit in a Texas courtroom spawned the Supreme Court's abortion decision, McCorvey confessed to Rowan that her claim to pregnancy as a result of gang rape was a lie. McCorvey told Rowan that she had created the story about being raped by four people while working at a Georgia circus in 1969 in hopes of receiving exemption from a state law that banned abortions except to save the life of the mother.

Attorney Sarah Weddington said she had agreed to take the case to the High Court because she believed McCorvey's youth, single status, and rape trauma would make a strong appeal. McGuigan said that early arguments in states for abortion on demand capitalized on "hard cases," such as the one claimed by McCorvey. "What this revelation demonstrates is that the pro-abortion movement was and is a lie at its very core," McGuigan said. "Without such lies I don't think the state legislatures which revised abortion laws in the late 1960s—let alone the Supreme Court in 1973—would ever have taken the steps they did to erode protection for unborn children."[245]

On September 9, the 15-member American Bar Association Standing Committee on the Federal Judiciary held a clandestine meeting in the New York office of ABA Chairman Harold R. Tyler Jr. After six hours of deliberation, the panel issued a verdict on Bork's fitness for the Court. The panel issued the highest ranking of "well-qualified", which, according to the ABA handbook, was "reserved for those who meet the highest standards of professional competence, judicial temperament and integrity." Though individual votes on judicial nominees were supposed to be kept confidential, Bork's opponents immediately seized on leaked information that four of the ABA panelists had found Bork "not qualified," while one had simply voted "not opposed."[246]

Conservatives were outraged at what they believed were the political motivations behind the dissenting votes, despite the ABA claim that in judging candidates the panel "does not investigate the prospective nominee's political or ideological philosophy, except to the extent that extreme views on such matters might bear upon judicial temperament or integrity." Senator Orrin G. Hatch (R-UT) called a news conference to question the integrity of the ABA members. "That's one of the problems we have had with the ABA in recent years, playing politics with the ratings. Questions about Judge Bork are raised in politically inflammatory terms, and the nominee is unjustly accused of favoring literacy tests or poll taxes or racial covenants," the Senator said. "I challenge the people opposing him to come up with facts and not just vilification." But ABA President Robert MacCrate insisted in a statement, "Politics is not a factor in the committee's deliberations."[247]

Reporters soon discovered that the ABA panelists who considered Bork "not qualified" were Joan M. Hall of Chicago, John D. Lane of Washington, D.C., Sam Williams of Los Angeles and Jerome J. Shestack of Philadelphia. Hall was an official at the Chicago chapter of the Lawyers Committee for Civil Rights Under Law, and a member of the Legal Assistance Foundation of Chicago. Williams, a black attorney influential in Los Angeles legal circles, was a former president of the California Bar Association and an adviser to Mayor Tom Bradley.

Lane's name was well-known to conservative legal analysts. His leftist politics, they believed, had led him to treat conservative judicial nominees unfairly in the past. When his name was being considered for a second three-year term on the ABA committee, a storm of internal ABA opposition was so fierce that he was turned down. But when another slot became available, Lane was there to fill it.

Shestack worked for President Carter as a U.S. representative to the United Nations Commission on Human Rights. He was also a former official with the Lawyers Committee for Civil Rights Under Law, the National Legal Aid and Defender Association, and the Mexican-American Legal Defense Fund.[248] Shestack's vote was the most controversial, as he admitted being aligned with the group of lawyers who had been working with Biden's presidential campaign. But he claimed: "Politics has never come up in any of the committee's considerations and political considerations do not play the slightest role in anyone's deliberations."[249]

However, committee member James Bierbower of Washington, D.C. "suggests that various lobbying by civil-rights groups and women's groups proved effective with some panel members," wrote Anne Kornhauser of the *Legal Times*, noting that Bierbower said panelists received about three times more literature from the opposing side than from the Bork forces. "We have a woman on the committee and we were literally bombarded by women's groups," Bierbower said. "We have a black man on the committee and we received a lot of material on race. And we have two strong active Democrats on the committee."[250]

Despite the careful leaks and the unprecedented four opposition votes, at the time most Bork advocates viewed the ABA verdict as a victory for their cause. In a statement from the White House, President Reagan said he "was especially pleased that the ABA's Standing Committee on Federal Judiciary gave its highest rating to Judge Bork

. . . Judge Bork is widely regarded as one of the most qualified individuals ever nominated to the Supreme Court, often compared to such great jurists as Justices Holmes, Brandeis, Frankfurter, Black and the man he is to replace, Justice Lewis Powell."[251] Justice Department spokesman Terry Eastland added: "The rating is certainly not unexpected . . . it is simply another piece of evidence for what we all know: that he is very well qualified."[252]

McGuigan observed that the committee's split decision was "more harmful to the ABA than Bork."[253] But Nan Aron of the Alliance for Justice called the dissenting votes "wonderful news, particularly in light of the '82 vote" where the ABA had given Bork a unanimous rating of "exceptionally well-qualified" to sit on the U.S. Court of Appeals.[254] Biden also saw the divided vote as a victory for his side. "It's amazing," he said. "I would have expected it would have been unanimous. They are timid usually about saying someone is not qualified."[255]

Weyrich had Mat West, who has worked with both of us for more than six years, track me down and deliver a note the afternoon we learned of the mixed ABA rating, which I'd feared and discussed with Paul in advance. His note was appropriately troubled:

The Bork deal is not going well . . . The ABA [rating] is a real problem— gives "moderates" an out. . . . Also, Nunn's deal [see below] is a disaster. The Administration cannot accept it. We need something dramatic—akin to the Burger endorsement, to change the atmosphere. This is slipping away.

With the ABA rating weighing heavily upon us, I still believed "Bork can win," as I had written to my allies in a pre-hearing action memo. In that missive, we did our best to predict what lay ahead for Judge Bork. The hearings were only five days away. The senators were returning from their Labor Day recess and our general assessment on Judge Bork's support had not changed much. Our vote tallies were holding at around 40 in favor, 30 in opposition and roughly 30 unde- cided. Like our first breakdown, we were classifying senators four ways. The categories were basically the same but with some slight differences. As of September 8, 1987 our breakdown constituted four groups again, but this time they were:

"Group 1—Assumed to be fairly solid;

Group 2—Can probably be considered leaning pro-Bork when all is said and done;

Group 3—Can probably be considered leaning anti-Bork but can possibly be gotten—maybe only on cloture; (and)
Group 4—Assumed to be solidly anti-Bork.''
We plugged the 100 senators into the four groups this way:

Group 1	Group 2	Group 3	Group 4
Armstrong	Bentsen	#Bingaman	Adams*
Bond*	Boren	Chafee	Bumpers
Boschwitz	Breaux*	Chiles	Biden
Cochran	DeConcini	+Dixon	Bradley
D'Amato	Ford	Graham*	Burdick
Danforth	Heflin	Nunn	Conrad*
Dole	+Johnston	#Pell	Cranston
Domenici	Shelby*	Proxmire	Dodd
Durenberger	Specter	Sanford*	Fowler*
Heinz	Stennis	#Weicker	Glenn
Garn	Cohen	Baucus	Daschle*
Gramm	Evans	Byrd	Harkin
Grassley	Hatfield	Exon	Inouye
Hatch	Stafford	+Pryor	Kennedy
Hollings		#Leahy	Kerry
Hecht		Reid*	Lautenberg
Kassebaum		Sasser	Levin
Helms		Gore	Matsunaga
Humphrey			Melcher
Karnes*			Metzenbaum
Kasten			Mikulski
Lugar			Mitchell
McCain			Moynihan
McClure			Packwood
McConnell			Riegle
Murkowski			Rockefeller
Nickles			Sarbanes
Pressler			Simon
Quayle			Wirth*
Roth			
Rudman			
Simpson			
Stevens			
Symms			

Thurmond
Trible
Wallop
Warner
Wilson

*freshmen
#voted for Rehnquist cloture but against him
+ voted against cloture but for Rehnquist

We suspected that the next two to three weeks would see heavy smoke from a barrage the opposition would lay on the Judge. Attacks on Judge Bork's character and integrity were, as we feared and expected, much worse than similar ones in the past.

The action memo called for a new wave of support letters to senators to counter the continued attacks. We had developed basic concepts we hoped would increase pro-Bork visibility in local media. The hope was to emphasize to the American public that this was a battle between democracy and judicial oligarchy—between representative government and the rule of judicial fiat.

The first was the simplest activity: encouraging greater activity among the troops in writing letters to the editor, the most widely read section in most newspapers. The memo instructed our troops to support Judge Bork by calling attention to all of the paid media the left was using and to castigate the anti-Bork senators who "caved" to the special interests—while praising the pro-Bork senators for standing up to them.

Second, we wanted to get the most mileage out of the legacy of the Fairness Doctrine. With all of the paid anti-Bork ads on the air, especially the radio, local stations could be asked to provide some "fairness doctrine" response time with a pro-Bork spot. (We were later able to send our own pro-Bork spots, aired on stations in the nation's capital, to a few local allies who secured such free time.)

A third suggestion was to join or form a local pro-Bork coalition. We passed on the example of Steve Baer's successes in forming state/local pro-Bork coalitions, from his offices at the United Republican Fund of Illinois, in Chicago. With that as a model, we hoped the more energetic of our troops in the local communities could get local law enforcement officials, corporate types and others to join a temporary alliance until the end of the battle.

Although the vote count was holding steady, our expectations for the hearings were that the Judge would do fairly well. More votes were *needed not only for nomination, but to prevent any Democrat attempt at filibuster. Because senators were coming out publicly and committing themselves to a full Senate vote, we were confident the nomination would make it at least that far. As the situation looked tougher and tougher, I kept saying to myself, and occasionally to friends, "Be not afraid."*

Senators returning from their month-long recess faced an uncharacteristically militant Sam Nunn (D-GA), who as chair of the Senate Armed Services Committee, declared he would hold the Bork nomination hostage until his GOP colleagues abandoned their efforts to block the 1988 defense authorization and campaign finance legislation. "I can't see bringing up Bork before a defense bill that's been pending for three months," Nunn said. "Until they let the [Department of Defense] bill come up . . . [Bork] can cool his heels. [The administration officials] have gotten themselves in a deep, dark hole on the ABM issue."[256] The following day, Senate Majority Leader Robert Byrd (D-WV) echoed Nunn's threats. "I'm not making a mark in the sand," he said. "I'm simply saying that the president and the minority party in the Senate could help get the vote on the Bork nomination up sooner than might otherwise be expected."[257]

Since the July 1 nomination, conservatives had been urging the White House to avoid allowing the opposition to frame the issues. They suggested that the Administration highlight Judge Bork's "tough on crime" record, and specifically highlight the larger, encompassing issue of judicial restraint.

However, it was not until the Left had spent three full months attacking Bork on issues such as civil and privacy rights that the White House released these talking points for Bork supporters:

• As Solicitor General, Bork argued for a broad view of consent as a valid basis for a police search, and that the Exclusionary Rule should not apply where police officers reasonably believed they had consent (*U.S. v. Matlock*, 1974).

• In *U.S. v. Edwards* (1974), Bork argued that the Fourth Amendment did not necessitate a warrant to search an individual who is already lawfully in custody.

• And in *U.S. v. Watson* (1976), Solicitor General Bork successfully argued that the Fourth Amendment's warrant requirement does not require police officers to obtain a warrant to make an arrest in a public place, so long as they have probable cause that the suspect has committed, or is committing an offense.

• Solicitor General Bork argued and won the major death penalty cases of the 1970s. In the 1976 case of *Gregg v. Georgia,* Bork argued in a "friend of the court" brief that the death penalty was not a violation of the Eighth Amendment's prohibition of cruel and unusual punishments. The Supreme Court agreed, in a decision supported by Justice Lewis Powell.

As a federal judge, Bork built a strong record on criminal justice issues:

• For example, Judge Bork's opinion in *U.S. v. James* (1985), upholding a conviction for narcotics possession, held that the federal "knock and announce" statute allows the police to enter and prevent destruction of evidence in situations where the accused is well aware of the purpose of the police visit.

• In another decision, Judge Bork affirmed a conviction for possession of a controlled substance and held that the government has properly refused in a criminal trial to reveal the location of an undercover police surveillance post (*U.S. v. Harley,* 1982).[258]

Interior Secretary Donald P. Hodel, one of the conservatives left in the Reagan Administration, told reporters on September 10: "Judge Bork's critics have totally politicized the process, hoping to turn votes against him without regard to the merit of his credentials or his abilities. It's not enough now just to defend Judge Bork. We've got an obligation to put out the word about how the left has transformed the debate into character attacks and is using it to raise money for its causes."[259]

Some in the White House preferred to keep the more conservative elements in the Administration away from the strategy sessions on Bork. Their tack was to advance the nominee as merely a mainstream jurist—to soften his image for acceptance in a hostile Senate. "Though the White House wants conservative social and religious groups to rally behind Bork it fears their embrace will repel moderate senators who hold the key swing votes," wrote Ronald Brownstein of the Los Angeles *Times*. "Because the White House strategy demanded that conservatives skirt such emotional issues as abortion, they were left to respond with civics-book arguments about Bork's qualifications."[260]

Direct-mail expert Richard Viguerie added: "Conservatives were told to cool it and not get too excited because that was the one thing that could lose the Bork nomination. The administration tried to package and sell Bork as a centrist and a moderate and de-emphasize his conservatism. How is that going to excite conservatives to go out and breathe and die for him?"[261]

For the most part, however, pro-Bork conservatives were undaunted by the cold shoulder treatment from the White House. They stressed Bork's "tough on crime" record with the press, and issued paper after paper detailing his academic writing and opinions from the bench to straighten out the inaccuracies spread by the Left. But they hoped their trump card would be the nominee himself. "When the American people see Robert Bork at the hearings, they will be offended—just like they were when they saw Ollie North—that liberal Democrats have made him out to be a raving lunatic," said Dan Popeo of the Washington Legal Foundation. "Everybody will be asking, 'Where's the nut they told us to expect?' "[262] Popeo added, "If they were smart, they wouldn't let him testify at all. Bob Bork is going to clean the floors with Joe Biden."[263] White House lobbyist Tom Korologos agreed that Bork would be their best playing card: "Lemme tell you something. Bob Bork ain't running for president. He ain't running for Miss America. He ain't running for Mr. Congeniality for the year. He's running for eight votes in the Senate Judiciary Committee and 51 votes in the Senate. Whatever gets us to that—this is the goal, and the witness himself is our secret weapon."[264]

On September 11, four days before the start of confirmation hearings, the National Federation of Business and Professional Women's Clubs held a news conference with 21 other women's organizations—including the American Association of University Women, NARAL, NOW and the National Institute for Women of Color—to announce they would activate their forces against Bork. "His recorded view is so outrageous from our point of view, we decided we couldn't sit this one out," said Monica McFadden of the federation, who argued that putting Bork on the Court would be "bad for the economy."[265]

Employees at NARAL Maryland used their office answering machine to lobby callers. One ring produced this hurried message:

> The U.S. Senate is about to make the most critical vote of this decade. Please call your Senators [Democrat Barbara] Mikulski and [Democrat Paul] Sarbanes and urge them to vote against the new nominee to the Supreme Court, Robert Bork. Bork has stated that *Roe v. Wade*, the decision legalizing abortion, was unconstitutional. Abortion rights is [*sic*] in serious jeopardy. If you can help, please leave your name and number at the tone and we'll get back to you.[266]

With three days to go before Judge Bork's testimony was scheduled to begin, Republican Presidential candidates Senator Robert Dole (KS),

Congressman Jack Kemp (NY), and Christian broadcaster Pat Robertson told the annual Iowans for Life convention that they were behind President Reagan's nominee. Kemp went one step further to promise that if elected he would nominate "pro-life, pro-family conservative judges to all the courts in America."[267]

Meanwhile, New York Governor Mario Cuomo told reporters that he had chatted with Joe Biden by telephone about anti-Bork strategy, and hinted he might rejoin his fellow Democrats in the war against the Judge:

> I believe the important thing for Biden to do is to make it clear that Bork was selected not for his objectivity but because the President believes Bork will give him the results the President desired politically—for example, cut back of affirmative action. The evidence that that's what the President wants and expects is in the statements by lobbyists on behalf of Bork, who are talking to conservatives and telling them that if Bork is selected, you'll get a change in criminal justice. That's the proof positive.[268]

What various Senators were telling my people in September

Cindy Antosh of Virginia

Cindy sent me copies of letters from Senators DeConcini, Reid, and Gore. Gore's July 28, 1987 response was lengthier and more in depth than most of the other senatorial replies. Gore noted that "Because a Supreme Court Justice is appointed for life and his decisions have far-reaching effects, it is essential that he be fair, open-minded and beyond reproach." Any decision he made was going to have to wait "Until Judge Bork is subject to the scrutiny of the Judiciary Committee during its hearings. . . ." As for the Nevadan, Reid was being very careful, leading me still to hope for his vote. I was getting more worried about DeConcini every hour.

Mary Eldredge of Vermont

The letter that Senator Stafford of Vermont sent out was also lengthy and held more substantial verbiage than most of the standard letters that allies sent in from the field. Stafford reiterated what he had told the Vermont press, and added: "I've always been somewhat of the George Aiken school of thought: that is, that any President is entitled to name somebody of his philosophical choice if the nominee is mentally competent and has the record and experience and is not guilty of any misconduct."

Stafford (whom I believed we would get until near the end) contin-
ued, "Were I to prejudge this nomination on the basis of that criteria,
I would certainly vote to confirm Judge Bork since he obviously is
mentally competent, surely has adequate legal and judicial experience,
and to my knowledge is not guilty of any misconduct. In this case,
however, I believe it best to wait and see how Judge Bork responds to
questions which will be raised during the confirmation process. Partic-
ularly important to me . . . will be Judge Bork's views on the rights of
women and minority groups."

Carole Dubbert of Kansas

Carole Dubbert of Shawnee, Kansas wrote Senator Nancy Kassen-
baum about Title X legislation and Judge Bork. Senator Kassenbaum
said that she planned to support our man.

Angela Grimm of California

Angela Grimm, my friend at the Free Congress Foundation's Cath-
olic Center, wrote several senators on her own. She passed along to
me copies of responses from Senators Thurmond and Simon. Thur-
mond, no shock here, told Angela she could be "assured" of him
giving "full consideration" to her comments.

On the other hand, Senator Simon went on about what a Supreme
Court Justice must be. He concluded his letter by saying that if after
careful review of Judge Bork's accomplishments and actions he was
"sure that Judge Bork will protect the rights of all citizens and will be
fair to victims of discrimination and injustice, I will support his
nomination."

(Paul Simon was running for President at the time, but my question
for this generally honest man is how—looking back now — he can
justify what he did to reject a man he knows was qualified, a man he
knows would be fair, a man consumed with passion for the rule of
law.)

Disaster struck for Democratic Presidential hopeful Joe Biden when
the New York *Times* printed on the front of its September 12 edition a
story revealing that he had used passages of British politician Neil
Kinnock's rhetoric for use during an August appearance in Iowa.
According to the *Times* account, the Kinnock campaign had run a
television ad during the 1986 British election that showed the Labor
Party leader saying:

Why am I the first Kinnock in a thousand generations to be able to get to university? . . . Was it because our predecessors were thick? . . . Was it because they were weak, those people who could work eight hours underground [as coal miners] and come up and play football, weak? . . . It was because there was no platform upon which they could stand.

Biden was then quoted during closing remarks at the debate:

Why is it that Joe Biden is the first in his family ever to go to a university? . . . Is it because our fathers and mothers were not bright? Is it because I'm the first Biden in . . . generations to get a college and a graduate degree that I was smarter than the rest? . . . Was it that they didn't work hard, my ancestors who worked in the coal mines of Northeast Pennsylvania and would come up after 12 hours and play football for four hours? . . . It's because they didn't have a platform upon which to stand.[269]

The media quickly figured out that Biden had borrowed from the speeches and writings of other liberal heroes as well, including Hubert Humphrey, John F. Kennedy and Robert F. Kennedy. For example, the press noted, a Biden favorite included heart-felt words uttered by Robert Kennedy during his 1968 Presidential bid:

The gross national product does not allow for the health of our children, the quality of their education or the joy of their play. It does not include the beauty of our poetry, or the strength of our marriages, the intelligence of our public debate or the integrity of our public officials. It measures neither our wit nor our courage, neither our wisdom nor our devotion to our country. It measures everything, in short, except that which makes life worthwhile, and it can tell us everything about America except why we are proud that we are Americans.[270]

This was compared to Biden's words at the California State Democratic Convention in February:

We cannot measure the health of our children, the quality of their education, the joy of their play . . . [economic strategy] doesn't measure the beauty of our poetry, the strength of our marriages, the intelligence of our public debate, the integrity of our public officials. It counts neither our wit nor our wisdom, neither our compassion nor our devotion to our country. That bottom line can tell us everything about our lives except that which makes life worthwhile, and it can tell us everything about America except that which makes us proud to be Americans.[271]

Biden campaign spokesman Larry Rasky was furious when his candidate, who had been banking on the Bork hearings to advance his prospects for the White House, suddenly became the focus of an intense and negative flurry of media coverage. "What really steams me is that here we are on the eve of the Bork hearings and another Democratic candidate is deliberately trying to undermine Biden who is going to battle on this thing," Rasky said. "Somebody has committed an outrageous act here."[272] The day after the *Times* story broke, Rasky explained that Biden "inadvertently didn't attribute his remarks. The Senator has quoted Mr. Kinnock's remarks, with attribution, both before and after the Iowa speech. One of our Democratic opponents deliberately provided the tape to the news media on the eve of the Bork hearings in an attempt to embarrass Senator Biden." In London, the British Broadcasting Corp. quoted an amused Kinnock as saying, "Imitation is the sincerest form of flattery."[273]

The Biden story nearly buried the Justice Department's entry (after being somewhat quiescent, apparently at White House direction) into the Bork debate. A 213–page report charged that the attacks from Bork opponents were "illegitimate and unwarranted," adding, "Their shoddy methodology and analysis seek to characterize a distinguished and fair-minded jurist as biased and closed minded." The report continued by saying that some 13 widely publicized position papers criticizing Bork "should be dismissed for the propaganda that they are and should not confuse the debate over Judge Bork's confirmation. . . . These reports criticize him as being motivated by his own political agenda. Yet Judge Bork neutrally applies the law. In contrast, the special interests evaluate judges precisely the way that they rank politicians—according to the number of times they deliver results desired by a particular special interest to further a political goal."[274]

Public Citizen lawyer William B. Schultz, whose group had distributed one of the more controversial anti-Bork documents, argued that the Justice Department's response "demonstrates that our analysis of Judge Bork's judicial record has done serious damage to the White House's claim that Judge Bork is a moderate." PAW's Art Kropp dismissed the report as "nothing more than a shabby last-ditch effort to whitewash the many serious problems in Bork's record."[275] Other anti-Bork analyses criticized in the DOJ report were produced by such groups as the Judiciary Committee, National Women's Law Center, the AFL-CIO and the Columbia Law Review.[276]

The White House wasn't the only one critical of the analyses produced by anti-Bork organizations. *Judicial Notice*, the Free Congress Foundation's regular newsletter on legal issues, " . . . reluctantly noted errors of methodology and fact so severe that they could have no other explanation than deliberate misrepresentation. Where methodology and facts were distorted, it always supported the anti-Bork position. . . . One conservative attorney was heard to mumble that an attorney who submitted materials so full of errors to a court of law would be vulnerable to severe professional sanctions."[277]

Meanwhile, activists on both sides were joining those who from the beginning had made best guesses of how individual senators would vote on the nomination. The week before the hearings, Administration officials said they counted 55 votes for their nominee, while Senator Patrick Leahy (D-VT) claimed the vote was an even 45–45 with 10 undecided. "A few months ago, there was no doubt of confirmation," said William Marshall, law professor at Case Western Reserve University. "But there's been so much pressure rallied against it, now nobody can be sure. It may happen, but it certainly won't be as clear cut." Leslye Arsht of the White House agreed, but remained positive. "There's no question that the 90 days of debate prior to the hearings have encouraged people to declare their positions early, and many have gone against us," she said. "But we're still confident the majority will support us."[278]

White House Chief of Staff Howard Baker continued to project Administration optimism during a September 13 appearance on NBC's "Meet the Press." "I think that what we have is a distinguished jurist who is widely supported, and . . . I think will be confirmed," he said.[279] Senator Howard Metzenbaum (D-OH), who appeared on the same program, said the nomination "will turn on his views. It will turn on his firing of Archibald Cox. It will turn on his opinions about the right to privacy."[280]

That same day, Senator Dennis DeConcini (D-AZ) warned viewers of ABC's "This Week With David Brinkley" that he would throw Bork "some hard questions . . . and they go beyond just his constitutional interpretation. They go to some of the integrity questions." DeConcini added, "I want to know what his answer is to Judge Gordon of Kentucky when he committed himself—according to Judge Gordon— and voted the other way. I want to know why he did not pay his taxes in Connecticut after he was a judge. I want to know what his excuse and rationale legally is for dismissal of Archibald Cox."[281]

We were growing more and more concerned about DeConcini's intentions, knowing full well his Committee vote could well be pivotal.

Casey believed, "We have to turn him politically with pressure from home. It's clear he's looking for some credible-looking reason to vote against Bork." Elizabeth Kepley continued seeking a meeting for several of us or for her people from Arizona.

As part of the accelerating smear campaign against Bork personally, the Left had circulated rumors that Judge Bork had a drinking problem, and was too lazy to handle the demanding case load of a federal court judge. DeConcini, further fueling speculation that he would vote against Bork, called the nominee's academic writings "very disturbing. He's got some problems; there's no question about it." On the same program, Senator Specter mused whether Bork "would turn the court sharply because a number of his writings suggest he is in sharp variance from justices from [Oliver Wendell] Holmes all the way to Chief Justice [William H.] Rehnquist." Specter said his vote will "turn on whether Judge Bork fits into the tradition of U.S. constitutional jurisprudence," and said he would attempt to determine whether Bork's writings were simply "matters of professorial theorizing and hyperbole in writing." Bork ally Senator Orrin Hatch (R-UT), who also appeared on "This Week," noted that Bork bashers had been forced to abandon attacks on his qualifications, and "so what they've done is play politics."[282]

Sunday newspapers were thick with Bork stories and full-page advertisements by groups such as the National Abortion Rights Action League, whose ad challenged: "You wouldn't vote for a politician who threatened to wipe out every advance women have made in the 20th century. Yet your senators are poised to cast a vote that could do just that." Another full-pager from Planned Parenthood declared: "If your senators vote to confirm the administration's latest Supreme Court nominee, you'll need more than a prescription to get birth control. It might take a constitutional amendment."[283] And on the day of the hearings themselves, People for the American Way began a million-dollar media blitz in newspapers across the country. Their full-page ad featured a large headline declaring: "ROBERT BORK VS. THE PEO-PLE." Under the picture of a gavel was written: "The nomination of Robert Bork . . . has a lot of people worried. With good reason." The ad went on to charge Bork with "sterilizing workers, billing consumers for power they never got, no privacy, no day in court, big business is always right."[284]

People for the American Way also ran a highly controversial, yet effective, anti-Bork television campaign throughout the month of September. The ad featured a stereotypical American family standing in front of what appeared to be the Supreme Court building. Actor Gregory Peck then warned viewers in a somber voice that their liberty would be in jeopardy if Bork was placed on the Court: "Robert Bork . . . defended poll taxes and literacy tests which kept many Americans from voting. He opposed the civil rights law that ended white-only signs at lunch counters."[285] Dan Casey of the American Conservative Union observed: "The American people should be outraged that the liberals are spending millions of dollars to try to buy a Supreme Court seat."[286]

But according to the September issue of *Broadcast* magazine, People for the American Way could not pay some television stations enough to air their messages. PAW budgeted $725,000 for its anti-Bork effort, $200,000 of which was slated for purchasing air time for the ads featuring Gregory Peck. But PAW media director Jackie Blumenthal said some of the money sat unused, as ABC affiliates in Chicago, Philadelphia and other cities refused her request to purchase time. The Fox network also turned her away, as did all TV stations in some areas, including Chicago.[287]

Meanwhile, Senator Edward Kennedy continued his attacks on the nominee. On September 13 he told an audience at the Georgetown University Law School:

> Rarely have we had such a combination of circumstances: a Supreme Court so closely divided—and a President so consciously seeking to bend it to his will; a justice resigned who held the decisive balance on many critical issues, yet who defied any ideological category—and a justice nominated who tilts consistently toward one narrow ideological point of view. . . . From the purchase of a home, to the ballot box, to the job site, to the indignity of "White Only" signs in public places, Robert Bork had made a career of opposing simple justice, and he does not deserve a new career on the Supreme Court of the United States.[288]

In introducing the Massachusetts lawmaker, Dean Robert Pitofsky of the Georgetown University Law Center had called repeated attention to the Kennedy family's long support for Georgetown University. After the Democrat arrived on stage with his entourage and began to speak, at least one listener in the audience found the tone of the speech, the presence of the television cameras and the pro-Kennedy student bodies all too convenient as stage properties for the Democrat's assault on Bork's integrity and jurisprudence.

Immediately at the conclusion of Kennedy's 40 minute speech, Paul

D. Kamenar of the Washington Legal Foundation, an adjunct professor of law at Georgetown who was in one of the box seats in the auditorium, leapt to his feet to ask the Senator the first question. But Dean Pitofsky told the audience that the Senator had business on Capitol Hill and could not take the time to answer questions. Kamenar remarked to the students seated around him that it was too bad no one would have a chance to rebut Kennedy's allegations about the nominee's fitness.

As Kamenar tried to leave through the exit, he was unable to open the door to that box, because some weight was blocking the door from the other side. When the door suddenly swung open, Kamenar was surprised to find himself face to face with the Senator who, startled, mumbled about whether his nephew was in that auditorium. Seizing the moment, Kamenar quickly asked Kennedy, "Now that you're here, can I ask you something? If Bork is such a bad guy, why is he being endorsed by Lloyd Cutler, Jimmy Carter's legal advisor, Griffin Bell and Justice John Paul Stevens?"

Before the engagement could begin, however, Kennedy's entourage surged around him, a phalanx of protectors pulled him back out the door and muttered that the Senator was too busy to take any questions, that votes awaited him on the Hill. Dean Pitofsky was among those escorting the Senator as the court followers surged toward the door and into the waiting limousine.

As Kamenar watched Kennedy and his aides leave, Brit Hume of ABC News hurried by, also seeking the senatorial quarry. Kamenar quickly told Hume of his belief that the entire Kennedy speech was a shamelessly staged event, with the law school and its students as props. Kamenar learned through University sources that the law school did not "invite" Kennedy to speak against Bork; Kennedy invited himself and Pitofsky was more than willing to oblige. Hume continued his pursuit, indicating he would ask the question if he had a chance.

After Hume disappeared, Pitofsky reentered the building as Kamenar was headed for the door. Still aggravated with the one-sided presentation on such an important issue, Kamenar confronted his dean. "It's a shame Senator Kennedy couldn't take any questions on anything," he said.

Pitofsky replied, "Well, Paul, you know how it is, he's so busy and he had to get going."

Kamenar rejoined, "Why don't you do something to get a little balance on this issue? Why don't you ask Senator Hatch to come present the other side?"

"Oh, well, Hatch didn't call us."

"So then, Kennedy did *initiate the contact so he would have a stage for his attack on Bork?" Kamenar challenged the dean—who rushed on at that point, saying, "Well, Paul, we did have Judge Bork out here recently."*

Kamenar later confirmed that no Senate votes were scheduled for the time the Senator was at the law school, or even later. He also called Judge Bork to ask if he had been to the Georgetown Law School recently. The jurist took the call in a rare quiet moment, and told Kamenar he was there in April for a Saturday morning conference on standing. There were 20 or so people in the audience.

A major law school's idea of equal time, no doubt.

Shortly before the hearings began, Lloyd Cutler's Lawyers' Committee for Civil Rights under Law parted company with Cutler himself when it released an analysis of Bork's civil rights record, which warned that confirming Bork to the Supreme Court "jeopardizes the continued vitality of civil rights and liberties long enjoyed by all Americans." The report continued: "Bork's record reflects strong and consistent opposition to many of the central principles for which the Lawyers' Committee has fought" and "places him well outside the territory occupied by the most respected advocates of judicial restraint in this century." An outraged Cutler, the self-described liberal who had infuriated his colleagues with his public defense of the nominee, considered leaving the Lawyers' Committee.[289]

Washington was not the only city in feverish anticipation of the hearings. The night before Judge Bork was scheduled to testify, a Philadelphia-based group of Bork bashers held a "funeral for justice"—complete with printed obituaries, pallbearers, and a choir.[290]

Chapter Five

"His Own Best Witness"

Normally, when I am upset, I take time to cool down before I act. However, an incident in mid-September—as the hearings were slated to begin—was an instance in which I acted immediately. My colleagues at Coalitions for America had shown me, first thing in the morning at the office, a newspaper article from the Washington Post. *In this article—a profile of Ralph Neas of the Leadership Conference on Civil Rights, a key Bork opponent—Tom Korologos, the private lobbyist working with the White House legislative staff, had disparaged the "organized groups" for not doing enough to help secure Bork's confirmation.*

I immediately called the office of a high ranking White House official with whom I had never talked, but whose staff had worked with me frequently. I began with the secretary: "Who in the hell is this guy Korologos, and what planet has he been living on? I want to know if he's *been working 16 hour days lately. How many weeks has it been since* he *spent time with his family? The man is an idiot if he believes what he said in the story is true. It is* only *the outside conservative groups who have delivered in the Bork fight so far." That last sentence was an overstatement, of course, in that I rushed past the central and ongoing work of the key Senate champions for Bork, as well as the non-stop efforts of the legislative operation in the Department of Justice. Nonetheless, my words obviously conveyed my anger.*

A secretary kicked me up to the next level, where I repeated this basic line. I went up yet another level, leaving messages all along the way.

Finally, the high ranking White House official himself called me to talk. I unburdened myself on this man, and asked him to communicate my displeasure to Korologos and Will Ball.

"Pat, my people told me you were very upset after you read that article. I went back and looked myself, and immediately understood that you misunderstood what Tom was getting at. I cannot speak for him, but I am certain he was not referring to the outside conservative groups," this official related to me.

Somewhat mollified, I replied, "Then who in the hell was he talking about?"

With surprising candor, this official replied, "Well, I believe he was talking about what you would call the corporate establishment—all the CEOs and public affairs officers who promised they would be there when we needed them, but who are not coming through now. The legal scholars, the Ivy Leaguers who promised to deliver for Bob Bork but who are now abandoning him. There are many others. It's starting to come apart, I'm afraid. I hope we can still win."

"Who are these people?" I demanded. There was no reply.

I offered, "As long as we're having this conversation, I have something to tell you. I'm not going to ask you for a penny for my organization or for my confreres in the conservative movement. We could use some help because we're all spending to the bottom of the barrel to support Bob Bork. But we'll get by. This nomination won't get by, however, unless some bucks get plowed into television advertising pronto." (I was referring to what by then had developed into a disaster. The California-based "We the People" organization was supposed to be a funnel for aggressive pro-Bork advertising. After announcing a $2 million objective, they raised $200,000, spent it on marginally useful media, and played only a small role in the Bork effort.)

I continued, "For God's sake, the other side has Abe Lincoln himself [Gregory Peck in the advertisements distorting Bork's judicial record] in their TV spots. You need to get the President on the horn to some of his rich buddies and the word needs to go out that this needs to happen."

"We can't do that. It's just not appropriate for the President to raise money for a lobbying operation," he replied.

I bluntly answered, "I don't care how you do it. I don't care if it's done with winks or nudges. I'm giving you my honest assessment. As your hard-working outside ally who is delivering the grass roots part of this effort, I believe that Bob Bork will lose unless, in addition to

*our stuff, there is a sophisticated, targeted media budget to offset the
negative advertisements. We don't have to match the other side, but
we do have to be visible and effective in paid media."*

*There was a long pause at the other end. Finally, he replied, "I find
what you say persuasive. I'll take a walk down the hall and run it up
the flag pole."*

*The conversation ended with my offer, "Call me if there's anything
you need us to do."*

*Massive dollars were never committed to a media effort. The "We
the People" media campaign continued to founder. The outside groups
continued to deliver the cards and letters to Senators, but it wasn't
enough.*

On September 15, the first day of hearings, spectators lined up
outside the Russell Senate Office Building to take turns watching Judge
Bork, and to determine for themselves whether he was—as his critics
said for months—really a villain.

While waiting for a chance to occupy one of the forty seats reserved
for the public in the marbled Senate Caucus Room, Georgetown
University law student Kevin MacIntyre noticed that his neighbor in
line, Phyllis D'Ermo of Bethesda, Maryland, was sporting a "Block
Bork" button on her shirt. The two began to debate. "If he's such an
extremist, how come none of his decisions have ever been overturned?" MacIntyre asked. "Read this," D'Ermo shot back, shoving
a People for the American Way ad at MacIntyre. "He sided with a
company that ordered women employees to be sterilized to prevent
birth defects from pollution." An incredulous MacIntyre asked, "Do
you really believe that?" D'Ermo argued, "Well, if it isn't true how
could they print it?" MacIntyre tested the waters: "Have you read any
of his opinions? I have. Tell me one thing you've read that he's
written." D'Ermo bristled. "You know nothing about me," she huffed.
"Don't make presumptions."[291]

The caucus room was jammed with reporters, onlookers, and television cameras. Judge Bork, squinting under the glare of 23 spotlights,
sat at a long table covered with green felt that directly faced the eight
Democrats and six Republicans on the committee. His wife, Mary
Ellen, and three children, Robert Jr., Charles and Ellen sat behind
him.

In unprecedented action before the Senate Judiciary Committee,
former President Gerald Ford introduced Judge Bork, praising him as
an "exemplary" candidate who is "uniquely qualified" to sit on the

Supreme Court. Ford, a friend of the Judge's for more than 20 years, challenged the criticism of Bork's actions during the "Saturday Night Massacre." "As solicitor general, Judge Bork was thrust into a situation not of his own doing," Ford said. "He acted with integrity to preserve the continuity between the administration and the investigation."[292]

Senate Minority Leader Robert Dole (R-KS) also applauded Bork, calling him a "man of unquestionable ability and integrity." In a subtle jab at Biden, Dole said, "We're all politicians and we know 1988 is next year."[293]

Following introductions and words of praise from Ford, Dole, and other political luminaries, Bork was left sitting alone at the table.

Each Judiciary Committee Senator then gave his opening remarks. As chairman, Biden spoke first. Claiming to be "deeply troubled" with Bork's writings, Biden questioned whether placing the nominee in the vacancy left by Justice Powell would rob Americans of their rights to use birth control, force state population mandates, and deny the right to enjoy various art forms. "We must pass judgment of whether your philosophy is an appropriate one in this century," Biden said.[294]

Biden's statements were but a subtle echo of charges made by Senator Kennedy during his opening remarks:

> Time and again, in his public record over more than a quarter of a century, Robert Bork has shown that he is hostile to the rule of law and the role of the courts in protecting individual liberty. He has harshly opposed—and is publicly itching to overrule—many of the great decisions of the Supreme Court that seek to fulfill the promise of justice for all Americans. . . . It is easy to conclude from the public record of Mr. Bork's published views that he believes women and blacks are second-class citizens under the Constitution. He even believes that in the relation to the executive, that members of Congress are second-class citizens. Yet, he is asking the Senate to confirm him. . . . In Robert Bork's America there is no room at the inn for blacks and no place in the Constitution for women; and, in our America, there should be no seat on the Supreme Court for Robert Bork. . . . Rather than selecting a real judicial conservative to fill Justice Powell's vacancy, the president has sought to appoint an activist of the right, whose agenda would turn us back to the battles of a bitterly divided America, reopening issues long thought to be settled and wounds long thought to be healed.[295]

Following the several hours of senators' statements, Bork used his opening remarks to explain his judicial philosophy to the packed hearing room:

The judge's authority derives entirely from the fact that he is applying the law and not his own personal values. . . . No one, including the judge, can be above the law. . . . How should a judge go about finding the law? The only legitimate way is by attempting to discern what those who made the law intended. . . . If a judge abandons intentions as his guide, there is no law available to him and he begins to legislate a social agenda for the American people. That goes well beyond his legitimate authority. . . . the judge must speak with the authority of the past and yet accommodate that past to the present. The past, however, includes not only the intentions of those who first made the law, it also includes those past judges who interpreted and applied it in prior cases. That is why a judge must give great respect to precedent. . . . My philosophy of judging is neither liberal nor conservative. It is simply a philosophy of judging which gives the Constitution a full and fair interpretation but, where the Constitution is silent, leaves the policy struggles to Congress, the president, the legislatures and executives of the 50 states, and to the American people.[296]

During what many media sources described as a dry and tiring seven hours of testimony, Judge Bork often found himself on the defense against hostile questioning from Committee liberals, questions which often ignored his previous responses. Senator Biden began the question-and-answer session with a probe into the nominee's criticism of *Griswold v. Connecticut*, a 1965 Supreme Court ruling that overturned a state law prohibiting contraceptives, on the grounds that the ban had violated a constitutional right to privacy. Bork had often been quoted as saying he thought the state law in question was "nutty," but explained during the hearings that it should have been struck down using other arguments, as he believed no general right to privacy existed in the Constitution.[297]

When Senator Orrin Hatch (R-UT) asked the Judge whether he personally had anything against artificial birth control, the nominee exclaimed: "Nothing whatsoever! I think the Connecticut law was an outrage and it would have been more of an outrage if they had ever enforced it against an individual."[298]

During the following exchange, Bork attempted to explain to Kennedy that he was not the racist and sexist the Senator had vociferously accused him as being. Using a prepared text from his staff, Kennedy said:

KENNEDY: I believe that in your world, the individuals have precious few rights to protect them against the majority, and I think this is . . . what the Bill of Rights is all about, that there are some things in America . . . no majority can do to the minority or to the individuals.

BORK: I have the greatest respect for the Bill of Rights, and I will enforce the Bill of Rights. I have enforced the Bill of Rights. What we are talking about here was a generalized, undefined right of privacy, which . . . is not in the Bill of Rights.

KENNEDY: I appreciate your support for the school [de]segregation decision in 1954. But I am troubled, because I believe that your clock on civil rights seems to have stopped in 1954. . . . When did you first publicly change your position on the Civil Rights Act?

BORK: One has also to know that as solicitor general, I enforced the rights of racial minorities in court, often further than the Supreme Court was willing to go. . . . On my present court, I have frequently voted for black plaintiffs in . . . civil rights or voting rights cases.

KENNEDY: At a time when men and women in the South and North, Republicans and Democrats, recognized that race discrimination had to be outlawed . . . you strongly and publicly opposed civil rights legislation, calling its underlying principle one of "unsurpassed ugliness," and it wasn't until 10 years later, when you were nominated to be solicitor general, that you publicly repudiated those views.

BORK: I don't usually keep issuing my new opinions every time I change my mind.

KENNEDY: I'm just wondering if you've changed your view that the Supreme Court was wrong . . . to hold that poll taxes are unconstitutional?

BORK: . . . I have no desire to bring poll taxes back into existence. . . . But if that had been a poll tax applied in a discriminatory fashion, it would have clearly been unconstitutional. It was not.

KENNEDY: You indicated June 10 of this year . . . "I think this court stepped beyond its allowable boundaries when it imposed one-man, one-vote under the equal-protection clause". . . . The people of this country accept the fundamental principle . . . even though they are not burdened with a law school education.

BORK: They can enact it anytime they want to. I have no desire to go running around trying to overturn that decision. But as an original matter, it doesn't come out of anything in the Constitution.[299]

Senator Hatch began his queries with a probe into Judge Bork's views on the Supreme Court decision to legalize abortion:

HATCH: How would you define judicial activism?

BORK: I would define it as a judge reading into a statute or the Constitution, his personal policy preferences. . . . No human being can sit down with words in a statute, with history and the other evidence he uses, and not to some extent get his personal moral view into it.

HATCH: You've been criticized for having been critical of this abortion case called *Roe vs. Wade*. Can you explain your apprehensions about this case?

BORK: *Roe against Wade* contains almost no legal reasoning. We are not told why it is a private act . . . and if it is, there are lots of private acts that are not protected. Why this one is protected, we're simply not told that.[300]

Bork went on to say that he didn't know if he would vote to strike down *Roe vs. Wade*. "It is safe to say you haven't made up your mind on that?" Hatch asked. "That's true," Bork replied.[301]

Under questioning from Senator Strom Thurmond (R-SC), the nominee answered Judge James Gordon's charges that he had acted unethically in writing an opinion in a case they had ruled on together. "There's nothing to the charge," Bork explained. "The memories of the people involved, the documentation, and the practicalities of the circumstances indicate it's just—I don't know what it is, but it's certainly a misunderstanding."[302]

Although McGuigan and other Bork supporters had predicted that the anti-Bork strategy would degenerate into a mudslinging campaign, they never envisioned that some would take it so far. Using anonymous sources (an increasing scourge of contemporary journalism), a newspaper reported during the start of the hearings that an FBI investigation of the nominee had revealed he was taken to the emergency room of Sibley Memorial Hospital in Washington, D.C. on two occasions in December of 1983 to treat a broken arm and sprained wrist he had suffered by falling on icy walkways. The account said that although Bork did not drive himself to the hospital, the alcohol found in his blood during the second visit had been one point less than the level considered safe to drive. Bork backers attacked what they considered an unfair story. "They know they can't beat him on the merits, so they have to resort to character assassination," said Jeffery Troutt of the Free Congress Foundation.[303]

Washington, D.C.'s *City Paper* published the titles of the video movies that Judge Bork and his wife had rented for the past two years. The only thing they could find was that the Bork's had viewed 146 tapes, many of them featuring Cary Grant. Senator Alan Simpson (R-WY) labeled the obvious attempt to find prurient or tasteless films among the jurist's selections "puerile, smug and pathetic."[304]

In a September 15 interview, Republican National Committee Chairman Frank Fahrenkopf said he believed that this nomination would help the public to realize that the Democratic Party was nothing more than a conglomerate of noisy special-interest groups. Fahrenkopf told reporters for the Washington *Times*:

> I think the nomination of Robert Bork blew the lid off the special interest pot on the Democratic party burner. We now see the real Democratic Party coming out. We see the radical feminist groups, we see the radical gay rights groups, we see the radical opponents of the right-to-life, we see all the organized labor groups, coming out and condemning Judge Bork before a hearing was ever held. The minute those special interests started to howl, Biden automatically took the position that he was going to vehemently oppose Judge Bork. Here is the individual charged under the Constitution of the United States with being the one to run the advice-and-consent hearing coming out, before a word is spoken, and condemning the nominee. That's a direct reaction to the special interests and their control over the Democratic nominating process.[305]

The first day of the hearings, swing-vote Senator Specter had two additional phone lines plugged into his office on Capitol Hill. Within the first four hours of testimony, his Washington staff had fielded some 2,000 calls, while an estimated 1,000 more calls were dialed to his Pennsylvania office. Callers to Specter's office were greeted with an exasperated: "Senator Arlen Specter's office. Are you calling about the Bork nomination? Are you for or against?"

As the first day of hearings progressed, I thought our guy was doing great. I remember Casey, who had not seen Bork perform publicly before, calling me and saying, "This guy is incredible. He's absolutely brilliant. I'm just afraid his answers might be too long."

The NBC television affiliate in Washington called Bill Kling, the Coalitions for America press guy, early that afternoon, September 15. They repeatedly asked him to ask me to do their news show that evening. Kling came to talk to me. I told him there was no way, but that we might be able to do something in front of our building. I believed my job was to stay at the desk and monitor the hearings, alerting the troops in the countryside, stay focused on the key issues, and get ready for tomorrow. But the station claimed they wanted our side presented.

They were very aggressive. They insisted I come to the station and do a debate with Ralph Neas. That got my interest. Bill recommended I do it, so I said yes.

I drove to the station. Due to traffic, I barely made the 5 p.m. start of the news hour, with me slated to go on about 5:20.

At that point I learned the station was the object of a labor strike and, as one NBC staffer put it, "Neas wouldn't cross the picket line, so we hooked him up remote from the Capitol."

Sitting under the klieg lights, it began to get warm. Across the studio were the two anchors. 5:20 came and went. 5:30 came and went as the news dragged on, with the station cutting a couple of times to the hearings, featuring the exchange between Senator Kennedy and Judge Bork.

At 5:40, the young woman who had met me at the door tapped me on the shoulder and asked me to join her in the hall outside the studio.

Outside, she told me, "The producer decided to cut the segment. I'm sorry we brought you all the way out here."

For one of the few times during those four months, I lost it.

"You're sorry? You're sorry?" I pointed to the television monitor, which was again featuring Kennedy and Bork, with Kennedy then on the screen. "That evil man is trying to destroy not only the chances for confirmation, but the reputation of my friend. I don't give a—about being on your show, except to the extent it helps my values. No one told me I could have done this remote two blocks from my office. I told you people I was busy and needed to do it from our place, but you promised a debate so I came here."

In fairness to her, she was apologetic. "I'm just a temporary employee here and I can only do what I'm told. They told me to get you, so I got you here."

I realized I'd misplaced my driving glasses. She helped me find them in the make-up room. As I walked out the door, she went with me. I parted this way, "I know it's not your fault. But I don't believe in these kinds of coincidences. Tell your bosses not to call me again."

They haven't.

On the second day of hearings, September 16, the New York *Times* printed a defense of the nominee written by attorney Lloyd Cutler:

The book against Robert Bork is that he is "outside the mainstream" of contemporary judicial philosophy. To locate the "mainstream" for us, the bookmakers cite such recent and current paragons as Justices Hugo Black, John Harlan, Potter Stewart, Byron White, Lewis Powell and John

Paul Stevens. They are portrayed as conservative moderates, in contrast to Bork the ideologue of the extreme right. But there is something wrong with this picture. It is at odds with the recorded view of these distinguished justices themselves. . . . While Judge Bork is by no means the mirror image of these distinguished justices (who are by no means the mirror image of one another), neither is he their exact opposite. Whether or not one agrees with his or their views on particular cases, they are all well within the mainstream.[306]

The Washington *Post* carried a small pro-Bork ad signed by a group called "New Yorkers for Bork." "Who should make social policy?" the ad asked. "Judge Bork says our elected representatives should—so does the Constitution. We agree. The Senate should also agree."[307]

As round two of committee hearings commenced, Senator Howard Metzenbaum (D-OH) harshly denounced Bork's firing of Watergate Special Prosecutor Archibald Cox: "You are up for confirmation to be a member of the highest court of the land. I wonder if Americans can say, 'I can commit an illegal act, too.'" Bork, who had received high praise from President Ford for his handling of the 1973 incident, refuted the Senator's charges that the firing was illegal, and that he had advised the White House how to handle Cox months before the incident. "I did not discuss executive privilege with the President," he said.[308] Metzenbaum whipped out a copy of a memo Judge Bork had written to White House Chief of Staff Alexander Haig on August 2, 1973. In the memo, Bork explained how he had decided to back President Nixon's refusal to release the Watergate tapes because of a letter that liberal law professor Charles Black had written to the New York *Times* supporting executive privilege. "You weren't simply passing on a letter, you were advising the president on your opinion," Metzenbaum challenged. "Of course I was, Senator," Bork replied. "The Justice Department advises the president on executive privilege all the time . . . But I never advised the White House on how to meet or how to deal with the special prosecutor force."[309]

A mini-controversy that plagued us for a few days in mid-September was a reporter's assertion that Bork was an agnostic—a description Bork himself never used. To counter it, Casey and I and many others did radio shows on Christian stations or networks with southern affiliates. The problems with key elements of our base faded rather quickly, but only after a period of several days during which unsigned fliers circulated in key states asserting Bork's alleged "agnostic" beliefs.

The only Senator who pretended to grant much credence to the reports was Heflin, who began referring, in his interviews with home state media, to Bork's allegedly *"strange"* beliefs. Heflin also claimed, as the confrontation dragged on, that Bork *"refused to discuss his belief in God or lack thereof."* The assertion was, first of all, untrue. Second, however, such questioning by any Senator would probably be unconstitutional, given the Constitution's explicit ban on a religious test for office.

Weeks after the hearings, when a devout Christian woman from Birmingham vigorously defended Bork and his Catholic wife in a visit to Heflin in his Washington office, the Senator challenged her: *"How can someone like you want a non-Christian agnostic on the Court?"* She replied, *"Senator, I don't know what his religious beliefs are—but I know he would rule for the law, and that's all any of us, Christian or otherwise, should hope for."* The meeting did not end on a friendly note.

The Bork hearings week brought other signs that the action memos to our network of *"true believers"* were yielding helpful action. On September 17, New Mexico Attorney General Hal Stratton's op-ed *"Principled Conservative Best Possible Choice from Reagan"* appeared in the Albuquerque Journal. Stratton's pointed arguments on the soundness of the nominee's legal reasoning were directed at Democrat Senator Jeff Bingaman.

Meanwhile, Howie Phillips revealed to me that his Bork mailings were roughly breaking even—similar to the input I was getting from others rolling out the mail in the battle. Although the other side was scoring a bonanza in dollars, our side was merely paying for its efforts—but we were successfully sparking a steadily increasing volume of mail to the swing vote Senate offices. We weren't sure it would be enough, however. Phillips shared his estimate that through September 17, he had *"mailed 266,190 pieces of mail at a cost of $147,327 with a return of $123,408."* He expected the gap between cost and net to close before the mail campaign ended.

Judge Bork denied the allegations of *Time* magazine reporter David Beckwith that he was an "agnostic." Under questioning from Senator Simpson, Bork explained:

I don't want to go into my religious beliefs but the report in a national magazine that I was an agnostic arose from the following conversation, and the reporter agrees that it rose from the following conversation. He

said, "You're not terribly religious, are you." And I said, "Not in the
sense you mean." That's it. He went bang, "He's an agnostic." And I
later denied that I was an agnostic, in the New York *Times*, when I got a
chance to. I took him to be talking about regular—you know, great piety
and regular church attendance, and that's what I mean . . . But agnostic
does not come out of that conversation in any way and I am not an
agnostic.[310]

Simpson then asked, "And so that word was never used?" Bork
replied, "No."[311]

In one exchange, Judge Bork explained to Senator DeConcini his
belief that the Equal Rights Amendment was constitutionally unsound
because it would rob from the people the power to decide sensitive
questions of sex:

DECONCINI: What troubles me, Judge, is why are the questions concerning sex discrimination any more difficult or any more complex and
undeserving of constitutional, judicial resolution than other questions
routinely subject to the Court for constitutional analysis?

BORK: My objection to the Equal Rights Amendment was that legislatures
would have nothing to say about those complex cultural matters and had
no chance to . . . express a judgment. People would go straight—you
know, straight to court and challenge a distinction and the Court would
have to write the complete body of what's allowable, discrimination or
whatever it is. A reasonable basis test allows a little more play in the
joints, I think, for the Court to listen to the legislatures and look at the
society and bring evidence in and so forth. If you want to say that the
Equal Rights Amendment really would enact the same thing as the
reasonable basis test, then my objection to the Equal Rights Amendment
drops out . . . [The reasonable basis test] can't apply just as it does to the
races. It is possible to say . . . for example, that there shall be no
segregated toilet facilities anywhere as to race. I don't think anybody
wants to say that as to gender. There are just differences that have to be
accommodated. That's why the difference.

DECONCINI: Yes, but well—but isn't that a bogus argument? We're not
talking about unisex toilets here, we're—we're talking about fundamental
rights that women for too, too long have not been provided. We're talking
about your interpretation of whether or not on the Supreme Court you're
going to look towards that equality for women, whether we have the
Equal Rights Amendment or not. And if you have a reasonable standard
that comes into play for women, because I'm referring just to women, or
for sex, but let's just say to women, but you don't apply that reasonable
standard to racial matters.

BORK: Oh, I do. Senator I do. It's exactly the same standard.

DECONCINI: You do have a standard?

BORK: Exactly the same standards, a reasonable basis test and there is no reasonable basis to segregate the races by toilet facilities. There is a reasonable basis to segregate the genders [in] those facilities. And when I said to you that you can't treat gender exactly the same as you do race, all I meant was some distinctions are reasonable as to gender, such as the one we mentioned . . . The same one would not be reasonable as to race.

DECONCINI: All right, but isn't that carrying it to an extreme Judge Bork?

BORK: No, Senator. All I am saying to you is that the various things we would prohibit in the law as to race—not all of those would be prohibited as to gender. Now, for example, you could not have a national law that said only blacks or only whites will go into combat. It may be and I don't want to arouse a philosophical argument here, but it certainly seems likely to me that you could have a national law, in fact the Supreme Court has said as much, saying that only males will go into combat. And that was a case about whether you could have an all-male draft . . . [T]he Supreme Court said you could. So that's an illustration of the fact that gender in some cases is treated differently than race.

DECONCINI: You leave this Senator unsatisfied as to how we . . . can conclude that you're going to protect the citizens of this country in interpreting the Constitution on the Court as it relates to sex.

BORK: The fact is that as Solicitor General I argued positions for the protection of women broader than those that the Supreme Court would accept. The other fact is that in the gender cases that I have decided as a Court of Appeals judge, I have decided more of them in favor of the female claim than I have the other way. I think substantially more. There is no reason whatsoever in my record to think that I have any problem protecting women or any other group.[312]

DeConcini also attacked Bork's quarter-century old and long-since repudiated criticisms of the public accommodations law and the voting rights act. "If you were a black man, wouldn't you be concerned about the remarks you have made on the public accommodations law and the voting rights act?" DeConcini asked. Bork replied: "If I were a black man who had heard those statements but knew my record on civil rights as solicitor general, I would not be concerned." Senator Gordon Humphrey (R-NH) later confronted the issue head-on. "Are you a racist, sir?" he asked. Bork confirmed, "No. I am not. You will not find in any of my writings or any of my statements any opinion favoring racial discrimination or segregation."[313]

Senator Howell Heflin (D-AL) charged that Bork had moderated his controversial views only when he realized they might inhibit his chances at a seat on the Court. "You changed your mind when a carrot was being dangled in front of your eyes," Heflin asserted. Bork then explained his gradual evolution from youthful flirtations with Socialism and libertarianism, an evolution not dissimilar from that professed by some members of the Senate, to his mature philosophy of judicial restraint. "Not one of the changes took place in relation to any carrot," Bork countered. "There was no reason for me to change my mind except that I changed my mind."[314] Heflin replied: "You've gone through a lot of changing ideas. I wish I was a psychiatrist rather than a lawyer and member of this committee to try and figure out what you would do if you get on the Supreme Court."[315] Senator Patrick Leahy (D-VT) reopened the issue by asking: "Is it safe to say then that there's been this metamorphosis of your views from '71?" Bork answered:

Oh, yes . . . [M]y views of the law have been changed . . . I can't say it as well as this quotation, I'd like to read it to you. It's what Benjamin Franklin said when he voted in the convention for the Constitution 200 years ago tomorrow. He said: "Mr. President, I confess there are several parts of this Constitution which I do not at present approve, but I am not sure that I shall never approve them. For having lived long, I have experienced many instances of being obliged by better information or fuller consideration to change opinions even on important subjects which I once thought right but found to be otherwise. It is therefore that the older I grow, the more apt I am to doubt my own judgment and pay more respect to the judgment of others.". . . . I think that says it.[316]

Under questioning from Senator Specter, Judge Bork stated publicly for the first time that he now believed civil disobedience was protected by the First Amendment unless, as stated in the Supreme Court's 1968 *Brandenburg v. Ohio* case, the actions were "directed to inciting or producing imminent lawless action."[317]

Bork also said despite claims that he would support prayer in public schools, he had "never thought through" his views on the subject, noting that he "would not in any way question the basic importance" of maintaining separation between church and state.[318]

Senator Charles Grassley (R-IA) guided the nominee into an explanation of his views on strict interpretation:

GRASSLEY: Don't legislatures do dumb things sometimes that only the courts can protect society—only the courts are in a position to protect society?

BORK: I'm bound to say Senator, yes they do dumb things sometimes and often those dumb things are unconstitutional . . . It's not a reason for making up a new Constitution. No, there is no clause in the Constitution that says, the legislature shall make no dumb law.

GRASSLEY: I want to give you a question that was put to Justice Fortas during his confirmation hearings to be Chief Justice in 1968 . . . I quote: "To what extent and under what circumstances do you believe the Supreme Court should attempt to bring about social, economic or political change?"

BORK: If the social change is mandated by a principle in the Constitution or in a statute, then the court should go ahead and bring about social change. *Brown against Board of Education* brought about enormous social change, and quite properly. If the social change is the *judge's* idea of what would be a nice social change, then Justice Fortas's answer is correct, "zero."[319]

After Grassley praised Bork for his patient and honest responses to often-hostile questioning, the Judge explained his interpretation of the role senators should play in judicial nominations: "I believe the Senate should assure itself that the candidate's judicial philosophy is an honorable one, but a senator should not reject confirmation because he believes the nominee will go a certain way on one or two cases."[320]

In a lighter moment during the long day of testimony, Senator Heflin asked Bork to "give us an explanation relative to the beard." Bork replied:

It's a very unromantic explanation. In 1968–69 academic year, I was on sabbatical leave in England with my family. I was writing a book . . . And I—we went on a canal boat trip . . . in the bathroom, the sink was right against the wall, so when you tried to shave, unless you shaved with your left hand, I couldn't do it. And for about a week I didn't shave. And by that time, my children had become fascinated with what was then the beginnings of a red beard, and they asked me to let it go . . . I've had it ever since.[321]

(Later Heflin would refer elliptically to the beard in home state public appearances, and explicitly in private conversations, as another example of Bork's "strange" life style, apparently as a justification for his negative vote.)

Following the second day of hearings, strategists speculated that Bork would probably win Heflin's vote and lose DeConcini's. "I think Heflin is looking for a reason to justify voting for [Bork] and DeConcini is looking for a reason to justify voting against," said one Democratic Senator.[322]

Meanwhile, Senator Biden's ethics troubles were far from over. As the nation watched him preside over the second day of hearings, Syracuse University Law School officials told reporters that during his first year in law school in 1965 Biden had been caught plagiarizing on a paper. An eager press reported that, according to anonymous sources, Biden "threw himself on the mercy of the board," begging them: "[It was] my aspiration for as long as I can remember to study the law, and now that there is a possibility that this desire will never be fulfilled, I am heartsick." The board chose not to kick him out.[323]

Biden interrupted the third day of hearings to hold a press conference during which he confessed to "mistakes," but reminded reporters that his hopes for the presidency were still alive: "I'm in this race to stay. I'm in this race to win." Biden explained that he had lifted five pages from a law review article without attribution, received a failing grade and was forced to retake the class. "I was wrong, but I was not malevolent in any way," he said. "I thought I was doing the right thing."[324]

The Senator also charged that the furor over the plagiarized passages in his campaign speeches was "frankly ludicrous" and "a matter of extra exuberance." He said it was no coincidence that the allegations arose while his Committee was holding the Bork hearings. Despite his decision to stay with the race, experts predicted that the scandal might hurt Biden's campaign. "Any ethical problem is a serious blow to a relatively unknown candidate in a field this large," said University of Virginia political scientist Larry Sabato. "People are looking for reasons to eliminate candidates."[325] Jeffery Troutt of the Free Congress Foundation said the Senator's problems would hurt public perception of his conduct in the hearings: "Biden's been talking about integrity on the court, then you see him lying about his academic record and plagiarizing. It causes people to question the integrity of the people judging the Judge . . . People outside Washington will take Biden with a grain of salt and indirectly that could increase Bork's support."[326]

Biden's colleagues on the Judiciary Committee from both parties rallied in support of their chairman. "I told him he should stay on," said Senator Thurmond. "I expressed my support. And nobody expressed their opinion to the contrary. I took that to be pretty solid support. We have found him to be fair and just. And we all think he's conducting the hearings fine." Senator Simon spoke for his fellow committee members: "There's a basic feeling that Joe is a person of integrity. Sure he made a mistake when he was a student. We've all made mistakes. For those of us on the committee, it's almost as if it didn't happen."[327]

The third day of testimony was an emotional trial for Judge Bork. A hostile Senator Leahy attempted to portray him as a greedy opportunist unconcerned about the needs of the poor. Leahy reminded the nominee: "In 1979 . . . you made approximately $197,000 that year for consulting work. In 1980 . . . around $250 to $300,000 a year for consulting work. In 1981 . . . around $150,000. Are those figures at least in the ball park?" Bork said quietly, "Those were the only years I made money. There was a reason I made money, but I don't want to go into it here." Leahy barely veiled his disgust with Bork for his failure during those years to provide the poor with free legal aid.[328]

As Leahy concluded his round of interrogation, Gordon Humphrey and Arlen Specter were seen huddled in consultation at their end of the Committee table. Humphrey nodded his head several times. When his own turn came to question the witness, he changed the thrust of the early questions.

In the wake of Leahy's questioning, Senator Humphrey asked Bork if his extra income "coincided with heavy medical bills in your family." Bork covered his eyes with his hand. "Yeah," he whispered, more softly than normal, trying to shield his eyes from the intrusive cameras. During that time, Bork's first wife, Claire, had been battling cancer. She died in 1980.[329] That night one of the television network reporters broadcast the sequence of Bork and Leahy, closing with Bork's response to Humphrey and concluding: "The Democrats are not expected to pursue this line of questioning."

During testimony Bork also said he believed women could be protected from discrimination under the Fourteenth Amendment's equal protection clause if a "reasonable basis test" was applied. "Distinction made between the genders in the 19th century . . . no longer seem to anybody to be reasonable. Those distinctions are beginning to fall," Bork said. "Now we see only a few distinctions that can reasonably and rationally be made between men and women." These "few distinctions" include physical strength and unisex bathrooms, Bork said, adding, "It's rational to have all-male combat." Bork further noted that he believed the protection clause was applicable only to racial groups, but that women "would be protected as adequately as they are now" if he were on the High court.[330]

Under intense questioning from Senator Biden, Bork said he "agrees with the concept" of a marital right to privacy, and called it "essential to a civilized society." When asked whether he would deny freedom of speech First Amendment protection, Bork replied, "I have no desire to disturb that body of law."[331]

Bork's critics often accused him of insensitivity over his ruling in a case involving the American Cyanamid Company:

METZENBAUM: Judge Bork, when we were talking about the American Cyanamid case, you said, "They offered a choice to the women. Some of them, I guess, did not want to have children." Apparently, that testimony was heard by one of the women, because a telegram has just been received by the Chairman and myself which reads as follows: "I cannot believe that Judge Bork thinks we were glad to have the choice of getting sterilized or getting fired. Only a judge who knows nothing about women who need to work could say that. I was only 26 years old, but I had to work, so I had no choice. It is incredible that [a] judge who is supposed to be fair can support a company that doesn't follow OSHA rules. This was the most awful thing that happened to me. I still believe it's against the law, whatever Bork says. Betty Riggs, Harrisville, West Virginia."[332]

BORK: I think it was a wrenching case, a wrenching decision for her, a wrenching decision for us, but the entire panel agreed on—the OSHA review commission agreed with us—agreed that it was not a violation of the hazardous conditions provision of the statute. The entire panel I sat on agreed. The full court, all eleven of us, did not sit to reverse it, and I don't know if anybody appealed to the Supreme Court, but if they did, the Supreme Court didn't take it.[333]

Liberal Judiciary Committee members harped over what they called Bork's "confirmation conversion"—his supposed readiness to change his views in order to win a seat on the Supreme Court. "I've been getting criticism because I never change my mind and now because I changed my mind," Bork said, adding, "I have got a lot of positions I've taken in the past that I've reaffirmed here which I have not converted."[334] But Specter pressed on: "The concern I have is where's the predictability in Judge Bork. Where's the assurances for this committee and the Senate of where you'll be?"[335]

The Leadership Conference on Civil Rights picked up this new theme, quickly pulling together a seven-page summary called "Bork

v. Bork" that highlighted his testimony of the past three days and compared it to statements from his past. An LCCR statement asserted:

> What the New Judge Bork now says differs significantly from the Old Judge Bork on free speech, discrimination on the basis of sex, privacy and contraception. The New Judge Bork has made statements in favor of the civil rights laws, and against restrictive covenants and forcible sterilization, which the Old Judge Bork, in all of his voluminous writings and speeches, never wrote or uttered. [His earlier writings, in which Bork] had little incentive to recast his views in a manner likely to be more palatable to the Senate, are a truer indication of what Judge Bork would do if he became a member of the Supreme Court.[336]

As the hearings recessed for a short break, White House lobbyist Tom Korologos observed: "On the first day he was jittery, on the second day he was looser and I think he did a hell of a job today. He answered questions honestly and forthrightly. His critics have charged that he is too rigid, and now they're saying he changed his mind too much. They can't have it both ways."[337] Korologos added: "Look at these guys up here [on the Judiciary Committee]. How many times have they changed their minds? Don't you want a living, flowing judge, rather than a predictable, dead one?"[338] Kate Michelman of NARAL had a different view: "He can't in 48 hours undo 30 years of legal reasoning. He is recasting his philosophy because he knows he has to win confirmation. It's simply not believable."[339]

Still trying to work with the White House

The hearings had finally begun. Four days into the hearings, on September 18, conservatives were at the White House meeting with some of the President's public liaison staff to discuss strategy. Many of the "top guns" in the conservative push to get Judge Bork confirmed were in the Roosevelt Room that day at 9:15 in the morning. There was Dan Casey (American Conservative Union); Donald Baldwin (National Law Enforcement Council); Doug Johnson, Kay James and David O'Steen (National Right to Life); Curt Anderson and myself (Coalitions of America); Jim Boulet (The Moral Majority); Shannon O'Chester and Rebecca Hagelin (Concerned Women of America); a representative of the National Right to Work Committee; and Gordon Jones (Heritage Foundation).

Coming in for the White House to meld minds with the twelve Bork crusaders were four of the President's key people in the fight. Kenneth

Cribb, Assistant to the President for Domestic Policy; Rebecca Range, Deputy Assistant to the President and Director of Public Liaison; Carl Anderson, Special Assistant to the President for Public Liaison; and Mildred Webber, Associate Director, Office of Public Liaison.

Everyone was provided an information folder that gave a broad overview of who-was-who and what-was-what in the confirmation battle. The handouts included a compilation of past and ongoing constituent activities that various groups were conducting on behalf of Judge Bork.

The various groups were engaged in fairly simple, traditionally effective things: mailings (to their own members and to Senators), writing articles and op-ed pieces, and visiting Senators.

As we sketched in that meeting, some of the more widely known groups, such as American Conservative Union (ACU), Concerned Women of America (CWA) and Focus on the Family were able to do a little more. Dan Casey participated in a debate with People for the American Way, National Abortion Rights Action League, the NAACP, the Heritage Foundation, and the Moral Majority that was covered by C-SPAN. Concerned Women for America, 500,000 strong, ran a few newspaper ads in Arizona and Pennsylvania (DeConcini and Specter country) and set up Western Union hotlines for mailgram responses to Senators. At James Dobson's ministry, Focus on the Family in California, they scheduled two national radio broadcasts on Judge Bork's nomination, one in August and one during September. With its audience of 4 million, Focus on the Family was undoubtedly part of the reason we had turned the tide in raw numbers of communications to the Senators.

Besides keeping tabs on what the pro-Bork people were doing, the White House was staying briefed on "Imminent Bork Events." These were events gleaned from UPI and AP regional daybooks. Despite the excellent works of Steve Baer's Free the Court! effort based in Illinois, in the rest of the country the other side was still doing a better job at "street theatre".

(On September 19, the day following our meeting, a teach-in and rally against Judge Bork was slated in Birmingham, AL. The rally was being organized by NOW, the Alabama New South Coalition, and the Alabama Democratic Conference.)

As the battle progressed, we were broadening the list of those willing actually to work for the Judge's nomination. The Cuban Women for Human Rights, Mexican-American Foundation, National Jewish Coalition, Order of the Sons of Italy in America, Renaissance Women,

Society of Former Special Agents of the FBI, and Victims Assistance Legal Organization, to name a few, supported Judge Bork.

For everyone's information at that meeting, copies were provided of the joint CWA, Coalitions for America and ACU mailing that had recently been sent to the 1700 daily newspaper editorial boards. (This was the third of four that Coalitions and ACU sent during the fight. Rebecca Range had given us a pat on the back for this particular effort.)

Along the same line, we discussed ways for the outside groups to spark favorable editorials or op-eds in the top 200 editorial pages among crucial swing vote Senators.

Senators Specter, Byrd, Heflin and DeConcini were still the key "suspects" among those we had targeted in the Senate. A cluster of the swing Senators came from six states: Louisiana (Breaux & Johnston); Florida (Chiles & Graham); Georgia (Fowler & Nunn); Tennessee (Sasser & Gore); Maine (Mitchell & Cohen); and Mississippi (Stennis & Cochran). On the swing Democrats list were: Bentsen (TX), Boren (OK), Ford (KY), Dixon (IL), Exon (NB), and Hollings (SC). And of the Possible Republicans, seven were considered potentially— in some cases likely—vulnerable: Durenberger (MN); Chafee (RI); Evans (WA); Weicker (CT); Stafford (VT); Wilson (CA); and Packwood (OR). Also on the list, but not in any particular category were Senators Heinz (PA), Rockefeller (WV) and Shelby (AL).

(These were the Senators, we learned, White House legislative operatives had targeted as of August 5, a good month before the hearings got started—but shortly after Casey and Curt Anderson pushed for shared target lists.)

We all endorsed a strategy to elevate the importance of the crime and law enforcement issue. To this end, everyone was given a copy of the list of strong law enforcement supporters of Bork, groups representing over 350,000 law enforcement professionals, under the heading "Judge Bork is Endorsed by Law Enforcement Groups." Those groups were: the National District Attorney Association; International Association of Chiefs of Police; National Sheriffs' Association; National Association of Police Organizations; Major City Chiefs Association; National Troopers Coalition; International Narcotics Enforcement Officers Association; and the Fraternal Order of Police.

The last item in the folder was a sampling of newspaper articles describing various aspects of Judge Bork's nomination. There were seven articles in all. With the sheer volume of work I'd not examined most of them until after that meeting. Reading them gave me modest *hope we were beginning to get some reverse "spin" on the issues surrounding Bork's struggle.*

In a September 17, 1987 New York Times *piece, Kenneth Noble gave a brief chronology of Judge Bork's involvement in the Cox dismissal. Critics of Judge Bork were suggesting that the Judge, who at the time was Acting Attorney General, dismissed Mr. Cox "to block the Watergate investigation and protect President Nixon's weakening grip on his office." But in his testimony the day before, as noted by Noble, the Judge reiterated "that he dismissed Archibald Cox, the Watergate special prosecutor, to spare the Justice Department a crippling series of resignations and to continue the Watergate investigations."*

Lars Erik Nelson did an interesting piece on the "bad taste of grilled Bork." In his September 16 New York Daily News *column, Nelson mused that some of the senators on the Judiciary Committee should have scrutinized their own integrity before they proceeded on Judge Bork. Nelson wrote that he didn't hear the senators ask questions like: "Judge Bork, did you ever drive a woman off a bridge? Did you ever cheat on your college Spanish test? Did you ever plagiarize a speech from a British Socialist candidate for prime minister?" Amidst all of the hyprocisy and hysteria of the first day of hearings, Nelson wrote, Judge Bork sat quietly in the center of it being held accountable "for vigorously expressing his thoughts over the past quarter century."*

Lloyd N. Cutler's excellent essay was included in the packet we shared with one another that day.

The New York Daily News *had another article on September 16 that described the first day of hearings as "fairly mild." But Joseph Volz, who wrote the piece, surmised that the first day questioning "may be the calm before the storm."*

In his September 14 commentary, William Raspberry highlighted a talk he had had with a black attorney who thought that Judge Bork "has been unfairly painted as a right-wing ideologue." Judge Bork was his former law professor at Yale and the man had agreed to testify in support of the nominee at the hearings. Although the attorney admitted he didn't agree with all of Judge Bork's thinking, he still felt that "his friend [the judge] has been unfairly maligned."

Raspberry wasn't convinced. He still felt that Judge Bork was out of "the American mainstream." He said that "Bork, on his record, is either a man who would do great harm to the cause of racial and sexual justice in this country or he is a hypocrite. Either is enough to disqualify him."

Senator John Danforth (R-MO) wrote an opinion piece published in

the September 13 Kansas City Times. *He said that he was looking
"forward to a vigorous debate." That debate, the Senator predicted,
would "be about basic philosophy—whether we want an activist Supreme Court or a court which practices judicial restraint. The question
put to the Senate" will be the extent to which legislatures can define
and enforce community values versus the readiness of the court to set
aside legislative action as unconstitutional. In a nutshell, Senator
Danforth said that the Bork nomination is "about democracy versus
elitism. It is about philosophy of the judiciary and about philosophy of
government."*

*The final article in the folder was by Theo Lippman, Jr. of the
Baltimore* Sun. *His September 16 piece dealt with popular opinions on
Judge Bork. According to a poll taken for the Associated Press and
Media General newspapers, Lippman said that only 30% of the people
polled had an opinion on Judge Bork. They had been asked "Do you
have a favorable opinion about [Bork], an unfavorable opinion, or
don't you know enough about him at this time to have an opinion?"
With all the smoke on this matter central to all of our lives, the bulk of
our countrymen, not surprisingly, were going about their day to day
business.*

*The same question was posed about the eight sitting justices. Based
on the poll Lippman cited, six of the sitting justices were even less well
known than Bork.*

*A continuing frustration for me, as a productive session of informa-
tion exchange concluded, was that there were still no signs of a real
media offensive to offset the mounting avalanche from Bork's enemies. My distinct impression was that the White House staffers in our
meeting had been raising this point for weeks—without success. Hud-
dling briefly with one of them in the corner as the others departed, I
repeated what I'd passed on a few days earlier to one of my friend's
senior colleagues: "We've got to get real bucks into this or we're
going to lose. It's as simple as that." My friend agreed, "I know, I
know. I'm doing everything I can."*

On Friday, September 18, the fourth and what committee members
hoped would be the last day of testimony, Bork defended his civil
rights record against harsh attack from Senator Metzenbaum. "The
women of America have much to be frightened about from your
appointment. Blacks as well. You're a man of frightening views," said
Metzenbaum. The Senator also challenged Bork for a record that
"allows government in the bedroom," favors big business, stifles free

speech and cripples equal rights. Bork said there was "no basis" for such accusations, and noted that, as a judge on the U.S. District Court, he had upheld decisions favoring minorities and women in seven of eight opinions. Bork assured the Senate panel that his integrity was intact. "This is a hearing which you gentlemen referred to as historic. I have expressed my views here and those views are now widely known. It really would be preposterous to say things I said to you and then get on the high court and do the opposite."[340]

Reading from questions prepared by his staff, Senator Kennedy used his turn at Bork to underscore the growing "received wisdom" interpretation that the nominee had moderated his views on controversial issues:

> KENNEDY: You've testified . . . that you see no constitutional basis for a number of landmark decisions by the Supreme Court upholding some of the most fundamental rights and liberties. . . . In the course of these hearings, you've expressed your strong disagreement with such decisions as the poll-tax case . . . one man, one vote . . . the decision invalidating restrictive covenants . . . striking down segregated schools here . . . recognizing that Americans have a right to privacy . . . key decisions protecting the freedom of speech. . . . You told us . . . that your views are changing in a number of controversial areas, but you told the *District Lawyer* in 1985, when you were a judge . . . "it's always embarrassing to sit here and say, 'No, I haven't changed anything,' because I suppose one should always claim growth. . . . My views have remained about what they were. . . . When you become a judge, I don't think your view point is likely to change greatly." You told the Federalist Society in 1987 that "an originalist judge would have no problem whatsoever in overruling a nonoriginalist precedent because that precedent, by the very basis of his judicial philosophy, has no legitimacy." And, finally, there is an audiotape of remarks which you made at Canisius College in Buffalo, Oct. 8, 1985.
>
> [Audiotape is played]
> QUESTIONER: Now the relationship between the judge, the text and precedent, what do you do about precedent?
> BORK: I don't think that, in the field of constitutional law, precedent is all that important, and I say that for two reasons. One is historical and traditional. The court has never thought constitutional precedent was all that important [because], if you construe a statute incorrectly, then Congress can . . . correct [it]. If you construe the Constitution incorrectly . . . everybody is helpless. . . . If you become convinced that a prior court has misread the Constitution, I think it's your duty to go back and

correct it. Moreover . . . willful courts . . . will take an area of law and create precedents that have nothing to do with the meaning of the Constitution. If a new court comes in and says, "Well, I respect precedent," which has a ratchet effect, with the Constitution getting further . . . away from its original meaning because some judges feel free to make up new constitutional law and other judges, in the name of judicial restraint, follow precedent, I don't think precedent is all that important. I think the importance is what the framers were driving at. . . .

[end tape]

KENNEDY: In light of what we have just heard, how can anyone have confidence that you'll respect the decisions of the Supreme Court with which you have disagreed?

BORK: Let me go down the items that you have mentioned. . . . You mentioned the *District Lawyer*, an answer about where I said, "It's embarrassing to sit here and say I haven't changed." The question was, "Has your view of the possible usurpation of political functions by courts changed since you ascended to the bench"—not all my views, my views about courts taking over areas that belong to the legislature. And I said, "It's always embarrassing to sit here and say, 'No, I haven't changed anything because I suppose one should always claim growth.'" The fact is, no, my views have remained about where they were. After all, courts are not all that mysterious, and, if you deal with them enough and teach their opinions enough, you're likely to know a great deal.

KENNEDY: Above all, a Supreme Court justice must be fair but, in a lifetime of [public] writings, Mr. Bork has shown his bias against women and minorities and in favor of big business and presidential power. And it's small comfort to minorities to know that, some years after the Civil Rights Act was passed over his opposition, Mr. Bork changed his mind and said that it had worked all right. . . . [He] asks us to judge him on his record as a judge, but, in his own speeches as a judge, he has shown little respect for the past decisions of the Supreme Court. Again and again, on the public record, he has suggested that he is prepared to roll back the clock. . . . And in these hearings . . . he has asked us to believe that he can make a U-turn. . . . Who is the real Robert Bork?

BORK: If those charges were not so serious, the discrepancy between the evidence and what you say would be highly amusing. I have not asked that either the Congress or the courts be neutral in the face of racial discrimination. I have upheld the laws that outlaw [it]. . . . I have never written a word hostile to women . . . hostile to privacy. . . . I have never written a word or made a decision from which you can infer that I am pro-big business at the expense of other people. . . . Nothing in my record suggests I have a political or ideological agenda.[341]

Months after the confrontaton, I sat with my father at the top of the hill at my house in Arlington, Virginia. My father was a Democrat until just a few years ago. Additionally, in our family we supported the first of the lettuce boycotts, thinking it was a way to help the migrant workers. My Dad, once an admirer of Martin Luther King, Jr., is still an admirer of Jack and Bobby Kennedy, and was a union president, to boot. He told me that day, "You know what bothered me more than anything else? Ted Kennedy never called him judge. He's not Mister Bork, he's Judge Bork. Any man who works hard and gets to where that man is—I don't care if you agree with him or not, he deserves the respect of his title. The way that man [Kennedy] treated Bork was wrong."

Bork explained gradual evolution in some of his views to the more hostile committee members: "It would really be preposterous for me to sit here and say the things I have and then go on the court and do the opposite. I would be disgraced in history. I also took an oath to tell the truth and I take an oath very seriously. I did tell the truth."[342]

After the hearings, Senator DeConcini raised the hopes of Bork supporters by saying, "It's still possible I could vote for him. The predictability or nonpredictability of Robert Bork is the biggest single question I have when you put it all together." And Senate Majority Leader Robert Byrd (D-WV), who had been believed to be leaning against the nominee, suddenly announced he would join the undecided trio of DeConcini, Heflin, and Specter.[343] Dan Casey of the ACU said he was "pleasantly surprised" by Byrd's apparent shift, but remained skeptical. "I would be surprised if Byrd voted in favor, but I'm hoping he will exhibit some statesmanship in terms of getting this to a full Senate vote."[344]

Meanwhile, another blow was dealt to Joe Biden's shaky presidential candidacy when the press reported that the Senator had lied to an audience during a campaign stop in Claremont, New Hamphire on April 3. When an unidentified man had asked him about his academic background, an indignant Biden had snapped as the television cameras rolled: "I think I probably have a much higher IQ than you do, I suspect. I went to law school on a full academic scholarship" and was "the outstanding student in the political science department" at the University of Delaware. Biden then went on to boast that he "ended up in the top half of my class" at the Syracuse University College of Law and "graduated with three degrees from undergraduate school."[345]

Transcripts of the Senator's records, which he released at a press conference, revealed that Biden had in fact graduated near the bottom—seventy-sixth in a class of 85—and had only received a partial scholarship. Records further showed that Biden had not, as he claimed, earned "three degrees," but one bachelor's for a dual major in political science and history. A humiliated Biden explained in a statement:

> As the complete record of my law school career indicates, which I released to the press last week, I did not graduate in the top half of my class at law school and my recollection on this was inaccurate. My reference to "degrees" at the Claremont event was intended to refer to those majors. I said three and should have said two. With regard to my being the outstanding student in the political science department, my name was put up for that award.[346]

At the close of the fourth day of hearings, Committee members who felt their concerns (about Bork, not Biden) had not been fully addressed asked that the panel convene for an unusual Saturday session. Judge Bork spoke to a mostly empty room, and press sources noted that Chairman Biden missed much of the day in order to watch his son play football in Wilmington, Delaware. Judge Bork sought to assure the senators that he would not abandon his philosophy to "interpret the law and not to make it." Again addressing concerns about his changed views, Bork noted: "I have received criticism in some quarters for being too rigid and from other quarters for being inconsistent or self-contradictory. Neither charge, in my opinion, is accurate."[347]

During much of that Saturday session, the Judge explained his views on the War Powers Resolution to Senator Specter. "Why should we confirm a nominee who is likely to find against us" in quarrels with the executive branch, Specter asked. Bork replied, "The impression that I always side with the president is wrong."[348]

When Senator Simpson asked Bork to explain why he wanted to become a justice, the nominee replied, "Our constitutional structure is the most important thing this nation has. And I would like to maintain it and be remembered for that."[349]

After he finished testifying, Judge Bork received a phone call from President Reagan, who told him: "You demonstrated yet again your qualifications to serve on the highest court."[350]

An exhausting and emotional 27 and a half hours of testimony was finally over.

September 18–19, 1987 joint statements by Pat and Dan on Biden's fairness and probable witness timing

Although he came across somewhat "cool" in the television medium, our own estimate was that Bork had done well in the hearings. But daily "spin control" from the other side was describing as supposed "reversals" in positions things which sounded to us like a guy explaining his positions. One thing Dan and I realized as the week went on is that the other side blanketed the media in the hearing room regularly with analysis and "spin" documents, serving their need for context for the sometimes convoluted discussions in the hearing room. It was dawning on us that we had missed the boat in that respect, but we had both believed, going in to the hearings, that it was most important for us to monitor the hearings and keep the troops pouring the phone calls and letters in to the right places. We issued another joint statement saying that "there can no longer be any credible, legitimate reasons—if there ever were—for any senator to oppose [Bork's] nomination."

In a subsequent statement, we praised Senator Biden for holding fair hearings even though a few weeks ago we had demanded that he step down from the chairmanship. At the same time we predicted that Biden would let opponents testify at the hearings in the morning while relegating Bork supporters to the late afternoon. With deadlines for the evening television news people and the newspaper boys coming before the pro-Bork people got to testify, guess how "informed" opinion on Judge Bork would be presented to the American public?

Our statement at the conclusion of the hearings declared Judge Bork had "candidly, openly and convincingly" responded to every question and criticism. Our own effort at (belated) spin control included a three page summary of highlights from some of Judge Bork's responses on key issues opponents had raised, such as freedom of speech, women's rights, race, and ethics. We believed that with such an outstanding performance "there can be no legitimate basis for the baldly ideological opposition [Judge Bork] has faced. His views on a variety of legal issues demonstrate that his nomination evokes the best in traditional American legal thought."

With the completed statements, we rushed to the Senate as the hearings were concluding. But I didn't know or understand the weekend routine in the Senate. Not having a Hill pass, I had no means of entry. A very kindly guard would not let me into the hearing room area as the session ended, but he did allow me to place copies of the statements so reporters could grab them as they left.

Casey, on the other hand, bluffed his way in. More than that, he hung around while a battery of cameras interviewed Neas. When they finished with Neas, Dan calmly stepped up to the cameras and fielded questions himself. Learning by doing.

Meanwhile, allies in the cause were creating some good "trouble" of their own. In a tough September 19 letter which attracted the attention of CNN, Peter Flaherty of Citizens for Reagan attacked Biden for hypocrisy through engagement in a smear campaign on Bork, and called on Biden to end his involvement in the hearings. Flaherty was the guest on Pacifica radio the morning of September 21, where he continued to attack the Democrats and Bork's aggressive liberal tormentors.

In Chicago, Steve Baer and the Free the Court activists stayed on track with constant activity. On September 14, 50 professional women involved in law, medicine, securities, armaments and education joined in a "Women for Bork" press event. In conjunction with celebration of the Constitution Bicentennial on September 17, 500 Bork supporters joined former Senator Paul Laxalt in recitation of the Preamble to the Constitution and the Bill of Rights.

A rally in Louisville, Kentucky on September 11 attracted 50 Bork supporters. In Cincinnati, Ohio, Deputy Mayor Ken Blackwell refuted NAACP distortions of the jurist's record. Television reporters gave good coverage to a September 15 press conference in Milwaukee, Wisconsin which attracted a dozen organizations, including the Catholic League for Religious and Civil Rights.

On the day Casey and I stayed in town for the final day of the Judge's testimony, September 19, many of our allies went to Charleston, West Virginia, where some 1,000 supporters gathered in the rain to demand that Senators Byrd and John D. Rockefeller IV support Bork. (The rally attracted uniformed law enforcement officers and a wide range of conservative and religious activists and garnered respectable coverage in the region. To the best of my knowledge, it was the largest pro-Bork rally held during the confirmation struggle.)

Chapter Six

The Tide Shifts

Four months after the Bork hearings, I was in Des Moines, Iowa. I had taken a leave of absense from the Free Congress Foundation for several weeks. Tired and burned out with Washington, I was regaining perspective and getting reenergized, working as Deputy Political Director for Pete du Pont's presidential campaign.

In the crowded du Pont headquarters one day, with the Iowa winds blowing bitterly outside as I worked on lists of undecided or uncommitted conservative activists, a call came.

The receptionist told me, "Pat, there's a lady on the line who is asking if you are the Pat McGuigan who worked to confirm Judge Bork last year. Should I put her through?" I said yes.

"Mr. McGuigan? You don't know me. I'm for Jack Kemp, so don't try to get me for du Pont [later I did any way—try, that is]. But I wondered if you are the same man whose name I saw occasionally in the news, who tried to defend Bork and get him confirmed?"

"Yes. I'm the one. It's the proudest thing I ever did."

"Do you know him?"

"Yes. I do."

"Could you please tell him how much he means to all of us?"

"What do you mean?" I asked.

She explained, "I have always been a conservative. I am a Christian and I believe in America. But I never have understood the law. Watching the Bork hearings changed my life."

This was getting interesting. "What do you mean?" I asked.

"I only have a high school education. I have four children and our

135

life is busy and hectic. I don't have time to think about big things much, but I read and I care. I never understood what a magnificent system of government the founding fathers set up," she began.

"When Judge Bork's hearings started, I turned the television on CNN. In between changing the little one's diapers, and cleaning up, and cooking and working in the house, I left the television on constantly. I listened to every word I could. Then, after dinner each night, I turned C-SPAN on," she continued.

"I can't explain it. I've lived here all my life. I love this country. But I never understood our system of government. I never understood what judges do. I never understood how the Constitution split the power up so we could be free. I never knew how incredible the whole thing was until Judge Bork explained it to me.

"It was so awful, what they did to him. I just want you to tell him that he means so much to people like me, conservative Americans who had no one to speak like that, for us, until he came along. I read what they said in the papers, that his answers made him lose. That's not true. He lost because he spoke for us. Will you tell him?"

I paused for a bit, rather moved by her brief narrative. "Why don't you tell him yourself?" I suggested that she write him a personal letter, telling him everything she had just said to me. She said she would.

In the flurry of news coverage following the end of Judge Bork's week-long testimony, strategists on both sides claimed that his appearance before the Senate Judiciary Committee had helped their cause. "To the extent that the White House thought Bork would portray himself as a flexible moderate, those hopes were dashed," said a Biden staffer. "Bork betrayed himself as Bork today."[351] William Schultz of Public Citizen said, "I think we made the most progress in presenting our case through his testimony and his responses."

But Assistant Attorney General John R. Bolton countered that "the most significant part to emerge from the hearings was five days of Bork testimony where he demonstrated the depth and richness of his intellect and why he is, as [former] Chief Justice [Warren E.] Burger said, the most qualified nominee in 50 years." Dan Casey of the American Conservative Union agreed: "I think Judge Bork performed magnificently, and any reasonable observer would have concluded that he has basically laid to rest all the outrageous charges against him. [But] the evening news clips gave a completely different picture. The picture was Judge Bork being accused over and over of being insensitive to minorities and women and not understanding why he wanted to go back to one man, one vote.''[352]

Bruce Fein of the Heritage Foundation expressed anger that committee liberals had ignored Judge Bork's tough law-and-order record during the hearings, while concentrating only on issues that concerned small, but loud special interests:

> Look at where the focus has been. *Griswold vs. Connecticut* is of interest to groups like Planned Parenthood and the National Abortion Rights Action League. Affirmative action and racial discrimination is of interest to groups like the ACLU and NAACP. Separation of church and state is the interest of groups like People for the American Way and Americans United for Separation of Church and State. [The Democrats] didn't ask any questions on the death penalty, notwithstanding that Powell was often the swing vote on death penalty cases. . . . The reason this skewed questioning is occurring is that on issues of criminal justice, the American people are all with Bork. [The Democrats] have taken one case like *Griswold*, and they've beaten it to death. But then cases like *Miranda vs. Arizona*—they make movies out of that case—why isn't there any questioning on how Judge Bork would change that? After a while . . . with Biden saying that First Amendment rights might tumble if nude dancing in the street isn't protected, you have to wonder . . . come on, are you really going to keep someone off the court for this?

Frank Carrington of the Sunny Von Bulow National Victim Advocacy Center echoed Fein's argument: ''The reason criminal law hasn't been mentioned is because they're trying to put the extremist label on [Bork]. When you have a judge whose speakings and writings are in accord on the death penalty with seven of nine justices, then you don't want to talk about the death penalty.'' But Nancy Broff of the liberal Alliance for Justice defended the committee Democrats: ''It may just be that [the senators'] constitutional concerns don't run that way. People can understand the concept of not having contraceptives or not being able to demonstrate against the government or being protected from discrimination on the job or any type of discrimination . . . I don't think criminal law is as immediate to most people.''[353]

Along with analysis of the hearings appeared commentaries on the players themselves. An editorial appearing in the September 22 edition of the *Wall Street Journal* reminded the public who was actually testifying against Bork:

> Consider Owen Fiss, Bork's successor as Alexander Bickel professor of public law at Yale Law School, who is one of several Yale professors

scheduled to testify against the nomination. The day after President Reagan's 1984 landslide victory, Fiss boasted to a class that "not only do I not know anyone who voted for Ronald Reagan, I don't know anyone who knows anyone who voted for Reagan." A first-year student from Utah stood up to broaden Mr. Fiss's horizons. "Here I am, Professor Fiss," he said.[354]

McGuigan questioned the motivations of those members of the Judiciary Committee who had attacked Judge Bork's ethics:

Judge Robert Bork is too tough on crime for some of the Senators. He's certainly too tough for Howard Metzenbaum, who earned and was forced to return a $250,000 finders fee for two telephone calls he made a few years ago—more than Judge Bork earns in two and a half years. Judge Bork is too tough on crime for a guy like Ted Kennedy, who was caught cheating at Harvard. Indeed, the Wall Street Journal notes that Yale law professor Burke Marshall, who testified against Judge Bork, is the very same man who advised Kennedy on how to beat the rap when he fled from the famed Chappaquiddick incident that left a girl dead. And certainly Judge Bork is too tough on crime for Joe Biden, an admitted plagiarist who misled Americans about his academic record; and for Pat Leahy, who resigned from a key Senate committee after it was revealed that he had leaked sensitive national security information to the press. Look who's judging the Judge![355]

Despite their praise of Bork's conduct and superior mind, the strategy by committee liberals to squelch the nomination by highlighting Judge Bork's "inconsistencies" seemed to work. After the hearings, freshman Senator John Breaux (D-LA), who had been elected by a majority black vote and was looking for a good reason to oppose Bork, said: "I'm troubled by his incredible inconsistencies. It seems to me the Judge has been all over the map."[356]

But White House lobbyist Will Ball claimed that Bork's philosophy of strict adherence to the Constitution would be the ultimate deciding factor for most swing-vote senators, particularly those from the South. "I think it is the kind of argument the overwhelming majority of senators would agree with," he said. "It is the major argument of these proceedings and when it is over the argument on which most senators will cast their votes."[357]

Meanwhile, conservative strategists expressed fear, as soundings on Capitol Hill grew more and more negative, that pressure from the organized Left might keep Bork from being confirmed. Casey noted,

"It has become apparent that some pressure from the labor unions has been put on a couple of key swing senators in the last couple of weeks. Because we hadn't anticipated such strong pressure, we are concerned." He declined to estimate the head count on a cloture vote to break the inevitable Democratic filibuster, but said that when the issue reached the full Senate, 40 senators would vote for, 30 against, and the 30 who were undecided would swing the decision one way or the other. "It's 50/50 whether or not we can get the 60 votes" needed to break the filibuster, Casey predicted.[358]

On Sunday, September 20, Senator Specter told viewers of CBS's "Face the Nation" that he remained undecided about the nomination. "I think we really have to hear the other witnesses who are coming on," he said. "There are some very complex questions which have to receive considerable thought. For example, Judge Bork has made significant shifts from his writings to what he testified about." DeConcini, who appeared on the same program, echoed Specter's hesitancy: "I share the same concerns. The Judge has made some very strong, what I consider radical, views known over his years of being a judge, and particularly before being a judge. And now he has changed."[359]

The endorsement of Bork triggered fierce attacks on the Southern Baptist Public Affairs Committee (PAC) from some elements in the denomination, including from Phil Strickland, executive director of the Texas Christian Life Commission. He argued the endorsement might endanger the church's tax-exempt status. But in a September 21 letter, Les Csorba, the conservative Baptist who had originated the endorsement, said he "smelled hypocrisy" in Strickland's attacks, noting that he "serves as a trustee of Americans United for Separation of Church and State, which is also a tax-exempt organization and which lobbied vigorously against Judge Bork's nomination."

With Judge Bork back in his chambers, day six of testimony, September 21, began the long parade of witnesses who had petitioned the committee to speak. In a pattern not unnoticed by Bork supporters (and predicted the previous week by McGuigan and Casey) witnesses against the nominee were scheduled to speak first—in time for the television reporters to make their deadlines—while pro-Bork witnesses were held until the end of the day. "Biden neatly kept the pro-Bork panels waiting past the evening television news deadlines, and yet managed to escape most of the blame for doing so," wrote Terence Moran of the *Legal Times*. "Biden pulled this trick off by having the . . . witnesses testify one at a time. This maneuver enabled the

Democrats to stall the proceedings. They carefully elicited testimony with time-consuming questions, while the Republicans, especially Senator Strom Thurmond of South Carolina, fell into the trap by strenuously challenging each [anti-Bork] speaker at length. Biden also kept Bork's forces on the committee off balance by refusing repeated requests to provide a complete witness list for the more than two weeks of expected testimony. The chairman finally acquiesced to the minority demands late in the afternoon on Tuesday, September 22. But the delay prevented the Republicans' sharpest debaters, Senators Orrin Hatch (R-UT) and Alan Simpson (R-WY) from readying themselves for the most highly publicized anti-Bork witnesses."[360]

Three prominent blacks—William T. Coleman Jr., transportation secretary in the Ford administration, former Congresswoman Barbara Jordan (D-TX), and Atlanta Mayor Andrew Young—opened the day's testimony by accusing Judge Bork of opposing the civil rights of minorities. "Here you have a man who in every instance on these great issues, publicly as a scholar, always comes out the wrong way," said Coleman. "In this day and age, can we really take the risk· of a man who fails to recognize the fundamental rights of privacy and liberty?"[361] Oddly enough, Coleman was a member of the American Bar Association committee that had voted Bork "exceptionally well-qualified" in 1981 to serve on the US Court of Appeals.[362]

Young, perhaps hinting Bork was a racist, charged that the booming cities of the South "could not be imagined in a segregated society or one where the race question was still open."[363] He went on to assert that if Bork's views on First Amendment protection had been in the majority, "I might have been branded a terrorist and jailed for my participation in the civil rights movement instead of becoming the first black elected to Congress from Atlanta in more than 100 years."[364]

Jordan said that "living for 51 years as a black American born in the South" had taught her to look to the High Court for help in advancing the rights of minorities, which she said Judge Bork would seek to reverse. Jordan further explained:

> We once had a poll tax in Texas. That poll tax was used to keep people from voting. The Supreme Court said it was wrong—outlawed it—outlawed it. Robert Bork said the case was wrongfully decided. . . . Judge Bork has this theory: If you can't find that right within the letters of the Constitution explicitly, it's not there, it doesn't exist. I believe that the presence of that point of view on the Supreme Court . . . places at risk individual rights. It is a risk we should not afford—we don't have to. . . .

I like the idea that the Supreme Court . . . is the last bulwark of protection for our freedoms. . . . I don't want to see the argument made that there is not right to privacy on the court. I don't want that argument made. And the only way to prevent its being made is to deny Judge Bork membership on the court.[365]

Others who testified against Bork were Yale Law School Professor Burke Marshall and former Attorney General Nicholas Katzenbach, who served under President Johnson.[366]

But Edward Levi, attorney general under President Ford, praised the nominee for his "inquiring, powerful mind," noting that "one of the consequences of having an inquiring mind is that you do change position." Levi assured Committee members, "His judicial philosophy is quite central. There is an inner consistency in what he has done."[367]

In a tough and aggressive presentation which earned him the respect too many conservatives had not previously afforded him, President Reagan's first attorney general, William French Smith, said Bork had unjustly become the target of "misrepresentations, distortions and lies." He went on to praise the nominee for his judicial temperament: "Judge Bork neutrally and fairly applies the law to the facts at hand. He does not approach a case by asking which side 'deserves' to win."[368] A heated exchange took place between Smith and Senator Metzenbaum over the distortions of Judge Bork's record:

SMITH: You are propagandizing it . . . The impression you're creating is that Judge Bork wants to control the use of contraceptives in the bedroom.

METZENBAUM: Propaganda, my eye!

SMITH: That is the image you are projecting and the kind of propaganda and distortions being thrown out. That is not true and I suspect and am willing to say you know it's not true.

METZENBAUM: Everything's just a figment of our imagination. Is that it, General Smith?

SMITH: That is false and it borders on dishonesty and it borders on lying to the American public. There are some very high people in this government who are lying to the American public.[369]

Former Attorneys General William Saxbe and William Rogers also testified for the nominee, but no one quite matched the intensity and substance of Smith's eloquent and impassioned defense of Judge Bork.

Wrapping up 13 hours of testimony, Harold R. Tyler Jr., head of the

American Bar Association committee, said the four members who had voted Bork "not qualified" to sit on the Court had "acted in good faith." In a letter to the committee, Tyler explained that the dissenters had "concerns as to his judicial temperament—for example, his compassion, open-mindedness, his sensitivity to the rights of women and minority persons or groups and comparatively extreme views respecting constitutional principles or their application."[370]

Meanwhile, the first Republican Senator to announce against Bork was pro-abortion champion Robert Packwood of Oregon, who noted: "I told Howard Baker two weeks ago that I had to be convinced 'beyond a reasonable doubt' that Bork would not vote to overturn *Roe v. Wade* and other rulings based on a right to privacy. . . . I am convinced that Judge Bork feels so strongly opposed to the right of privacy that he will do everything possible to cut and trim the liberties that the right of privacy protects."[371] Packwood also said he would join a filibuster to stop the nomination, prompting President Reagan to tell reporters: "I don't think I'd better say what I think about that."[372]

Assistant Attorney General John R. Bolton, increasingly vocal in Bork's defense as the White House legislative team practiced restraint, said he was not overly concerned about Packwood's announcement, observing: "It's entirely possible we'll hold all the other Republicans."[373]

On September 22, the next day of hearings, 20 witnesses testified for nine hours. Chairman Biden, who had promised a committee decision by October 1, announced that the vote would be delayed by at least a week.

Harvard Law Professor Laurence Tribe, perhaps the most widely quoted Bork opponent, spoke for an entire morning. "Unless he has unusual respect for precedent, putting [Bork] on the court may spell chaos," Tribe said, adding, "Not one of the 105 past and present justices in the Supreme Court has ever taken a view as consistently radical as Judge Bork's on the subject of liberty, or lack of it, underlying the Constitution. Judge Bork has a uniquely narrow interpretation that runs counter to the entire 200–year tradition of the Court."[374] He also claimed:

> Judge Bork has basically said that nothing in the Constitution authorizes judges to treat a married couple's intimacies in the bedrooms any differently from a business enterprise's economic decisions in the board room. And, understandably, that notion that judges can't draw that line, has led some to be fearful. And in response, Judge Bork tells this committee that

he will listen to new arguments designed to show that some of those rights. . . . I wouldn't count on it. . . . Now, with respect to the crucial area of equality . . . the threat is clear in speeches right up through this June, Judge Bork indicated that the equal protection clause should have been kept to things like race and ethnicity. That leaves out such vital matters as sex, poverty, illegitimacy and handicap.[375]

Four law professors led by Carla Hills, Housing and Urban Development Secretary under President Ford, spoke on behalf of the nominee. "Judicial activism has harmed women in the past and will harm them in the future," said Hills. "In the first third of the 20th century, it was an activist court which tried to overturn legislation that protect women's rights in the workplace such as in the Lockner case and in the Atkins case on minimum wages and working hours."[376] Hills explained, "By allowing democratically elected bodies to make these distinctions, Judge Bork is not being less serious about women's rights, as his opponents charge; he is being more sensitive. In letting legislatures, which are directly responsive to female voters, take into account special needs of women, Judge Bork aligns himself with leading feminist legal theorists."[377] Hills, who said she had known Judge Bork since the Watergate era when she worked as an official in the Justice Department, praised Bork for his conduct during the troubled days of the Nixon Administration:

> During that period, Judge Bork displayed an uncommon capacity to listen with an open mind, a relentless fairness, in all of his actions and an enormous dedication to intellectual effort. Given my deeply held views of Judge Bork's splendid character and capacity, I was startled and saddened by the proliferation of reports from interest groups contending that his presence on the Court threatens that group's particular interest. Rather than reason with his considerable intellect, too many have used highly selective quotations from his writings and skewed tabulations of his opinions to brand him anti-labor, anti-First Amendment, anti-feminist and, in particular, anti-the-social-objective of the writer.[378]

After Hills finished speaking, Senator Hatch observed, "Women ought to pay attention to you instead of the extreme misrepresentations put out by special interest groups."[379] Hills caused a brief sensation when she speculated that Bork might not vote to reverse *Roe v. Wade*, the controversial decision giving legal protection to abortion on demand. She reversed herself later, explaining she had gone futher than she intended in speculating on her friend's possible rulings on the sensitive case.

Washington, D.C. lawyer Gary Born, a visiting professor at the University of Arizona, disputed charges that Judge Bork was a racist and a sexist: Bork "takes equal-protections guarantees for all people—blacks, whites, men, women—very seriously."[380]

University of Chicago law professor Michael McConnell said that on First Amendment protection cases Bork's rulings were "as strong if not stronger than the current Supreme Court doctrine."[381] Addressing Bork's supposed "confirmation conversion," McConnell said:

> Now there's a new twist in the controversy about Judge Bork.
>
> Some nominees in the past have been accused of being rigid ideologues, who will have some set and unacceptable view of constitutional law. Others have been accused of being shifting sands, changing their opinions all too often, and not being rooted in any firm principle at all. I think I can confidently say that Judge Bork is the first nominee ever to be accused of both of these things at the same time. I think that there's a reason for this impression as well, which is that the criticisms of Judge Bork have tended to be so extreme, so inflated as to create an impression coming into this chamber that the nominee is some kind of a monster, some kind of a threat to our civil liberties. And then, when you see Judge Bork in the flesh and you find out that he's in fact a moderate, sensible, intelligent, liberal—in the sense of honoring liberty—sort of person, there is an inclination to assume that he's the one who has changed.[382]

The Judiciary Committee members reviewed an anti-Bork letter signed by 32 law school deans and 71 constitutional law professors, and heard testimony from artist Robert Rauschenberg and author William Styron, who charged that if Bork was placed on the Court their art would no longer receive First Amendment protection. Many Bork supporters were outraged that people who were not legal specialists had been allowed to testify. Indeed, artist Rauschenberg's speech was different than that of most witnesses:

> Young, old, rich and hopeful are united by repulsion that a neauveau changeling by his tongue and his unproven change of ideology might entrap decades of innocences [sic]. The artistic freedoms and artistic freedoms. Law is not a fixed point of view. Even supremely. But a just love of people. There must be persons with less controversial and destructive qualifications to assume this highest office. Art is the nourishment of society and the energy leading to the continuation and the universality of life.[383]

Styron, author of the best-selling novel, *Sophie's Choice*, asserted: "I do not believe that Judge Bork's appointment would lead to book burnings. I do believe, though, that his pronouncements about free speech . . . leave us in much doubt about how he would treat a case where the dark areas of obscenity are raised."[384]

Late in the day, long after the departure of such analysts as Rauschenberg and Styron—and much too late to make the evening news—nine law enforcement officials spoke on behalf of the nominee.

Committee staffers, and some of the Democrat Senators themselves, encouraged the law enforcement officials, who had been kept waiting for hours, merely to submit their statements into the record and bring the day to an early end.

Don Baldwin, Executive Director of the National Law Enforcement Council, told me later there was never any question of submitting to the not-so-subtle entreaties. "Everyone of the guys said, a couple of them in rather colorful language, that they were going to put every word they intended to into the record. They did."

Baldwin stressed to his allies, who had come at their own expense from all over the country to support Bork, that "they've buried us late in the day, as we expected. But there are many Americans watching on C-SPAN and some of the heartland newspapers will give us a fair shake." In all, the nine Bork supporters took about an hour to express the views of their rank and file: Despite the fact that he had only ruled on a few criminal justice cases, Bob Bork looked like their kind of judge.

Dewey Stokes, president of the Fraternal Order of Police said, "Judge Bork's record indicates he is both tough and fair" in criminal cases.[385] Representing nearly 200,000 law enforcement officials, Stokes continued, "Judge Bork interprets the Constitution in such a way that criminal defendants receive the full measure of protection afforded by that document. He does not reach beyond the Constitution, however, and create rights that were not granted by the Framers. . . Judge Bork has been characterized in these hearings and the attendant news and commentary as a conservative and a radical. We believe, based on his record as a public servant, that he is and will remain a reasoned, principled jurist whose decisions on criminal justice are fair. Further, we find Judge Bork. . . to be in the mainstream of contemporary judicial thought."

Johnny L. Hughes, a 20 year veteran of the Maryland State Police, endorsed Bork on behalf of the 45,000 members of the National Troopers Coalition. Hughes declared Bork "has avoided legal gymnastics and interpreted applicable constitutional provisions and statutes according to their intent and purpose."

Joining Baldwin, Stokes and Hughes on the pro-Bork panel were Robert R. Fuesel of the Federal Criminal Investigators Association, L. Cary Bittick of the National Sheriff's Association, Jerry Vaughn of the International Association of Chiefs of Police, John Bellizzi of the International Narcotics Enforcement Officers Association, John Duffy, a sheriff from San Diego County, and Frank Carrington, a private attorney long associated with a variety of victims rights groups, including the Sunny von Bulow Victim Advocacy Center.

Also on day seven, Supreme Court spokeswoman Toni House told reporters that Justice Byron White had commented to television talk show personality John McLaughlin that "it would be all right with me" if Bork were placed on the Supreme Court.[386]

Day eight of testimony was fraught with tension for Chairman Biden, who left the proceedings to announce that his quest for the Democratic presidential nomination was over. The Senator said his decision to step down was simply a choice "between running for President and doing my job, which is to keep the Supreme Court from going in a direction I consider harmful." Biden said he hoped to stop "Ronald Reagan's efforts to reshape the Court" by killing the Bork nomination. He admitted that he had made mistakes by not citing sources for his borrowed rhetoric and for overstating his scholastic record, but hinted that "exaggerated" reports by the press were the reason his campaign failed.[387] Grinning bitterly at the reporters, Biden quipped: "Lest I say something that might be somewhat sarcastic, I'd better get back to the Bork hearings."[388]

Humiliated over his failed Presidential campaign, Biden was testy and impatient during the rest of the day. When he accused Committee Republicans of purposely ignoring Bork's writings, Hatch jumped in to object. Biden shouted with a bang of his gavel, "I have the floor! I am misstating nothing. You all can make your statements when it is your turn." As Biden sat red-faced, Hatch told the committee he believed that it was the Democrats who were guilty of disregarding what Bork had written. Biden calmed himself and said he disagreed.[389]

Former Chief Justice Warren E. Burger, the first man in his position to testify on a judicial nomination, told the committee he had never watched a confirmation process "with more hype and more disinformation," and asserted that "if Judge Bork is not in the mainstream then neither am I." Burger said he had thought Bork's superb qualifications would assure an easy confirmation; but, "when the opposition mounted" from the left, he "sent a message that [he] would be available" to testify on Bork's behalf."[390] The former chief justice said he did not believe Bork would seek to strike down past Supreme Court rulings. "He couldn't do it if he wanted to. There are nine people there and they listen to each other."[391]

Lloyd Cutler, former counsel to President Carter and a self-described liberal, called Bork a "conservative jurist who is closer to the center than to the extreme right," noting:

> I do agree that if all of the findings of the Warren court upholding rights of individuals and the press were overturned, that would be a disaster. I don't think that's going to happen. Those who prefer the status quo ought not to convert this preference into a rigid orthodoxy that bars the confirmation of any nominee who has at some times been critical of a prevailing majority view.[392]

Duke University law professor Walter Dellinger, University of North Carolina history professor William Leuchtenburg, and Duke University history professor John Hope Franklin charged that Bork was insensitive to the needs of women and minorities. Franklin asserted: "One searches [Bork's] record in vain to find a civil rights advance he has supported from its inception." And Leuchtenburg asked: "Has the nominee ever supported the claims of blacks or of women at the time they were litigated, or is his support always retrospective?"[393]

Defending the nominee's record on criminal justice cases, former federal prosecutor and Illinois Governor James Thompson noted: "There has been the smallest amount of attention paid to Judge Bork's views on one of the most important issues to consistently come before the court which not only involves the public but individual rights as well."[394]

Even at this late stage in the game, various groups were still making public statements on the nomination. Jackie Presser, General President of the international Brotherhood of Teamsters, announced on September 23 that his union was "unalterably opposed to the nomination of Bork." In a letter to Chairman Biden, Presser explained:

> A review of Judge Bork's record in cases involving labor relations issues makes it readily apparent that he has little respect for either the rights of labor unions or those of the American worker, whether represented by a labor union or not. In view of Judge Bork's record on such issues, his appointment to the United States Supreme Court could result in catastrophic consequences for employees and the rights which Congress has

bestowed upon them. Judge Bork's record on labor relations issues demonstrates his hostility to the American worker and stands as a sufficient reason alone to prevent his appointment to the Supreme Court.[395]

Several environmental organizations—including Friends of the Earth, the Sierra Club Legal Defense Fund and Greenpeace—announced opposition to Bork in late September. Durwood Zaelke of the SCLDF explained, "We decided to take some action. We had watched Reagan appoint 300–plus judges. And this was it. This was the final straw." Finally, even disabled groups decided to jump on the bandwagon as well, as representatives from several organizations declared against Bork. (The announcements were late, but important, in building a more "mainstream" looking opposition to the nominee.) These are "mainstream groups which cannot be characterized as liberal interest groups by anyone's definition," claimed Leonard Rubenstein of the Mental Health Law Project.[396]

Ms. magazine got into the act in its September issue with an attack on Bork:

Women stand to lose the right to abortion and also may lose on sexual harassment and affirmative action cases. . . . Gay rights are also at stake. . . . If a Reagan nominee is rejected, there is a chance that a new President could appoint a judge even more progressive than Powell and we could begin to win back some things already lost, like gay rights and Medicaid abortion.[397]

Meanwhile, the anti-Bork strategy entered what Nan Aron of the Alliance for Justice called "chapter two," explaining: "At this point, the strategy is to go as broadly as we can to reach as many senators as possible, not limit it to those on the Judiciary Committee. All these Senate offices want information: 'How's it going, where are the problems, what's the response?' So we are getting large numbers of calls from Senate offices asking for information." ACLU lobbyist Jerry Berman said the Bork offensive included educating senators on Bork's "confirmation conversion": "We have to make the case that the so-called new Judge Bork is not very different in degree from the old Judge Bork. If it's not an issue of credibility for the senators, it's an issue of predictability: knowing who is Robert Bork. Is he an intentionalist or is he a new person? We think that on the whole his judicial philosophy remains the same."[398]

"Chapter two" of the pro-Bork strategy was outlined by McGuigan: "It's very interesting to judge a man by his enemies." Direct-mail expert Richard Viguerie explained it this way: "I think for the most part the conservatives are attacking the opponents of Bork and tying the senators who are going to be opposing Bork into the opposition. So the senators who oppose Bork are going to be identified now and forevermore with Planned Parenthood, People for the American Way, the ACLU, Jesse Jackson, all these other wild people out there."[399]

A Washington *Post*/ABC News poll released on September 24 showed that 48 percent of the public said they opposed the Bork nomination, while 44 percent were in favor. The survey also found that 60 percent said the Supreme Court would not tilt to the right if Bork were confirmed. Of most significance was the finding that 80 percent of the blacks polled opposed the nomination. According to strategists, Bork's fate was in the hands of two groups, comprised of about two dozen Republicans and Southern Democrats—who in many cases felt indebted to the black vote that had put them in office. These included the nine senators that McGuigan and Casey estimated were still uncommitted: John Breaux (D-LA), Lawton Chiles (D-FL), J. James Exon (D-NE), Wendell H. Ford (D-KY), Bob Graham (D-FL), Howell Heflin (D-AL), J. Bennett Johnston (D-LA), Sam Nunn (D-GA), and Lowell P. Weicker Jr. (R-CT).[400] Breaux noted that "the people who most strongly supported me are the most strongly opposed to Bork. That has to be a factor—not a political factor but a representative factor," adding, "I better have a hell of a good reason" to vote for Bork. The pressure against Bork's nomination "was intense," observed Senator David Pryor (D-AK). "It permeated into the black churches of the south. Ministers were talking about it, choirs were singing about it."[401]

The *Post*/ABC poll's findings were too insignificant to be a major concern, said Will Ball, chief White House legislative liaison. "There ain't but one vote that counts on this one. And that's the [Senate] roll call."[402] But Dan Casey of the ACU said he was heartened by the poll's results "What I find amazing is that these figures are not worse in light of the fact that most Americans received their information about Bork from the terribly imbalanced evening newscasts. As the hearings continue and the true record gets out, those numbers will shift dramatically in Bork's favor."[403]

The media may have structured the public's negative perception of Bork, according to *Media Monitor* researchers at George Washington University, who noted that a full 72 percent of sources used by the

Washington *Post* and television reporters found Bork's judicial philosophy to be "detrimental to the court." According to the *Monitor* report, Bork was considered well-qualified for the Court by 58 percent of the sources used by the media, while 68 percent said the Senate should review the nominee's ideology before making a decision.[404]

While the liberal Democrats were successfully looking south for their votes, I looked unexpectedly to New England. Pete du Pont's campaign had called and asked if I'd be willing to visit Manchester, New Hampshire formally to endorse Pete, whom I'd supported for the presidency for some time.

As much as I wanted to do it, I told Jeff Eisenach, who'd called early in the second week of the hearings asking me to go up on the weekend of September 25–27, I just could not leave the fight for that long.

As I turned back to the desk from the chat with Jeff, it hit me as I began to revise one of the target lists after discussions with Casey: Rudman had never come through with his promise to help; Cohen was still in the undecided category; we still hoped we might get Stafford. Perhaps even Democrat George Mitchell of Maine, the former judge, was conceivable.

So I called Eisenach back.

"Jeff, I'll do it if, instead of flying to Manchester I fly to Portland, Maine. Can the campaign have someone meet me there with a car? If so, I could probably pull together a meeting with some Bork supporters there. What do you say?"

He said yes. Thus began the most frenzied 48 hours of my life.

With Curt Anderson's help we called such allies at the American Conservative Union, National Right to Work, and National Right to Life. I reserved in my name lunch for 10–15 people at the Holiday Inn Zachary's Restaurant in Portland, Maine. I gave to my allies in the key groups the name of the hostess, the details on the place and time and asked each one to select their best local activists and tell them to be there at noon on Friday, September 25. In addition, I asked for the recommendations of Don Baldwin on law enforcement officials I might see or call while moving through the region.

The whirlwind planning and execution of the trip resulted in one of the most useful "quick hits" during the confrontation. Bill Kling, news director at Coalitions for America, worked over the phone and secured promises of media contacts while I moved through the state.

I flew to Maine and met David Tille, a young volunteer with the du

Pont campaign, at the Portland airport early that Friday morning. In his car, we rushed to WPOR AM-FM, the largest country music station in the state, where I did a 45 minute interview with an aggressive news directer, Al Diamon. The interview went well and we parted on reasonably good terms, with his promise to track the course of the battle with me over the phone.

I then rushed down the street to the combined offices of the Portland Press Herald, Evening Express *and* Sunday Telegram. *Dieter Bradbury interviewed me for nearly an hour. Bill Kling had prepared press kits, which I left at both media stops. Then, David and I rushed to the Holiday Inn, where a gathering of about 20 grass roots conservative leaders from ten different organizations and from three states met us.*

We then drove to Manchester, New Hampshire, where we arrived in time for me to spend some time with Pete du Pont before the press conference. Pete graciously drew the attention of the gathered reporters to the Bork battle, with the result that my sketch of the course of the confrontation drew nearly as much attention as the endorsement itself, ostensibly the reason for the trip. The event received substantial coverage the next day in the Union Leader, *and on the local radio station. In addition, I met reporters from all over the country who planned to write on the Bork angle of my trip, including the Dallas* Morning News.

That evening I networked at a Republican fundraiser with activists from five states (Vermont, New Hampshire, Maine, Rhode Island and Massachusetts), giving out a one-pager I'd prepared on remaining swing vote Senators in the region.

The next morning David drove me to Boston, where I spent two hours with John Barnes, a friend and editorial writer at the Herald, *discussing themes for his ongoing editorials supportive of Judge Bork. I also left materials for the* Herald's *political reporter. With the paper's modest circulation into both Rhode Island and Maine, I hoped these efforts might contribute not only to Senator Kennedy's problems, but also effect the ultimate choices of both William Cohen and John Chafee.*

That quick swing through the region gave me hope that we could yet reverse the negative tide, and it certainly acquainted me with an active network of conservatives. And, after the Portland meeting, we established communication between local conservative leaders and law enforcement officials.

The trip had one down side, however. I had to miss President

Reagan's speech to Elizabeth Kepley's rowdy cohorts at the Concerned Women for America national convention.

Speaking to members of Concerned Women for America on September 25, President Reagan delivered a rousing denunciation of the liberal attack against Bork, noting: "It's clear now that charges that Robert Bork is too ideological are themselves ideologically inspired," he said. "[Bork's critics] are themselves so far outside the mainstream that they've long ago . . . lost sight of the moderate center." As the 1,500 women cheered and cheered, Reagan said, "It's wonderful to see you all here. It makes me feel as if the reinforcements have just arrived." An optimistic Reagan told the crowd that Judge Bork would "go down in history as one of the finest Supreme Court justices our nation has ever known."[405]

During day nine of the hearings, September 25, two former American Bar Association presidents—Robert Meserve of Boston and Chesterfield Smith of Lakeland, Florida—spoke against Judge Bork. "This is a political determination, but not a partisan one," said Meserve. "We have here a doctrinaire gentleman . . . I don't think we want a right-wing radical on that court."[406]

New York Bar Association President Robert Kaufman also testified against Bork, along with a group of women lawyers that included Shirley Hufstedler, Education Secretary under President Carter. "I gravely question his ability to transform himself into a man of moderate views who will respect the opinions of others with whom he does not agree," Hufstedler said. "I do not believe he will be able to abandon his continuing search for absolutes in favor of a search for tempered justice."[407]

Black economist Thomas Sowell spoke on behalf of the Judge, labeling criticism against Bork as "hysterical and dishonest." Senator Specter took offense to Sowell's belief that Bork's "confirmation conversions" were legitimate and should not be blown out of proportion. "I think Judge Bork has a perfect right to modify his position, but when you make representation on where he stands, I have a real question on how much you know about Judge Bork," the Senator said.[408]

After several days of testimony alternately depicting Judge Bork as a close-minded racist and a sensitive, highly-qualified jurist, the public began to ask, "Who is the real Robert H. Bork?" A column by Joseph Goldstein published in the New York *Times* on September 27 attempted to answer that question:

Who is the real Robert H. Bork? This is the question "all of us are asking," Senator Edward M. Kennedy said after listening to 27 hours of Judge Bork's testimony. I believe I know the answer. I know Judge Bork well. I have been a member of the Yale Law School faculty for more than 31 years, and was a colleague of his during his entire tenure at Yale. . . . I have been a registered Democrat for all of my voting life and, for many years, I have supported the work of the American Civil Liberties Union, the NAACP, and the Planned Parenthood Association. I take Senator Kennedy's question to mean that he and other Senators who publicly committed themselves in advance of the hearing are prepared to change their minds if they learn they have wrongly assessed the nominee. In essence, the Senator is asking these questions: "Is the real Robert Bork the person I have described as racist, sexist and an opponent of individual liberty and equal justice, who will disregard Supreme Court precedent, roll back the clock and uproot decades of settled law in order to write his own ideology into law?" Or, "Is the real Robert Bork the person whose testimony before the committee and whose record as Solicitor General and as court of appeals judge demonstrates that he is sensitive to the rights of minorities and women, understands that every person is entitled to the equal protection of the law, recognizes the importance of precedent, even if developed in a manner contrary to his judicial philosophy, and strongly believes there is no place for a personal political or social agenda in the way Justices must carry out their work?" The real Robert Bork is the latter.[409]

Some claimed the hearings failed to accomplish their real purpose—a search for the truth about Judge Bork. "As a senator, you really can't get a clear sense of what your vote means in this process, so you end up guessing about where Bork will come out or stereotyping him—which everyone, including Metzenbaum and Kennedy, knows is not entirely fair," said Ohio State University law professor David Goldberger. Added Larry Sabato, a University of Virginia political scientist who had opposed the nomination: "These hearings are not really about any search for truth. They are about senators posturing and searching to defend previous prejudices. The specter of having Judge Bork having his judicial integrity questioned by the likes of cheaters Joe Biden and Teddy Kennedy—and Metzenbaum with his allegations of improprieties over the years—would be funny if it weren't sad. Maybe Bork shouldn't be confirmed. But our politics suffers when good people are mishandled like this. In a way, he comes out seeming like a victim of the political process."[410]

Meanwhile, Senator DeConcini all but cemented his position on the nomination. Ironically, in light of the intense pressure he was getting behind the scenes from organized labor, the Arizonan did this by expressing disapproval of what he called a "sleazy" and "overzealous" White House attempt to win his vote. The Senator was referring to a list of 100 pro-Bork academics that had included Paul Marcus, the University of Arizona Law School's dean. Marcus asked that DeConcini have his name taken off the pro-Bork list. White House lobbyist Korologos explained that when Bork called Marcus, the Dean had expressed his support, leading the White House to assume that his name could be included on the list. Marcus said the confusion was a "reasonable misunderstanding," but DeConcini used it to bash the Reagan Administration's efforts for Bork. "It is almost embarrassing that the White House thinks that kind of petty approach will be successful," he said.[411]

The switchboard at DeConcini's Capitol Hill office was deluged with calls on the nomination—one day late in September the office handled 1,520 phone calls, most of them in support of the nominee.[412] A group called Arizona's Citizens for America took out a full-page ad in the Arizona *Republic*, which was headlined: "We told Senator DeConcini what we think about JUDGE BORK!" The body of the text read: "On behalf of millions of Americans who care about our Constitutional form of government and its guarantees of freedom of speech and freedom of religion, a representative group of Arizona citizens met with Senator DeConcini at Sky Harbor Airport, Sunday, September 20. The Senator promised to give serious consideration to this letter, which now carries the signatures of hundreds of Arizonans who support President Reagan's nominee to the Supreme Court."[413]

Elizabeth Kepley had secured a meeting with DeConcini for herself and three members of Concerned Women for America from Arizona. She asked me to join them and add my perspective. I went early and sat by myself in one of the hallways of the Hart Building, praying that we might still turn DeConcini around. I was increasingly pessimistic, however, not only because of DeConcini's public comments and antagonism toward the nominee, but also because an Arizonan "in a position to know" had told me that organized labor in the state had explicitly threatened DeConcini with a primary opponent in 1988 if he supported Bork. Even though the state is substantially conservative and the Republicans were increasingly disarrayed, the prospect of first a primary challenge from the Left and then a general election challenge from the Republicans on the right would carry serious weight with DeConcini.

We met down the hall from his office in the Hart Office Building. Briefly, we rehearsed talking points. I would cover constitutional issues (DeConcini was alternating between the Ninth and Fourteenth Amendments as his bases for worry about Bork) whereas Kathy Herrod would emphasize the support her 9,000+ members felt for the jurist, and Elizabeth would underscore CWA's national membership of 500,000.

While we waited in the Senator's anteroom, the phones rang non-stop.

"Senator DeConcini's office, please hold. Senator DeConcini's office, please hold. Senator DeConcini's office, please hold," the harried receptionist said to caller after caller. Once every line was on hold, she would ask each caller in turn: "Are you for or against the Bork nomination?" After receiving a response (one of his aides told us the calls were running overwhelmingly in favor of Bork) which she tallied, the receptionist moved on to the next line and covered what incoming calls she could.

We were ushered into the Democrat's office. He greeted the ladies warmly. Without smiling, he greeted me with a harried look in his eyes. Introducing each of us, his staff started to sketch my background and DeConcini waved them off: "I know Pat."

The half hour went quickly, with these key points made.

Kathy Herrod: We resent Senator Metzenbaum's assertion that Judge Bork frightens American women. He does not frighten us. We are working women. We are mothers. We are professionals, and lawyers and homemakers. We resent the insinuation that Howard Metzenbaum or the National Organization for Women speak for us. We support Judge Bork and we want you to support him.

DeConcini: How can I be confident he will uphold equal protection for women? I'm not sure we can count on him to grant my own daughter the protection she deserves.

McGuigan: How many times does he have to say that the only legal distinctions permissible are those based on reasonableness—in rest-rooms, in the draft and so forth? He's explained the levels of scrutiny until he is blue in the face.

Then DeConcini seized on the Ninth Amendment as a source of the right of privacy, and Elizabeth's allies politely scored their Senator for suddenly advocating a legal doctrine he had criticized throughout most of his career (DeConcini had a generally pro-life voting record before the Bork confrontation).

Kepley: "Senator, Beverly LaHaye, whom you know, has spoken

out on behalf of Judge Bork repeatedly. Our 500,000 members feel
very strongly about this and we want you to support him."

DeConcini: "I'd like to, and I generally support the President's
nominees, as Pat knows. But how can I be sure he will uphold the
law?"

It went like that. DeConcini did agree to work on Senator Biden to
find a slot for LaHaye to testify. (Biden's staff had avoided a response
on the matter for weeks and the Arizonan said he thought she should
get her say on the nomination.)

On the way out, I argued the historic meaning of the Fourteenth
Amendment and equal protection with two of DeConcini's staffers,
still deluding myself that the criticisms of Bork had something to do
with the merits of his views.

In the hallway outside, the four Bork supporters gathered in a circle.

"Ladies, that man is going to vote against Robert Bork, unless you
can make him change his mind with more sheer numbers. We're
already beating the other side in direct communications from our
people. I'm not hopeful but we cannot give up," I summed up the
picture.

As her friends turned to go, Elizabeth grabbed my hand: "You're
doing a good job. We'll keep it up. We can win," she said. I responded
simply, "I just don't know. I just don't know."

Senator Specter was also the target of heavy lobbying in his home
state. Some 60 members of the University of Pennsylvania College
Republicans, carrying signs with slogans such as "Don't Be a Dork;
Confirm Bork," waited for the Senator to arrive at a September 25
meeting of the Republican State Committee. When the organization's
president, Guy Ciarrocchi, handed Specter a button supporting the
nominee, he reminded the Senator it was from "those people who
elected President Reagan and yourself."[414]

Senator Humphrey, who attended the Republican State Committee
meeting with Specter, addressed the crowd: "Let's hear from all of
those who believe we should vote to confirm Bork." As the crowd
cheered its agreement with Humphrey, Specter replied, "I'm hearing
you."[415]

By late September, some 50,000 letters and nearly 50,000 phone
calls had been handled by Specter's office showing a 2 to 1 preference
for Bork. "I can't go anyplace without people coming up and saying
have Arlen vote for or against," complained the Senator's wife, Joan.
One of the letters Specter received was from conservative Pennsylva-

nia Congressman Robert S. Walker concerning a promise Specter had made to some 50 religious leaders while running for reelection in 1986. "I think he made a firm promise to the religious conservatives that he would not oppose any of Reagan's nominations on the basis of philosophy," Walker said. "I was in the meeting when he made that pledge."[416]

One of the more poignant, if underpublicized, letters sent to Judiciary Committee members came from by Doris Tate, a board member of Parents of Murdered Children. She wrote:

> In 1969, my daughter, Sharon Tate, was murdered by the infamous Manson Family serial killers . . . I have had to continually fight to assure that my daughter's murderers are not released into society again . . . I ask the Senate Judiciary Committee members . . . to support me and millions of other citizens who have been hit by violent crime in the United States by confirming Judge Robert Bork to the U.S. Supreme Court.[417]

Meanwhile, the White House was beginning to think their nominee might not make it to the Supreme Court. Republican Presidential hopeful Pat Robertson said Administration officials had asked one of his aides to rally evangelical forces for Judge Bork. "I haven't heard personally from the White House, but an aide of mine got word from the White House that they were planning to mobilize more support and that I was one of those they'd like to call on," he said. "Now that the nomination is in trouble, the White House is talking about bringing all these coalition groups together. Regretfully, it may be too late." Robertson articulated the frustrations of many conservatives when he told the press:

> [The] first mistake the White House made goes back to the appointment of Judge Antonin Scalia. Some White House aides suggested the President should have picked Bork first because he would be the most controversial and hold Scalia until the second round because he would be easiest to get confirmation on. [Another] mistake was that Howard Baker felt he had the confirmation proceedings sewed up, and he deliberately did not call on either the conservatives or the evangelical Christians to assist him in the process.

But Robertson lost the concurrence of many conservatives when he claimed that because Bork had "gone before the television cameras and said he is [in the judicial] mainstream and wouldn't do anything different from anybody else . . . some people are wondering why they should go to the mat for him."[418]

Judge Bork met with Administration strategists on September 26 to tell them he believed the White House was not doing enough to advance his nomination. Bork was assured that the President would begin meeting personally with undecided senators, as well as lobbying audiences to support the nomination wherever he spoke. A top aide noted, "When he left, he had a better feeling that things were being handled, probably better than he thought."[419]

As day ten of the hearings opened on September 28, Griffin B. Bell, a former attorney general in the Carter Administration testified that Judge Bork was "principled and rational . . . not a radical," adding, "I don't think he'd wear anyone's collar. He's searching and growing all the time." Bell also said he hoped that the Senators who were not on the Judiciary Committee would not be swayed by polls showing an increasing public disapproval of Bork. "The Senate ought to rise above all this," said Bell. "It's one of the worst things going on in this country. People don't know as much [about Judge Bork] as the committee."[421]

Former Pennsylvania Governor Richard Thornburgh praised Bork, with whom he had worked in the 1970s, as "committed to ensuring high standards in government" and "an extremely able and intelligent lawyer." The future Attorney General described the nominee as "a man of personal integrity and a man of commitment to the rule of law" and "a staunch believer in our Constitutional system . . ."

In the wake of Bell's comments and a Louis Harris Survey of September 17–23 which claimed that 57 percent of the public opposed the nomination while only 29 percent supported it, Chairman Biden insisted the committee would only "vote on the strength of the testimony." Senator DeConcini chimed in, "I am not going to make my judgment on this issue based on the polls."[422]

Jewel LaFontant, Judge Bork's first black female deputy solicitor general, disputed the critics who had accused him of racism and sexism: "I sincerely believe he is devoid of racial prejudice or I wouldn't be here. As a woman, as a black woman, I have no fear of trusting my rights and privileges to Robert Bork."[423] Under questioning by Senator Humphrey, LaFontant relayed how she had been pressured not to appear on the nominee's behalf:

HUMPHREY: I've heard, only hearsay, that you were under some pressure not to appear and testify on behalf of Robert Bork, is that correct?

LAFONTANT: I don't know that I like the word "pressure." Let's say on the Hill we call it lobbying, don't we.

HUMPHREY: You were lobbied—.

LAFONTANT: Yes.

HUMPHREY: By some mainline minority groups, is that it? Or do you care to say? Individuals or groups?

LAFONTANT: Primarily individuals representing various groups, yes.[424]

Speaking against Judge Bork was University of Chicago Law Professor Philip Kurland, who argued that placing the nominee on the Court would "help effect the constitutional revolution that has been part of the Reagan platform since he entered office. The claim that Bork is a middle-of-the-road jurist . . . was an afterthought and without much, if any, basis in fact."[425]

Former Senator Thomas F. Eagleton (D-MO) charged Bork with supporting an "overwhelmingly powerful executive—the second coming of George III," adding, "When it's a dispute between the president and the Congress, as far as Judge Bork is concerned, the president is always right and Congress should always be deprived of its power to challenge him in court—even on matters of deep institutional conflict. Judge Bork believes not only in an all-powerful president, but in an omnipotent president."[426] University of Chicago law professor Cass Sunstein added: "Judge Bork's positions . . . should be a source of concern to conservatives, liberals and moderates interested in the constitutional system of checks and balances."[427]

The Reverend Kenneth Dean of Rochester, New York reinforced the impression of Bork as bigot by relaying to the committee a conversation he claimed he had with the Judge during a meeting in 1985. Dean said he had told Bork about a Jewish teen whose parents asked school officials to allow their child to be excused from reading required religious materials. According to Dean's account, Bork remarked at the time: "Well, I suppose he got over it, didn't he?" The Judge assured the panel members during his testimony that he had never said such a thing.[428] No other witnesses offered any stories similar to Dean's.

At the end of the day's testimony, Senate Majority Leader Robert Byrd (D-WV) said he would pressure fellow committee members not to give the nomination a positive or negative recommendation.

Meanwhile, White House spokesman Marlin Fitzwater remained hopeful that Judge Bork would be confirmed, but noted: "It's clear the liberal Democratic leadership on the committee has taken a number of actions designed to foster a special-interest led public referendum on this issue. The Judiciary Committee had done some real damage to itself in diminishing its own power and its own authority . . . in trying to make this into a public referendum." Fitzwater, who said he believed the Senate was split evenly on the nomination, admitted, "We've been getting a lot of criticism lately for not doing enough in getting involved in the public arena in the debate."[429] Another White House official said, "We're beginning to realize that we've got a terrible fight on our hands. Initially we laid back too much."[430]

Conservative strategists said that despite the President's declaration that Bork's confirmation was his "number one domestic priority," the White House was moving too little, too late. "They came to the realization too late that this was going to be trench warfare," said Dan Casey of the American Conservative Union. "They failed to shift gears in time and recognize the need to get the president more frequently out front." Finally saying publicly what he had said privately for some time, McGuigan concluded: "The White House was figuring out that this was a real fight in September. We figured out it was a real fight in July."[431]

On the eleventh day of testimony, September 29, former Watergate prosecutors Henry S. Ruth Jr. and George T. Frampton Jr. claimed before the Judiciary Committee that Judge Bork had lied when he testified that following the Saturday Night Massacre he had worked quickly to ensure that the special prosecutor's investigation would be independent. "I don't want to see history rewritten just to confirm a Supreme Court justice," Ruth said, adding that after the firing of Watergate Special Prosecutor Archibald Cox, "We were totally tenuous in operating. We did not know what was going to happen. . . . It was only after a week and a half that we thought we were going to be back in business." Frampton added, "More troubling than the reworking of the facts is the attitude of Judge Bork toward unrestricted executive power."[432]

However, former Attorney General Elliott Richardson, who had quit his job to avoid firing Cox, praised Judge Bork's conduct during the 1973 incident. "The nation owes a substantial debt to Robert Bork for his service in that situation. . . . From the outset, Bob Bork was first of all determined to make certain the Watergate special prosecution force was kept intact," he said, adding that the problems in the Justice Department "turned out all right . . . in significant part because of the role played by Robert H. Bork." The committee also reviewed affidavits from Cox's counsel, Philip A. Lacovara and then-DOJ official Henry E. Petersen, who said the nominee's recollection of the incident was correct.[433]

Senator Simpson chastised the anti-Bork witnesses for using a long-ago incident to crush Bork's confirmation: "To thrash around in that like we've been doing about something that happened 14 years ago is the most bizarre exercise."[434]

Senator Biden announced that the Judiciary Committee would not vote on the nomination until October 7, while Senator Byrd said the full Senate would not begin its debate over Bork before November 1. At a time when events before the committee were feeding modest hopes for a tie or better, McGuigan said he hoped that Byrd—who remained publicly undecided—would vote to confirm Bork, but believed the Senator's actions were an effort to buy time for his fellow Democratic Senators who opposed the nomination. "It's very clear that if a committee vote were to be held today" on the merits of the nomination itself, "we'd at least have a tie, or we'd win 8 to 6," McGuigan declared optimistically. "Byrd is giving the Democrats more time to create the illusion that the fight for Bork is a losing one. But it's very close and it can be won, especially since President Reagan is beginning to get personally engaged."[435]

Observing, "I think he's licked," Senator Alan Cranston (D-CA) said he counted 49 senators who would vote down the nomination, 40 who would support it, and 11 undecided. "It might prove easier to get 51 votes against in an up-or-down vote than 41 votes to sustain a filibuster," he said.[436] McGuigan, who along with several GOP Senators charged that Cranston had inflated the numbers to meet his own ends, said he counted 39 senators as solid votes for, 27 as definitely opposed, while 34 remained undecided.[437] White House Chief of Staff Howard Baker said he counted "40 plus" votes for Judge Bork, "30 plus" against, and 25 to 30 "genuinely undecided" senators. Cranston is "the worst vote counter in the United States Senate," Baker charged. Cranston shot back, "Howard has lost touch with the Senate . . . I have a reputation for being able to vote-count pretty accurately."[438]

It was during these final days before the Committee vote that Casey remarked to me one day, "Cranston's got the spin going, and his going in front of the cameras with the tote sheet is brilliant theatre. It's slipping away."

Some in the White House must have felt it slipping, just as we did.

On September 29, a memo to Judge Bork came from White House aide John Tuck, listing the things they believed Howard Baker and the White House staff had done for the nominee in the past several months. But one person who saw the memorandum and who was familiar with the record described it to me as full of errors and distortions overstating the White House role at key points in the battle.

Casey and his people refused to give up. As dollars became available, he deployed them into the heartland. One ad ran on a few West Virginia stations, arguing:

> *. . . Judge Bork's opponents, liberal special interest groups like the ACLU, seem to think the Constitution is just a piece of paper for them to bend to suit their political agenda. Why, the ACLU even claims that published child pornography is protected by the Constitution. Judge Bork doesn't believe that and neither do you. . . It's our Constitution too, Senator Byrd, and we'd rather have it guarded by Judge Bork than gutted by the ACLU.*

The final effort to reverse our fading hopes for DeConcini's vote included Dan's radio spot calling on the Arizonan to "Stand Tall . . . the people of Arizona know you are a man of principle. They know you wouldn't knuckle under to the ACLU . . . [T]hese are the same leftists who are threatening you, Senator DeConcini. Stand Tall. Vote for Judge Bork."

OK. We can be forgiven. We were still trying to get his vote.

Senators Bill Bradley (D-NJ) and Paul Simon (D-IL) surprised few people with their announcements they would vote down the nomination. Bradley said, "I doubt that [Bork] has the commitment to civil rights and individual liberties on which the decency and well-being of our American community depends."[439]

As the twelfth and final day of hearings began on September 30, Roy Innis of the Congress of Racial Equality told the panel:

> Judge Bork's presence in the Supreme Court can . . . mitigate one of the most pressing problems facing black America today—urban crime. Judge Bork's firm approach to criminal law is a matter that should be of interest to the civil rights community, for crime preys most savagely on the poor . . . of our major urban centers . . . who bear the brunt of the enormous costs of rampant crime in our society.

Innis added that Bork's critics were making too much of his supposed "confirmation conversion" over civil rights legislation. "Many who oppose the Civil Rights Act of 1964 for considerably less noble reasons than the libertarian rigor that Judge Bork was pursuing have later become great allies of civil rights—of the civil rights movement," he said. "People change."[440]

Concerned Women for America President Beverly LaHaye disputed the charges of feminist leaders by testifying that Bork would indeed rule to protect the rights of women. "He does not view women as a special interest group to whom he must cater," she said. "He views women and men as equal citizens under the law."[441]

Several of the witnesses speaking against Judge Bork were concerned with his positions on anti-trust. "If we ended up with five gigantic corporations, he would say 'so what,' " said Georgetown Law Center Dean Robert Pitofsky.[442]

Biden told the panel members he had received letters signed by 1,925 anti-Bork law professors, which comprised about 40 percent of the teachers in American Bar Association accredited law schools.[443]

Another letter read by the committee was written by former President Jimmy Carter who said he opposed the nominee for his "particularly obnoxious" views on civil rights. "Only recently," the letter said, "with the vision of a seat on the Supreme Court providing some new enlightenment, has Judge Bork attempted to renounce some of his more radical writings and rulings."[444]

When it was over, 62 witness had appeared in favor, 48 in opposition. (Conservatives worried among themselves, however, that the position and timing of the witnesses had created an impression the nominee was widely opposed. As McGuigan and Casey had feared, Biden had the best of all worlds: raw data to support assertions of fairness, combined with a clear media-conveyed, deadline-distorted atmosphere of opposition.)

On the Senate floor, Majority Whip Alan Cranston (D-CA) and Patrick Leahy (D-VT) announced they would vote against the nomination, while Senator Richard Lugar (R-IN) said he would support it.[445]

While the final days of the hearings were in session, Judge Bork was busy meeting with uncommitted Senators David Durenberger (R-MN) and Arlen Specter (R-PA), and President Reagan was speaking to a group of Bork supporters at a White House briefing. Encouraging them "not to give into noisy, strident pressures" from the leftist "campaign of disinformation and distortion," the President assured the group, "I do not believe the United States Senate will succumb to allowing the special interests to choose court members."[446] The Senate must choose "between liberal judges whose decisions protect criminals or firm judges whose decisions protect the victims," Reagan continued. "A president, whether Republican or Democrat, liberal or conservative, seeks out the best-qualified person who generally shares the president's judicial philosophy. The Senate then decides whether the nominee meets the qualifications to serve . . . Now is not the time to change the standard, to break that tradition."[447]

As the White House briefing concluded, Reagan responded first with surprise and then with personal warmth to Rev. George Lucas, a black cleric present at the briefing, who told the President—standing only a few feet away in the auditorium of the Old Executive Office Building— of his strong support for the embattled nominee. Lucas' closing exchange with Reagan electrified the room full of Bork supporters, including movement conservatives and religious activists.

An hour or two after the White House briefing, Don Baldwin of the National Law Enforcement Council, Kepley, Casey and I gathered at Don's suggestion in the Senate Capitol dining room, for a late lunch and what turned out to be one of the few relaxing moments we shared during those months. '

We rehearsed roles for the upcoming meeting with Minority Leader Robert Dole and some of his staff. Worn out from weeks of energy-sapping long days but exhilirated and hopeful after the upbeat briefing at the White House that morning, for a time the four of us turned away from the battle and talked of family, parents, friendship and things other than the confrontation at hand. Don Nickles of Oklahoma, whom I had supported in his first run for the Senate in 1980, stopped by to say hello, and took time to chat with all of us.

After Nickles walked away I made Casey chuckle because my wandering thoughts turned, as they often did, to my home state. Casey had a committment back at the ACU office, and he had to leave us. However, Dave O'Steen and Doug Johnson of National Right to Life Committee joined us in time for the meeting.

The meeting with Dole was curious, if cordial. Friendly at the outset and conclusion, with a group photograph Dole subsequently inscribed to each of us, the body of the meeting consisted of a description of all the grass roots mail and phone calls our people were pouring in already, and planning to unleash in the days before the floor vote. Then we followed with impassioned requests, as we'd planned at lunch, for his specific action.

Senator Dole remained vaguely noncommittal through much of the meeting, raising an eyebrow or arching his head now and then after an idea had been expressed. On three occasions, I recall, he nodded his head at the aide joining us in the meeting, directing follow up on one point or another without words. One of those nods came after I made an impassioned plea to trigger action from Senator Rudman.

"Senator, Casey and I met with your colleague more than a month ago and he committed to speak or write publicly in support of Bork, yet nothing has been heard from him since. He even claimed he was 'more conservative than Bork' on some of the legal questions. Couldn't you get him to speak out for Bork soon, to help stem the tide of announcements against him?"

Head nods. Aide writes.

Rudman spoke. But not right away.

Later, Dole did become more engaged in the final joust on the floor, after meetings with Bork and his wife. Perhaps some personal sympathy for the jurist's plight brought the final surge of action.

Long after the confrontation was over, a long time friend of Dole's who is also a movement conservative told me of a conversation in which he pushed Dole during those days in September. After making clear his lack of enthusiasm for the effort that would be required to win, Dole informed my discouraged ally, "Look, he's your nominee. You'll have to confirm him."

Also on September 30 it was revealed that officials in the Democratic presidential campaign of Massachusetts Governor Michael Dukakis had given New York *Times* reporter Maureen Dowd the "attack video" that destroyed Biden's campaign. Dukakis, who called Biden to apologize, said in a statement: "Although I had no knowledge of this . . . I accept full responsibility." Campaign manager John Sasso and issues director Paul Tully quit over the incident.

Bork supporters in the Southern Baptist Convention, meanwhile, recognized that the quick action of the Baptist Joint Committee's lobbyist James Dunn had undermined the effectiveness of the pro-Bork resolution among the southern Senators. In an October 1 letter, Les Csorba asked Dunn why he had failed to mention, in his own letter to Senators three weeks earlier, "that the five dissenting . . . votes [on the pro-Bork resolution] were not against Judge Bork's nomimination, but were against the [Public Affairs Committee of the Southern Baptists] taking a stand on the issue." Csorba hit Dunn hard: "Why did you fail to mention that there hasn't been any Southern Baptist leader who has publicly opposed Judge Bork? . . . Is it because you serve as trustee member for Americans United for Separation of Church and State which has taken a stand opposing the nomination?"

As noted by writer James Carl Hefley, "Several [Baptists who supported Bork] noted that the leadership of the Progressive Baptist Convention, which gave less than 1/100th of what the [Southern Baptists] allocated to [Dunn's Baptist Joint Committee], was on record as opposing Bork. Yet Dunn had *not* written a letter to the senators qualifying their stand."[448] Dunn's earlier letter had undercut among the Senators and among analysts throughout the south the impression of Baptist support conveyed in the original pro-Bork resolution Csorba had written.

October 1 brought a big blow to pro-Bork forces when three undecided Southern Democrats—Senators Terry Sanford (NC), David Pryor (AK) and Bennett Johnston (LA)—told their fellow Senators they would not support the nomination because of the judge's narrow view toward privacy rights, women and minorities. Sanford said the nominee "does not stick with his views. He reversed himself on civil rights. He reversed himself on the protection afforded by the First Amendment. He reversed himself on the protection of women against discriminatory legislation."[449]

Despite a private meeting with Bork on September 30 and a phone call on behalf of the nominee from Lloyd Cutler later that evening, swing-vote Republican Arlen Specter called Judge Bork at 11:45 a.m. to tell him he would vote against the nomination. "I'm disappointed to know that," Bork said. "I thought I addressed your concerns." The Senator then said: "You did address my concerns, but you didn't resolve the doubts that I had."[450] Later, in a speech on the Senate floor, Specter said: "I will be opposing my president, my party and a man of powerful intellect." A triumphant Joe Biden said, "Clearly, the momentum is with us." But Senator Thurmond said he believed "this nomination is winnable," because "the president has indicated he's in the fight to the end." President Reagan, who summoned Senator Heflin to the White House for a chat, refused to give up: "I'm working my head off to make sure that we don't lose it." And Attorney General Edwin Meese insisted, "We are looking as good as we did 48 hours ago."[451]

The President also met with Judge Bork and top aides to plan strategy. Columnists Rowland Evans and Robert Novak explained how the White House chose to deal with a nomination that looked bleaker by the day:

When the Reagan Administration's high command met [October 1] in an atmosphere heavy with doom. . . . Attorney General Edwin Meese urged that the nomination not be pulled. Chief of Staff Howard Baker responded that it would not, save under two circumstances. First, if Bork himself requested withdrawal; second, if there is "substantial" hemorrhaging among Republican senators, removing political benefit from a roll-call vote.[452]

Meanwhile, the Atlanta *Journal* and *Constitution* published results from a survey taken September 18–28 which showed that 51 percent of Southerners did not support the nominee, while 31 percent did. Southern Democrats were all given copies of the survey.[453]

McGuigan then took a step only publicized among conservative media and on Christian radio outlets such as Contact America, Bott Broadcasting, and USA Radio. He asked allies to make October 4 a day of prayer for Judge Bork. "We will continue to work without ceasing, but it is time to, as the Bible says, 'pray without ceasing,' " he said. McGuigan called on these Christian broadcasters and pro-Bork political associates to begin a vigil for the nominee to "pray for Judge Bork himself—a good and decent man who in a decent town would not have to endure such attacks—and his family, that God give them peace and the strength not to become embittered. Please also pray for our country, that never again will Americans allow the established government in Washington to so effectively distort the career and the record of a just and righteous man."[454]

On October 2, Southern Democrat Lloyd Bentsen (TX) joined the opposing forces, prompting Charles Green of the Miami *Herald* to observe: "Democrats are responding to the most potent demonstration to date of black political clout in the South." Senator Howard Metzenbaum (D-OH) noted that "blacks have had a potential force for years. The Bork nomination has transformed that into an effective force." Polls taken after the 1986 election cycle had indicated that without the black vote freshman Democratic Southerners Richard Shelby (AL), Wyche Fowler Jr. (GA), Terry Sanford (NC) and John Breaux (LA), would not have been elected. Strategists noted that the mass defection of Southern Democrats was due in part to pressure from this constituency.[455]

My colleague Jeffery Troutt, director of the Free Congress Foundation's Judicial Reform Project, was frustrated at times during the confrontation because of our strict policy of only engaging in educational activities as a Foundation. As a lawyer, however, he certainly understood our conservative position in interpretation of IRS guide-

lines on 501 c 3 involvement in lobbying activities. Jeffery was not regularly an employee of Coalitions for America, Paul Weyrich's lobbying organization, and therefore engaged in direct lobbying only on his own time.

However, during the months of the Bork confrontation he handled a staggering load of press inquiries and engaged in debates with Bork's opponents. From July through October 2, when he sent me a memo summarizing his activities, he had averaged several radio talk shows a week, including nationally broadcast appearances on Pacifica Radio, Contact America, CBS Radio and Christian Science Monitor Radio.

And, his own visibility with the print media had gone through the roof, with frequent appearances defending Bork in the Wall Street Journal, *Boston* Globe, *Washington* Times, *Portland* Oregonian *and* USA Today.

Among his varied debate opponents were Jenny Piser of NARAL, Martha Jimenez of the Mexican-American Legal Defense and Education Fund, Chris Brown of the Maryland ACLU, Jan Levine of PAW and Paul Levy of Public Citizen.

Also on October 2, David Boren of Oklahoma became one of Robert Bork's announced supporters when he put a simple statement in the record. On October 6, Paul Weyrich wrote Boren, with whom he'd clashed all that year over Boren-supported proposals to heighten Federal Election Commission regulation of campaign financing. Weyrich wrote:

> *... I want you to know we will never forget what you did last Friday. As a veteran of politics, I know that you knew then as well as I did what lay ahead. Despite this, you made the decision to stand by a decent and principled man in his hour of need. I don't mind the rough and tumble of politics, in fact I thrive on it. But what has been done to the reputation and record of Judge Robert Bork in the last few months is criminal ... Judges are indeed part of a political system, but traditionally they have played an important and uniquely elevating role in our politics. That unique role was imperfectly filled at times in our history, but at least the ideal of fair and principled jurisprudence remained the goal. During your lifetime and mine, judges have increasingly become the engine of anti-democratic social reform. In Robert Bork, the country has a chance to restore the rule of law and the important, appropriate role of judges in upholding both individual rights and separation of powers.*

Weyrich wrote again to Bill Proxmire, his fellow Wisconsin native, with whom he'd exchanged several calls and letters as the battle dragged on. The end of the battle was coming now, and our hopes of July were fading as the fall advanced. But Paul made a last try at "Prox", his home state Senator:

> I am horrified by what has happened to this good man. A principled jurist of the first rank has been subjected to the most vicious and distorted assault I've ever seen. There may be room for disagreement about some of his decisions, but there is no room for disagreement about the thrust of his life as a scholar and judge: he rules for the law, understanding its nuances and reflecting them in his decisions. Bill, I hope you will stand on principle—the principle of balance and fairness—and vote for Judge Bork. Stand with him as the curtain falls.

October 2, in addition, brought a Wall Street Journal *report on an effort by White House Deputy Chief of Staff Ken Duberstein to assemble a group of private lobbyists to augment the sinking official effort. "Eight weeks too late," lamented one of the participants. In a curious development, some in the Administration apparently planted stories that Heflin might be considered as the next nominee—in the hopes that might make it harder for the portly southerner to vote no.*

We still hoped to gain the backing of the formally undecided Senators. A memo to me from Dan Casey marked "as of noon, 10/2/87" listed 10 Senators "assumed leaning pro-Bork". With the 39 votes we felt sure of, we believed these 10 would put us in range: Boren, Cohen, Dixon, Evans, Hatfield, Reid, Shelby, Stafford, Stennis and Heflin. The "unknowns" at that point were Byrd, Chiles, Exon, Graham, Nunn and Weicker. Finally, Dan considered 12 senators "assumed leaning anti-Bork—or might be good on cloture." I had sketched them simply "fading fast": Baucus, Bingaman, Chafee, DeConcini, Ford, Gore, Melcher, Mitchell, Pell, Proxmire, Sasser and Breaux.

In his weekly radio address on October 3, President Reagan spoke forcefully for his nominee and against anti-Bork liberals whom he said were engaging in "a constant litany of character assassination and intentional misrepresentation." Reagan continued:

> Now, liberal special-interest groups seek to politicize the court system, to exercise a chilling effect on judges to intimidate them into making decisions not on the basis of the law or the merits of the case, but on the basis of a litmus test or response to political pressure. . . . There was always one area [liberals] controlled so long they never thought they

would have to give it up. They thought it was a sort of private preserve, and that was appointments to the federal courts.[456]

With Senator Thomas A. Daschle's (D-SD) announcement on the Senate floor that he would not support Judge Bork, the gap narrowed between the 32 Senators who said publicly they would endorse it and the 28 who had publicly pledged opposition. According to the count from the White House, 40 supported, 42 opposed, and 18 remained undecided.[457]

Appearing October 4 on NBC's "Meet the Press," Senator Hatch said President Reagan still believed the nomination had a chance and would urge a full floor vote no matter what the outcome from the Senate Judiciary Committee. "The President has authorized me to say on this program . . . that he's going to press through to conclusion," Hatch said. Senator Heflin said on the same program: "It's what you might call a plank-walker. You walk to the end of the plank to take off your blindfold, and you see a bunch of barracudas on one side and swarming sharks on the other. . . . You go on to decide that your vote should be what's best for the United States of America and what's best for the Supreme Court."[458]

Chapter Seven

Liberal Victory

Many strategists on both sides declared the nomination legally dead when Judiciary Committee swing-vote Senators Dennis DeConcini (D-AZ) and Robert Byrd (D-WV), announced on October 5 that they would vote against it, bringing the number of Judiciary Committee members opposed to eight. Senators John H. Chafee (R-RI) and Lowell P. Weicker Jr. (R-CT) also declared their opposition. Claiming that it was "one of the toughest decisions" he had ever been forced to make, DeConcini told White House Chief of Staff Baker that President Reagan should withdraw the nomination immediately. "In my judgment, no other potential Supreme Court nominee in history has been as strident in his criticism of the way the Constitution has been used to protect individual liberties," DeConcini said. "That is the difference between the previous Reagan nominees and Judge Bork." But Reagan insisted, "I'm going to continue with his nomination. I'm fighting a . . . war [for] Bork." When ABC News correspondent Sam Donaldson shouted to Reagan that it "looks like the Bork nomination will fail in committee," the President retorted, "Over my dead body."[459]

Nancy Kassebaum (R-KS) was the lone Senator to throw her support behind Bork. "It's a judgment call, but the vitality he would bring, the dedication and integrity he would bring is important to the Supreme Court," she said.[460]

With the tide of announcements against Bork, Senator Cranston declared that he counted 52 Senators opposed, 42 for, and six undecided.[461]

Judge Bork's son, Robert Bork Jr., sickened and disgusted by the campaign against his father, wrote this defense of him in the October 5 edition of the Washington *Post*.

Three months ago the President honored my father by nominating him to become an associate justice on the U.S. Supreme Court. Since then our family has endured a relentless and bitter campaign against my father. . . . Week by week the campaign has mounted. As the distortions were repeated over and over again, we watched my father portrayed as some villainous ideologue, a racist and a sexist. For his opponents the more he is made to look like a crazed neanderthal, the better for them. Indeed, one particularly ugly rumor spread by his opponents to injure him is that my stepmother, Mary Ellen, doesn't believe that the Holocaust happened. These characterizations, these rumors, are vicious slander and they hurt. They hurt because the people I meet on the street who took the trouble to watch and listen to his testimony before the Senate Judiciary Committee know that they are untrue. My stepmother, brother, sister and I— who know him better than anyone—know they are untrue. And what's more, the special-interest groups that so masterfully have spread these lies know it, too. . . . I know a different picture. I know that: He never has harbored any biases or prejudices. Our home was always open to our friends no matter who they were or where they came from. He, as a junior associate, fought for and won a place at his Chicago law firm for a lawyer whom the senior partners didn't want to hire because he was Jewish. He came to the aid of a black female lawyer in the Justice Department who charged that she was being excluded from meetings by her white male colleagues.[462]

Pro-Bork groups held out for their nominee, hoping to change wavering Senators' minds. Although it was late in the confrontation, the final weeks saw a surge in print ads such as this one by Citizens for America that appeared in the Washington *Post* on October 5. "THIS TIME THEY'VE GONE TOO FAR," declared the headline. The ad continued:

They have called him a racist. They have accused him of wanting a return to back alley abortions. They have labeled him a major threat to the civil liberties of all Americans. They have poured money into a direct mail campaign and slick television ads. They have applied unprecedented pressure to the Senators who must confirm him. But Robert Bork bears no resemblance to their untruths.[463]

In one of the few manifestations of what had been the much-touted west coast effort to secure funds for paid media, the October 6 edition of *USA Today* carried a full-page ad by the group We The People that declared:

> For the past several months you have been subjected to a stunning use of propaganda . . . extremists in groups such as the ACLU and NOW . . . spent millions of dollars to conjure images and perceptions of a one man court turning back accomplishments of an entire nation. They lied. They threw ethics and integrity out the window.[464]

October 6, 1987 A letter to Bork; radio spots by the Coalitions for America & the American Conservative Union.

The final push was on. Dan's latest analysis still showed Bork with about 41 favorable votes. Our "solid" count never exceeded 43 votes. Those of us laboring in the vineyard continued to demand from White House friends that they find a way to trigger an infusion of big dollars into television, where the battle had been lost in September, as well as a visible, prime time presidential address.

At the end of one gathering of the those working day to day in the battle, 23 of us signed an emotional appeal to Bork:

> *We have been and are continuing to work without ceasing for your confirmation. We admire you, respect you and thank you for the honor it has brought us to strive for your confirmation. We encourage you to stay in this fight until the Senate takes a recorded roll call vote on your nomination . . . Be assured of our unceasing efforts and undying admiration for your principled jurisprudence and devotion to country.*

Those signing the letter included Curt Anderson and Kimberly Roberts of the Coalitions for America staff, Grover Norquist of Americans for Tax Reform, John Kwapis of the Center for Peace and Freedom, Morton Blackwell of the Leadership Institute, James Boulet of Moral Majority, Paul Kamenar of the Washington Legal Foundation, March Bell of Americans for Robertson, Ray LaJeunesse of the National Right to Work Committee, Jack Clayton of the Christian Legal Defense & Education Foundation, Shannon O'Chester of Concerned Women for America, Dan Peterson of the Center for Judicial Studies, the ubiquitous Jo Billings, Don Baldwin and others.

In a most welcome gesture, Washington radio station WMAL-AM, its sister station WRQX-FM, and WNTR in Silver Spring, Maryland had informally adopted the "fairness doctrine" even though it was no longer in effect. They even asked Coalitions for America for spots to balance the ones People for the American Way had been putting on. One media ad placement person told us PAW's spots were too "strident to stand without an opposing viewpoint." After calls from the stations, Bill Kling and Curt Anderson of the Coalitions drew some of our people together and cut the spots in the Contact America studios.

One of the spots contended that Judge Bork's testimony exposed the lies and distortions brought against him by the liberal left. Thus there couldn't be any legitimate or credible grounds to vote against him. The other spot took a "friends" and "enemies" approach. "You can tell a lot about a man by who his enemies are, and who his friends are," the spot ran. It was pointed out that the ACLU, who opposed Bork, believed that the Constitution protects child pornography and bans the death penalty for even "heinous" murders. On the other side, the spot noted what Chief Justice Warren Burger and Justice John Paul Stevens had to say of Judge Bork. They said, respectively, that Bork was most qualified for the Court and if nominated, he would be a welcome addition to it.

Coalitions for America sponsored one of the two-minute spots while the American Conservative Union got the tag line for the other. The spots also ran eventually on some of the Christian radio stations. It wasn't enough, but at least some Americans got to hear our story as the end came.

One light note from those days came in a postcard mailed October 6 from Professor Henry Mark Holzer of Brooklyn Law School. Holzer had joined the "Beards for Bork" campaign, and asked me: "How do I get rid of this bloody beard if he isn't confirmed?"

As the end of the confrontation loomed, the decentralized and underfunded conservative movement was beginning to kick in with high voltage attacks on Bork's foes, including Jack Clayton's letter to supporters of the Christian Legal Defense & Education Foundation, in which he said, "All Americans should be outraged that the slander of these radical hate groups is about to cause the Senate to deny confirmation to the best qualified nominee for the Supreme Court in the past fifty years."

And, Mr. Conservative, from his mountaintop in Arizona, was echoing our anguished critiques of the White House performance. Barry Goldwater criticized his old friend Ronald Reagan for mishandling the nomination fight: "It was very apparent to me from the opening day that they were out to get Bork and I kept wondering when is the President going to put more effective troops on this?"

The Republican National Committee also ran a full-page ad in the Washington *Times* on October 7. The ad, "AN OPEN LETTER TO THE MEMBERS OF THE UNITED STATES SENATE," featured hundreds of signatures of citizens supporting Bork. "We the undersigned join millions of Americans and ask you to confirm Robert H. Bork to the United States Supreme Court," it read. "End the politically motivated, self-serving partisanship which has been an embarrassment to the American people. Do the job to which you have been elected."[465]

Though they knew the chances for Bork's confirmation were fading, Bork supporters pushed for a full Senate vote anyway. "Senators who thought they had a free vote will have to think again," said Richard Viguerie, who handled several of the pro-Bork mailings. "We are going to make it the most expensive vote they ever cast. We will be able to take a vote against Bork and equate it with supporting the homosexual lobby agenda, the radical feminist agenda, with the AFL-CIO, Jesse Jackson, and Ted Kennedy."[466] The reason "it's very important we have a floor vote is that the people of each state have a right to know who voted against a Supreme Court nominee who opposes racial quotas and supports victims' rights," said Senator Phil Gramm (R-TX). "And that won't happen if the nomination is withdrawn." Senator Gordon Humphrey (R-NH) added: "We're going to win this either by confirming Bork or making it a tough political issue for certain senators in 1988 and 1990."[467]

Meanwhile, the White House was complaining that conservatives had not done enough to advance the nomination, but Bork supporters felt they were the ones that had been let down. Gary Jarmin, a political consultant for Christian Voice, explained that his group had lessened its campaign for Bork because "there was pressure from the White House not to politicize it."[468] McGuigan put the blame on one particular cog in the White House wheel: "The White House congressional relations office has had a marked lack of aggressiveness in this battle. They didn't do their job for the most principled judicial nominee ever."[469]

Senator Grassley charged President Reagan with the failure of the Bork nomination:

This may be his last opportunity to change the Court and instead he was riding horses in California in August. It was very definitely the fault of the White House, which went on vacation in August while the [Bork] opposition was working. Instead of building coalitions to support Judge

Bork, they were writing briefing books and caught asleep at the switch. The Bush and Baker loyalists in the White House may have been at fault, but in the final analysis the buck stops with the president. There's a lackadaisical air about governing in the White House in general, and the best example is the Friday afternoon when Ron and Nancy are waving from a helicopter on the way to Camp David.[470]

Senator Humphrey said the strategic errors were "a reflection of the people [Reagan] put [in] place [in the White House], and of course Howard Baker has to shoulder his share of the blame." Humphrey continued: "The White House erred in trying to softball Bork and play down issues which unite conservatives with a good many moderates, [such as] opposition to homosexual rights, forced busing, racial and sex quotas and the complete obliteration of religion in the public school systems."[471]

But Bork supporters turned the criticism on themselves as well. "The conservatives have no media program at all," said James McClellan of the Center for Judicial Studies. "They totally underestimated the power and influence of the vicious civil rights industry that vented [against the nomination] all their wrath and disappointment that has accumulated since 1981." Consequently, he said, the right "ran no full-page ads that rise to the level of sophistication and prominence or high profile of People for the American Way. The electorate right now is grossly misinformed about this nomination and Bork in particular."[472]

At 6:30 p.m. on October 5, Joe Biden placed a call to the White House. The Senator told Howard Baker that a 9 to 5 vote against Judge Bork in the Committee was certain, and asked him if he would like to withdraw the nomination. Baker turned the Senator down.[473]

On October 6, President Reagan reinforced his pledge to stand behind Judge Bork and expressed anger at the barrage of liberal attacks against him. "I am going to continue to do everything I can to get him confirmed," Reagan said. "Our work is cut out for us. We have a lot to do before the floor vote. We simply have to work together." The President added that Bork bashers "have made this a political contest by using tactics and distortions that I think are deplorable . . . [Bork is] without question one of the most qualified candidates for the Supreme Court that we've ever had."[474]

October 6, 1987

The 721 Group meeting opened with prayer. The floor vote was about two weeks away. We hoped the president would make an address soon, and another just prior to the vote. The White House could also help by getting a big name speaker for the Americans for Bork rally Friday, October 9. Jo Billings, a "temp" nurse who had volunteered for the pro-Bork effort several weeks earlier, had worked draconian hours voluntarily. She'd given up her profession in order to work for Bork's confirmation. Her enthusiasm and intensity was infectious and at times of discouragement—and that certainly describes early October—she picked our spirits up.

At that October 6 meeting, we tentatively decided to do a "48 hour special" and sponsor a rally on the ellipse the following Friday. The object would be to get the hundreds of people working in the various conservative groups together for a big, visible sign of the support and affection we felt for the nominee. Jo Billings was put in charge.

Dan Casey gave us the latest low-down on how the Senate figured to vote. His tally had 41 senators assumed to be pro-Bork, 39 assumed to be anti-Bork, and the remaining 20 uncommitted, with half of those on the record with plenty of statements sufficient to make us doubt our chances for victory. Of the 20 uncommitted, Dan thought we might still have a shot at nine, while eight were leaning against him (but could be good for cloture if a filibuster developed). The other three simply could not be figured out.

The nine we thought might still be brought towards Judge Bork were: Cohen, Dixon, Evans, Hatfield, Reid, Shelby, Stafford, Stennis, and Heflin. Senators Breaux, Ford, Gore, Melcher, Mitchell, Nunn, Proxmire, and Sasser were assumed to be leaning the other way. But they might be good on cloture. And the three impossible to figure out were Graham, Chiles (the Florida boys) and Exon.

The 721 Group had the largest participation in its four years of existence, with 30 individuals and organizations attending every session. Regular coordination with the other coalitions groups, Library Court (the social justice/moral issues, 40 groups) and Kingston (economics, 20 groups) was expanding our impact and triggering more and more paper and calls into the Senate—but no one had the money or other resources to counter the paid media barrage of September. And none of us had the ability to undo the Senate elections of 1986.

As people on both sides of the battle across the country held a collective breath, members of the Senate Judiciary Committee issued 90 minutes of statements before voting 9 to 5 to send the nomination of Judge Robert Bork to the full Senate with a negative recommendation. After a 10–minute statement, the lone "undecided Senator" on the panel, Howell Heflin of Alabama, cast his vote against the nominee. "I am in a state of quandary as to whether this nominee would be a conservative justice who would safeguard the living Constitution and prevent judicial activism or whether he would be an extremist who would use his position on the court to advance a far-right, radical judicial agenda," Heflin said. "I am not sure I have the answer. I am reminded of an old saying, 'When in doubt, don't.' . . . Because of my doubts at this time and at this posture of the confirmation process, I must vote no." Heflin noted that he still might change his mind before the floor vote.[475]

Claiming that he felt "badly" for Bork, Biden said after the roll call was over: "I don't think there's a reasonable prospect that Bork will be confirmed."[476]

President Reagan said he was determined to press on: "I am saying that I am not going to withdraw this nomination under any circumstances. Robert Bork is without question one of the most qualified candidates for the Supreme Court that we've ever had and I'm going to continue to do everything I can to get him confirmed."[477]

Meanwhile, Senator Robert T. Stafford (VT) joined four of his Republican colleagues in denouncing the nomination, while Democratic Senators Claiborne Pell (RI), Brock Adams (WA), Wendell Ford (KY), and Christopher Dodd (CT) also said they would vote against. "I'm not sure it's over, but we're in trouble," said White House lobbyist Tom Korologos. "It's not unreasonable that we could win half the remaining uncommitted votes."[478]

Following the committee vote, Senator Simpson called Judge Bork on the phone. According to the Senator's account, the nominee said: "Did you call to cheer me up? Don't feel any anguish or despair for me. I'm a big boy and I know full well what's happening. I have a fine job, and I'll be doing it for the rest of my life if I don't go to the Supreme Court."[479]

Senator Cranston issued another pronouncement on the full Senate vote: 54 against; 42 for.[480]

The following day, October 7, President Reagan and Robert Bork held a 25-minute meeting at the White House while lawmakers and strategists wondered whether the Judge would withdraw his name. "I urge you to stay in it," Reagan told his nominee. "I urge you to keep going."

Ten more Senators—Lawton Chiles (D-FL), Bob Graham (D-FL), J. James Exon (D-NB), Alan J. Dixon (D-IL), John Breaux (D-LA), Richard C. Shelby (D-AL), Wyche Fowler Jr. (D-GA), Jim Sasser (D-

TN), Albert Gore Jr. (D-TN), and Kent Conrad (D-ND)—came out against the nomination. The lone Senator announcing support was Mark O. Hatfield (R-OR). Vote-counter Senator Cranston gleefully claimed that his tally had reached 56 "no" votes, 40 "yes" votes, with four remaining undecided.[481]

The steady announcements from Southern Democrats made at least some of their constituencies unhappy, as evidenced by this editorial that appeared in the Ville Platte (LA) *Gazette* and other newspapers across Louisiana:

> "Those who helped us get elected—the black voters—are united in their opposition to Bork, and don't think for a moment that we are going to ignore that." So spoke Louisiana's freshman U.S. Senator John Breaux last week in explaining why he will more than likely oppose the appoint-ment of conservative Supreme court nominee Robert Bork. So, just who is Breaux choosing to ignore? Will it be his constituents who have indicated a seven-to-one sentiment in favor of Bork's nomination? Or, the so-called special electorate he credits for getting him elected? Political favoritism and campaign "pay backs" should not be an issue in his decision. Rather, the underlying issue should be whether Bork is immi-nently qualified to serve or not. If Breaux wants to play politics, the alternative should be the overwhelming voice of his total constituency.[482]

Speaking to a gathering of minority business leaders, President Reagan made an eleventh-hour appeal for his nominee, whom he said would be "a widely respected force for justice and civil rights on our highest court." The group was reportedly unimpressed.[483]

Meanwhile, sixteen Republican Senators gathered in Senate Minor-ity Leader Dole's office to give encouragement to the embattled nominee and his wife, Mary Ellen. The Senators applauded Bork as they walked him to his car. Senator Phil Gramm (R-TX) commented: "The American people know what the people who cheated in college think. We want to hear from the straight-A student." After the Judge left the meeting, Senator Dole observed that Bork "feels much better about it. If he was on the fence when he walked in, I think he's more determined to hang in there," he said.[484]

The Marlin Maddoux Shows, October 1, 6 & 7, 1987

Thursday, October 1, 1987.
It all started when Marlin asked me how the fight was going. Marlin had invited me on his "Point of View" show to talk about the hearings

and the committee. (Early in the show we talked about the intense scrutiny the Committee was putting Judge Bork under. I told Marlin that I didn't know what to say when you have someone like Ted Kennedy casting "moral aspersions" on anyone. I repeated to Marlin and his audience what Jo Billings of Women for Bork said: she didn't know of any women who were afraid to get in a car with Judge Bork.)

But in response to how the fight was going, I admitted the fight had slipped over the past two weeks. "What can I say?" I told Marlin. "On our side all we've got is America and a lot of good people writing cards and letters and making phone calls. The other side has an awful lot of money and high powered paid political advertising. . . ."

They even had Gregory Peck, "you know, Abe Lincoln himself," I said, doing the "voice over" for one of the television spots People for the American Way put on. In a brief digression from the seriousness of the situation, I admitted to the nation, live via satellite, that I liked Gregory Peck westerns, but added "he should be ashamed of himself" for making such a distorted commercial.

We talked further about the tactics the liberals were using, the agenda they were operating under and how uncertain the vote seemed to be this late in the game. At the time of my October 1 appearance, there had been no vote in the Committee to either kill the nomination or send it up with no recommendation at all. Marlin had just begun to say that people still might want to get involved when a staff member handed him a telephone number. One of his secretaries had checked it out and it was none other than the Judiciary Committee Opinion Line. Anyone could call and register their opinion on Judge Bork's confirmation hearings.

Marlin passed the number along to his nationwide audience. He announced, "I'm going to give it to you and I'd like for you to write it down. Because after we give the number out the chances are they'll be flooded with calls. So it may be later on today or tomorrow before you'll be able to get in."

No words could have been more prophetically spoken. They had that Biblical "and it shall come to pass" ring to them.

Now that had been Thursday. The following Tuesday, five days later on October 6, Marlin was back at it giving out more phone numbers. On this particular show he had been talking about Senator DeConcini coming out against Judge Bork. I wasn't on this show. But from what Marlin said, during a press interview DeConcini had given out a White House number for people to call and register their opposition to the Judge.

Well, come to find out, the Senator had given out the wrong number. Marlin found out the correct number, the one to the President's opinion line, and gave it out. But he said he wouldn't be as narrow as DeConcini and urged everyone to call regardless of whether they favored the Judge or opposed him.

In Marlin's view, it was important that America let the President know what was going on. But more important than calling the President was calling senators. Marlin emphasized that "whatever state you're in, you have two senators. And all you need to know is their names. I'm going to give you their phone number." Live via satellite went the number to the Capitol Switchboard.

"And it came to pass" that the flood prophesied by Marlin hit the Senate Judiciary Committee in Noahic proportions. A tsunami was more like it. From reports Marlin was given, more than 900 calls an hour triggered by his show went into the Senate Judiciary Committee. In my time in Washington I'd never seen anything like it. The crowd had gone crazy.

The Committee staff apparently was not pleased with this outpouring of citizen involvement. So they decided to get back—giving out The Marlin Maddoux Show's 800 number and telling people that was the right number to call to register your opinion on the Bork nomination.

I didn't find out about this until the October 7 show. Marlin had me back on the show and I was telling him that it was hard to see the path that led to victory and that things looked bad, but I was going to fight until there was a vote in the Senate. Then Marlin said, "Well, you know the program we did the other day and gave out the phone number of the Senate Judiciary Committee caused a storm in Washington DC. And newspaper reporters called me, the National Public Radio called me and wanted to know what was going on; that they hadn't seen anything hit that town like that in a long time."

I responded that "[The liberals] control all of the levers of power . . . within the beltway, the road that circles Washington DC. . . . And because of that power, that dominance, they . . . sometimes forget that there is a country out there that has values that are quite a bit different than the values which prevail in the centers of media power and in the halls of the Congress. And I'm sorry they were upset but I'm thankful to every single listener who participated the other day because they got a message."

The good news was that their message got through. The bad news was that the message of "the other side" got there first.

The "campaign of disinformation" Marlin called it.

The way he saw it, the campaign waged against Judge Bork by the left was a "classic con on the American people." A new phase in the battle for the minds of the American people.

Although their efforts in most of the battle were a heart-breaking disappointment, after the hopes of the summer, perhaps the California group, "We The People" said it best in their full-page ad in the October 6 USA Today. Marlin read the ad's headline on his show the same day—"The Assassination of Judge Robert Bork: How Politics Stink and You Lose."

On October 8, President Reagan continued to maintain that he would back his nominee "all the way," and that "it would be impossible for me to give up in the face of a lynch mob." Meanwhile, according to one source close to Bork, the Judge was "miserable. He's not a politician; he's not used to getting the hell kicked out of him. He can't figure out what happened."[485]

Five more Senators—Dale Bumpers (D-AK), Paul S. Sarbanes (D-MD), George J. Mitchell (D-ME), Tom Harkin (D-IA), and Daniel K. Inouye (D-HI)—said they would vote down the nomination, bringing the official count of "no" votes to the fatal 53. Announcements in support of Bork came from Senators Ted Stevens (R-AL), William S. Cohen (R-ME) and Ernest F. Hollings (D-SC).[486]

The grassroots, meanwhile, refused to give up the fight. Waving signs that read "Women for Bork," "Students for Bork," and "America Wants Bork," about 500 (at the peak when Congressman Kemp spoke) people gathered at the Ellipse near the White House on October 9 to cheer for Judge Bork and urge him to continue his battle. The crowd heard support speeches for Bork from Congressman Jack Kemp (R-NY), Congressman Bob Dornan (R-CA), Pat McGuigan, Dan Casey, representatives of several groups—including several uniformed law enforcement officers—endorsing Bork, and Conservative Caucus director Howard Phillips.[487]

In a dramatic statement at the White House Judge Bork said:

The process of confirming justices for our nation's highest court has been transformed in a way that should not and indeed must not be permitted to occur again . . . Federal judges are not appointed to decide cases according to the latest opinion polls . . . But when judicial nominees are assessed and treated like political candidates, the effect will be to chill the climate in which judicial deliberations take place, to erode public confidence in the impartiality of courts and to endanger the independence of the judiciary. . . . Far too often the ethics that should prevail have been violated, and the facts of my professional life have been misrepresented. . . . Were the fate of Robert Bork the only matter at stake, I would ask the President to withdraw my nomination. The most serious and lasting injury in all of this, however, is not me . . . Rather, it is to the dignity and the integrity of law and of public service in this country. I therefore wish to end the speculation. There should be a full debate and a final Senate decision.[488]

In a statement released to the press after Bork's remarks in the White House press room, and after his own departure from the White House for the weekend, President Reagan replied:

I am pleased by Judge Bork's decision to go forward with his nomination for the Supreme Court. . . . Our efforts will be focused on setting the record straight with the American people. It is time to remove the special interests from the judicial selection process . . . The American people want a Supreme Court justice who interprets the law, not makes it: who is concerned about victim's rights, not just the rights of criminals.[489]

It was a beautiful day, all day, for the rally. Jo Billings had worked like a dynamo getting bodies down to the ellipse near the White House, calling on Casey, myself and friends on the Hill and in the Administration to secure "name" speakers.

Pastor Wellington Boone, a black Baptist from Richmond, Virginia, had called Jo a couple of days before and asked if he could help. When we talked before his prayer on the day of the rally, he told me, "I've watched this unfold, and God put a burden on my heart. This is a righteous man, and I will stand with him as this ends." It was almost too much for me, talking to Boone that day, after all the cynicism and inaction I'd encountered in the three months preceeding. He wasn't even a conservative, just a man who'd watched the hearings and decided this was one for which he would go on the line. He and an aide drove up from Richmond to be with us that day.

A battery of more than a dozen cameras—and the rally did secure some of the best coverage Bork's supporters gathered throughout the confrontation—recorded the words spoken from the platform beginning after 2:30 p.m., as every Republican presidential campaign sent a representative—and Jack Kemp came himself to raucous cheers from the crowd. We'd heard about the Kemp campaign's plans to commit some money to pro-Bork ads, a rare example of the application of substantial resources to paid media, and I told him, before he addressed the enthusiastic crowd, how much his help meant to those of us who were working around the clock to turn the thing around. Mari Maseng came for Dole, and I introduced her with a personal "witness" about her dedication to conservative values. B–1 Bob Dornan can go on too long sometimes, but he was perfect representing Bush that day (and I reminded him of the St. Patrick's holy card he inscribed for me in 1978). My old friend from the Free Congress, Doug Shaddix, represented Pat Robertson. I read a letter from Pete du Pont.

Perhaps the toughest words of the day came from Howie Phillips of the Conservative Caucus, but his aggressive tirade had the ring of truth to it. In remarks directed to the heads of the Republican campaign committees and the National Committee, Phillips declared:

> *For the past seven years, the Republican committees over which you preside have, using the signature of Ronald Reagan, collected hundreds of millions of dollars from hundreds of thousands of Republicans who believed in the causes for which President Reagan campaigned. As a result of your fund-raising success . . . conservative organizations have had less money available to them and have not been in a position to counter the expensive television and newspaper advertising underwritten by the Hollywood humanists, the big-profit pornographers, the multi-million dollar abortionists, and the others who had a selfish, pocketbook interest in financing the unprincipled campaign of character assassination directed against the good and honorable Judge Bork. . .*
>
> *. . . The small contributors who sacrificially entrusted you with those resources have a right to inquire why you declined to invest those funds in Judge Bork's cause and whether, in the future, you will sit on their money, or commit it to battle. When the left is shooting at us with loaded guns, it does little good to fire back shooting blanks.*

The uniformed cops, all from Virginia, D.C. and Maryland spoke briefly with intensity and dignity of their belief that Judge Bork would support the working policemen of America, by simply upholding the Constitution. Jo had orchestrated appearances from spokesmen and representatives for the entire spectrum of the conservative movement, from law enforcement, and from the Republican establishment. One after another, Chinese, Hispanic, white, black and other Americans—including Mildred Jefferson, a founder of the National Right to Life Committee—spoke to us about their reasons for backing Bork. We even had a group of homosexual activists hang around at the edge of the crowd to harrass us, but they did not keep us from having our say.

Jo and her troops served the media as best we could in the hectic atmosphere, giving them copies of the prepared statements we'd been able to pull together.

At the end, I told the crowd most of them were cleared (as a result of intense negotiations by Casey and Billings) to enter the White House grounds for a rally to send the President off to Camp David and cheer for Judge Bork.

Cameras surrounded Casey, Boone, Jo, the cops, myself and others as the rally concluded. The words weren't always eloquent, but the questions were nearly always the same. How can you keep fighting? Is there any possibility for victory? In my concluding prayer, I'd put it simply: "Father, we have worked so hard. We accept your will. But we dare to pray for a miracle finish."

A group of women who had listened to me on Marlin's show a few days before, when I'd mentioned the Friday rally, stopped me as we headed toward the White House, to say they'd never been involved in politics until this fight. I told them, "Just keep listening to Marlin."

A camera man from one of the major networks stayed until the end, recording the words of every speaker. He told one of the girls who had volunteered to handle logistics for the rally: "I just have to tell you something. This was awesome. Where were you people two months ago?"

In the beautiful sunshine, the groups went around the southeast side of the White House complex, to enter the grounds through the east gate. Reporters followed some of the crowd, asking them where they were from, why they'd come, if they really thought there was a chance to win.

At the gate, the guards told us we could not bring the signs in with us. However, they quickly conducted checks on the many people who had come to the rally without pre-clearance, and all but a handful were cleared into the grounds. Those not cleared were disappointed but understood. It seemed as if we were getting a nearly perfect day after all the disappointments.

As the week had progressed, I'd been told by White House officials that the President had prepared two statements for the send-off—one if Bork stayed in, one if he withdrew. I'd indicated as much to Morton Blackwell, the former White House aide and friend of a decade who had come down for the rally. He told me, "Pat, after this rally we just had, if Bork stays in and the President gives a stem-winder before he takes off, we could get a new spin going."

After getting inside the gate, I sought out a restroom. A Marine *guard directed me down a long hall in the east wing of the White House. Emerging from the restroom, I heard Bork's voice in the air. Rushing down the hall, I entered a small room where three marines were watching a television. Bork was in the White House press room, where he had just begun his statement.*

As Bork's statement progressed, a young marine a head taller than me stared intently at the screen. Bork's words penetrated every one of us in the room, and the fellow I was watching looked at me and said, "What a man he is. What a great man."

Bork was going to stick with it.

I rushed back out through the gardens, onto the grass behind the White House where not only our rally group but hundreds of others had gathered to see the President off. I saw Mary Lewis, a colleague of mine from the Free Congress who had worked two nights in a row with volunteers to make signs for the rally.

"Mary, Bork was just in the White House press room. He's going to stay in. It's not over!" I told her.

"Oh Pat, My God," she answered, hugging me. "I'll be right back." She ran off toward the gate our group had entered.

I saw Rebecca Range, our ally in the Public Liaison office and told her. With us on the lawn, she'd not heard either. I described for her the front row of reporters in the press room, their stunned faces as Bork completed his remarks and headed for the door. "Becky, for once even they were speechless."

Fired up as I was, she admonished me, "Don't tell everyone, that will make it more exciting when the President tells them Bork's hanging in there."

Suddenly, I noticed pro-Bork signs popping up in the crowd (the visuals that night on the evening news were priceless). I saw Mary giving out the signs.

"How did you get those in here?"

"I told them I'd been sent to bring them in! The guards said OK."

Someone's little boy could not see as the President and Mrs. Reagan emerged. I held the little one on my shoulders so he could see them.

Reagan muttered a couple of sentences, to the effect that Bork had decided to hang in there.

The crowd went crazy, waving the signs, cheering in pandemonium (in a scene that would secure as much coverage as the earlier rally on that evening's television news).

Reagan said he would keep working to help Bork. One or two sentences. That was it.

As the helicopter blades began to rotate, the couple boarded the vehicle. Morton found me in the crowd.

"What an outrage! An incredible opportunity was just lost. He could have sent these people through the atmosphere if he'd said the right words," Morton told me.

I agreed. "I don't know why he didn't say more. They must have thought Bork was going to withdraw."

I contended, "But this is a great day regardless."

Feeling rejuvenated and happy, if mildly perplexed by Reagan's performance, I walked away from the White House by myself, accepting congratulations from friends who caught up with me.

That night I watched NBC, one of the first times I'd watched one of the networks during the battle. From a black screen, the picture of Bork's face emerged. They broadcast nearly all of his statement. At the conclusion, with no comment, they cut to their trademark music and the statue of liberty. Pam was sitting with me.

"Wow," she said.

Yeah. Wow.

We could never have sustained our energy in those final weeks without the example the nominee himself offered that day. It was time for the final push.

The conservative leaders who had campaigned intensely for Bork's confirmation said that their movement remained strongly unified despite brutal treatment of Bork by liberal Senators and special interest groups. "If this nominee is defeated, there will be the same unanimity behind a new conservative candidate as there was on the Bork nomination, and this time it will be helped along by a more engaged President," said Dan Casey of the American Conservative Union. "Besides, you don't see anyone blaming the conservatives for what happened with the Bork nomination. We gave our all—we won the mail and phone campaign in most Senate offices, we energized the grass roots." McGuigan added: "The [pro-Bork] rally was a good example. We had representatives from many factions in the movement. Conservatives are still slugging away and will continue to unite no matter happens."[490]

Indeed, direct-mail expert Richard Viguerie said that minutes after Judge Bork pledged to stay in the fight, pro-Bork groups sent 350,000 letters exposing the tactics of the left on the Bork nomination "to raise money for 1988 campaign ads." Viguerie explained: "The left was very effective in the last three months in framing the debate their way and making Judge Bork the issue. Now we're going to make the liberal left—the Teddy Kennedys, the Jesse Jacksons, the Joe Bidens—the issue.''⁴⁹¹

In his weekly radio address on October 10, President Reagan said that his nominee's record had been "subjected to distortions and misrepresentations." The President continued: "While I refused to withdraw his name, I understood why Judge Bork himself might choose to do so. I know that any decision made by Judge Bork would be made on solid grounds of principle, in contrast to those who would politicize our courts, jeopardize the independence of the judiciary and hold our courts and Constitution hostage.''⁴⁹²

A Saturday strategy meeting among White House officials produced a decision to "maximize the vote, to frame the debate and set the record straight on Bork, and to set the stage so the next nominee doesn't have to go through the Bork agony," said one attendee. "It's a fight for the judicial system. Those senators [supporting Bork] do not want to allow this nomination to be the standard by which other nominees are to be judged in the future. Is this how we're going to name Supreme Court justices?''⁴⁹³

Meanwhile, pro-Bork leaders Casey and McGuigan said they had not given up hope on their nominee's chances. "If you can crack a Howell Heflin, you can hopefully open up the floodgates, because whatever it is that eventually changes Heflin's mind will probably be a substantial enough hook for other senators." Casey said his group was continuing to lobby Senators in Nebraska, Mississippi, Louisiana, Alabama, and Georgia.⁴⁹⁴ McGuigan added: "We've got to maximize the pro-Bork showing in the Senate so if we don't win, we make the next conservative nominee's fight a bit easier." McGuigan believed that Bork could win confirmation if he gained the votes of the remaining undecideds, and if moderate Senators who had said they would oppose Bork can be persuaded to change their minds.⁴⁹⁵

On Face the Nation that Sunday, October 11, Senator Biden—with what Judge Bork's son later said was "the smile of the Cheshire Cat"—said he did not understand Judge Bork's assertion of two days earlier that the confirmation process had been unduly politicized. Biden countered, "He sat before our Committee for 30 hours, he looked me straight in the eye and told me how fair he thought the hearings I was conducting were."

On October 12, White House Chief of Staff Howard Baker told a group of newspaper publishers at a meeting in West Virginia: "I'm sorry he's not going to make it," expressing White House sentiment that the nomination had no chance of survival on the floor. An angry McGuigan criticized Baker specifically in interviews with the press. "They've already taken the high road and all it's gotten us so far is the defeat of Judge Bork," said McGuigan. "It's time to start playing rough. When is the TV time they're talking about? I want to know when it's being scheduled."[496]

Presidential hopeful Jack Kemp—not anyone linked with the White House—spent $50,000 for a pro-Bork cable television ad to run the week beginning October 12. "The liberals in the United States Senate have attacked and smeared a man of decency. A man of law and order," the ad showed Kemp saying. "It's not too late to help Judge Bork be confirmed to the United States Supreme Court," Kemp said. "Please write your senator today."[497]

The last "regular" meeting of the 721 Group before the Senate voted was October 13. A last push effort was being put together to re-energize the grass roots support and go after targeted senators. Morton Blackwell of the Conservative Leadership PAC was seeking last minute media ideas for the outside groups. Demands on the White House to give a presidential speech and to deliver at least one Republican "get back" vote were also made. Maintaining solidarity among the remaining Republicans was crucial.

"Don't count him out until the count is in" was our internal battle cry. My dear friend Connie Marshner, working at home since leaving the Free Congress in July, spoke for many of us in her "Weekend" commentary for Jim Dobson's Focus on the Family:

Every once in a while, even here in Babylon on the Potomac . . . the human spirit shows itself to be courageous and noble. The behavior of Robert Bork under the intense pressure of the final days of the Judiciary Committee hearings is such an example . . . The liberal establishment knew that Robert Bork would not bend, that he has too much respect for the law to bend, and so they knew he had to be destroyed . . . [S]o deeply does Bork believe in the rule of law, so profoundly does he believe in the constitutional process, that he resolved to see the constitutional process through . . . Robert Bork, in what must be one of the most courageous acts of political self-sacrifice I have witnessed, refused to spare himself and his family and his career that humiliation of the [coming] defeat. He refused to give the jackals their prey. He said he was not withdrawing. The Senate would have to vote on his nomination. It was the way the Constitution ordained it, and Robert Bork is the good servant of the Constitution, even when he must pay the price . . . [M]ay your heroic defense of the Constitution not be forgotten.

In quiet moments together, between the frantic times of those weeks, we prayed. But in our hearts we knew realistically that if the votes were not there, preparation for the next choice had to be an immediate focus. In my notes at the October 13 meeting, I scribbled that "the Senate is a bully pulpit, but it's not a bully's pulpit."

I was surprised when, that week, an October 9 letter from Dennis DeConcini arrived in the mail. Thanking me for the copy of The Judges War *I had given him during our meeting, DeConcini told me:*

> Your efforts and strong commitment to a constructive change in the Judiciary is welcome, I can assure you. Please be assured that my view and judgment on Judge Bork was based on what I believe is fair to this country, to Judge Bork, to President Reagan and, of course, to my state. I was careful in my deliberations and did not make them based on political fallout. Rather they were based on what my conscience told me I should do. I was fortunate, as a young man, to have a father who not only set a good example but who offered a value system that I have tried to attain. He always said, "Whenever in doubt, do what is right." That sounds simple but, indeed, it is often difficult because of the pulls and strains and because of the respect you have for other people's judgments. When it comes down to it, however, my judgment was based on my father's advice.

In another note, Newt Gingrich encouraged President Reagan to choose an effective strategy for the end of the Bork battle and the presumed beginning of the next confrontation. In his October 13 letter, he told Reagan "it is vital you decide which vision of America you want the country to rally to" and continued:

> If you want the vast majority of Americans who share your values to join you in an all-out struggle to save the Supreme Court and Senate from a left-wing lynch mob, you will have to systematically focus attention, arouse allies and encourage supporters. This process will take months but may isolate and defeat the corrupt left-wing minority which today dominates Congress. The best historical example of a President who aroused his majority against a bitterly opposed Congressional leadership may be Andrew Jackson.
>
> Alternatively, if you want to wage a solid fight but gracefully accept the probable defeat of Judge Bork so you can get a judge approved this year, then you must follow very different vision of White House Congressional relations. Approval of a conservative justice who shares your values but also meets the Democratic Senate leadership standards will require an insider strategy of accommodating power in Washington. The

best historic example of a conservative President working with a liberal Congressional leadership may be Dwight Eisenhower.

The worst possible course is for you to use the language and outline the vision of an assault against the corrupt left-wing lynch mob, but then to try to pull your punches so you and they can find an accommodation. That zig-zag policy will simply confuse your followers, enrage your opponents and cripple your presidency. The best historic example of the confused zig-zag approach is Jimmy Carter.

Gingrich argued *"We owe it to Judge Bork to vindicate that sincere and decent man."* But, he maintained, *"If you decide you cannot follow the path of Jackson, I deeply hope you will follow the path of Eisenhower . . . Please, under no circumstances zig-zag between the two visions. Either approach can work if pursued systematically. A zig-zag between the two will lead to disaster."*

At a speech in Wippany, New Jersey on October 13, an angry President Reagan vowed, if Bork were defeated, to give the Senate liberals a nominee "that they'll object to as much as they did to this one." Meanwhile, over in the Senate, GOP Bork supporters said they wanted to wait several days before holding a vote, while Senator Harry M. Reid (D-NV) became the fifty-fourth to announce opposition to Bork's nomination.[498]

Promising he would "keep this Senate open all night" to get a final vote on Bork by the end of the week, Majority Leader Byrd asked Republicans to "stop beating a dead horse" and allow a quick vote on the nomination. Bob Dole responded, "I find it a little unique that the Democrats, after waiting 72 days to start hearings on this nominee," are now offering with "great generosity . . . to have this immediate vote on Bork."[499]

October 13, 1987 priority action memo

"[I]t is do-able." By now the vote was less than two weeks away and nomination prospects looked bleak. Never one to lie to those who worked hard, in this memo I told my allies, *"On the surface and 'on paper,' it looks impossible to win."* Encouragement wasn't oozing out of the walls. But Bork himself had re-energized us all with his announcement a few days before that he would stick with it and see the vote through.

A realistic analysis of the situation that faced us made it clear how difficult was the path ahead. The goal was to secure the votes of the *five "undecided senators," the five "unannounced Republicans (believed leaning in favor but not on the record yet)," and four of the "get backs (announced against but we believe possible reversals)." The five Senators clinging to an "undecided" position at that time were: Nunn (D-GA), Evans (R-WA), Proxmire (D-WI), Reid (D-NV, who announced his opposition the morning the mailing went out), and Stennis (D-MS). Of the "unannounced Republicans" there were: Warner (VA), Roth (DE), D'Amato (NY), Murkowski (AK), and Heinz (PA).*

And we had deemed Stafford (R-VT), Bingaman (D-NM), Heflin (D-AL), Chafee (R-RI), Chiles (D-FL), Shelby (D-AL), Exon (D-NE), Melcher (D-MT), Graham (D-FL), and Dixon (D-IL) as our only hopes for "get backs." Targeted senators were hit with immediate letters and we asked local people to conduct high quality personal lobbying by October 19 in anticipation of the vote.

Beyond all of this, there was going to be a new media effort (primarily radio) if the dollars came in. (They never did.) Otherwise, pro-Bork demonstrations were strongly recommended. The Americans for Bork rally on October 9 had boosted all of us, as several days later we were still reaping results— it got coast to coast coverage and helped frame the coverage later that day of his announcement that he would stick with the fight.

From October 13 onward, the leadership group, ranging in size from four to ten, depending on the day, met somewhere every morning, frequently on the Hill over a cup of coffee in Humphrey's office or in one of the cafes.

On October 14, President Reagan gave a televised speech—in the middle of the afternoon—which all major networks except Cable News Network refused to carry. "If the campaign of distortion and disinformation is allowed to proceed . . . it will mean that on critical issues, like the fight against crime and drugs, each of us will be the loser," Reagan said. The President continued: "My agenda is your agenda . . . we want judges who don't confuse the criminals with the victims . . . who understand the principle of judicial restraint. . . . This is not just one vote on one man. It is a decision on the future of our judicial system."[500]

That same day, Senators Thurmond, Simpson, Hatch, Danforth and Rudman sent a letter to Harold Tyler of the ABA Standing Committee on the Federal Judiciary asking that the bar disclose the names and views of the justices interviewed in forming the panel's judgment on Bork. The ABA refused the Senators' request.

On October 14, Newt Gingrich angrily wrote again to the President, saying the New York Times coverage of his New Jersey speech had demonstrated the confused present path of the Reagan presidency. As Gingrich put it, the Times' coverage:

> suggests your senior staff wanted to follow a conciliatory path and you had accepted that strategy in your speech. Then in a quip you raised your personal values which force you to confront the left-wing lynch mob. The result is a story which irritates your opponents and confuses your friends and allies. You must either impose your strategy of confrontation on your senior staff or you must discipline yourself to stay within the bounds of a conciliatory strategy as designed by them. Either will work. The chaos and confusion exemplified by the attached article is simply crippling your presidency.

On that Wednesday evening, I was slated to appear on Fox Television's "A Current Affair", with host Maury Povich. I was opposite Senator Alan Cranston of California, a leader of the anti-Bork forces in the Senate and the chief vote counter for the other side.

Over a week before, the Judiciary Committee had rejected the most qualified judicial nominee in this century on a vote of 9 to 5, with all the Democrats joined by Republican Arlen Specter of Pennsylvania. As the floor vote approached and pressure grew for Judge Bork to withdraw his name from nomination, Cranston issued increasingly optimistic (for his side) vote counts. A few days before, Chief of Staff Baker had told an audience at the White House he did not buy Cranston's inflated figures. But "unnamed White House sources" continued to hint that Bork should withdraw. Bork himself had rejected that counsel the previous Friday.

The dam broke, there was little doubt, with the decision of liberal southern Democrat Senators to oppose Bork's confirmation. But Bork's decision to hang in there gave his supporters a chance to shore up the dam and do their best in the closing days. This was the context of our appearance on the show.

Before and after the interview, Cranston and I talked. I don't know if he meant it, but he told me, "I'm sorry the way this has turned into such a smear of Bork himself. That's not fair." I replied, "It's not surprising given how much money your friends had to trash his reputation." I told him my count gave his side only 47 truly solid votes, with my side at 42 and 11 or so Senators undecided or potential reversals.

At that point he surprised me by reaching into his pocket and pulling out his famous tote sheet (a list of all the Senators with notes on how they would go on the Bork vote). So, I pulled out mine and we compared notes. Our counts coincided except that I still counted a few Senators as "undecided leaning against", truly undecided or possible reversals, while he was counting those as solidly against. Included in that last category were the two Senators from Florida, Democrats Lawton Chiles and Bob Graham. Although they had announced against Bork, I still hoped to bring them back, and I still believed we could get the votes of the handful of undecideds—at least we could make it interesting.

I grinned a little and told Cranston we were both pretty good counters. I had had Chiles and Graham as truly undecided until recently, along with several of the others. I asked him, "When did you put them in your solid 'no' camp?" Cranston replied, "Just in these last days. I talked with both of them. In all honesty, I had them leaning in favor of Bork" until they came out against him.

Life is a game of inches. There are no guarantees in politics, of course. The momentum and the objective totals were clearly against Bork at the time I saw Cranston in mid-October, and had been for weeks. But perhaps, if the hopelessness and despair our enemies intended for us to feel had been stemmed, the fight might have been sustained more effectively. Perhaps those Democrats—whom Cranston himself said only broke in his direction late in the game—could have been captured for the pro-Bork side. In fact, though, the despair was reaching epidemic proportions. Only Judge Bork's dramatic speech in which he announced he would stick with the fight sustained our energy in the final weeks. At least we were going to get a recorded vote and put the SOBs on record, in the hopes they could be held accountable and responsible for their actions.

On October 15, Senator Daniel Evans (R-WA) announced he would support the nomination.[501]

A Washington *Post*/ABC News poll released October 16 revealed that 65 percent of the public believed the confirmation process had, in the words of Judge Bork, "been changed in a way that should not . . . be permitted to occur again."[502]

Meanwhile, some conservatives (not McGuigan or Casey) who were furious over Howard Baker's treatment of the Bork nomination, demanded that the Chief of Staff turn in his resignation. "I'm not leaving. I'll be here to lock the door and turn the lights out," Baker said.[503]

On October 15, Dan and I participated in a meeting with Gerry Carmen and some of the field men of Citizens for America. They had become increasingly active in the final weeks of the battle, and were helping to increase the direct grass roots surge into the Senate offices. Also present were Jack Clayton, a key religious conservative organizer, Maiselle Shortley, Richard Viguerie and Howie Phillips, as well as a representative of the National Right to Work Committee. In these closing days, everyone seemed completely engaged on a personal level and able to spark hits from the heartland into the various Senators— but we were all obsessed by the reality of severely cramped resources in a confrontation where the other side was still outspending us and the media "spin" seemed to have been lost long ago.

A later White House briefing with Rebecca Range and Ken Cribb brought to each of us the same sense that the situation was not salvageable.

But after the White House meeting came one of the first optimistic times for me in final weeks of the battle. Casey, Richard Viguerie, Howie Phillips and I accepted the invitation of Leonard Garment and his wife Suzanne to return with him to his offices at Dickstein, Shapiro & Morin. While we'd talked a few times, Garment and I moved in completely different orbits—me concentrating on the world of journalism, legal research and the conservative grass roots, he, on the other hand, representing the quintessential Washington lawyer/insider.

We wound up spending several hours with Garment and Suzanne at his office. We carried ongoing discussions on final strategy and themes while sitting around a large circular coffee table, each of us with a phone in front us, each making calls all over the city, including several to Senators who were sketching their final strategies in the battle.

Garment had secured financing for rapid research and packaging of detailed responses to the most egregious of the liberal distortions of Bork's record. While Garment described the research teams he'd constructed to perform that work in Washington and in New York, we continued to brainstorm—and Howie settled on an idea which, while ultimately costing his Conservative Caucus only some $10,000 in print media buys, resulted in nationwide press attention and, eventually, a starring role in the final Bork debate on the Senate floor.

Howie's eventual idea was to craft ads, under the heading "You Can Tell a Man by the Company he Keeps", which featured a key Senator in his home state newspapers, noting that he was agreeing with groups and individuals such as the National Abortion Rights League, American Civil Liberties Union, Coalition for Lesbian & Gay

Rights, National Lawyers Guild, National Organization for Women, Feminist Men's Alliance, Ted Kennedy, Howard Metzenbaum, Joe Biden and others. Particularly in states like Louisiana, Montana and Kentucky, we concluded, those sorts of affiliations might raise an eyebrow or two among the typical reader.

In discussions months later, it became clearer and clearer that just such obnoxious and aggressive "hits" as these—perhaps in July and August and September—could have offset the mendacious ads of People for the American Way, Planned Parenthood and the others.

October 16, 1987 media packet

The vote on Judge Bork's nomination was nearly upon us. This was the last packet of clippings, analysis and so forth the editors would get from Casey and myself. I wish more could have been sent out but the money just was not there.

Although the outcome of the vote was all but assured, hopefully this material would remind editors across the country that more was at stake than Judge Bork's career advancement. The integrity of the confirmation process itself was at stake.

The goal for this last minute mailing was to set the record straight. Filled with 31 pages of excerpts from Judge Bork's testimony, plus columns and articles from the "establishment" press, this packet was an attempt to dispel all of the disinformation on Judge Bork.

As the end of this confrontation approached, even my mother and father—Bruce and Bonnie McGuigan of Oklahoma City—grew increasingly involved. Earlier in the fall, they had expressed delight when Father David Monahan, editor of The Sooner Catholic, *wrote an endorsement of Bork. Then, they felt rewarded when their letters (and thousands of others) to David Boren had secured the Democrat's support for Bork.*

On October 4, however, The Sooner Catholic *letters section carried blistering attacks on Monahan, who was my high school principal at Bishop McGuinness. I knew Monahan to be a sincere liberal of the old school, so the charges of one writer that Bork's judicial philosophy contradicted Catholic principles must have hurt.*

Momma and Daddy called me about the situation. Together over the phone late one night the three of us drafted a strong defense of Monahan which was printed in the November 1 issue of the newspaper. We noted that Bork's philosophy of judicial restraint, with its emphasis on powers reserved to the people and the states, "places Bork squarely in conjunction with the Church's traditional, wise teachings—that social services shall be provided and governmental decisions should be made at the level closest to the people." We concluded: "Father Monahan and The Sooner Catholic *can be proud that they did not join the mob seeking to lynch Judge Bork. Monahan stands for fair play and political responsibility—attributes of the best in American traditions."*

On October 17, Secretary of State George Shultz distributed letters to all U.S. senators in defense of the nominee, saying Bork was in the "mainstream of . . . legal thought." He hoped his support and that of other prominent Americans might help persuade some of the 54 Senators who had announced opposition to Bork's nomination to vote otherwise during the floor vote. The letters included a statement from 128 pro-Bork professors, including Allan Bloom of the University of Chicago and John McCarthy of Stanford University. Shultz told the Senators that he was angry with the campaign of disinformation waged by anti-Bork liberals. "These attempts pose a significant threat to free intellectual debate in America and to the healthy future development of constitutional doctrine," he wrote.[504]

Judiciary Committee Chairman Joe Biden wrote an opinion piece defending the liberal attack on the Bork nomination, which the Washington *Post* printed on October 18:

> The Senate Judiciary Committee has just completed a great constitutional debate on an issue as old as the republic: the role of government in the lives of individuals and the rights that individuals cede to their government. . . . But as the Senate prepares to vote, President Reagan and Judge Bork's proponents ignore this debate. Instead, they imagine that a "lynch mob" has swayed the Senate, and public opinion too, by a campaign of lies and distortions. President Reagan is wrong. . . . Perhaps there have been distortions outside the Senate debate . . . But the excesses of the right—the fear-and hate-laden telephone campaigns, the character assassination, the "lynch mob" charges—have been no less strident.[505]

Meanwhile, conservatives were outraged at reports that Senate Judiciary Committee aide Linda Greene had intimidated John T. Baker, a black witness who favored the nominee and who had planned to testify, into refusing to testify during Bork's confirmation hearings. Greene, a staff lawyer appointed to the committee by anti-Bork Senator Howard Metzenbaum, called Baker to warn him that his testimony might be unpleasant because of his May 1986 resignation from Howard University. Baker left the school because he believed graduation standards for Howard law students were too low. Baker, a professor at the Indiana University Law School, did not speak at the September 28 hearing, but insisted the decision not to appear was his alone.[506]

Gordon Humphrey called Greene's tactics "highly offensive . . . perhaps illegal," and asked for an investigation of the incident. "I just don't find credible the explanation given by the aide who says she called this professor out of concern for his well-being," he said. "The effect clearly was intimidation, and it worked. It's simply unacceptable for Congressional witnesses to be intimidated by staff. Black leaders have been intimidating black Americans, suggesting that Bork would turn back the clock on civil rights."[507]

"In these instances we finally have documentation of what we had heard in whispers from both Democratic and Republican staffers . . . of intimidation and sleazy, hardball tactics on the part of the Democrats," said McGuigan. "In my view, this could really turn the Bork vote around. I'm hoping that several Senators will refuse to continue to sustain their alliance with Bork's unprincipled opponents."[508] McGuigan pointed out that if only eight or nine of the 54 Senators who had declared opposition either voted "yes," or protested the intimidation tactics by voting "present," Bork would be confirmed.[509]

On October 18, Senate Minority Leader Robert Byrd stalled debate on the floor for a third time. Senator Hatch, who with other Bork supporters was counting on the debate to clarify distortions of the nominee's record, remained optimistic. "I can feel things finally shifting for Judge Bork," he said. "I think more than a few senators believe they may have spoken out too early against him and could reverse themselves when the vote is finally taken."[510]

Like Orrin, those of us on the outside continued to hope the tide might turn. Late on October 18, I walked four draft speeches to Jade West at the Senate Steering Committee, for possible use in the floor confrontation about to begin. Gary McDowell of the Center for Judicial Studies had written a lengthy constitutional-oriented piece, whereas I'd crafted three sets of remarks which could be delivered within five minutes. As hopeless as things looked, we were working through the end.

On October 20, Senate Judiciary Committee Chairman Joe Biden said he would order a probe into allegations that Greene intimidated

Baker. Committee Senators questioned Greene for two hours, but members refused to reveal what was said.[511]

A group calling themselves Criminals Against Bork (CAB) held a boisterous rally in Washington, D.C. to protest the Supreme Court nomination of Judge Bork on October 21. A dozen "criminals"—Bork supporters in costume—dressed in prison uniforms, clenched hand-cuffs in their right fists and chanted, "More crime! More victims!" and "No Bork! No Jail!" to amused passersby. The CAB's demands, displayed on a banner in block lettering, included abolition of the death penalty, low or no money bail, light sentencing, early release, and color televisions in jail. Highlights from the criminals' anti-Bork message included: "Welcome to the largest open meeting of alleged criminals since the Zacarro family reunion early this week. . . . In decisions that Bork has made he has shown the sort of 'firm but fair' [boos from the criminals] application of the laws that the criminals here find so objectionable."[512]

Organizer Eugene Delgaudio said that the high point of the demonstration occurred when Bork's most vocal enemy in the Senate, Ted Kennedy, walked within 25 feet of the demonstration. The criminals chanted, "Thank you, Senator Kennedy, thank you!" Kennedy waved mechanically, smiled, and hurried off to the Capitol to cast a floor vote. When he returned minutes later, he stopped dead in front of the protesters, perhaps thirty yards away. Upon reading the signs, he turned beet red. One of the criminals yelled, "Chappaquiddick—way to go, Senator!" An outraged Kennedy ran up the steps of the senate office building.[513]

Weyrich wrote Bork on October 21:

. . . Your determination to see this through will enable those of us on the outside to see that there is, ultimately, an appropriate measure of political accountability for those who joined the lynch mob. . . I will never forgive myself and the rest of the conservative movement for not being ready. We did our best with limited resources, but we could have done better with a more realistic assessment of what lay ahead. . . You dared to defy the Washington rules. You dared to stand for your principles to the end. It has been my honor to know many good men in my years in politics. In politics, we hear words like "courage" and "dignity" and "principle" used all too lightly. Words always convey our meanings imperfectly, just as these words convey mine all too inadequately. You are the embodiment of the most precise meanings of the words courage, dignity and principle. It has been our high privilege to support your

nomination for many years, and to coordinate the efforts for your confirmation these last three months. Your commitment to principled jurisprudence and the highest civic virtues will stand as our example in the years ahead.

The bitter floor fight on the nomination of Judge Robert Bork began on October 21, and the man about whom fierce debate had swirled for months said he was disgusted with a system that allowed politics to determine who sat on the bench. Even Senator Specter, the lone Republican Judiciary Committee member to announce his opposition to Bork, said he was unhappy that Senators had publicly chosen sides before the debate. Friends said that Bork was "disgusted by the political hoopla and wishes it was over already," but did not regret his decision to stick with the nomination because he "wants to make sure that the kind of politics we've seen in this confirmation aren't repeated for future nominees."[514]

A reporter for a major northeast daily called me as the final debate began in the Senate, to ask for my interpretation of how that would play out, what the President might do next and so forth.

We'd been talking to one another regularly for two years, and she had always been fair to me, to my point of view, and she had been fair to Judge Bork in this fight.

After finishing her questions, she said, "Pat, I'm putting my pen down. End of interview. Can we talk?"

"Of course," I answered, a bit surprised.

"You are sad, I've never heard you like this before. Do not be sad. You did your best. You guys were magnificent. No one worked harder. No one could have worked better. Judge Bork had no better friends."

My throat tightened, and, unbidden, the tears welled in my eyes, one of a few times that happened in those days.

I responded, "All that may be true, but the bottom line is we're going to lose. My values are losing, and the finest man nominated to the Court in our lifetimes is being rejected."

She persisted, persuading me to "keep your chin up. You know there will be other days, other things you believe in and can fight for. This isn't the end of the world. Keep it in perspective."

I was surprised at another demonstration of the times and unexpected ways life can demonstrate the decency that lies, sometimes hidden, in many hearts. "Your words mean a great deal to me, and I'll never forget this conversation," I concluded as we hung up.

I still don't know if she was for Bork herself.

Senate Republicans said they hoped to use the debate to clear Bork's record. "It is profitable to create a monster and cast yourself as the only knight," Senator Hatch said, pointing to an anti-Bork advertisement by People for the American Way. "This . . . is the art of character assassination."⁵¹⁵ When Senator Kennedy stood up to deliver his remarks, the Judge's wife and son, Robert Jr., who had been observing the debate from the visitors section, stood up and exited quietly.⁵¹⁶

In those final days, we did the only thing we knew to do. Over coffee every morning we discussed little signs of hope and divided up the action of working to maximize the showing for "our man." We organized thank you calls to Senators who delivered their floor statements supporting Bork. Jo Billings issued continuous statements as the debate progressed. Casey and I returned every press call we could. Baldwin kept the letters coming from his law enforcement allies. Kepley monitored staff level developments and reported them to us.

Among those I talked with regularly in the final push were Howard (Howie) Phillips of Conservative Caucus and Morton Blackwell of the Conservative Leadership Political Action Committee. (Blackwell had first trained me in youth campaign techniques a decade earlier during my years at Oklahoma State University.) Both he and Howie were involved in aggressive last ditch efforts to turn up the pro-Bork volume in radio and print media advertisements.

Although the efforts enjoyed at best scattered success, modest purchases were made in a few of the hoped-for "get back" states— Montana, Kentucky, Louisiana and North Carolina. Howie's work in particular struck a raw nerve with one of its targets. To our surprise, Senator John Melcher, Montana Democrat, actually devoted a portion of his remarks on the floor to a critique of the advertisement the Conservative Caucus had placed in the Helena Independent Record on Monday, October 19. Melcher's convoluted and rambling attempt to disassociate himself from the anti-Bork forces (The ad was entitled, "You Can Tell a Senator by the Company He Keeps") merely reinforced the aggressive anti-Melcher/pro-Bork thrust of the advertisement. The ad listed the Senator's phone numbers in both the nation's capital and his home state—and we understand he was among those swamped with pro-Bork calls in those closing days.

As the end approached, Casey prepared a target list, which we had ready for distribution to our allies within hours of the next nomination.

He established three basic categories: Column one consisted of Sena-tors "who voted FOR Bork who may be soft." Column two were those who "voted AGAINST Bork but should be priority targets." Column three were Bork opponents who were "secondary targets." Our final Senate analysis of the Bork confrontation had Boren, Cohen, D'A-mato, Evans, Hatfield, Murkowski and Hollings in the first group. In the middle category were Senators Bentsen, Heflin, Shelby, Breaux, Chiles, Graham, DeConcini, Bingaman, Reid, Stafford, Warner, Dixon and Stennis. In the "secondary" category (column three) were Nunn, Proxmire, Chafee, Weicker, Specter, Johnston, Melcher, Gore, Ford and Sanford. All other Senators we assumed solidly in one camp or the other.

After the Senate debate had gone on for a day or so, Paul Weyrich entered my office at Coalitions for America and asked my secretary, Lisa Kai, "Where's McGuigan?" She wasn't sure, but called four places before finding me in the office of George Smith, Senator Humphrey's Judiciary Committee aide.

Weyrich told me, "Pat, Jim McClure [the Idaho Republican Senator] just got me on the phone. He wants our advice. He thinks he and the others can keep this alive for a few more days, if there's any chance to sustain it. What should I tell him?"

I was standing and felt a great shudder as I said, after pausing only a few seconds, "We did our best. Bork is tired. It's time for it to end and there's no need for it to go beyond making sure all of our guys get a chance to go on the record, and we respond to the worst of the other side's speeches."

Paul told me, "I'll pass it along. Don't get down. He's still going to be there fighting for the law. He's a good man. We worked hard for him. I don't think the other side can sustain this intensity. So long as the Administration stays focused, you'll get a good jurist yet."

"Yeah, but it won't be Bork."

Following three days of intense debate, the Senate voted at 2 p.m. on October 23 to reject the nomination of Judge Robert H. Bork by a margin of 58–42, ending months of bitter debate and producing conservative vows to fight harder for Reagan's next nominee. Senators John Warner (R-VA), John Stennis (D-MS), and William Proxmire (D-WI), the three remaining Senators who had refused to announce their positions prior to roll call, all cast their votes against Bork. In a speech to an unusually hushed group of Senators, Warner said he would vote against confirmation because he "could not find the necessary compassion for a Supreme Court nominee" in Bork's record. In the final tally, 52 Democrats and six Republicans cast "no" votes, while 40 Republicans and two Democrats voted "yes."[517]

As mid-day on the day of the vote came, I walked to Judge Bork's office at the U.S. Court of Appeals. I entered his office and gave Judy Carper, his secretary, several copies of the statements Paul Weyrich and I had prepared for release upon completion of the vote.

Standing with Bork's clerks watching the television as the debate closed was Doug Ginsburg. I shook his hand and said, "It was our fault. Not his fault. Not his fault."

I walked then through the bright sunshine to the Hill, where I left copies of the statement in both the House and Senate press galleries.

After doing some odds and ends at the office, I called Pam and told her I would be home at a reasonable time, but that first Dan and I were gathering for a drink.

The agony ended on October 23, 1987. Paul Weyrich told reporters, "Whatever lies ahead . . . for the Supreme Court, Judge Robert Bork's example will stand for decades to come as the height of civic virtue and citizen courage. He dared to defy Washington rules. He stood for his principles to the end."

After getting a handshake and a pat on the back from Kennedy— fellow engineer of the Bork defeat—Biden told reporters in the Senate gallery: "If [President Reagan] sends [another nominee] who feels the same way as Judge Bork on major Constitutional issues, [the President] will not only have trouble, but will not have another nominee."[518]

Conservatives were shocked and outraged by Warner's action — the only surprise in the proceedings—as he had voted with Reagan on most major issues. "John Warner just started to write his own obituary," said Dan Casey of the American Conservative Union. "What made Warner's vote even more unforgivable is that when every other Bork opponent was backing off on the personal attacks, Warner phrased his objections in personal terms, implying that somehow Judge Bork lacked humanity." McGuigan said that the fight was lost because conservatives did not have anywhere near the funding for the project that liberals spent. "Leaders in the movement are all saying how outraged they are, but they did not respond with money," he said. "We had good will, energy and creativity, but we had a White House asleep and no money. And we're going to lose again if we don't get it."[519]

It was early evening, just a few hours after the vote ending the activity which had been my prime focus for so many months. Dan Casey and I were sitting at the bar of the Joseph Story Society, an educational and fraternal organization of conservative lawyers and legal researchers, behind the Supreme Court on Second Street, N.E.

We came to the club, as we call it, quite determined to finish a bottle of Irish Whiskey, and we were making a respectable effort to do exactly that.

I called Himself. To my surprise, he answered himself. "This is McGuigan," I said. "Oh, hello, Pat. I'd like to talk, but I'm on the phone right now. Could you try later?"

A half hour or so later, I got him on the line again.

"Counsellor, I have a problem I need your advice on," I intimated. "What's that?"

"Well, you see, this friend of mine got nominated to the Supreme Court. This damn reporter called me and asked me what I was going to do to make sure my friend got confirmed. Like an idiot, I said I was going to grow a beard and not shave until he was confirmed."

Bork began to laugh.

"My trouble is," I continued, "my wife hates the beard. She didn't mind me growing it for my friend, but she doesn't want me to keep it. What can I do, I gave my promise?"

He replied, "As you might guess, I am aware of your problem. I hear rumors that the principal involved here might, himself, be contemplating at least a down-sizing of the beard. And, no one would expect you to retain your beard in those circumstances. So I think people will understand. I will."

"I thought you might be interested to know that Dan Casey and I are sitting here at the bar plotting the political demise of one John Warner, our fellow Virginian," I told him.

Bork startled me then. "He came to see me, you know."

"You're kidding."

"No. Said he had just a few questions to ask me. We talked about some innocuous things for 15 minutes or so, maybe less. Then we shook hands and he left. I didn't feel great about it but thought there might be a chance for his vote. Guess he just came to see me so he could say that he'd done that."

"Bob, why don't you come have a drink with me and Dan? We've still got a ways to go on this bottle of Irish Whiskey." It was not the first time I'd ever called him Bob, but it felt a little easier than in the past.

"Hmmm. Your offer is of some interest. What are you drinking, Bushmill or Jameson?"

"Dan says we're drinking Jameson, that's what we've got."

"No. If it was Bushmill I'd come, but I just sat down with a good detective novel and I'm not going to get dressed and go back out just for Jameson."

After I relayed his words to Casey, my fellow Irish Catholic declared in a loud voice, "What's a good man like you doing drinking that Prod whiskey?"

After a chuckle, there was a pause in the conversation. "I worked so hard."

"I know you did, Pat, I know you did."

"We'll have that drink another time. Enjoy the book."

A few days later I bought a bottle of Bushmill and put it behind the bar. I sent word through his secretary that it would be waiting for him when the time was right.

Afer his rejection by the Senate, Judge Bork issued the following statement:

The Senate has now made its decision. . . . There is now a full and permanent record by which the future may judge not only me but the proper nature of a confirmation proceeding. . . . Now I simply wish to express my deep gratitude to President Reagan, to the senators who supported me so magnificently, to all those in and out of government who assisted me, and to the many Americans I will never meet who expressed their support so warmly. Finally, I owe a special debt of gratitude to my wife, Mary Ellen, and to my children, Robert Jr., Charles and Ellen. Their love and counsel sustained me throughout the extended process we have been through together.[520]

Afterword

Despite the ultimately happy ending for conservatives in the confirmation of Justice Anthony Kennedy, and the reality that his judicial philosophy appears largely to mirror Robert Bork's, the months between the retirement of Justice Lewis Powell and Kennedy's eventual confirmation will be regarded by historians as one of the more tragic periods in the modern era. For in those months came the sad fulfillment of what many people had worked to prevent, and what I had mournfully predicted, in my well-intentioned Judges War, would be the result of continued warfare over judicial nominations: "the domestic, political equivalent of the Iran-Iraq War."

In a paper presented at the fall 1988 annual meeting of the American Political Science Association, Professor Frederick L. Morton of the University of Calgary succinctly sketched a strong case that liberals wrought a fundamental change in the American system of government with their incredible assault on Robert Bork. First, as Morton observed, the scale and scope of the Bork confrontation was without precedent. It represented a qualitative, not merely a quantitative, change in the nature of judicial confirmations. Second, the current conflict over judges in general ("the judges war", as I call it) occurs against a backdrop of crisis in constitutional interpretation. Third, what essentially became an election for a Supreme Court jurist represented part of what Morton believes is "an ongoing dismantling of Republican governmental structures."

Perhaps even more troubling was the following observation from a scholar who critiqued drafts of this book for me. Comparing the course of the 1988 presidential campaign with the earlier Bork battle, this analyst argued Bush "took the initiative" from Dukakis, just as the liberals had taken it from us in the Bork battle: "[Ninety percent] of *the battle is getting in first to define the issue. . . This basically is what the Bush campaign did to Dukakis. And now that game is to be extended to judicial nominations. And conservatives must play, and play to win. But isn't it enough to make a granite column weep? The fears of the founders, about the dangers of too direct a democracy, coming true before our eyes.''*

I do not agree with all the observations of fellow conservative scholars and analysts on the meaning of the Bork battle. I do know that despite the aggressive efforts of hundreds of conservative leaders and organizations from the first moment of this confrontation, the Left had the initiative from the first moment of the battle. In fact, their preparations for the Bork confrontation began in the mid–1980s, as Reagan's presidency advanced and he elevated more and more advocates of judicial restraint to key slots on the federal bench. The confrontations over Wilkinson, Meese, Reynolds, Kozinski, Fitzwater, Ellingwood, Manion and Rehnquist were rehearsals during which tactics and themes were tried out and honed for the next confrontation. Effective liberal judicial watchdog groups had sprung up as the list of Reagan judicial nominees topped the 300 mark. The Alliance for Justice had tracked Reagan nominees since 1985.

In confrontations which never secured massive press attention, liberals developed techniques for effective distortion and raised the price for any thorough-going conservative raised to high position. And, they seemed to have a better sense than conservatives on what particular positions (not merely people) to target. When Herbert Ellingwood, an evangelical Christian, was nominated for the Assistant Attorney General spot responsible for weeding out candidates for federal judgeships, People for the American Way (PAW) took notice and decided it had better give conservatives a fight over the President's pick, in order to prevent a firm evangelical from standing in the slot most influential on the thinking of the Attorney General on judicial selection matters.

Years before conservative preparation began, liberals were collecting information on prospective candidates, including Judge Bork. The work on the one liners and facile distortions of the record began long before the eventual nomination of the conservative jurist.[521] Another outfit, Supreme Court Watch, began compiling and analyzing Judge Bork's record in 1986 when they realized then that he was a likely nominee.[522]

They took the initiative. They framed the debate. To the extent Judge Bork's supporters anticipated the onslaught he would face, we acted *in a misdirected, if well-intentioned, manner. While I was spending nine months writing a book* (The Judges War)*, my friends and I hoped would promote fairness toward future conservative nominees among the national press and in academic circles, our opponents were getting ready for the domestic issues political fight of the Century. Whereas we thought, and I still would like to believe, the battle ahead was primarily intellectual and moral, our foes were getting ready to pull out all the stops in a raw, political confrontation, accuracy be damned.*

One can fault the accuracy of the words, symbols and content of the attacks which Bork's opponents used to shift many citizens away from either neutrality or soft support for the nominee. But it is important to stress that, although they frequently lied in their advertising, Bork's key opponents largely understood exactly what his nomination meant for the liberal jurisprudence and politics which dominated America for the quarter century preceeding the 1980s. Larry Tribe quite probably realized that playing the part he did in the Bork opposition would nearly eliminate his own chances of ever securing nomination to the High Court. He did it anyway because, as one scholar who read this manuscript advised me, "Tribe correctly perceived *the extent of Bork's intellectual challenge to everything he, and the academic culture that sustains him, stands for."*

After the nomination, Judge Bork's supporters in the outside groups began a conventional build-up for a garden variety (but more intense than in the past) judicial war—but found ourselves increasingly utilizing "guerilla warfare" tactics as the confrontation slipped away from us. The organized Left, on the other hand, engaged from the beginning in guerilla warfare, making unexpected and surprising assaults into what should have been elements of support for Judge Bork—all the while engaging in a massive conventional build-up for what they understood would be a major political war.

Even what we thought was an outrageously excessive speech— Kennedy's incredible polemic within an hour of the nomination in July—had the effect, as Dan Casey remarked to me the night of the defeat, "of freezing everyone in place. After that speech, no Democrat who felt in the least bit beholden to their core liberal constituencies was going to jump on board the Bork Bandwagon." When we got excited because moderates like Gerald Ford threw soft ball encomiums in support of Bork, we did not understand we needed—from the beginning of the battle—more angry, righteous men like William French Smith, to counter the memory of Senator Kennedy's diatribe.

As I noted ruefully on one of Marlin Maddoux's shows—Judge

Bork's opponents wrote a script for this one and followed it unfailingly. While Bork supporters reacted to the nomination—and, perhaps more importantly, to Justice Powell's resignation—nuanced, slow and late, those committed to continued judicial activism and to Bork's defeat reacted hard, fast and early.

Joe Biden framed the debate when he backed off of his "I'd have to vote for him [Bork] even if they tear me apart" statement, deciding not to take his medicine. He framed an important early point in the debate when he reversed himself on the Senate's role in advise and consent in confirming judicial nominees.

Bork's opponents cross-pollinated the varied themes employed by the outside groups and the key opposition spokesmen effectively from the beginning of the confrontation. (Bork's supporters did this somewhat effectively toward the end of the battle, when it was too late.) For example, Biden's "new" position on the Senate's role in confirmation was reflected in the first ads that PAW put out. Their initial focus was on the confirmation process itself. They questioned the exclusivity of personal morality, intellect, qualification and judicial temperament as the sole factors for confirming nominees. PAW suggested that a candidate's philosophy and ideology might also be considered.[523]

In following PAW ads, "candidate's" general became Judge Bork, particular. Full page ads in newspapers ranging from the New York Times *to the Los Angeles* Times *argued that the Senate must examine the Judge's political views and "ideology" as they consider his nomination. At the same time, PAW was framing the debate around controversial issues like personal privacy and civil rights. Particularly vulnerable to these "issues ads" were the Southern Democrat swing votes.*[524]

Once we had a nominee for Powell's slot, Bork's supporters concentrated on the Senate vote—while the opposition was out attacking the man. Our side was in there battling for the process whereas their side was out there hacking away at the man's supposed ideology and political views. While the other side was organizing the raw political power it had, we were trying to organize persuasive, intellectual argument for our troops, when we probably should have been asking them to hit the streets.

Ted Kennedy set the tone of the debate as he stood on the Senate floor proclaiming what Robert Bork's America would be like. It was his way of catching the attention of the American public in "everyday language," he told Joe Klein of New York[525] *magazine following the*

Committee vote. Klein observed that "after a quarter century adrift in his own agony, Ted Kennedy finally—inexplicably—got a wake up call: Bork."[526]

Kennedy woke up both liberal America and the supporters of Judge Bork. This resurgence of energy made Kennedy, in Klein's view, the key to public opposition and I suspect Klein is right. Klein described how the newly energized Ted Kennedy immediately set out to mobilize opposition to the nomination. He began by hiring the founding president of PAW, Tony Podesta, to help in organizing anti-Bork forces (Podesta, like Biden, had once said he could support Bork).

Kennedy wrote a "warning" letter to 6,000 black elected officials cautioning them on Judge Bork's civil rights "record."[527] *Herman Schwartz, in his book* Packing the Courts *noted that Kennedy also made a conference call to over forty state and regional AFL-CIO leaders to "energize" them.*[528] *And from what Klein reported, the Massachusetts Senator called every Democratic fundraiser he could think of, but particularly those in the South, to spread the word on Bork and enlist support for the opposition.*[529]

Meanwhile Biden, the other leading figure in Bork's opposition, remained active solidifying support against the Judge's nomination. He was working with the Leadership Conference on Civil Rights developing strategy. He spent weeks attempting to harvest the southern swing votes. Polls he had seen, in wake of the early attacks, indicated a noticeable concern among Southerners that an Associate Justice Bork would mean revived race relations battles. Schwartz mentions in his book that Biden pursued J. Bennett Johnston, Jr. (LA) to get an assist on the Southern Democrat swing vote because Johnston was hoping for a Senate Democrat leadership slot. Biden understood that. Biden also knew that Johnston claimed he was afraid that a Bork confirmation would reopen old civil rights wounds. As the fight went on, Biden played up the polls and the power grab to Johnston with good results.[530]

Eventually it was learned that in late July Gerald McEntee, president of the American Federation of State, County and Municipal Employees, met with the Leadership Conference and agreed to provide $40,000 to hire a polling firm to research what aspects of Bork's record to emphasize. Marttila & Kiley gathered polling data in August and in early September which was packaged in a confidential report entitled, "The Bork Nomination and the South." The report concluded that a way to keep the public skeptical about Bork's "fair-mindedness" was *to hit his record on civil rights. Whereas that would be the emphasis in the south, the report advocated a "Yuppie Strategy" targetted to the northeast and northwest, playing up Bork's opposition to a generalized right of privacy.*

Biden spent weeks going over Judge Bork's writings with the help of Professor Laurence Tribe of Harvard. Afterwards they held a mock hearing. For the rehearsal Larry Tribe posed as Judge Bork. Herman Schwartz made the comment that Biden knew all of the right issues to touch on and all of the right questions to ask. The result for Bork's enemies was "good" politically, if questionable morally. Schwartz claimed that "Biden . . . bested Bork in the legal exchanges. . . ."⁵³¹ That is an absurd assertion—but the presentation of the Biden-Bork (and Kennedy-Bork) exchanges on the evening news, those 30 second sound bites, certainly accrued to the advantage of the jurist's enemies.

Knowing who we were up against still did not make it easier to determine what we were up against. Although the various special interest groups, from the fringe to the mainstream Left, were similarly urging their people to write their senators, sending mailgrams and telegrams and making phone calls, they did so with differing agendas. Although many of the liberals set out deliberately to smear the reputation "of an individual who I consider to be the leading constitutional scholar of our generation," ⁵³² some of the anti-Bork leadership— notably Ralph Neas of the Leadership Conference—cautioned his allies not to demonize Bork. They did any way, but some liberals sought to exercise a degree of restraint.

And, Bork's opponents at times exercised another sort of restraint for the sake of their values. Part of the opposition leadership's strategy was keeping the more visible special interest people behind the scenes. They did not want to risk feeding the conservative claim that the nomination was really a fight between middle America and the most liberal special interest groups. Thus, many of the most notable and visible activists, including the organized homosexuals and lesbians, supporters of abortion on demand and some civil rights activists, were relegated to a role behind the scenes. Admittedly, advocates for these viewpoints received plenty of print coverage, but in this visual media-dominated age, they did not become central figures, no doubt a situation they did not relish, but one they made the most of. Although they never shared the spotlight with the Hill staffers, the lawyers and the academics during the hearings, they made up for it with other organized activities—and with victory in the final vote.

Because Bork's supporters did not understand that during the actual hearings the opposition was essentialllly implementing a pre-written script, we got hurt. I said as much on "Point of View" in early October 1987 when I confessed to Marlin Maddoux: "as one of the political tacticians in the middle of this battle . . . I didn't understand that going in. I understand it now after they've managed to create a lot of false impressions, and negative headlines, and they've spent a lot of money. I understand they were not interested in a dialogue. They were interested in raw judicial power."

Terry Eastland put it well in an article in Legal Times *when he explained the unfortunate verb:* to bork. *He wrote:*

> *What does it mean to be borked? Simply this: Your opponents attack you on a matter involving law and criticize you in terms of policy outcomes. You defend yourself by discussing the issue in legal jargon. With Bork, for example, it was said that he was against civil rights. He responded with legal arguments, but he was never able to overcome what had been stated in laymen's language.*

Entirely aside from the rhetorical incisiveness of the other side in contrast to both the nominee and his supporters, the resource gap between the two sides was ultimately breathtaking. According to the July 20, 1987 Newsweek, *there were 75 special interest and civil rights groups (including the NAACP and NOW) who had joined forces with Senator Biden to oppose the nomination. A month later,* Newsweek *was reporting in its August 24 issue that 185 liberal organizations from abortion to civil liberties had become involved. By the end of it all, over 300 groups (including feminists, labor and environmentalists) had heeded the call and over $2 million had been raised to protest Judge Bork, according to Herman Schwartz.[533] (This spending estimate is probably low.)*

Contrast those numbers with a simple reality. The organized conservative movement in the nation's capital consists of some 110 organizations, fewer than the number of groups that concentrate on civil rights issues alone.

On legal issues, 15–20 groups meet regularly on legal issues in the 721 Group. During the height of the Bork battle, that grew to about 30 groups which had made his confirmation a top or nearly top priority. Another 80 or so groups considered it important, but their battles (whether Central American policy or family issues or whatever) had not gone away. Here's the political bottom line: The most generous reading possible (to conservatives) pits 300+ liberal groups against 100+ conservative groups (and a dozen or so law enforcement groups) engaged rather substantially in the battle.

But that may understate the resource differences. Whereas the total annual budget for People for the American Way and its action fund exceeds $10 million, the total annual budget for Coalitions for America (Paul Weyrich's 501 c 4) was $150,000. The Free Congress Foundation, not wanting to push the edge of IRS interpretations, has never devoted substantial resources to legislative confrontations. But even granting, as some would, that the money spent to write, produce and market The Judges War *book (envisioned and largely completed before the battle ever began) should be counted in the "pro-Bork" total for organizations with which I am affiliated, the resource gap remains clear.*

Comparisons between any of the roughly analogous liberal and conservative groups—data I know scholars and others will develop for public consumption in the years ahead—will yield results similar to the foregoing sketch.

So we found ourselves in Ted Kennedy's America. "Ted Kennedy's America," Joe Klein estimated, "apparently was a place where a senator could spend a half-hour grilling a Supreme Court nominee with questions provided by his staff, not listen to the answers, then sum up with a 30–second epigram intended for the evening news that had nothing to do with either the questions asked or the answers given: 'In Judge Bork's America, there'd be no room at the inn for blacks and no place in the Constitution for women.' "

(Some might believe that a year after the Bork battle, in October 1988, liberals found themselves in George Bush's America. Claiming their presidential hopeful, Mike Dukakis, was the object of inaccurate "negative" advertisements focusing on his criminal justice record, they complained bitterly as the hopes of summer 1988 faded with the approaching election. But one analyst, Charles Krauthammer, recalled the Bork smear in an October 28, 1988 essay in the Washington Post:

> *Liberal forces hatched the meanest national campaign of this decade. Their attacks on Bork set a standard that the Bush campaign cannot hope to match. Now they are allied with Dukakis and find themselves on the receiving end of a withering negative campaign. And they are crying foul. Who says there is no justice in this world?*

Who says, indeed? Richard Cohen of the Washington Post, *in his essay "Pardon Me, Mr. Bork", seemed to recognize the enormous shift which occurred in contemporary American political civility with the*

Bork defeat. It is hard to quibble with the conclusions reached in a National Review *editorial looking back at the 1988 campaign:*

All the indignation would carry more conviction if the phrase "negative campaigning" had been heard in connection with the negative campaign of 1987: the concerted defamation of Robert Bork. People for the American Way (a real mainstream outfit, that one) poured megabucks into TV and newspaper ads in an unprecedented attempt to block a judicial nomination. Liberals who fret about what campaign spending does to elections didn't reflect on what Norman Lear's money was doing to the independence of the judiciary. Not to mention the vileness of the actual charges and innuendos heaped on Bork by the Bidens, Kennedys, and Metzenbaums. Nothing Bush has said of Dukakis approaches the scurrility Bork was subjected to. The memory of it makes the liberals' current self-pity simply disgusting.)

The liberals were not the only ones at fault, or in credit, for the outcome of the Bork battle. For a long time, conservatives in Washington could say to each other, and to the conservative grass roots: "Well, at least the Administration is picking and getting confirmed the right kinds of people as judges." A combination of the political calendar, the length of the confirmation struggle to fill Powell's seat and an astonishingly complete collapse of political will in the White House legislative operation combined to make even that assessment invalid.

If central blame for the worst domestic political defeat of the Reagan presidency could be placed on both the White House and its political enemies, it is only fair to note serious weaknesses in the political foresight, strategy and determination of Bob Bork's best friends—Ed Meese at the Department of Justice, and the various conservative organizations who should have had the moxie and political determination to carry forward the Bork struggle with or without the help of the White House and other elements of the Reagan coalition.

Ed Meese, with all his personal troubles, remained the steadfast field general throughout most of Reagan's second term, at least in terms of the selection of first rate federal judges. Meese and his team managed, during the second Reagan term, to select and elevate principled, qualified men and women for federal judgeships, individuals capable of earning the praise of even liberal political scientist (and judicial analyst) Sheldon Goldman.

But Meese himself must bear responsibility for one disastrous aspect of the Bork defeat, actually the legacy of a decision he made in 1985.

Early in his tenure at the Department of Justice, over the objections and against the advice of his closest friends in the conservative movement, the Attorney General decided to retain the American Bar Association's (ABA) involvement in evaluating federal judicial nominees.

The ABA Standing Committee on the Federal Judiciary is a growing national scandal. This Committee meets in secret and is unaccountable to the American people and to our elected representatives. With a marked bias in favor of liberal judges in the Jimmy Carter years, the ABA Committee has grown increasingly obnoxious toward principled conservative nominees during the Reagan years, dramatically increasing its offenses since Democrats seized control of the Senate in 1986.

The bitter fruit of Meese's bad choice—to retain the ABA involvement for the sake of ephemeral, occasional advantages for certain nominees, and to keep the liberal Democrats from being even more overt in their partisan "investigations" of judicial nominees—was tasted in the Bork confirmation. Four members of the ABA Committee, incredibly, rated Robert Bork unqualified for the Supreme Court. Thus did the intellectual pygmies and leftist diletantes of the American legal establishment do their bit to sully the reputation of one of the most dignified men to grace American life in this century.

At least Ed Meese made sure that Bob Bork was the nominee. Whatever the faults reflected in Meese's early choice to retain the ABA's role in judicial selection, victory remained achievable even in the face of the action of four of the ABA Committee members.

Which brings me again to the White House. It is unfair to focus indeterminately on that institution and not be quite clear on who, and what, deserves particular credit or blame for the non-intense and unserious manner in which Bork's confirmation was approached. It was the job of the White House legislative operation, under Will Ball, to see that Bork had a realistic shot at getting confirmed. Throughout the Bork battle, Ball consistently refused to consult with the President's strongest allies on the Hill and in the conservative movement. Ball and his people relied on the classic Washington "insider" strategy. He honestly seemed to believe that quiet dinners and gentle conversations in the halls of Congress would somehow persuade liberals and moderates to support conservative judicial nominees.

On the rare occasions when indirect communication did occur, it was merely to send signals that conservatives should not emphasize conservative issues, lest they endanger the Bork nomination's prospects. In all too many ways, it fits.

When Robert Bork was nominated, conservatives realized this much: *"That for which we exist is upon us."* That's why conservative organizations spent hundreds of thousands of dollars, and thousands of man hours, making the calls and stuffing the envelopes—an operation which proved decidedly inadequate but which nonetheless resulted eventually in pro-Bork mail heavily outweighing anti-Bork mail in 80 to 90 of the 100 Senate offices. As impressive as the sheer volume of mail was eventually, in the early stages (as opposed to in September, when those of us on the outside had crafted common themes and utilized them in a more or less rational order) support for Bork was expressed in an unfocused and diffuse way, whereas Bork's enemies were focused and specific in their criticisms.

Further, the confidence that Bork would *"do an Ollie [North]"* on the Committee ignored two realities: first, a judicial nominee can't respond politically and at the gut level (Bork's answers were invariably nuanced and balanced), and second, there was no real dialogue between liberals on the Committee and Bork—just set questions, Bork's legally profound but lengthy responses, and set rejoinders designed for the evening news.

The Bork defeat and its aftermath sparked widespread introspection among conservatives and a generally civil debate about what might be done to prevent a recurrence in a future judicial confrontation. Perhaps the most penetrating, and frequently correct, early critique came from Amy Moritz, writing in the Heritage Foundation's Policy Review.[534]

Moritz is absolutely on the mark when she asserts that conservatives cannot compensate for weakness with *"frequent, blustering threats."*

I find fault, however, with Moritz's charge that the movement is inappropriately *"obsessed"* with the press. The problem is, rather, that too many conservatives feel that the press is so important to their success that conservative spokesmen feel compelled to comment on literally everything that happens. Not every story is *"our story,"* nor is it possible or appropriate to get in on every single political or policy development in the nation's capital. The most effective way to purchase long-range authority with the press is to comment insightfully, accurately, and honestly on developments in which you or your organization have an actual interest and expertise.

The working press, with whom I interact regularly in my dual roles as a conservative legal policy spokesman and a journalist covering American politics, is not so much biased against conservatives (although elements of it certainly are) as it is cynical about politicians *and those in public life in general. The majority of reporters are looking for the "real thing," someone who actually understands the story they are pursuing. The sort of restraint I am counseling here may mean that weeks, even months, will pass without a given individual or organization appearing in news stories—but when that individual's or organization's area of expertise jumps to the news forefront, most reporters will treat them seriously.*

Too many conservative brethren still fail to recognize that the political struggle is but a subset of the larger battle for the soul of America—its economic ethos, its politics, its culture. Conservatives need to carry their message into all aspects of American society. There is frequently insufficient appreciation for the role conservatives need to play in the media and in academia—not only as writers and scholars but as active members of professional associations. This is territory conservatives cede to liberals all too easily.

Pat Buchanan pointed to this larger struggle in our society when he noted that those most committed against Bork regarded his nomination as a matter of "good and evil, morality and immorality." In the April 1988 issue of Columbia, *the magazine of the Knights of Columbus, reporter Russell Shaw, a veteran observer of events in the nation's capital, ruminated on the "persistence" in American politics of the moral issues as reflecting a conflict taking place at a deeper, more profound level.*

Both Buchanan and Shaw understood what many of Bork's supporters perceived only dimly during the confirmation fight. Yes, the smear of Bork's reputation among the bulk of Americans only generally aware of legal policy issues was an important factor in his defeat. But Bork was "borked" in the advertisements not because he was misperceived by his opponents, but because he was correctly *perceived. The top elites of American political, intellectual and legal life are still quite comfortable with a federal (and, increasingly, a state) judiciary that implements policies that could never be legislated. Further, many legislators today are content to have jurists do things for them they would find it awkward to vote for themselves. The American establishment likes judicial activism just fine.*

Judge Bork not only threatened that establishment view as Lewis Powell's replacement, he had committed the unforgivable "sin" of tirelessly confronting that elite establishment with the extra-constitutional bases of its modern "constitutional" jurisprudence. This reality gave an extra edge of ferocity to the attacks on Bork throughout the summer and fall of 1987. Perhaps the clearest lesson of October 1987 is that Tribe and other cultural radicals misused words and symbols ("civil rights," "equality," "privacy," "choice") which Americans cherish to make the case against the jurist most likely to thwart continued advances for cultural relativism and anti-democratic elite policy objectives. They knew exactly what they were doing—and they did it well.

In her analysis of the grass roots aspects of the Bork confirmation battle, Amy Moritz asserts conservatives were "out-mobilized at the grass roots level by the Left." I'm not sure that's true. The battle was not lost in the trenches of heartland America, but in the halls of power in Washington, D.C. Moritz's point raises an interesting corrollary: The Left did mobilize faster and on a broader front than did Bork's conservative supporters.

Nevertheless, by the end of the battle conservatives delivered the grass roots of America to the in box of the United States Senate. But that was never enough: To win, Judge Bork needed the all-out support of not only the working class and middle class soldiers of the movement, and the vigorous hard work of the Department of Justice's legislative people, which he got except when their hands were tied (that's another book someone else will have to write). He also needed the help of conservative and other elements in the rest of the Reagan coalition: corporate America, the Republican establishment (the Republican National Committee, the Senatorial Campaign Committee and so forth) and a total effort from the entire Senate GOP leadership, not just the usual champions. None of these elements delivered at a level equal to that of the conservative movement, and even the outside pro-Bork coalition delivered imperfectly (for example, never developing the capablity to do any meaningful paid advertising).

Why did Will Ball and other moderate elements in the Reagan Coalition not deliver, why did Chief of Staff Baker and others in the Republican establishment fail to deliver in this most important nomination? I cannot answer all the questions, and frankly I still don't have enough evidence on Baker to speculate fairly.

But for Will Ball and company, the answer is simple. For them, the Bork battle was just another little moment in their career in Washington politics. When this "Supreme Court thing" was over, Will and his friends needed to go back to their quiet dinners, where they cut deals and trade principles for the sake of ephemeral "victories". When Ronald Reagan is long gone, these guys will go back to cushy Washington consultants' jobs where they can quietly—and a bit less conspi-

culously than Michael Deaver—sell their expertise to the highest bidder.

Such judgements may seem harsh, but it is hard to find another explanation for the studied neglect the White House legislative operation afforded the confirmation of Bob Bork.

A final criticism, of President Reagan himself, is in order. A magnificently capable politician, he nonetheless did what was easy at several points in his presidency. As his conservative allies noted at the time, the selection of a moderate conservative woman jurist in 1981 was easy politics. And, the selection of a conservative Italian-American in 1986—with Robert Bork still in the wings—was, as his allies noted at the time, easy politics. Selecting Robert Bork third (fourth, including Rehnquist's elevation to Chief) was doing it the hard way. A politician with Reagan's remarkable political instincts should have known better. For the sake of constitutional restoration on the Supreme Court, the order of selection should have been exactly the opposite—or at least Bork should have preceded Scalia. These observations come despite the general defense I have offered in numerous settings for the jurisprudence of both Justices Scalia and O'Connor.

Reagan himself must bear responsibility not only for the belated nature of Bork's selection, but for the lack of determination and clarity in the subsequent White House strategy for confirmation. The twin facts of Democrat control of the Senate and Ronald Reagan's political vulnerability in the wake of the Iran-contra hearings led to months of uncharacteristic detachment and lackluster performance by the President. In essence, he picked a fight, then left the field, leaving the battle to out-numbered guerilla fighters who continued desparately to hope, until his disappointing performance at the door of the helicopter on October 9, that he would lead us up the Hill one more time. Sincere appreciation for the leadership and principles of this man, whom I supported for the presidency beginning in 1975, cannot restrain this judgment of his performance on the most important domestic policy confrontation of his presidency.

(For all that he bore in the President's poor performance in his own confrontation, Judge Bork himself critiqued the "unjustified loss of morale" afflicting conservatives at the end of the Reagan era. Giving Reagan the credit he is due for generally keeping his eye on the ball, Bork wrote for National Review [August 5, 1988]:

A major achievement, due in large measure to the much-maligned Ed Meese, has been the re-orientation of the federal judiciary. Care was taken to select judges who understand that judging is not politics. The constitutional philosophy of original understanding, and the judicial restraint it begets, have become a public issue. A time may even come when the liberal policy-making of modern courts will be as discredited as the conservative policy-making of the courts before 1937 now is.)

In a wide-ranging interview in Policy Review in the fall of 1988, former Secretary of Education William Bennett compared the defeat of Bork to the late collapse in Ronald Reagan efforts to support the Nicaraguan freedom fighters. Commenting on the Administration's failure to push aggressively for Bork when the nomination struggle became difficult, he told Adam Meyerson:

> *For some reason, we didn't make the case, we didn't get our team together, we didn't push hard enough . . . I would guess as with the Contras, it was because some people in the administration didn't have their hearts in it. It was disgraceful what the Senate did to Judge Robert Bork. It was a terrible thing to happen to one of the most distinguished legal minds in America. It was a real job of sabotage and smear. There is a lesson here: in politics, sometimes you have to think low and act high. You can't underestimate the degree of self-interest and politicization in the Senate and House. As Justice Brandeis told his daughter: As soon as you believe that life is difficult and hard, things will be all the smoother for you. Assume there is going to be trouble with everything, that nothing is going to go through unchallenged. Assume that the nomination of a very distinguished legal mind is going to be controversial. And be ready. Prepare more of the case than you think you are going to need, because you are probably going to need it.*

Some conclusions[535]

In sum, what lessons can conservatives draw, looking back on the Bork battle? We should never, in order to "grow up" in politics, give up our ideals. But there are some clear modes of operation, principles of politics or whatever, that stare me in the face as I look back on the Bork confrontation.

The first is clear: "If you would have peace, prepare for war." The great historian Gibbon put it this way: "They preserved the peace by a constant preparation for war and while justice regulated their conduct, they announced to the nations on their confines that they were as little disposed to endure as to offer an injury."

While conservatives can hope for a restoration of a civil and principled judicial confirmation process, they must prepare for every confir-

mation battle to be the legislative equivalent of a senatorial campaign, complete with high dollar media expenditures, vigorous negative advertising and polemical theatrics. The very act of preparation may prevent such confrontations, and I hope it does. (I speak as someone who spent nearly a year of my life focusing on crafting the arguments to prevent the emergence of a baldly political judicial confirmation structure.)

A critical part of this preparation includes assembling broad ongoing coalitions in the states comparable to those formed on the Left. In order to be effective, such coalitions must include representatives from disparate conservative interests—businessmen, Christian activists, law enforcement and others.

The second lesson is drawn from the teachings of my friend Dan Casey: It's time to hang some scalps on the wall. The conservative movement got used to relying on the Republican political structure to achieve many of its goals—but what do you do, then, when the third ranking Republican in the Senate joins the assault on your nominee? Presumably you don't give him the primary "pass" John Chafee got in the 1988 election that followed the Bork battle.

Politics is about many things: idealism, realism, policy, people. But in the real world of governing, politics is ultimately about elections. Even legislative politics is ultimately about elections. Even if the pro-Bork forces eventually outdid the other side at the grass roots, the combined force of the paid media advertising (which did shift "soft" popular opinion away from Bork) and explicit threats of political retaliation from the Left led the typical southern Democrat to conclude, with John Breaux of Louisiana: "If I vote against Bork, I'll make the conservatives mad for a week, and civil rights groups happy for ten years."

Although conservatives cannot point to dramatic short-term scalps from the Bork battle, some modest results appear reasonably clear. George Bush demonstrated (as discussed above) an ability to define judicial and legal issues with clarity in his contest with Michael Dukakis. In the 1988 senatorial elections, the pro-life movement supported Montana Democrat John Melcher's opponent for the first time, telling allies in the Reagan-Bush-Quayle coalition that Melcher's opposition to Bork was their primary motivation. Melcher was defeated by Republican Conrad Burns. Further, Wyoming Republican Malcolm Wallop, who has had only a mixed pro-life voting record throughout his career, for the first time received ardent support from the pro-life movement in his reelection campaign against a Democrat whose record on abortion was at least mixed. Wallop won with only some 1,000 votes to spare. Finally, William F. Buckley and (late in the campaign) George Will pointed to Republican Lowell Weicker's opposition to Bork as a key factor in the decisions of thousands of Connecticut conservatives to support Democrat Joseph Lieberman (who had indicated he could have supported Bork, and who ran distinctly to Weicker's right on moral and cultural issues).

Third, conservatives should assume that some liberals, at least such organizations as People for the American Way and unprincipled demagogues such as Ted Kennedy, will lie. They will lie because they correctly perceive *the threat conservative victories hold for the substantial "territory" liberals still control. Further, they will lie with big multi-million dollar megaphones called paid advertising and free media (the evening news and so forth). In her* Fortune *magazine analysis of the battle entitled "Winning One from the Gipper", Ann Reilly Dowd described the Judiciary Committee's rejection of Judge Bork as "partly a Norman Lear production." Conservatives must accept the burden of acquiring media megaphones just as big as Norman Lear's, and using those megaphones to tell the truth.*

A friend, Peggy Noonan, wrote me after the Bork battle. A veteran of the news business, she thanked me for my strong efforts for Bork, saying she was "quite moved not only by the size of your efforts but by the passion with which you worked. When I saw [in the first memo of the battle], 'That for which we exist [is upon us]' I thought: Oh boy, is this going to be a fight." But she admonished me:

> *I'm more sensitive to the rhetorical elements of a fight than the strategic and organizational aspects, and for all the right's complaining about the wild unfairness of Ted Kennedy's speech on the Senate floor "In Robert Bork's America . . . ", we may have missed this central fact: It worked. That sound bite of Kennedy's speech was repeated over and over and nice, average, not-too-political citizens saw it and heard it and the steady drum beat finally convinced them . . . [The next] time the right should answer in kind, matching tone for tone and blow for blow. I think this is one of those rare cases in which if the left gets mean the right should be just as mean, if not more so. In nice neat soundbites that can be easily cut and used by network producers who want to make tonight's show more dramatic and compelling.*

A fourth lesson is closely related to the foregoing point about the use of symbols and media. It is simply this: Conservatives should have the wherewithall to win the truly essential battles even without the help of the incumbent Administration and the party organizations. Bork's confirmation was so important it deserved ultimate expenditures from his supporters at least the equivalent of what the opponents made. The conservative dependence upon the woefully lethargic decision-making process in the Administration and the Republican party committees proved fatal.

Fifth, eradication of the American Bar Association from the judicial evaluation process must become a unified "no negotiations" position for principled advocates of both fair play and conservative political views.

Sixth, counter productive and counter intuitive non-starters such as Will Ball should be dismissed immediately in future administrations, before they have a chance to be central inactive figures in important policy and personnel confrontations. Losing a good fight is one thing— refusing to engage in a good fight is another.

Seventh, Ronald Reagan never marshalled the army only he could have deployed in this confrontation—the army encompassing the entire Reagan Coalition of 1976, 1980 and 1984, all elements of the conservative movement, the Republican party apparatus and the financial wherewithall to prevail. He did not take counsel as to whether he could prevail in anything other than an all-out fight for restoration of the Constitution, the rule of law and traditional American values.

Eighth, for all the foregoing it is conceivable that the Bork battle was lost on Election Day 1986. Senate control was arguably the central deciding factor in the most significant domestic policy confrontation of the Reagan presidency. When it counted, there turned out to be two Democrats who valued the rule of law more than — or at least as much as—their own futures in the Democrat caucus. When, despite Iran-contra, it was clear that Ronald Reagan himself would not follow Lyndon Johnson, Richard Nixon and Jimmy Carter into the political despair of failed presidencies, the organized Left steeled itself for an all-out struggle to deny Reagan at least one fundamental accomplishment. Not surprisingly, Judge Bork was a convenient target.

A ninth lesson I draw from a Wall Street Journal *editorial (February 21, 1989) during the controversy surrounding the Senate's consideration of John Tower's nomination to serve as Secretary of Defense. While not concurring in the* Journal's *conclusions on John Tower, it is hard to quibble with the writer's succinct description of the meaning of the Bork battle for conservatives—and potentially ominous implications for the nation:*

Senate confirmation procedures lost the presumption of seriousness in the Bork lynching . . . To anyone left of center the Bork defeat has become the kind of totem the Hiss case once was: a hypocrisy that must be defended precisely because it was so monumental. Yet the bottom line remains: a majority of Senators decided that although Judge Bork participated in more than 400 cases on the nation's important appellate court without a single reversal, he was outside the "mainstream" of judicial thought. Or at least, so the Senators professed.

Tenth, and finally, conservatives who believe God is in control need to remember another aspect of struggles like these. The apostle Paul observed for believers: "We are not among those who draw back and perish, but among those who have faith and live." (Hebrews 10:39) Despair can have no permanent place in the vocabulary of those seeking, not perfection on earth, but a political system a bit better than the one we inherited. At the height of the battle, after the Judiciary Committee rejection of Bork, the editor of Conservative Digest called me and asked, "Pat, what do you do when you've done everything you can do?" With a peace I'd not felt in days, I told him, "I pray." Those committed to the rule of law in our beloved land—and who also believe God is in control—need to remember the spirtual and personal dimensions of such battles on this earth. It is all too easy to become embittered beyond recognition by the heartbreak of losses such as that which Bork endured.

Yes, those committed to reforming the law should be ready to do the practical work of making sacrifices of time, writing letters and making phone calls, and sending money to those most actively engaged in the confrontations which still lie ahead. But from here on in, I for one will remember Paul's admonition, "pray without ceasing." (1 Thessalonians 5:17) Politics and public life, even something so fundamental as the restoration of constitutional law, is not what is most important in our lives. As the Christian writer Gerry Rauch observed, "We do not seek utopia but God himself, who is greater than any utopia."

This story of the Bork battle, and the compilation of recollections, impressions and lessons drawn from it, is preliminary and utterly incomplete. And much of the stress is, perhaps too heavily, on the shortcomings of The White House's part of that pro-Bork effort.

The dedication and fervor of Bork's most principled Senate champions (Hatch, Humphrey, Simpson, McClure, Danforth and many others) is neglected here, primarily because my objective was to tell the story of the "outside" groups, and to draw what lessons I could from that story and from data generally available through 1988.

There are no words to express the sadness I felt personally for Judge Bork and his family at the end. The pain lingers in my heart more than a year later, as I close this text. When I finally, intellectually, accepted the inevitable before the final vote, I wept not only for Judge Bork, his family, his friends, his supporters; not only for myself and my colleagues in the cause of judicial reform—not only for these, but also for my country.

Many of us are weeping still.

References

1. Washington *Post*, June 28, 1987, p.A10.
2. *ABA Journal*, August 1, 1987, p.48.
3. Washington *Post*, June 27, 1987, p.A1.
4. *Id.*
5. *Id.*
6. Washington *Post*, July 2, 1987, p.A1.
7. Washington *Post*, July 12, 1987, p.A7.
8. Washington *Post*, June 29, 1987, p.A1.
9. The Senator said then: "I think the advise-and-consent responsibility of the Senate does not permit us to deprive the president from being able to appoint that person who has a particular point of view unless it can be shown that his temperament does not fit the job, that he is morally incapable or unqualified for the job, or that he has committed crimes of moral turpitude . . . I do not think that under the Constitution I have a right to say I will not vote for someone to be on the Supreme Court . . . because I disagree with the view that he holds on a particular issue." *See also,* McGuigan and O'Connell, eds., *The Judges War: The Senate, Legal Culture, Political Ideology and Judicial Confirmation* (Washington, D.C.: Free Congress Foundation, 1987), p. 22, n. 41.
10. Washington *Times*, June 29, 1987, p.A1. Biden's reversal of his previously statesmanlike stance might have been triggered by devastating critiques of his past performance on judicial nominations. The most notable of these was Andrew Kopkind's essay "Down and Out in L.A.," *The Nation*, March 14, 1987. Kopkind, whatever his political inclinations, cannot be accused of lack of intestinal fortutitude. When Arthur J. Kropp of People for the American Way wrote a letter to *Nation* defending Biden, Kopkind responded:

> . . . Ted Field, a board member of People for the American Way, is one of the biggest contributors to Biden's presidential campaign and . . . Field's money-dispenser and political adviser, Bob Burkett, was an important figure in the early years of the organization, when he held a similar advisory position with Norman Lear. He is now a member of the organization's board and executive committee. Readers of the "Letters" column should know that these epistles don't float in from some unseen hand, but often come carrying excess political baggage, and entail real interests of money and position.

Kopkind then went on to articulate his complaints about Biden's performance as a legislative tactician. See *The Nation*, May 9, 1987.

11. New York *Times*, July 3, 1987, p.A1.
12. Washington *Times*, June 29, 1987, p.A1.
13. Washington *Post*, July 1, 1987, p.A9.
14. Washington *Post*, July 2, 1987.
15. Richmond *Times-Dispatch*, July 2, 1987, p.A16.
16. New York *Times*, July 3, 1987.
17. New York *Times*, June 29, 1987, p.A14.
18. Washington *Post*, June 30, 1987, p.A7.
19. Washington *Times*, June 29, 1987, p.A1.
20. Washington *Post*, June 30, 1987, p.A7.
21. *Time*, July 13, 1987, p.10.
22. Washington *Post*, June 30, 1987, p.A7.
23. New York *Times*, June 29, 1987, p.A14.
24. *Eleanor Smeal Report*, June 28, 1987, Vol. 5, No. 1, p.1.
25. Washington *Post*, July 1, 1987, p.A1.
26. *New York Times*, July 9, 1987, p.A24.
27. Washington *Times*, June 30, 1987, p.A1.
28. New York *Times*, July 2, 1987, p.A1.
29. *Time*, July 13, 1987, p.10.
30. Washington *Times*, June 30, 1987, p.A1.
31. *Time*, July 13, 1987, p.10.
32. *Id.*
33. Statement of President Reagan during nomination of Judge Bork, July 1, 1987. Readers desiring a relatively brief exposition of Judge Bork's mature judicial philosophy are encouraged to read Appendix B in this book, the transcript of a long interview I conducted with Bork in September 1985.
34. New York *Times*, July 2, 1987, p.A1.
35. Washington *Post*, July 2, 1987, p.A1.
36. New York *Times*, July 2, 1987, p.A1.
37. Washington *Post*, July 2, 1987, p.A1.
38. *Id.*
39. Washington *Times*, July 3, 1987.
40. *Congressional Record*, Senate, July 1, 1987, p.S9188.
41. Washington *Times*, August 14, 1987.
42. Washington *Times*, July 16, 1987.
43. New York *Post*, July 7, 1987.
44. Washington *Post*, July 2, 1987, p.A1.
45. Washington *Times*, July 2, 1987, p.A1.
46. People for the American Way press release, July 1, 1987.
47. *Judicial Notice*, May 1986. (*Judicial Notice* is now incorporated into the monthly newsletter, The Free Congress *Family, Law & Democracy Report*.) For most of the material from the exchange between Nan Aron and myself, *see C-SPAN Update*, July 20, 1987, and the recording of that July 2 show.
48. Philadelphia *Inquirer*, November 16, 1986.
49. *Congressional Quarterly*, July 4, 1987, p.1429.
50. Washington *Post*, July 12, 1987, p.A7.
51. Washington *Post*, July 3, 1987.

52. Baltimore *Sun*, July 3, 1987, p.8A.
53. Washington *Times*, July 9, 1987, p.A2.
54. Washington *Times*, July 14, 1987.
55. *Newsweek*, July 20, 1987, p.30.
56. Washington *Post*, July 9, 1987, p.A21.
57. *Legal Times*, July 13, 1987, p.1.
58. *Id.*
59. *Id.*
60. *Id.*
61. *Id.*
62. *Judicial Notice*, June 1986, p.18. The incident prompted us to hold a contest offering "the reader who finds the greatest number of typos in this issue. . . dinner at the moderately priced Washington restaurant of his or her choice, at the Editor's expense." A New York psychiatrist won the contest, finding a handful of typos in the 16 page issue.
63. *Legal Times*, July 13, 1987, p.1.
64. *Id.*
65. Washington *Times*, June 27, 1987, p.A1.
66. *USA Today*, July 3, 1987, p.A4.
67. Washington *Post*, July 7, 1987, p.A4.
68. *Id.*
69. Washington *Times*, July 27, 1987, p.A1.
70. Washington *Post*, July 7, 1987, p.A4.
71. Washington *Times*, July 27, 1987, p.A1.
72. Washington *Post*, July 6, 1987, p.A3.
73. Washington *Post*, July 7, 1987, p.A4.
74. Washington *Times*, July 7, 1987.
75. Washington *Times*, July 8, 1987.
76. Washington *Times*, July 7, 1987.
77. Washington *Times*, July 8, 1987.
78. New York *Times*, July 10, 1987.
79. Washington *Post*, July 10, 1987, p.A1.
80. Washington *Times*, July 6, 1987.
81. Washington *Times*, July 27, 1987, p.A1. However, see n. 238 below.
82. St. Petersburg *Times*, July 3, 1987, p.18A.
83. Raleigh *News & Observer*, July 3, 1987, p.24A.
84. Washington *Post*, July 2, 1987, p.A1.
85. Washington *Times*, July 1, 1987, p.A14.
86. Arlington (VA) *Journal*, July 2, 1987, p.2.
87. Bismark *Tribune*, July 2, 1987. Robert Bork had worked for President Nixon as U.S. Solicitor General for only four months before Nixon, in the heat of the Watergate crisis, demanded that Attorney General Elliott Richardson fire special Watergate prosecutor Archibald Cox. Richardson resigned rather than do so. The job fell to Deputy Attorney General William D. Ruckelshaus, who also refused and quit. On October 20, 1973, Bork obeyed the order, fired Cox, and became acting attorney general. Leon Jaworski was named Cox's successor.
  The day before the White House announced Bork as the nominee, Richardson, who now practices law, broke years of silence on the incident to go public with his defense of Bork's action. "I had asked the legal counsel to check whether Nixon had the right

to fire Cox,'' Richardson said. ''The legal counsel concluded that he did. Therefore, we thought Bork could do the right thing and deliver that message: Bork deserves a lot of credit for standing up to Nixon and telling him to appoint another special prosecutor.'' (Washington *Times*, June 30, 1987, p.A10.) Bork critics said that Cox had become Bork's victim during his ''Saturday Night Massacre.'' Bork said he toyed with the idea of quitting after the Cox firing because ''I did not want to be perceived as a man who did the President's bidding to save my job.'' (*USA Today*, July 2, 1987, p.A2.) Richardson explained that he had had to convince Bork to stay with the Justice Department:

''On the so-called ''Saturday Night Massacre,'' [Bork's] original intention was to resign, along with [Deputy Attorney General William D.] Ruckelshaus and me, but we convinced him not to do so. We told him the [Justice] Department was under great pressure and needed his leadership, and that he had no comparable reason to resign. We eventually persuaded him to stay, which meant he had to fire Cox. Bork thought the firing of Cox wasn't justified, because Cox was carrying out his function under the charter guaranteeing independent investigation and it was a mistake for the White House to try to get rid of him.'' (Washington *Times*, June 30, 1987, p.A10.)

During Bork's confirmation hearings for the U.S. Circuit Court of Appeals in January 1982, Senator Max Baucus (D-MT) had asked him to explain the Watergate episode to the Judiciary Committee. ''There was never any possibility that the discharge of the special prosecutor would . . . hamper the investigation or the prosecutions of the special prosecutor's office,'' Bork testified. ''Neither the President nor anyone else at the White House ever suggested to me that I do anything to stop or hinder in any way those investigations. If I had been asked to do that, I would not have done it.'' Bork explained that he had had ''to contain a very dangerous situation, one that threatened the viability of the Department of Justice and other parts of the executive branch.'' With the resignations of Richardson and Ruckelshaus, ''there was nobody after me in the line of succession,'' Bork said. ''The only thing that weighed against doing what I did was personal fear of the consequences, and I could not let that, I think, control my decision.'' (Washington *Post*, July 2, 1987.)

88. *Time*, July 13, 1987, p.11.

89. Washington *Post*, July 2, 1987.

90. Boston *Globe*, July 26, 1987, p.72.

91. Washington *Times*, July 27, 1987, p.A1.

92. *USA Today*, July 3, 1987, p.A4. Somehow these remarks conveyed to some readers the impression that I expected the conservative efforts to be well-funded. In fact, I learned yet again to watch what you say to reporters—my words were used in a People for the (un)American Way fundraising letter mailed out a short time later as supposed evidence of how well-funded the pro-Bork effort was going to be.

A short time later, *Legal Times* reported Coalitions for America would have ''$150,000 to spend'' in support of Bork. I wrote the editor a note explaining, ''I have no plans to spend $150,000 on the Bork fight. In contrast, the *total annual budget* of Coalitions for America is roughly that figure. If I am lucky, I will be able to massage (other than my own time) a few thousand dollars for the Bork fight. Beyond that, I have a xerox machine and an intern . . . [T]hat may not be particularly glamorous, but it reflects the realilty of how I operate in these confirmation battles.'' The impression that conservative organizations were loaded in advance of the battle, in conjunction with initial beliefs among most donors that there was no way Bork could be defeated, combined to thwart permanently the desperate efforts of those of us in the pro-Bork leadership to convince our allies that huge infusions of cash were needed to offset the steadily building liberal advantage in resources.

93. Washington *Post*, July 7, 1987, p.A4.
94. Washington *Times*, July 27, 1987, p.A1.
95. Washington *Times*, July 2, 1987.
96. Washington *Post*, July 7, 1987, p.A4.
97. Washington *Times*, July 27, 1987, p.A1.
98. Washington *Post*, July 7, 1987, p.A4.
99. Washington *Times*, July 27, 1987, p.A1.
100. *Id.*
101. Washington *Post*, July 7, 1987, p.A4.
102. *Legal Times*, July 13, 1987, p.1.
103. Washington *Times*, July 16, 1987. Neither Kennedy nor Metzenbaum dwelled, of course, on the fact that Bork had never been reversed by the High Court—and that the justices had adapted many of Bork's views in their own opinions. Months after the confrontation, Dewey Stokes of the Fraternal Order of Police (FOP), who worked extensively in support of Bork (including several meetings working on Metzenbaum himself), stressed to me his view that "the Democrats feared Bork's brain-power, his ability to persuade those other guys, more than anything else."
104. Washington *Post*, July 6, 1987, p.A1.
105. New York *Times*, July 16, 1987, p.A27.
106. *Legal Times*, September 14, 1987, p.12.
107. Washington *Post*, September 14, 1987, p.A3.
108. *Legal Times*, September 14, 1987, p.12.
109. Washington *Times*, July 3, 1987. Ironically, the two pillars of judicial reform thought had not personally met until a 1982 conference in Washington, D.C. For Berger's glowing praise of Bork on that occasion, *see* Patrick B. McGuigan and Claudia A. Keiper, eds., *A Conference on Judicial Reform: The Proceedings* (Washington, D.C.: Free Congress Foundation, 1982), pp. 127–31.
110. Washington *Times*, July 3, 1987.
111. Washington *Times*, July 6, 1987, p.D1.
112. New York *Post*, July 6, 1987, p.1.
113. Washington *Post*, July 2, 1987, p.A20.
114. Washington *Times*, July 7, 1987, p.A1. DeConcini took increasing side-swipes at Bork throughout the summer, suggesting the Committee look into his alleged "heavy drinking".
115. Washington *Times*, July 7, 1987, p.A1.
116. *Legal Times*, August 10, 1987, p.1.
117. *Id.*
118. *Id.*
119. Washington *Times*, July 7, 1987, p.A1.
120. *Id.*
121. Washington *Times*, July 9, 1987, p.A2.
122. "Transcript of Proceedings," United States Senate, Committee on the Judiciary, S.332, S.789, S.430, S.558, Business meeting, Washington, D.C. July 9, 1987, p. 47.
123. Washington *Times*, July 9, 1987, p.A2.
124. Washington *Times*, July 10, 1987.
125. Detroit *News*, July 10, 1987, p.14A.
126. San Gabriel *Valley Tribune*, July 14, 1987.

127. Washington *Times*, July 9, 1987.

128. Washington *Times*, July 16, 1987.

129. This retroactive application of selective liberal "ethics" became characteristic of liberal tactics during the battle. The idea seemed to be "throw it against the wall and see what sticks. Even if it doesn't stick, it helps muddy the waters and undermines Bork's greatest strength—his reputation for integrity."

Christic Institute lawyers had asked the U.S. Circuit Court's three-judge panel to force then-Attorney General William French Smith into launching an investigation of what they claimed was the Justice Department's participation in a Ku Klux Klan attack in 1979 on civil rights activists in Greensboro, North Carolina. In a June 4, 1984 ruling against the institute, Bork had said there was no private right of action to compel use of the Ethics in Government Act, which allows special prosecutors to conduct inquiries on top government personnel. Sheehan, who had not protested Bork's hearing of the case at the time, complained to reporters that Bork should have excused himself because he had fired special prosecutor Archibald Cox during the Watergate scandal, the incident which promted passage of the independent counsel law. Sheehan also argued that Bork had engaged in conflict-of-interest because in 1973 he had spoken before the House and Senate Judiciary Committees on proposed bills that in 1978 became the Ethics in Government Act. Bork "had a judicial and professional responsibility to recuse himself," Sheehan argued. "Nobody ever suggested that [I rescuse myself], including counsel," Bork said. "It was never brought up." Besides, there was no conflict-of-interest involved in relation to his testimony before lawmakers on ethics issues, said Bork. "The statute involved [in the 1984 case] was not the same statute I testified on 14 years ago," he said, adding, "Constitutionality was not an issue in this case." Geoffrey Hazard Jr., a judicial ethics expert and professor at Yale Law School, agreed with Bork. "If he's expressed an opinion on the [independent counsel] issue, then involvement in the same legal issue is not disqualifying." (*Legal Times*, September 13, 1987.)

The Christic Institute was among the more bizarre participants in the Bork opposition coalition. The organization has concocted an incredible conspiracy theory about CIA and other governmental involvement in drug trafficking. Their assault on former Army Major General John Singlaub—a Racketeer Influenced and Corrupt Organizations (RICO) civil suit dismissed in June 1988—was described by legal analysts as "legal terrorism." For more on this organization, adept at raising money for itself while forcing its targets to spend hundreds of thousands of dollars to defend themselves, *see* Michael Hedges, "Christic's 'fairy tale' lawsuit called 'legal terrorism,'" June 28, 1988 and Mark Hosenball, "The Ultimate Conspiracy," Washington *Post*, September 11, 1988. Eventually, the Christics were hit with a devastating judgment against their legal terrorism, when federal District Judge James Lawrence King ordered them to pay Singlaub and other victims $1 million in legal costs. *See* William Bole, "Christic Institute Fights to Survive," Washington *Post*, February 11, 1989, and Reed Irvine, "King Crushes Christics," Washington *Inquirer*, February 10, 1989.

130. *Legal Times*, July 13, 1987, p.2. *See also* McGuigan and O'Connell, eds., *The Judges War*, pp. 21–34.

131. *Legal Times*, July 13, 1987, p.2.

132. The cases involved: *Russoniello v. Olagues*, in which it was argued that a probe of voter fraud had included only foreign-born voters who used bilingual ballots; *Hartigan v. Zbaraz*, challenging an Illinois abortion law; *Webster v. Doe*, on whether the Court should review the circumstances around the firing of a "gay" employee; *Reagan v. Abourezk*, on the denial of United States visas to communists; *Karcher v. May*,

challenging a moment of silence law in New Jersey's public schools; *McKelvey v. Turnage*, challenging the Veterans Administraton's refusal to provide educational funding to an alcoholic. (*Legal Times*, August 3, 1987, p.1.)

133. *Legal Times*, July 13, 1987, p.2.
134. New York *Times*, July 13, 1987, p.A12.
135. Washington *Times*, July 15, 1987.
136. Washington *Post*, July 16, 1987, p.A9.
137. Washington *Times*, July 17, 1987.
138. Denver *Post*, July 19, 1987, p.8A.
139. *American Press International*, August 11, 1987, p.16.
140. Washington *Post*, July 23, 1987, p.A9.
141. For the Weyrich comments on Bork in mid-July, *see* UPI story in *Deseret News*, July 15, 1987, p. A4. The Yard comments are in Washington *Times*, July 20, 1987, p.A5.
142. Washington *Times*, July 20, 1987.
143. Washington *Post*, July 23, 1987, p.A9.
144. Washington *Post*, July 18, 1987, p.A4.
145. *USA Today*, July 23, 1987, p.4A.
146. *United Press International*, July 23, 1987.
147. New York *Times*, July 23, 1987.
148. Washington *Post*, June 23, 1987, p.A9.
149. New York *Times*, July 24, 1987, p.A12.
150. Washington *Post*, July 29, 1987, p.A23.
151. Washington *Times*, July 27, 1987, p.A4.
152. New York *Post*, July 27, 1987.
153. Washington *Times*, July 28, 1987, p.A3.
154. Washington *Post*, July 30, 1987.
155. Washington *Times*, July 30, 1987.
156. Washington *Times*, August 3, 1987.
157. *National Law Journal*, August 10, 1987, p.S–2.
158. Washington *Post*, August 4, 1987, p.A3.
159. Washington *Times*, August 3, 1987.
160. Washington *Post*, September 4, 1987, p.A23.
161. Washington *Post*, August 11, 1987, p.A4.
162. Washington *Post*, August 11, 1987, p.A4.
163. *USA Today*, September 4, 1987.
164. Washington *Post*, August 11, 1987, p.A4.
165. Washington *Post*, August 5, 1987, p.A20.
166. Washington *Times*, August 5, 1987.
167. Washington *Times*, August 5, 1987.
168. *Id.*
169. Washington *Post*, August 4, 1987, p.A3.
170. Washington *Times*, August 5, 1987. The New York *Times* noted (August 6, 1987) that "One of the last beneficiaries of the 38–year-old 'fairness doctrine' was a man who had questioned its constitutionality and had helped pave the way for its demise on [August 4]: Judge Robert H. Bork." The News Director at Coalitions for America, Bill Kling, thought this "angle" was irresistable to reporters, and he proved right. We had developed the technique of seeking fairness doctrine or personal attack rule time during the effort to confirm Dan Manion to the Seventh U.S. Circuit Court of Appeals in 1986.

See McGuigan and O'Connell, *The Judges War*, Chapter 1, especially pp. 21–34, and p. 39, n. 68.

171. Washington *Post*, August 4, 1987, p.A3.

172. Washington *Times*, August 6, 1987. It is interesting to note that the anti-Bork advertisements sapped liberal groups of much of their Bork budgets, but conservative organizations, such as Coalitions for America, received free advertising under the Fairness Doctrine, which was repealed during the later months of the Bork battle. However, the overall liberal resource advantage remained overwhelming.

173. Washington *Post*, August 6, 1987, p.A8.

174. *Id.*

175. Washington *Times*, September 8, 1987.

176. Washington *Post*, August 11, 1987.

177. Washington *Times*, August 18, 1987, p.A2.

178. Washington *Times*, August 11, 1987.

179. *Id.*

180. Washington *Times*, August 12, 1987.

181. *Id.*

182. *Time*, August 24, 1987, p.16.

183. New York *Times*, August 12, 1987, p.A17.

184. Washington *Post*, August 13, 1987, p.A3.

185. Ralph Adam Fine, "Justice Bork: Helping to Restore a Proper Balance," *Wall Street Journal*, August 12, 1987. *See also*, Washington *Times*, August 12, 1987.

186. Washington *Times*, August 14, 1987.

187. *Id.*

188. *Id.*

189. *Id.*

190. *National Review*, August 28, 1987, p.11.

191. Washington *Times*, August 18, 1987, p.A2. Eventually, however, communications supporting Bork overwhelmed the opposition—but too late for Bork's sake.

192. Washington *Times*, August 19, 1987, p.A4.

193. Washington *Post*, August 23, 1987.

194. Washington *Post*, August 23, 1987, p.A4.

195. *Time*, August 24, 1987, p.16.

196. UAW-CAP-CDAC ALERT, August 24, 1987.

197. *American Press International*, August 21, 1987, p.17.

198. Washington *Post*, August 26, 1987, p.A4. The failure of this effort to come anywhere near its announced objectives was a crucial factor, in the month that followed, in the collapse of hope among the pro-Bork coalition.

199. Washington *Times*, August 26, 1987.

200. Washington *Times*, August 24, 1987, p.A3.

201. Washington *Times*, August 28, 1987.

202. Dallas *Morning News*, August 29, 1987, p.20A.

203. New York *Times*, August 30, 1987.

204. Washington *Times*, September 2, 1987.

205. New York *Times*, August 30, 1987.

206. Washington *Inquirer*, August 28, 1987, p.1.

207. James Carl Hefley, *The Truth in Crisis, Volume 3: Conservative Resurgence or Political Takeover?*, p. 132, available from Hannibal Books, 31 Holiday Drive, Hannibal, MO 63401. *See also*, American Legislative Exchange Council, resolution regarding the

Bork nomination, August 30, 1987. Executive Director William Myers wrote the ALEC measure.

208. Washington *Post*, September 1, 1987, p.A4.

209. *Wall Street Journal*, March 11, 1986.

210. San Francisco *Chronicle*, August 31, 1987.

211. *American Press International*, August 31, 1987, p.1.

212. Los Angeles *Times*, September 3, 1987.

213. *Knightline*, September 1, 1987, p.2.

214. National Legal Aid & Defender Association, letter to supporters, September 2, 1987, p.1.

215. Washington *Times*, September 3, 1987.

216. Washington *Post*, September 4, 1987, p.A3.

217. Washington *Post*, September 4, 1987, p.A2.

218. *American Press International*, September 4, 1987, p.1.

219. *USA Weekend*, September 4–6, 1987, p.6.

220. James Carl Hefley, *The Truth in Crisis*, Volume 3, p. 132. *See also*, New York *Daily News*, September 6, 1987.

221. Richmond *News Leader*, September 8, 1987, p.15.

222. *Legal Times*, September 14, 1987, p.6.

223. Philadelphia *Inquirer*, September 13, 1987, p.6A.

224. *USA Today*, September 8, 1987.

225. Philadelphia *Inquirer*, September 13, 1987, p.6A.

226. Philadelphia *Inquirer*, September 13, 1987, p.7A.

227. *Legal Times*, September 14, 1987, p.2. The last comment indicated either a complete lack of familiarity with Bork's productivity level, or deliberate and mean-spirited distortion.

228. *Legal Times*, September 14, 1987, p.2.

229. Washington *Post*, September 15, 1987, p.D1.

230. *Legal Times*, September 14, 1987, p.6.

231. *American Press International*, September 14, 1987, p.1.

232. Washington *Post*, September 9, 1987, p.A3.

233. Washington *Post*, September 9, 1987, p.A3.

234. Washington *Post*, September 10, 1987, p.A20.

235. *American Press International*, September 7, 1987, p.8.

236. *American Press International*, September 7, 1987, p.8.

237. Washington *Blade*, October 2, 1987, p.1

238. *American Press International*, September 7, 1987, p.8. Despite Mike Edwards' indications about low expenditures, lobbying filings later showed a $70,000 NEA contribution to PAW's effort against Bork, in addition to the "in kind" items sketched here.

239. *NEA Today*, September, 1987, p.19.

240. *American Press International*, September 7, 1987, p.9.

241. *American Press International*, September 7, 1987, p.10.

242. New York *Times*, September 11, 1987.

243. Washington *Times*, October 6, 1987, p.A5.

244. *National Law Journal*, September 21, 1987, p.4.

245. *American Press International*, September 9, 1987, p. 1.

246. Washington *Times*, September 11, 1987.

247. Washington *Times*, September 11, 1987.

248. Washington *Post*, September 25, 1987, p.A23.
249. New York *Times*, September 11, 1987.
250. *Legal Times*, September 14, 1987, p.15. For background on the ABA committee's treatment of Reagan judicial nominees, and the left-leaning record of Committee members determined to see that many Reagan nominee became "controversial" nominees with "mixed ratings", *see especially* Daniel J. Popeo and Paul. D. Kamenar, "The Questionable Role of the American Bar Association in the Judicial Selection Process," in McGuigan and O'Connell, eds., *The Judges War*, pp. 177–191.
251. Washington *Times*, September 10, 1987, p.A1.
252. Houston *Chronicle*, September 10, 1987.
253. *USA Today*, September 10, 1987, p.4A.
254. Washington *Post*, September 10, 1987, p. A1.
255. Washington *Times*, September 10, 1987, p.A11.
256. Washington *Post*, September 10, 1987, p.A1.
257. Washington *Times*, September 11, 1987.
258. White House issue brief, "Judge Bork and Criminal Justice," p.1.
259. Washington *Times*, September 11, 1987. Hodel spoke at the Coalition for America at Risk meeting organized by Scott Stanley of *Conservative Digest*.
260. Los Angeles *Times*, October 4, 1987.
261. Dallas *Morning News*, October 4, 1987, p.H–2.
262. Washington *Times*, September 11, 1987.
263. Washington *Post*, September 13, 1987, p.A39.
264. Washington *Post*, September 15, 1987, p.D10.
265. *Legal Times*, September 14, 1987, p.20.
266. *American Press International*, September 11, 1987, p.17.
267. New York *Times*, September 13, 1987, p.A14.
268. *Id.*
269. Washington *Post*, September 13, 1987, p.A7.
270. New York *Times*, September 17, 1987, p.B12.
271. New York *Times*, September 17, 1987, p.B12.
272. Washington *Post*, September 13, 1987, p.A6.
273. Washington *Times*, September 14, 1987.
274. New York *Times*, September 13, 1987, p.A14.
275. Washington *Post*, September 14, 1987.
276. New York *Times*, September 13, 1987, p.A14.
277. *Judicial Notice*, September 1987, p.3.
278. Cleveland *Plain Dealer*, September 13, 1987.
279. *USA Today*, September 14, 1987.
280. Washington *Times*, September 14, 1987, p.A1.
281. Washington *Times*, September 14, 1987, p.A1.
282. Washington *Post*, September 14, 1987, p.A3. Specter's views as the hearings began are also sketched ably in Philadelphia *Inquirer*, September 13, 1987.
283. Washington *Post*, September 17, 1987, p.A27.
284. Washington *Post*, September 15, 1987, p.A19.
285. *Wall Street Journal*, October 14, 1987, p.72. What appeared in the TV ad was actually the Senate steps at the U.S. Capitol. Supreme Court security guards would not allow filming at the High Court. In fact, Capitol police almost ran the director off the Capitol grounds—but Senator Byrd, passing by, gave permission for the filming.
286. *American Press International*, September 23, 1987, p.16.

287. *American Press International*, September 29, 1987, p.6.
288. Georgetown *Law Weekly*, September 14, 1987, p.1.
289. Washington *Post*, September 14, 1987, p.A3.
290. *Newsweek*, August 24, 1987, p.12.
291. *USA Today*, September 16, 1987, p.8A.
292. *American Press International*, September 15, 1987, p.1.
293. *Id.*
294. *Id.*
295. Washington *Post*, September 16, 1987, p.A14.
296. Washington *Times*, September 16, 1987. For a readable, relatively brief sketch of Judge Bork's judicial philosophy, read my interview with him (conducted in 1985), printed here as Appendix B.
297. Washington *Post*, September 16, 1987, p.A14.
298. Washington *Times*, September 16, 1987, p.A11.
299. Washington *Post*, September 16, 1987, p.A14.
300. *USA Today*, September 16, 1987, p.8A.
301. Washington *Times*, September 16, 1987, p.A1.
302. Washington *Post,* September 16, 1987, p. A14.
303. *USA Today*, September 16, 1987, p.8A.
304. *USA Today*, September 29, 1987.
305. Washington *Times*, September 16, 1987.
306. Washington *Post*, September 16, 1987.
307. *Id.*
308. *American Press International*, September 16, 1987, p.4–5.
309. Washington *Times*, September 17, 1987, p.A11.
310. New York *Times*, September 17, 1987, p.B10.
311. *Id.*
312. *Id.*
313. Washington *Times*, September 17, 1987, p.A11.
314. *Id.*
315. New York *Times*, September 17, 1987, p.A1.
316. New York *Times*, September 17, 1987, p.B10.
317. New York *Times*, September 17, 1987, p.B11.
318. *Id.*
319. New York *Times*, September 17, 1987, p.B10.
320. *American Press International*, September 16, 1987, p.5.
321. New York *Times*, September 17, 1987, p.B11.
322. Washington *Post*, September 17, 1987, p.A16.
323. *American Press International*, September 18, 1987, p.8.
324. *USA Today*, September 18, 1987.
325. *American Press International*, September 17, 1987, p.2.
326. *USA Today*, September 24, 1987.
327. Washington *Post*, September 18, 1987.
328. Washington *Times*, September 21, 1987.
329. Washington *Post*, September 18, 1987, p.A10.
330. *American Press International*, September 17, 1987, p.1.
331. *American Press International*, September 17, 1987, p.1.
332. Transcript of Senate Judiciary Committee hearings on Bork nomination, September 17, 1987.

333. *Id.*
334. Washington *Post*, September 18, 1987, p.A10.
335. Washington *Post*, September 18, 1987, p.A1.
336. Washington *Post*, September 18, 1987, p.A10.
337. Washington *Times*, September 18, 1987, p.A11.
338. Washington *Post*, September 18, 1987, p.A10.
339. Washington *Times*, September 18, 1987, p.A11.
340. *American Press International*, September 18, 1987, p.6.
341. Washington *Post*, September 19, 1987, p.A10.
342. Washington *Post*, September 19, 1987, p.A1.
343. Washington *Post*, September 19, 1987, p.A11.
344. *American Press International*, September 21, 1987, p.16.
345. Washington *Times*, September 22, 1987.
346. *Id.*
347. Washington *Post*, September 20, 1987, p.A16.
348. Washington *Post*, September 20, 1987, p.A17.
349. *Id.*
350. Washington *Post*, September 20, 1987, p.A16.
351. Washington *Post*, September 16, 1987, p.A14.
352. Washington *Post*, October 5, 1987, p.A4.
353. Washington *Times*, September 22, 1987, p.A3.
354. *Wall Street Journal*, September 22, 1987.
355. *American Press International*, September 24, 1987, p.2.
356. Detroit *Free Press*, September 20, 1987, p.7B.
357. Washington *Post*, September 20, 1987, p.A17.
358. *American Press International*, September 21, 1987, p.3.
359. New York *Times*, September 21, 1987, p.B14.
360. James Carl Hefley, *The Truth in Crisis*, Volume 3, p. 131. *See also*, *Legal Times*, September 28, 1987, p.10.
361. Washington *Post*, September 22, 1987, P.A8.
362. Washington *Times*, September 22, 1987, p.A11.
363. Washington *Post*, September 22, 1987, P.A8.
364. *USA Today*, September 22, 1987, p.10A.
365. Washington *Post*, September 24, 1987, p.D3.
366. *USA Today*, September 22, 1987, p.10A.
367. *Id.*
368. *Id.*
369. Washington *Times*, September 22, 1987, p.A1.
370. Washington *Post*, September 22, 1987, p.A1.
371. Washington *Post*, September 22, 1987, P.A8.
372. *USA Today*, September 22, 1987, p.10A.
373. Washington *Post*, September 22, 1987, P.A8.
374. Washington *Times*, September 23, 1987.
375. New York *Times*, September 23, 1987, p.A28. For my discussion of Tribe's mendacious testimony, see Appendix A.
376. Washington *Times*, September 23, 1987.
377. Washington *Post*, September 23, 1987.
378. New York *Times*, September 23, 1987, p.A28.
379. *Id.*

380. Washington *Post*, September 23, 1987.
381. Washington *Post*, September 23, 1987.
382. New York *Times*, September 23, 1987, p.A28.
383. *Id.*
384. Washington *Times*, September 23, 1987.
385. *USA Today*, September 23, 1987.
386. Washington *Post*, September 23, 1987.
387. *American Press Interational*, September 23, 1987, p.1
388. *Id.*
389. *American Press International*, September 23, 1987, p.3.
390. *Id.*
391. Washington *Times*, September 24, 1987, p.A1.
392. *Id.*
393. Washington *Post*, September 24, 1987, p.A3.
394. Washington *Times*, September 24, 1987, p.A1.
395. Teamsters news release, September 23, 1987.
396. Washington *Post*, September 25, 1987, p.A16. Some of the groups later recanted their opposition, or denied it had ever been offered, but the damage had been done.
397. *Ms.*, September 1987, p.111.
398. Washington *Post*, September 25, 1987, p.A16.
399. *Id.*
400. *American Press International*, September 24, 1987, p.17.
401. *Wall Street Journal*, October 7, 1987, p.1.
402. Washington *Post*, September 25, 1987, p.A1.
403. *American Press International*, September 28, 1987, p.4.
404. Washington *Times*, September 24, 1987. For a more detailed and critical analysis of media coverage of the Bork battle, see R.H. Bork, Jr.'s essay in this book.
405. Washington *Post*, September 26, 1987, p.C1. *See also,* Manchester (N.H.) *Union Leader* September 26, 1987, p. 5.
406. Washington *Post*, September 26, 1987, p.A6. Ironically, at the same conference where Robert Bork and Raoul Berger first met, Meserve gave a very "Borkian" summary of reasons for opposing the congressional use of Article III, section 2 powers in the Constitution to restrict the powers of federal courts. *See* McGuigan and Keiper, eds., *A Conference on Judicial Reform: The Proceedings*, pp. 31–35.
407. Washington *Post*, September 26, 1987, p.A6.
408. *Id.*
409. New York *Times*, September 27, 1987, p.D23.
410. The *Plain Dealer*, September 27, 1987, p.A1.
411. Arizona *Republic*, September 28, 1987, p.A1.
412. *Id.*
413. Arizona *Republic*, September 28, 1987, p.B5.
414. Washington *Post*, September 29, 1987, p.A10.
415. *Id.*
416. *Id.*
417. Washington *Times*, October 21, 1987, p.A6.
418. Washington *Times*, September 29, 1987, p.A10.
419. *Wall Street Journal*, September 30, 1987.
420. Washington *Post*, September 29, 1987.
421. Washington *Times*, September 29, 1987, p.A1.

240   REFERENCES

422. *Id.*
423. Washington *Post*, September 29, 1987.
424. *Congressional Record*, September 28, 1987, p.1467.
425. Washington *Post*, September 29, 1987.
426. *Id.*
427. Washington *Times*, September 29, 1987, p.A1.
428. Washington *Post*, September 29, 1987.
429. Washington *Times*, September 29, 1987, p.A1.
430. Washington *Times*, October 1, 1987, p.A1.
431. Washington *Post*, September 29, 1987, p.A1.
432. Washington *Post*, September 30, 1987, p.A1.
433. *Id.*
434. *Id.*
435. *American Press International*, September 29, 1987, p.1.
436. Washington *Post*, September 30, 1987, p.A4.
437. *American Press International*, September 30, 1987, p.2.
438. Washington *Times*, October 1, 1987, p.A1. Among those coming out against Bork in the last days of September was Senator Daniel Patrick Moynihan of New York. Although we had always listed him as a probable no, we continued to hope his intellectual vigor might bring him our way—but when he announced his opposition on September 29, he linked it to the pedestrian, traditional Senate pork barrel, saying part of the reason was the Administration's refusal to nominate Columbia University Law Professor Peter Strauss to the U.S. District Court in Manhattan.
439. Washington *Post*, September 30, 1987, p.A4.
440. Washington *Times*, October 1, 1987, p.A1.
441. *USA Today*, October 1, 1987, p.4A.
442. *Id.*
443. Washington *Times*, October 1, 1987, p.A1.
444. *USA Today*, October 1, 1987, p.4A.
445. Washington *Times*, October 1, 1987, p.A1.
446. *American Press International*, September 30, 1987, p.5.
447. Washington *Times*, October 1, 1987, p.A1.
448. *USA Today*, October 1, 1987. *See also*, James Carl Hefley, *The Truth in Crisis*, Volume 3, p. 133.
449. Washington *Times*, October 2, 1987, p.A1.
450. *Wall Street Journal*, October 7, 1987, p.1.
451. Washington *Times*, October 2, 1987, p.A1.
452. Washington *Post*, October 5, 1987, p.A15.
453. Washington *Times*, October 2, 1987, p.A1.
454. *American Press International*, October 2, 1987, p.17.
455. Miami *Herald*, October 4, 1987, p.16A.
456. Of the 28 Senators listed in our analysis of October 2, we actually secured the votes of only four: one Democrat (David Boren) and three Republicans (Cohen, Evans and Hatfield). Reagan's radio address was covered in Miami *Herald*, October 4, 1987, p.16A.
457. *USA Today*, October 5, 1987.
458. Washington *Post*, October 5, 1987, p.A4.
459. *American Press International*, October 5, 1987, p.2.
460. Washington *Post*, October 6, 1987, p.A1.

461. *Id.*
462. Washington *Post*, October 5, 1987, p.A15.
463. Washington *Post*, October 5, 1987, p.A7.
464. *USA Today*, October 6, 1987, p.9A.
465. Washington *Times*, October 7, 1987, p.F5.
466. Washington *Times*, October 6, 1987, p.A5.
467. Washington *Times*, October 7, 1987, p.A1.
468. Dallas *Morning News*, October 4, 1987, p.H–2.
469. Washington *Times,* October 6, 1987, p.A5
470. Washington *Times*, October 7, 1987, p.A1.
471. *Id.*
472. Washington *Times*, October 6, 1987, p.A5.
473. *Wall Street Journal*, October 7, 1987, p.1.
474. *American Press International*, October 6, 1987, p.1.
475. Washington *Times*, October 7, 1987, p.A1.
476. *Wall Street Journal*, October 7, 1987, p.66.
477. Washington *Times*, October 7, 1987, p.A1.
478. *Id.*
479. Washington *Post*, October 7, 1987, p.A1.
480. *USA Today*, October 7, 1987.
481. Washington *Post*, October 8, 1987, p.A1.
482. Ville Platte (LA) *Gazette*, October 8, 1987.
483. *USA Today*, October 8, 1987, p.6A.
484. Washington *Post*, October 8, 1987, p.A1.
485. Washington *Post*, October 9, 1987, p.A1.
486. *Id.*
487. *American Press International*, October 9, 1987, p.1.
488. Washington *Post*, October 10, 1987.
489. Boston *Sunday Globe*, October 11, 1987.
490. *American Press International*, October 9, 1987, p.17.
491. Washington *Times*, October 12, 1987, p.A1.
492. Boston *Sunday Globe*, October 11, 1987.
493. Washington *Post*, October 11, 1987, p.A1.
494. Washington *Times*, October 12, 1987, p.A1.
495. *American Press International*, October 12, 1987, p.16.
496. Washington *Times*, October 13, 1987, p.A1.
497. Id.
498. Washington *Post*, October 14, 1987, p.A1.
499. *American Press International*, October 14, 1987, p.1.
500. *American Press International*, October 14, 1987, p.17.
501. *USA Today*, October 16, 1987, p.4A.
502. *American Press International,* October 16, 1987, p.4.
503. *USA Today*, October 16, 1987, p.4A.
504. *American Press International*, October 17, 1987, p.14.
505. Washington *Post*, October 18, 1987.
506. *American Press International*, October 19, 1987, p.7.
507. New York *Times*, October 19, 1987, p.A31.
508. *American Press International*, October 19, 1987, p.7.
509. *American Press International*, October 21, 1987, p.16.

510. Washington *Times*, October 19, 1987, p.A1.

511. *American Press International*, October 20, 1987, p.1.

512. *American Press International*, October 21, 1987, p.1.

513. *Id.*

514. *American Press International*, October 22, 1987, p.1. In the pages that follow, I have not sketched in any detail the course of the final Senate debate. Whereas Bork's outside supporters reacted still with hope during the hearings before the Judiciary Committee—thus making the hearings a central part of this story—by the time of the final confrontation on the Senate floor we knew we would lose, and I, too, was largely a spectator. In this book my purpose has been explicitly to tell the story of the outside groups who worked for Bork. I must leave to others the no doubt intriguing tale of the internal Senate discussions about the course of the nomination. For the historical record, I must say, however, the Congressional Records for October 21, 22 and 23 are must reading.

515. *Id.*

516. Washington *Times*, October 22, 1987.

517. *American Press International*, October 23, 1987, p.1. Here, according to the New York *Times* (October 24, 1987), is the final vote on the Bork nomination:

FOR CONFIRMATION—42

Democrats—2

Boren, Okla.   Hollings, S.C.

Republicans—40

Armstrong, Colo.	Dole, Kan.	Hatfield, Ore.	Lugar, Ind.	Roth, Del.
Bond, Mo.	Domenici, N.M.	Hecht, Nev.	McCain, Ariz.	Rudman, N.H.
Boschwitz, Minn.	Durenberger, Minn	Heinz, Pa.	McClure, Idaho	Simpson, Wyo.
Cochran, Miss.	Evans, Wash.	Helms, N.C.	McConnell, Ky.	Stevens, Alaska
Cohen, Me.	Garn, Utah	Humphrey, N.H.	Murkowski, Alaska	Symms, Idaho
D'Amato, N.Y.	Gramm, Tex.	Karnes, Neb.	Nickles, Okla.	Thurmond, S.C.
Danforth, Mo.	Grassley, Iowa	Kassebaum, Kan.	Pressler, S.D.	Trible, Va.
	Hatch, Utah	Kasten, Wis.	Quayle, Ind.	Wallop, Wyo.
				Wilson, Calif.

AGAINST CONFIRMATION—58

Democrats—52

Adams, Wash.	Cranston, Calif.	Harkin, Iowa	Melcher, Mont.	Riegle, Mich.
Baucus, Mont.	Daschle, S.D.	Heflin, Ala.	Metzenbaum, Ohio	Rockefeller, W. Va.
Bentsen, Tex.	DeConcini, Ariz	Inouye, Hawaii	Mikulski, Md.	Sanford, N.C.
Biden, Del.	Dixon, Ill.	Johnston, La.	Mitchell, Me.	Sarbanes, Md.
Bingaman, N.M.	Dodd, Conn.	Kennedy, Mass.	Moynihan, N.Y.	Sasser, Tenn.
Bradley, N.J.	Exon, Neb.	Kerry, Mass.	Nunn, Ga.	Shelby, Ala.
Breaux, La.	Ford, Ky.	Lautenberg, N.J.	Pell, R.I.	Simon, Ill.
Bumpers, Ark.	Fowler, Ga.	Leahy, Vt.	Proxmire, Wis.	Stennis, Miss.
Burdick, N.D.	Glenn, Ohio	Levin, Mich.	Pryor, Ark.	Wirth, Colo.
Byrd, W.Va.	Gore, Tenn.	Matsunaga, Hawaii	Reid, Nev.	
Chiles, Fla.	Graham, Fla.			
Conrad, N.D.				

Republicans—6

Chafee, R.I.	Specter, Pa.	Stafford, Vt.	Warner, Va.	Weicker, Conn.
Packwood, Ore.				

518. *American Press International*, October 23, 1987, p.3.

519. *American Press International*, October 23, 1987, p.1.

520. *New York Times*, October 24, 1987, p.A1.

521. Ann Reilly Dowd, "Winning one from the Gipper," *Fortune* Magazine, November 9, 1987, p. 128.

522. Herman Schwartz, *Packing the Courts*, (New York, Charles Schribner's Sons, 1988), p. 132.

523. Dowd, "Winning one from the Gipper," p. 128.

524. *Id.*

525. Joe Klein, "The Old Frontier," October 19, 1987, p. 26.

526. *Id.*

527. *Id.*

528. Schwartz, *Packing the Courts*, p. 135.

529. Klein, p. 26.

530. Schwartz, *Packing the Courts*, p. 136.

531. *Id.*

532. Transcript, "Point of View," October 6, 1987.

533. Terry Eastland, "What Next for Justice Department?" *Legal Times*, October 31, 1988. *See also*, Schwartz, p. 132.

534. Amy Moritz, "Conservatism's Parched Grass Roots," *Policy Review*, Spring 1988.

535. As this book was finished in 1989, a variety of shorter studies of the Bork confrontation appeared, as well as two other books: Robert H. Bork, *The Tempting of America*, Free Press; and Ethan Bronner, *Battle for Justice: How the Bork Nomination Shook America*, W. W. Norton. Useful shorter works include Grover Joseph Rees III, "The Next Bork," *National Review*, December 9, 1988; Stanley C. Brubaker, "Rewriting the Constitution: The Mainstream According to Laurence Tribe," *Commentary*, December 1988; F. L. Morton, "The Bork Affair: Politics as Usual or Constitutional Crisis?" revised version of paper presented at the 1988 Annual Meeting of the American Political Science Association, Washington, D.C.: September 1–4, 1988; Stephen M. Griffin, "Politics and The Supreme Court: The Case of the Bork Nomination," Journal of Law & Politics (Spring 1989). pp. 551–604.

The Media, Special Interests, And The Bork Nomination

R. H. Bork, Jr.

"[A] good deal of our reporting was sloppy and simply inaccurate. Sometimes we journalists take great joy and pride in challenging (or attempting to challenge) the statements of high government officials. I feel it is quite clear that we failed to challenge many of those who made statements regarding your nomination. . . . [W]riting a story for a network news broadcast is somewhat akin to writing a majority opinion. We have half a dozen editors who feel they have not earned their salaries unless their two cents worth of editorial wisdom appears in every story. Most of what we write is often written in haste. And, as with occasional opinions at the Court, sometimes the finished report produces neither heat nor light, only smoke."

> —From a March 1988 letter to Judge Robert Bork
> by Tim O'Brien, Supreme Court Correspondent,
> ABC News

Doubtless everyone seeing these words has read a newspaper story or viewed a television piece, and, having an intimate personal knowledge of the subject, realized how inaccurate, biased, shallow, or otherwise inadequate the journalist's account is.

In the city where I live and work, Washington, D.C., such occurrences are common. Yet they never fail to upset because they point out simply and directly the awful reality of the business: There is no truth, only impressions and opinions filtered through the minds of the source,

245

the writer, and the editor. I suppose that is why most reporters I know seldom read their own work after it is published and do not linger in those chilling moments of realization.

As a member of the Washington press corps for two years, the experience was more frequent than I liked. During the four months between June 26 and October 23, 1987, it was almost a daily unpleasantness. These were 120 days when I had to balance my allegiance, affection, and belief in the essential integrity of my chosen profession with the constant misguided, unintelligent, and dishonest reporting about my father, Judge Robert Bork.

The problem of the poor reporting about my father and his views is more important than the anguish it caused our family to see him pilloried day after day in the press. The reason it remains important two years after his defeat by the Senate and the ultimate confirmation of Justice Anthony Kennedy is that in 1989 a new administration took office. President Bush most likely will have three Supreme Court vacancies to fill, perhaps more. Three justices were over 80 years old on January 20, 1989. The Left, pleased with the results of my father's confirmation, says it will employ the same tactics and techniques again if conservative candidates are nominated. (In fact, they were used in 1988 in the case of federal appeals court nominee Bernard Siegan.) The Right, stung by its defeat, has sworn vengeance and will no doubt plagiarize the methods used against my father should the nominees be liberals. Both sides will look to the media to carry their disinformation to the people. By showing how and why the media failed, it is my hope that the press will be more skeptical next time.

Let me be clear that by examining the relationship between special interests and the media I am not arguing that my father should have been confirmed; there could be, and was, honest opposition to his nomination. And I am not suggesting that the media was solely responsible for the outcome; I have been in the news business too long to think that the messenger should be held exclusively culpable for the results of a negative message designed and propagated by others. However, I contend that my father was caught in the politics of the media age in which image becomes reality. In this way, the media became an unwitting accomplice in some cases, and a willing ally in others, of those special interest groups that did not want an honest debate and in that way contributed to the outcome.

Partisan Press

There were not many black and white cases of the most egregious sorts of unethical behavior by the press. There were not, for example, cases of breaking and entering, or theft of documents. The hoards of reporters and photographers who kept a sporadic vigil outside my father's house generally were polite and did not trample the flower beds. Even the two motorcyclists and a driver who tailed us constantly for the television networks during the week of the Judiciary Committee vote, were very nice. Attempts to shake our pursuers at changing traffic lights and with unsignaled turns provided the few light moments of that tension-filled week. One of motorcyclists—*CBS's* I believe— even gave us a "thumbs-up" as we left the White House after my father's October 9 statement that he would carry on to a full Senate vote.

There were, however, a few serious instances of journalistic mendacity worth noting:

• Nina Totenberg, legal affairs correspondent of *National Public Radio*, deliberately used a sound-bite from an interview with former Associate Attorney General William Ruckelshaus out of context, creating a false impression that he was contradicting former Attorney General Elliot Richardson's and my father's version of events during the Saturday Night Massacre. She stuck to her fiction despite Ruckelshaus' repudiation of her version.

• Al Kamen, Supreme Court reporter of the *Washington Post*, refused to print my father's response to an accusation of misconduct made against him by another federal judge even though he had interviewed my father and one of his clerks. Kamen had both sides of the story and chose to print only one.

• David Beckwith, *Time's* White House correspondent, mistakenly described my father as an "agnostic." He subsequently refused to change that depiction even after my father corrected it. Consequently, my father's later statements about his faith were cast in the media as "denials" of his agnosticism.

• Finally, the *City Paper*, a free Washington weekly, invaded my father's privacy when it obtained his video rental records and published them.

These pieces were not without consequence. Ms. Totenberg's fabrication provided "proof" of my father's dishonesty about his role in the Massacre to which senators and other critics pointed. Mr. Beckwith's mistake allowed Senators Howell Heflin (D-Ala.) and Bennett Johnston (D-La.) to include my father's supposed lack of religious belief and their constituents' concern in their bogus litany of reasons to vote against his confirmation (despite the fact that considering a nominee's religious beliefs is unconstitutional). This was no small thing in the South as the *Washington Post* pointed out in a prominently placed front-page story. And Heflin even tried to cover his backside by issuing a radio actuality (that is, a recorded statement) in which he cited my father's "strange lifestyle" and "refusal to discuss his belief in God, or lack thereof."

Worse than these examples of journalistic misconduct, however, was an insidious and pervasive lack of objectivity that can be attributed to the influence of powerful special interest groups on the mind of the media.

Some of my colleagues in the press have warned me not to use the "O-word," or if I do, to define it. Indeed, objectivity can be a slippery term, for what is objective reporting to one observer is biased and subjective to another. Let me then offer a simple, and I hope non-controversial definition: By objectivity I simply mean fairness; applying equal scrutiny to the statements and claims of both sides during the debate for accuracy or truthfulness, not just one. That was a first principle of journalism when I got into the business in 1976.

This lack of objectivity took many forms. Often it was a sin not of commission but of omission—the absence of fairness, indeed the absence of any critical coverage of the claims made by the well-funded special interest machine. Other times it was an unbalanced presentation of opposing views; the trouble here was that too often the media applied different degrees of scrutiny leading to unfair coverage. Always, it seemed that it was a state of mind in which reporters allowed their biased expectations to invade their coverage.

How that state of mind was cultivated by my father's opposition is critical to understanding the coverage. While it was happening there were few overt signs. But in the months since the nomination was defeated, the architects of the strategy have been unable to restrain themselves and now are outspoken about their methods. In fact, one of the leaders taught a course at Harvard's Kennedy School of Government in the autumn of 1988 which was essentially a primer on the subject.

By some accounts, the anti-Bork planning effort was established after Ronald Reagan's election in 1980. Liberal law and special interest groups worried that my father would be the new president's first choice for the Court. Indeed, it was well reported that he had been on the short list for the vacancy created by William O. Douglas' retirement in 1975 which was filled by John Paul Stevens. And when Sandra Day O'Connor was nominated in 1981, administration officials told the media that but for the president's promise to name a woman to the Court, my father would have been the choice.

Planting Seeds

The concentrated and coordinated anti-Bork planning began in November 1984. American University law professor Herman Schwartz in his book *Packing the Court* (Charles Scribners Sons, New York) explains that fear of four more years of Reagan judicial appointments led to a meeting at which he, Nan Aron of the Alliance for Justice and William Taylor decided to organize the "public-interest community." The meeting was held on November 19, 1984 and a new organization, the Judicial Selection Project, was formed. Its members included many of those who would take prominent roles in the Bork opposition: the Leadership Conference on Civil Rights, the NAACP, the Women's Legal Defense and Education Fund, and others.

During the next three years, the groups grooved their organizational and rhetorical strokes on the controversial but ultimately successful nominations of Alex Kozinski, Sid Fitzwater, and Daniel Manion to the federal bench, and Justice William Rehnquist to be chief justice of the Supreme Court. Others they were able to block included Jefferson Sessions III, Kenneth Porter, Michael Horwitz, and Lino Graglia (the latter two were not even officially nominated).

So when my father was named on July 1, 1987, those who would oppose his nomination were energized, practiced, and ready. The Judicial Selection Project prepared a three-page memo for editorial writers which was mailed by People for the American Way along with one of its own to 1,700 newspapers. In fact, the day before the White House announcement, the Leadership Conference on Civil Rights (LCCR), under the direction of Ralph Neas, its executive director, organized the first meeting of a coalition of 40–plus special interest groups to oppose my father. Before long the coalition under Neas' direction had enlisted some 300 groups, thus proving Alexis de Toqueville's axiom, "The effective force of any power is increased in proportion to the centralization of its control."

Had Toqueville been prescient about American politics in the 1980s, he might have added, "and the bounty in its coffers." Money poured in to LCCR's offices. The AFL-CIO and the United Auto Workers each contributed $40,000. The Service Employees Union donated $20,000 as did the United Food and Commercial Workers. There were also large donations from individuals like Aaron Fischer, a St. Louis businessman, who gave $58,500, and Washington, D.C. author Phillip Stern who donated $10,000. Counting only contributions of $500 or more, LCCR received almost $260,000 in the three months from July through September and another $74,000 from October through December. That was far more than the group had collected in the preceding six months.

Norman Lear's People for the American Way proved to be the real money machine; from July through September it collected $1.6 million. Much of it came in large chunks like the $75,000 gift from the National Education Association and $20,000 from the AFL-CIO.

And the American Civil Liberties Union, which provided much of the legal manpower for the opposition, raised $1 million.

Exactly how much was collected isn't known. But Arthur Kropp, PAW's executive director, said his group sent out a test mailing to 541,000 potential contributors in July. The response was so strong that it quickly mailed another 3.8 million appeals for donations. Dozens of groups kept the presses rolling day and night issuing appeals for cash. The National Abortion Rights Action League got actress Joanne Woodward to ask its disciples for a quick $500,000.

"It's a fundraising bonanza," one political consultant marveled at the time. And Roger Craver, a direct-mail specialist who worked with several anti-Bork groups, said the Left collected $6 million through early September. He guessed that the figure would double by the final Senate floor vote.

Spending estimates for all the groups have been as high as $15 million. It is impossible to know the precise figure because virtually all the groups who lobbied against my father have failed to fully complete lobbying reports required by Congress and the Senate Secretary's office says it doesn't have the manpower to enforce the law. For example, ACLU operatives Morton Halperin, Jerry Berman, and Leslie Harris posed for a frontpage photograph in the *Legal Times of Washington* that declared them "ACLU shock troops," but there is no ACLU filing at the Senate Secretary's office detailing what the group spent in the offensive. In fact, the ACLU is listed as an inactive organization. This example is repeated by other groups such as NARAL, the Alliance for Justice, NAACP, and others who actively worked against my father's confirmation.

Despite the fact that many anti-Bork groups refuse to reveal how much they raised and spent in the effort, we do know where some of the money went. The Bork opposition put its overflowing warchest to good use. A $40,000 donation by the American Federation of State County and Municipal Employees was used to finance a survey by the polling firm of Marttila & Kiley—a company with close links to the Biden presidential campaign—to identify issues that most frighten

Americans. It set out to measure not only public opinion about the nomination and related issues, but also "to gauge the potential effect on voters' attitudes of many elements of Bork's record and background that have been subject to criticism in recent weeks." This was discerned not by honestly stating my father's views in the questions, but by twisting his opinions into a mean, almost Hitlerian tone. As most of those polled said they had little or no information or opinion about my father, this was easy to do. In other words, the task fell to the pollsters to find out which lies produced the biggest bang, or in the lingo of the political symbolism game, the most "cultural resonance."

There were three perfect harmonics, a supplemental analysis of the 47-page report determined. Not surprisingly, and as the groups clearly had expected, "Resistance to Bork seems to cluster around three main issue areas: civil rights; privacy, and individual freedom; and big business vs. the individual." Consequently the decision was made to focus on these.

This had to be done "without the traditional saber rattling and protest marches because that was not the impression we wanted," Arthur Kropp, executive director of People for the American Way, in April 1988 told an audience of public management students at the Stanford Graduate School of Business. "What the camera always focuses on is the most outlandish person in the demonstration. It detracts from the issue. . . . I believe we won because we had a good cause and because we presented it so that we didn't alienate but rather attracted people.

"It was an example of how mass media and marketing now play a dominant role. Once the progressives started using mass media and moving away from the old-fashioned politics of confrontation, the right wing began to lose its grip. What we did was be innovative in the area of marketing."

Beginning the first week in August, members of the coalition and Senate staffers began holding weekly meetings in Senator Kennedy's office to map strategy and share information. The scheme they devised was a masterwork of deceptive packaging that would have made Madison Avenue jealous. Hot-button issues like abortion rights, affirmative action, and gay rights that would have alienated the majority of Americans were cast in more palatable terms as marital right to privacy, right to use contraceptives, and civil rights. Therefore, divisive special interest issues of the late-1980s became, by proxy, the "old wounds"—settled issues of law and public policy—that my father would "reopen."

Shortly after the blueprint was drawn up, a blitzkrieg of anti-Bork television, radio, newspaper, and direct-mail advertisements began to appear. They were accompanied by a tidal wave of anti-Bork studies and press releases by such groups as the American Civil Liberties Union, the Feminist Men's Alliance, the Nation Institute, the National Abortion Rights Action League, and Planned Parenthood, all focusing primarily on the three areas Marttila & Kiley determined would most scare the public.

Marketing savvy was crucial to their success, but what the groups were selling the American people were false symbols based on lies about my father's record and philosophy. Indeed, as Thomas Sowell points out in his book *Conflict of Visions: Ideological Origins of Political Struggles,* dishonesty is a cornerstone of the "unconstrained vision," of the law, that is, judicial activism.

"The first thing a man will do for his ideals is lie," according to J. A. Schumpeter. It is one reason why sincerity is given such light weight in the constrained vision. A modern defense of judicial activism by Alexander Bickel clearly put more weight on sincerity than on fidelity, when it urged that "dissimulation" was "unavoidable" and referred to "statesmanlike deviousness" in the public interest.

Pulling Weeds

Conservative groups on the other hand were fewer in number, less well funded, and nowhere near as organized. At the time of my father's nomination, the conservative movement counted about 110 organizations among its ranks. Only about 15 of these had any interest or expertise in legal questions. The result was that at the height of the battle, odds were about 30 to 1 against him. In terms of manpower, they were even worse. Ralph Neas of LCCR and John Buchanan of PAW didn't have to lick envelopes. The principal leaders of the pro-Bork forces, Dan Casey, executive director of the American Conservative Union, and Pat McGuigan of Coalitions for America spent many nights stuffing envelopes.

And while People for the American Way was buying $100,000 spots on CNN, and placing $30,000 full-page ads in the *New York Times,* the *Washington Post* and other major market newspapers, the conservative Concerned Women for America—one of the most active pro-Bork groups—was able to purchase only a $425 newspaper ad in the *Montgomery Advertiser* and a $406 ad in the *Allentown Morning Call.* What PAW spent on one TV spot amounted to almost the Coalitions for

America's entire annual budget. McGuigan joked about it at one early press conference saying, "We haven't budgeted any money. Our [effort] may be low-tech, but it's high-brain."

There was a great deal of disarray on the right. For example, the National Rifle Association, one of the most powerful and sophisticated conservative lobbying organizations, never got behind my father. Despite his belief in the rights of gun owners and support of the death penalty, he opposed the exclusionary rule. This rule disallows the use of certain illegally obtained evidence in criminal trials. But it has been extremely useful dismissing charges against NRA members caught illegally transporting firearms across state lines.

While the Left launched a barrage of about 10 negative studies of my father's legal philosophy, the Right's counterattack was a single slim volume by the Center for Judicial Studies. Poor resources and production problems meant that it was issued virtually without notice the day before the hearings began. The Justice Department's thorough and masterly dissection of the anti-Bork studies also arrived too late, just four days before the hearings.

The only possible source of leadership, manpower, and conduit to money that could have drawn all the disparate efforts together, was the White House. But throughout the battle, virtually no substantive help and little encouragement was forthcoming. White House legislative boss, Will Ball, refused to consult with the President's strongest allies on the Hill and in the conservative movement, according to McGuigan. Even after a peace meeting between conservative groups, congressional aides and the White House staff at the Heritage Foundation, communication and coordination was sparse.

Chief of Staff Howard Baker was anxious about allowing the Justice Department to have any visible role in the confirmation. Consequently, Justice's staff—some of whom were intimately familiar with my father's record, having clerked for him—were forbidden from publicly representing the judge's views. Perhaps the press officer best suited for planning and executing a pro-Bork media plan, Terry Eastland, essentially was given a gag order by the White House.

As for political advertising to counter the Left's specious claims, the White House wanted no part of it. People For the American Way had Lincoln himself in the voice of Gregory Peck, to narrate its radio and TV messages. The White House could have had Moses or Dirty Harry. Both Charlton Heston and Clint Eastwood sent word that were ready and anxious to help. Neither was called.

Of course, the ultimate responsibility for the debacle rests with

President Reagan. When PAW began running newspaper and television advertisements against Manion's 1985 confirmation, the President got angry. He stopped in at a senior staff meeting in the Roosevelt Room one morning and told then Chief of Staff, Don Regan, "Don, those guys aren't going after Dan Manion, they're going after me. Confirm him." Regan may have been a son-of-a-bitch, but he knew how to play hardball with Congress and so did Patrick Buchanan, then director of communications. Manion was confirmed by a vote.

Yet during the Bork battle, despite Reagan's public statement that the confirmation was his "top domestic priority," no such order ever came. Even if it had, the President could field a team only capable of throwing marshmallows, from Baker and his deputy Ken Duberstein, to legislative aide Ball and communications adviser Tom Griscom. Compared to the studious research and planning by the anti-Bork coalition, it took Griscom more than a month to come up with a media plan for the nomination which then went largely unused. It should be remembered that as head of the Republican Senatorial Campaign Committee in 1986, Griscom presided over the GOP's loss of the Senate. His strategy then, as in my father's confirmation, was to avoid confrontation, avoid divisive issues, to punt.

Why was that? The only coherent explanation comes from McGuigan. "For most of the White House staff," he writes, "the Bork battle was just another little moment in their careers in Washington politics. . . . When Ronald Reagan is long gone, these guys will go back to their cushy Washington consultants' jobs. . . ." Translation: they didn't have passion; they weren't believers in the importance of the nomination. The conservative groups had passion. And to their credit, so did the Left. But they also had money, manpower, organization, and most of all leadership.

While conservatives could do little beyond organizing the grassroots, the liberals were able to do that effectively plus direct their attention at influencing the media. What's more, they were able to generate huge amounts of fresh, newsworthy analysis; there seemed to be a new "newspeg" for another anti-Bork story every few days. By contrast, the conservatives seemed to be singing a tired refrain. Nothing bores the media more than people who keep repeating the same argument, even if it is true.

Harvesting the Crop

What effect did mendacious market research have on the media? Lyndon Johnson once said that, "Reporters are puppets. They simply respond to the pull of the most powerful strings." From my special perspective as both a journalist and a witness to this event, I think LBJ was right.

For example:

• Newspaper and television advertisements by People For the American Way said that my father favored racially discriminatory poll taxes, and literacy tests. He never has. What he did do was criticize *Harper v. Virginia Board of Elections,* a 1966 Supreme Court case which invalidated Virginia's $1.50 poll tax. However, the decision had nothing to do with race or racial discrimination, as Justice Hugo Black wrote in his dissent. The accusation against my father regarding literacy tests stems from his criticism of the Court's 1966 *Katzenbach v. Morgan* decision. His sole objection to the case was over the issue of separation of powers between Congress and the Court to interpret the Constitution. This is also why he testified against the Human Life Bill which sought to apply *Katzenbach* to give Congress power to define fetuses and persons, thereby overruling the Court's 1973 *Roe v. Wade* decision. He never has favored discrimination in any form and in fact has a strong pro-civil rights record. You didn't read a critique of PAW's attack in the press or see one on the nightly news.

• An advertisement by Planned Parenthood said "Bork upheld a local zoning board's power to prevent a grandmother from living with her grandchildren because she wasn't part of the nuclear family. Is this the sort of extremist we want on the Supreme Court?" He never did any such thing. The case referred to is *City of East Cleveland v. Moore.* Not only was it an Ohio state court case that was appealed to the federal circuit for Ohio, but the case was finally decided by the U.S. Supreme Court in 1978. My father did not become a judge on the District of Columbia Circuit until 1982. He did not decide the case, has never written about it, taught it, or even spoken privately about it. You didn't see this exposed by the media.

• The Public Citizen Litigation Group—a Ralph Nader organization—issued a study characterizing my father's record on the bench as unwaveringly pro-business and pro-government. But in case after case, the study twisted the facts to support its premise. In a case in which my father ruled in favor of a labor union and against a federal agency, the PCLG determined it was pro-business because the union is in the business of representing workers. His expansive decisions upholding First Amendment freedom of the press cases were described as pro-business because newspapers, and other media are businesses. In two other cases, the study says he ruled in favor of business but fails to mention that all the parties in both cases were corporations. You didn't read about this either.

• The studies employed spurious methodology such as focusing on split decisions by the three-judge appeals court panel on which my father sat. These cases amount to only about 10 percent of his decisions. So when Public Citizen or ACLU says ". . . 92 percent of the time . . ." what they mean is that in 92 percent of 10 percent of his cases, or merely 9.2 percent of his overall record of decisions. If reporters had examined my father's complete record instead of accepting the studies as accurate, they would have discovered that he was part of a unanimous panel 90 percent of the time and in the majority 95 percent of the time. Therefore, he was in the minority in merely 5 percent of the cases before him. In addition, he had ruled with so-called liberal Judges Ruth Bader Ginsburg, Abner Mikva, Harry Edwards, and Patricia Wald 91, 82, 80, and 76 percent of the time, respectively. The media never explained these important qualifications to its readers and viewers.

The few times when the media chose not to simply accept his critics' assessment of his record and philosophy, and attempted its own pre-hearing analysis, the result was feeble and biased.

One of the worst attempts was *Time* magazine's piece entitled "The Law According to Bork," by Richard Lacayo in its cover package dated September 21. The piece announced "[O]ne thing is clear from his 25 years of unflinching and outspoken legal advocacy: he is not the mainstream legal thinker that the White House is now painting him to be." It was a premise Lacayo proved only by ignoring my father's record or twisting facts to suit his purpose. For example, Lacayo used the Ninth Amendment to prove that his refusal to find rights in the Constitution not intended by the framers was unfounded. Although Lacayo did note in passing that the Court had ignored the Ninth Amendment for 200 years, he declared that the justices had discovered it in the mid–1960s; something that is patently false. In fact, my father's reading of the Ninth Amendment has been that of the Supreme Court since its adoption. In so doing, Lacayo either demonstrated his own legal understanding to be outside the mainstream or that he was listening to those who were.

Lacayo was also master of the backhand slash, that is, parenthetically making a point not only without substantiation but in clear contradiction of the facts. Witness: "Because the core value of a free press is clearly part of the original intent of the First Amendment, he argues, judges in this instance can play an activist role—though he rarely advocates that role in most matters pertaining to the core value of racial equality." Had Lacayo investigated my father's record he would have found that as a federal appeals court judge he ruled for the minority or woman in civil rights cases before him 7 out of 8 times. And as solicitor general during the Nixon and Ford administrations he took the position of the civil rights plaintiff in 17 of 19 substantive cases that did not require him to defend the federal government.

Mr. Lecayo's article was accompanied by two caricatures by Seymour Chwast of my father. The first was a simple illustration of him speaking and gesturing; the second placed his head upside down on his shoulders. Mr. Lecayo can not be held responsible for this, although his article established a tone legitimizing the artistic interpretation, but *Time* went beyond illustrating that my father differed with other legal scholars about the Constitution. The implication was clear: my father was crazy.

The media also was obsessed with my father's background in personal life, culminating ultimately in the issue of his "compassion." (Never mind that judges are supposed to administer the law fairly and dispassionately.) Consequently, I gave several hours-long interviews to reporters who wanted to know about his paternal skills and our family life in New Haven. At first, this seemed reasonable to me and a way to help illustrate that my father was not the ogre he was being portrayed as.

However, I have since changed my mind about this media-measure of character. George Will has remarked that America's fascination with the personal lives of its leaders is the nation's way of determining whether or not to trust them. The issues that our leaders must resolve are so complex and beyond the ability of the average citizen to comprehend, in Will's formulation, that they now invest their trust in persons with whom they believe they would enjoy eating dinner.

I would go a step further: This now strikes me as a further sign of America's and the mass media's growing anti-intellectualism. Jacques Barzun called this the media's "technique of casualness" which is "derisive, suspicious, [and] faintly hostile . . . which characterizes the democratic ego when faced with Intellect."

Therefore, it shouldn't have been a surprise to me when my journalistic colleagues like Carl Cannon of *Knight-Ridder Newspapers* and Dale Russakopf of the *Washington Post* used virtually nothing of this son's proud recollections of his father. In fact, now that I think back on it, their questions were a quest for his failings, flaws, and foibles.

Barzun's analysis of this aspect of the media was made nearly thirty years ago, but seems even more apt today:

> Intellect, unless redeemed by the mystery of science or art, or again by the courage of adventure, as in the successful voyage of the Kon-Tiki, is equated with pretension and must even while acknowledged, be "whittled down to size." This is done by clever doubt—"raised eyebrows"—by understatement, or by interjecting a biographical fact calculated to lessen or inhibit admiration: the Nobel Prize winner wears a dirty sweater before lunch. This does duty for criticism and makes the subject seem "human." Never, in truth, has the educated population needed to be so often reassured about its distinguished fellow members being human. The world greets with approval any discovery of shortcoming, applauds the confession of mistakes, and indemnifies the spectator for any fleeting sense he may have of diminution by someone else's accomplishment. A truly modern dictionary would add an entry under "human": "The opposite of admirable". . . .

Hearings, But Not Listening

Having uncritically, unobjectively, and in some cases dishonestly reported the campaign against my father before the hearings, the reporters—some 100 of them—arrived on the morning of September 15 at the Senate Caucus Room to begin covering the confirmation hearings.

Immediately, the Democrats' not so subtle plan to manipulate the media coverage was apparent. Only weeks before, Lt. Col. Oliver North had won the hearts and minds of the American people in the same room. On television, clad in his Marine uniform and ribbons, photographed head-on and from slightly below, he was an heroic and sympathetic character. Meanwhile, the rows and rows of pin-striped senators and their staff appeared as ominous inquisitors. Fresh from that debacle, the Democrats on the Judiciary Committee dismantled their tiered desks, put themselves on the same level as my father and banned full-frontal shots of him. The cameras were moved off to one side and mounted on platforms so that they could peer down on the judge in profile, making him seem smaller, less formidable. A camera mounted in the rear of the room, however, could still get the full-facial expressions of the senators as they showed disbelief or dissatisfaction at his testimony.

The Democrats even assigned the seating behind my father so as to keep our family off camera. We tolerated this the first day but moved on the second so that the country could see that my father had a family.

The influence of the special interest machine on the senators immediately showed itself once the hearings began. Their opening statements were virtually verbatim recitations of the anti-Bork studies and advertisements.

Senator Kennedy: "It is easy to conclude from the public record of Mr. Bork's published views that he believes women and blacks are second-class citizens under the Constitution."

Senator Howard Metzenbaum: "Judge Bork says he is neutral and even-handed in applying the law. Yet, in split decisions involving disputes between the government and an individual, he has voted for the government almost 100 percent of the time. When citizens wanted access to the courts, he has always voted against them. Yet, when a business is challenging a regulatory agency of the government, has been on the corporate side in virtually every case . . . Now new information has come to light which suggests Judge Bork may not have been completely forthcoming regarding his role in [the Saturday Night Massacre.]"

And Senator Joseph Biden: "I will question you in several areas . . . whether it was wrong for the state courts to enforce a covenant that prohibited a black couple from buying a house in a white neighborhood; whether the United States Congress can stop the use of literacy tests to protect voting rights . . . whether anyone can be subjected to sterilization . . . whether the government can prohibit a married couple from using birth control . . . whether Americans can be denied the right to create and enjoy literature, painting, sculpture, dance, the movies and the music of our choice."

This is not surprising. As liberal columnist Mary McGrory noted in the *Washington Post*, the senators, particularly Biden, worked very closely with the special interest machine in preparing for the hearings.

At the hearings, the propaganda-altered consciousness of the press also emerged.

For example, the *Post* wrote after the first day of testimony that "Bork, under questioning by committee Chairman Joseph R. Biden Jr. and Kennedy did not back away from his controversial positions against Supreme Court rulings involving abortion, affirmative action or one-man, one-vote or the right to privacy in general." This sentence suggests that the reporters were listening more to what they expected my father to say than to what he actually said. Nowhere during Biden's or Kennedy's question was there any mention of affirmative action.

The *Post* also wrote that my father "defended his assertion that the Court had improperly extended the equal protection clause of the 14th amendment to cover sex discrimination claims." Even if it were true that he had made such an assertion, which he did not, it is certainly not true that he defended it in the Q&A session referred to. In fact, he had taken a position completely contrary to what the *Post* reported.

Television did an even worse job, mixing editorial opinion with falsehoods to cook up biased accounts that, were they souffles, would have collapsed with a thud.

Charles Kuralt, host of *CBS Sunday Morning* said on September 20: "[Judge Bork's] record on discrimination against women, against other minorities, is, at least judging from his writings, not very good." Wrong. Actually, he argued in the Supreme Court for the rights of minorities more times than any nominee since Thurgood Marshall. And the NAACP Legal Defense Fund sided with my father in nine of the ten cases where they both filed briefs before the Supreme Court.

Carl Stern, *NBC*'s legal affairs correspondent said on September 14: "The difference is that Bork has spent a quarter century sharply attacking fundamental Supreme Court doctrine long after others stopped arguing about it." Long after others stopped arguing about it? That is simply wrong, for as a lawyer himself, and his network's legal reporter, he has covered the multitude of arguments in the courts over such questions. (Stern would later write in a jacket blurb for *Packing the Court:* "In the 1990s—if the federal courts become closed to the claims of many Americans—Herman Schwartz's book will remind us of how it happened and precisely how it was done.")

Ted Koppel, anchor of *ABC's Nightline* program, on September 15 called my father "a constitutional fundamentalist" with all the negative implications that carries.

It was also at the hearings that the media's third failure of objectivity blossomed to full flower. The examples that follow are misrepresentations by presenting one side of the story and not the other.

The *Post* reported that Senator Byrd "questioned Bork closely on his view that members of Congress should have no legal standing to bring suit against" members of the other branches of government. "You're saying to members of Congress 'You ain't never going to get into this court,'" Byrd said. Nothing is said in the *Post* article to put this statement about congressional standing in perspective. (Congressional standing is a doctrine unknown until 1974, a doctrine unknown in any appeals court except the District of Columbia Circuit and a doctrine upon which the Supreme Court has never ruled. Byrd chose words to make my father's view appear unique and extreme.) By presenting only one side of the issue, the *Post* made itself the mouthpiece for the senator. The exchange is mentioned again in the *Post* on September 20. More space is given to Senator Byrd's position; again nothing is said about my father's position.

The worst butchery of the facts and subsequent press coverage was instigated by Senator Metzenbaum. He charged during the hearings that my father somehow conspired or encouraged the sterilization of female workers when he ruled in Oil, Chemical and *Atomic Workers Union v. American Cyanamid* in 1984. The senator was parroting the line taken by People for the American Way, Planned Parenthood and others. The press, which had never carefully examined this serious charge when it was made before, again failed to look at the record. On September 19, Edward Walsh and Al Kamen reported in the *Post* that my father had written an opinion "upholding a chemical company's decision to offer some of its female employees a choice between being sterilized or losing their jobs."

That characterization implies that my father found that the company violated no law and because of him, innocent women were mutilated. That was not the case. The opinion cannot be read as an approval of the company's policy, and his testimony made this clear: "My opinion is not an endorsement of a sterilization policy. As I noted . . .—in the opinion—the policy might be an unfair labor practice or a form of employment discrimination under Title VII."

Indeed, the company did violate discrimination and labor laws for which it settled out of court with the women. The case that the ACLU brought to my father's court was only about whether or not—after paying the women sizable damages—the company should pay an additional $10,000 fine for violation of an OSHA regulation. In fact, the sterilizations took place three years before my father was a judge.

Later in the same article it is stated that "Bork upheld an administrative law judge's ruling that the company had the right to offer female employees of child-bearing age a choice between sterilization and dismissal." Once again the decision is falsely described as having found a "right" in the company to give the sterilization option. The decision clearly did not do this and the judge's testimony stated that it did not. Whether wittingly or not, the *Post* presented false information in the guise of objective background, leaving the reader with the impression that Senator Metzenbaum's skewed view of the American Cyanamid case was the correct view.

The *New York Times'* story by Linda Greenhouse also misstates the holding of the American Cyanamid case. My father was said to have "ruled that the American Cyanamid Company did not violate Federal law when it required women to undergo sterilization in order to continue working in jobs that exposed them [*sic*] chemicals likely to harm a developing fetus." Again, the court, in its opinion, and my father, at the hearings made clear that the court did not decide that federal law had been violated. The company may have violated labor or civil rights laws. Given the disposition of the case, the court had no power to decide those questions. The most it could do was note, as it did, that the decision was not a finding of a "right" or legality with respect to those schemes. The *Post* and the *Times* accounts accept as fact allegations originally planted by the special interest machine and allied senators.

Incidentally, the three-judge panel that ruled unanimously in the case included then-Judge, now-Justice Antonin Scalia. Not a word about this case came up at his confirmation hearings.

The real shame of the press and television news accounts, was not what they showed but what they suppressed. What was not reported were the many instances when the senators betrayed their ignorance of the Constitution, Supreme Court cases, and even their own legislation.

Senator Biden's hilarious questioning of my father on the potential abuse of an anti-contraceptive law like the one struck down in *Griswold v. Connecticut,* was just such an instance.

JUDGE BORK: Nobody ever tried to enforce that statute, but the police simply could not get into the bedroom without a warrant, and what magistrate is going to give the police a warrant to go into search for signs of the use of contraceptives? I mean it is a wholly bizarre and imaginary case. . . .

SENATOR BIDEN: If they had evidence that a crime was being committed—

JUDGE BORK: How are they going to get evidence that a couple is using contraceptives?

SENATOR BIDEN: Wiretap.

JUDGE BORK: Wiretapping?

SENATOR BIDEN: Wiretap.

JUDGE BORK: You mean to say that a magistrate is going to authorize a wiretap to find out if a couple is using contraceptives?

SENATOR BIDEN: They could, could they not, under the law?

JUDGE BORK: Unbelievable, unbelievable.

Television news did not show this exchange. Neither did the press report it. And because of the directional microphones at the witness table, those watching the live broadcast could not hear the roar of laughter from the press and the audience at Senator Biden's outrageous statement.

On the second day of the hearings, Senator Arlen Specter got himself mired in a line of questions that would have been embarrassing to the average second-year law student. Specter somehow got it into his head that my father's view that the First Amendment should not protect obscenity implied that the First Amendment should not protect anything that the government chooses to call obscenity. Midway through these questions, a confused Senator Specter said, "Judge Bork, with all due respect, I think you are putting the rabbit in the hat." If there was any news here it was that Senator Specter did a good job of appearing to know what he was talking about when he was completely lost.

Senator Kennedy's exchanges with my father followed a predictable pattern. Kennedy: Accusation. Bork: Refutation. Kennedy: Change subject. Accusation. Bork: Refutation. Kennedy: Change subject. Accusation. Bork: Refutation. Kennedy: Prepared statement repeating charges with no mention that the judge's testimony had just disproven his charges.

For example, on September 17, my father's third day at the witness table, Senator Kennedy began questioning him about the presidential power. It must be read to capture the delicious dishonesty of Kennedy's tactics.

SENATOR KENNEDY: Judge Bork, the framers of the Constitution recognized the unchecked powers in the executive branch of government as perhaps the greatest threat to liberty, and that is what the fight for independence was all about. . . . Isn't it true, that in an article in *The Wall Street Journal,* in 1978, you stated that the War Powers Act was—and I quote—"probably unconstitutional, and certainly unworkable? . . ."

JUDGE BORK: . . . I think I can clarify that, not that I am going to take it back. I am just going to clarify it. That was a sentence leading to a different topic, and I do not recall that I ever made any extensive analysis of the War Powers Act. . . . When I say it was probably unconstitutional, that is a very complex act, and let me say, I think the consultation requirements probably seem constitutional to me. The notice requirement seems constitutional. But you know, that Act, as I recall, contains a legislative veto, which, at the time, I thought was probably unconstitutional, and the Supreme Court in the Chada case has since said that it is unconstitutional. . . . There is one other area of possible problems with the act, and that is this. The major questions of war, or peace, or questions affecting that, are most certainly for Congress. Only Congress can declare war. In fact, the Congress need not give the president a single soldier. There is no constitutional requirement that it do so.

SENATOR KENNEDY: . . . So the War Powers Act simply insures that the President has the support of Congress, and the country for these sorts of military actions, but you say the Congress does not have any such power in this absolutely vital area of war and peace.

JUDGE BORK: Senator, I just said precisely the opposite. I just said the question of war and peace is entirely for Congress. Only Congress can declare war.

SENATOR KENNEDY: Let's go to the Foreign Intelligence Surveillance Act. It requires that a warrant be obtained from a special federal court before electronics surveillance can be conducted on United States citizen in the course of a national security investigation. It contained an exception for a limited number of top-secret wiretaps by the president. In June 1978 you testified before the House Judiciary Committee: "The plan of bringing the judiciary a warrant and a criminal violation standard into the field of foreign intelligence is, when analyzed, a thoroughly bad idea, and almost certainly unconstitutional as well. . . ."

JUDGE BORK: Let me explain that view. We are talking now about electronic surveillance of people we have good reason to believe are agents of a foreign power. Every president since Franklin Roosevelt has claimed the power to engage in electronic surveillance of foreign agents without a warrant. Every president has claimed it.

In addition to that, the United States has won two court cases at the court of appeals level. . . .

What troubled me about this new warrant procedure was that it is a secret court. There is no chance to challenge the procedure unless somebody is arrested, which may not be the case because you are just surveilling for intelligence purposes—there is no change to procedure and you have got a secret body of law growing up, that nobody knows about except the judges on the court and the government people who go to talk to that court.

SENATOR KENNEDY: Well, the fact is, under Article II, Congress must have the power to limit the surveillance of U.S. citizens.

JUDGE BORK: I quite agree with you senator. The president has no power just to violate the privacy of American citizens.

SENATOR KENNEDY: Let's talk about another area. That is the role of special prosecutors. . . .

In November, 1973, a few weeks after you fired Mr. Cox, you testified, "The question is whether congressional legislation appointing a special prosecutor outside the executive branch, or empowering the courts to do so, would be constitutionally valid, and whether it provides significant advantages that make it worth taking a constitutionally risky course.

"I am persuaded that such a course would almost certainly not be valid, and would, in any event, pose more problems than it would solve."

JUDGE BORK: . . . I think those proposals were very different statutes than the one that is now in effect. They were contemplating judicial appointment and judicial control, and judicial termination of the special prosecutor. The present one does not. . . . And as I recall what I said then . . . was that congress probably could protect the special prosecutor from discharge except for cause. . . . So I made that distinction back then.

SENATOR KENNEDY: That is a welcome one because as you very well know, the special prosecutor statute has been invoked several times, both by the Carter and the Reagan administrations. . . .

Moving to another area, I would like to ask you about congressional standing to bring lawsuits challenging the abuse of the Constitution by the president. . . .

In a dissenting opinion in 1985, is it not true you said, "We ought to renounce outright the whole notion of congressional standing"?

JUDGE BORK: . . . That is an entirely novel constitutional doctrine which I think was never heard before 1974 in the case you brought, *Kennedy v. Sampson* and it is confined to the circuit court on which I sit. I do not think that any other circuit has ever picked up that doctrine. So it is a constitutional novelty, and it is by no means settled. And the Supreme Court has not passed on it.

The reason I am troubled by it is as follows: What it will lead to is, I think, utter domination of the government by the judiciary. . . .

This went on for two more exchanges. Then Kennedy began a lengthy summation.

SENATOR KENNEDY: Just to summarize, Judge Bork, the American people rely on the Congress to protect them from abuses of power by the executive branch; but Judge Bork, whenever Congress has tried to curb the power abusers, you always seem to side with the president. You broke the law in Watergate when you obeyed President Nixon and fired Archibald Cox. You have testified that court appointed special prosecutors are unconstitutional, which suggests you would let the administration investigate itself when corruption is the issue.

You oppose limits on the national security power of the president, even when the issue is wiretapping and eavesdropping of on American citizens. . . . You believe that Congress can never use the courts to challenge the president when he abuses his power. You wrote that the War Powers Act was probably unconstitutional. You suggested that Congress has no power to stop the president from taking us into a wider war in Vietnam. And that same reasoning would apply to sending U.S. military aid to the contras in Nicaragua or even selling arms to the Ayatollah in Iran.

The Constitution calls for checks and balances. You seem to feel when it comes to the relation between congress and the president, instead of checks and balances the president has a blank check and the congress exerts no balance at all. . . .

JUDGE BORK: Senator Kennedy, I must say I think those are most unfair characterizations of my views. Let me start—I hardly know where to start. . . .

All that television news showed was this last manuever of Kennedy's examination. My father's responses were not shown. All that was aired was his statement calling the charges "unfair characterizations." The media had no time for context or clarification. Senator Kennedy knew that and took advantage of it. What also went unseen and uncommented upon was steady supply of hastily scribbled notes handed the senator by his staff when, as was usually the case, he was unable to comprehend the most rudimentary discussion of the law. As Joe Klein of *New York* magazine put it: "Ted Kennedy's America apparently was a place where a senator could spend a half-hour grilling a Supreme Court nominee with questions provided by his staff, not listen to the answers, then sum up with a 30–second epigram intended for the evening news that had nothing to do with either the questions asked or the answers given."

A similar lack of context came about because of a quotation taken by the media from the questioning of my father by Senator Dennis DeConcini, also demonstrates how the media suppressed context. "You leave this senator unsatisfied on how this senator can conclude that you are going to protect the citizens of this country in interpreting the Constitution on the Court as it relates to sex." This statement made on September 16 sounds like a thoughtful wrap-up of a probing discussion. In fact, it came at the end of one of the most incoherent lines of questioning launched by any senator.

Senator DeConcini mischaracterized my father's position on the Voting Rights Act (as did People for the American Way and others) having transformed his objection to *Katzenbach v. Morgan* into a denunciation of bans of literacy tests. When my father asked, "Was I discussing *Katzenbach v. Morgan*?" DeConcini responded, "Excuse me. The ban of literacy test, excuse me, and it is the *Katzenbach*—". The senator clearly had no idea what *Katzenbach* was, and only after repeated prompting from his staff was he able to respond that my father indeed had been discussing that case. Furthermore, Senator DeConcini asked no question that suggested he understood anything about *Katzenbach*. The senator went on to confuse my father's comments about the Equal Rights Amendment with the equal protection clause and seemed unable to grasp the distinction between them.

My father did his best to make some sense out of Senator DeConcini's questions in order to answer them. But what was reported was only the senator's concluding comment: "You leave this senator unsatisfied . . . ."

Round Two

After my father's five days of testimony, came the two-week parade of anti-Bork and pro-Bork witnesses.

Consistently, the Democratically controlled Judiciary Committee pushed pro-Bork panels late into the evening to avoid news coverage of their testimony. The media accepted this manipulation and so, in many cases, my father's witnesses got little or no coverage of their supportive testimony. In fact, the *Post* consistently gave front-page play to critics while reserving the inside pages for testimony of my father's supporters such as former Chief Justice Warren Burger. Indeed, very little coverage was given to the fact that not only did the former chief justice speak out for my father but seven former U.S. attorneys general and eight past presidents of the American Bar Association testified on his behalf. And they did not notice or report that the distinguished lawyers and law professors who testified for the confirmation constituted a political and ideological smorgasbord while those who spoke against the judge were politically well to the left.

The opponents made a lot of what they claimed was the Reagan/ Meese/Bork agenda for the Court. My father had no agenda for the Court, but that's unimportant in this forum. The press picked up this line but seldom if ever asked what the constitutional agenda of the left/ liberal special interest groups was. The groups that were trying to portray my father as anti-family themselves have little sympathy with the religious, moral and family values. For example, the ACLU has argued to prohibit the singing of "Silent Night" in public schools and to ban the posting of the Ten Commandments in classrooms. It has tried to end tax exempt status for churches and synagogues and to halt public funding for busing to Catholic schools. The ACLU also has fought for a student's right to bring his male lover to a high school prom and has argued in the Supreme Court that the right to privacy prohibits a mother from being informed that her 14–year-old daughter has requested an abortion. It also opposed a local zoning law which prohibited porn dealers from locating their shops and theaters near schools and churches.

Harvard Law Professor Laurence Tribe, who was an adviser to Senator Biden before, during and after the hearings, in 1986 argued before the Supreme Court in *Bowers v. Hardwick* that the constitutional right to privacy protects homosexual sodomy. Yet, he told the Senate Judiciary Committee that the right to privacy "just relates to the most down-to-earth fundamental things about marriage, family, parenthood. . . . I do not accept the characterization that is a vast and undefinable right." Tribe also has said that there may be a constitutional protection for the use of drugs like marijuana. Stanford Law Professor Barbara Babcock, who also testified, criticized my father's view on dangerous vagueness of the generalized right to privacy. She became flustered when Senator Gordon Humphrey reminded her that she had written in 1973 that prostitution could be protected by it. New York University Law Professor A. J. Richards, who testified against my father, has said "the right to use many drugs currently criminalized is one of the rights of the person which the state may not transgress." He also has stated that local control and financing of schools is "a sign of our moral immaturity as a people" and is "outrageous." Shirley Hufstedler, a former federal appellate judge, criticized Judge Bork's record as a judge. However, she holds one of the worst records of reversal by the Supreme Court of any federal judge. None of this was reported.

Some reporters to whom I spoke during the hearings, like Reginald Stuart of the *Philadelphia Daily News,* apparently did not perceive what was happening. After my father's lengthy testimony about his record as a judge and as solicitor general, I asked Stuart—a black reporter—if my father had proved to him that he was not prejudiced against minorities and women. "Not really," Stuart said. When I again rattled off example after example that contradicted what had been alleged, Stuart smiled at me in a condescending manner and said simply, "It's not convincing."

Other reporters, however, like Lyle Denniston, the *Baltimore Sun's* Supreme Court correspondent, expressed their contempt for the brainpower of the Judiciary Committee but never wrote a word critical of the process. Denniston told me that he was impressed with testimony of the several witnesses who testified about how my father's reached out to help them overcome racial and religious prejudice against them and planned to write a piece about that. Ultimately, no such piece appeared. When I asked Denniston why not, he said that the "newspeg" had passed.

After the hearings concluded, the coverage devolved to little more than tallies of the growing number of senators announcing their opposition to the judge and reports of polls showing public disapproval of the nomination. Some in the media have pointed to these polls as proof that their coverage only reflected the national mood. But this is a tautology as Michael Ignatieff has noted:

> Millions of households look out through the screen in search of their collective identity as a national society and as citizens of the world. The media now play the decisive role in constituting the "imagined community" of nation and globe, the myth that millions of separate "I"'s find common identity in a "we." . . . News editors act as ventriloquists of this "we" serving up a diet of information that is legitimized as being what "we" need to know; in fact, what we get to know is what fits the visual and chronological constraints of the genre. In this circular process, the news is validated as a system of authority, as a national institution with a privileged role as purveyor of the nation's identity and taker of its pulse.

In addition, the questions asked by these pollsters were universally biased against my father. How could anyone respond positively when asked a question like: "Judge Bork has been critical of decisions expanding the rights of women and minorities. Do you think he should be on the Supreme Court?"

It was this sort of thing that caused me finally to write an op-ed in the Monday, October 5 *Washington Post* entitled "An Evil Caricature of the Nominee." If the media wouldn't tell the other side of the story, then I would. The piece was picked up in hundreds of newspapers nationwide. Suddenly, I was besieged by television and radio programs that wanted interviews and by print reporters. I flew to New York that afternoon to appear on ABC's *Good Morning America,* the following morning.

The experience further illustrates how some in the media were interested less in the facts than in the spectacle of a Bork fighting back. At the same time I agreed to appear, Barbara Walters of *ABC's 20/20* program was negotiating with the White House to get my father and/or step-mother for an interview. When Walters found out that I was going to be on Tuesday morning—four days before *20/20* would air—she called the White House and threatened to withdraw her offer of an interview. At *ABC,* an internecine battle of epic proportions ensued. The White House staff were in a dither: I could go on the morning of the committee vote, or my father (who was refusing to be interviewed) could go on four days later. The negotiations went on late into Monday night. I even was called at my hotel in New York at 9:30 p.m. by a panicked administration official who told me not to go on. I responded that it was very late in the day to withdraw, but that I would if the official would first confer with the White House public affairs office. Only the fact that the official could not find anyone from public affairs, kept the plan from changing.

In the end I went on. My interviewer, Charles Gibson, was not interested in the tale of distortions outlined in my *Post* piece, but asked me in four of my six questions whether my father would withdraw if the committee vote was negative as expected. Walters never carried out her threat. Instead, she continued to leave long, rambling pleas on his answering machine. After all, there was still some pathos to be wrung from the story.

Chain Reaction

So there is the chain reaction: Interest group research/ads setting the agenda and tone of the debate, infiltrating the senators statements, and finally insinuating themselves into the media which delivers the message and reports, with amazement, that it has been absorbed. Maybe, for the sake of argument, the press discounted what the groups said—I do not think that they did—but they had important United States senators, who they did cover, parroting the same line. Perhaps the *ABC/Washington Post* poll that said people didn't read the ads, was right. No matter, they heard the identical line from the senators, from the so-called experts and from the media.

The distortions that I have just outlined were never investigated or challenged by the press until after my father's nomination was rejected by the Senate Judiciary Committee on October 6—a full two months after some of them first appeared—and then only in passing references to one or two examples. In many cases, as I have noted, these almost verbatim excerpts from anti-Bork literature were inserted matter-of-factly into the coverage and this led to further unbalanced coverage. To my mind there is little difference between fabricating information and accepting fabrications as fact without checking them, particularly when verification is fairly easy. This practice is damnable because they were unfairly inserted in without balancing comments. But passing that, it was contemptible because the details were untrue as anyone taking the time to study the record would have known. As John Hohenberg of Columbia University's journalism school once wrote, "What use is it to spell the name of the speaker correctly and fail to report what he said is a tissue of lies?"

Furthermore, had my father made statements as blatantly incorrect as these, the press would have had a field day taking him to task. That's another indication, I would argue, of the media's evaporated objectivity.

As a result, during the my father's confirmation the line between journalist and propagandist became seriously blurred. Journalists and politicians counter that the public at large made up its mind about my father by watching the hearings. Yet the evidence suggests that the vast majority saw little, if any, of the hearings live or unedited. *C-SPAN's* data for the period shows that while the live hearings were available to 37 million households about 7.8 million, or 20 percent, watched any of the hearings. Of those, the average viewing time was a 6.9 hours of my father's 32 hours of testimony.

PBS's figures show that only 17 of 318 stations carried at least one day of the judge's five days of testimony. And only 28 of 318 public television stations carried at least one day of the network's one-hour edited highlight program.

Clearly, most Americans were getting their impressions of my father's testimony from television news accounts and newspapers.

Patterns

Are these merely a few isolated examples or do they represent a pattern of unfair coverage?

The Center for Media Studies in Washington is the only organization that has done any statistical analysis of the media coverage. It examined the network television and *Washington Post* coverage of the nomination between July 1 and October 9, 1987. Several of its findings stand out:

• "The topics covered [by the media] most often reflected the major concerns of Bork's critics. Civil rights dominated with almost twice as much coverage as any other topic. Women's rights, privacy, abortion and First Amendment issues were also prominent." Overall, "of 381 source judgments that clearly indicated praise or blame, 63 percent were negative and 37 percent were positive."

• "Anti-Bork statements came from a much broader range of sources than pro-Bork sentiments. President Reagan stood virtually alone as a regular source of support. Criticism was dispersed much more widely among senate opponents and interest groups."

• "Sources discussing his ideology ran 4–to–1 negative at the *Post* and 6–to–1 negative at the networks . . . 8–to–1 negative at CBS. Throughout the entire three months, only 16 sources defended Bork's ideology on TV news compared with 89 critical source statements." Joseph and Stewart Alsop once wrote "The whole truth is only revealed or approximated by a long public debate; the realistic estimate is only reached after viewpoint has been tested against viewpoint, and all the facts, pro and con, have weighed against each other. And in the United States, the debate about the nation's situation and the nation's policy is mainly carried on in the press." However, as the statistics illustrate, neither were opposing viewpoints nor all the facts pro and con, tested against each other. The media largely ignored the opinions and factual testimony of the pro-Bork forces.

I find this fascinating because witnesses at the hearings ran about 7–to–5 in favor of my father and mail and telephone calls received by senators ran "20–to–1" in favor, by Joe Biden's own admission during the floor debate.

Granted that Senator Biden is prone to hyperbole (sometimes even his own), but clearly, while the press could have found persons to interview who favored my father, it simply chose not to. Combine that with the media's role as conduit for information provided by the special interests that opposed my father's confirmation, and it is clear that the media played a vital role in the political process. However, its role was not as investigators or establishers of objective truth.

At my own magazine, *U.S. News & World Report,* attempts I made to get legal writer Ted Gest to call experts for the other side of the story were virtually ignored and only loud complaints caused editors to amend blatantly biased writing that bordered on defamation. Even after my father was defeated, Gest persisted. In a November 1987 story about the nomination of Judge Anthony Kennedy, Gest wrote:

The 51–year-old Kennedy clearly is not a conservative theorist of the likes of Robert Bork. "Kennedy is fair-minded and compassionate," says law Prof. John Oakley of the University of California at Davis, a friend of the nominee's and an avowed liberal Democrat. "But he has no agenda." At McGeorge Law School, where Kennedy taught constitutional law, Dean Gordon Schaber says his 14 years of law practice before he became a judge "gave him a good understanding of ordinary affairs and an empathy for people."

I came across this slander after the story was already in page proofs and complained to an editor that Gest's juxtaposition was unfair. He agreed and changed the paragraph.

I should note that Chief Political Correspondent, Michael Kramer, a lawyer, immersed himself in my father's writings for several weeks and interviewed him for several hours after which he wrote a very fair and thorough cover story. Interestingly, this generally favorable—but not uncritical—analysis caused him to come under severe criticism from his colleagues within and without the magazine. I am not aware of any similar criticism being leveled at any writer who took a negative slant in his or her reporting.

The Journalist's Morality

The ultimate question is, why didn't the press challenge the claims of the special interest machine, its proxy senators, and the other "experts?"

I think publishing deadlines were an important factor in some cases. Certainly, this was a reality upon which the Democrats depended during the hearings as the Senate Caucus Room emptied just as pro-Bork witnesses were called to testify. However, the media had more than enough time and information for a correct evaluation of the allegations coming from the Left in the 77 days before the hearings began.

Incompetence also was a factor. Many of the reporters covering the confirmation were not even remotely conversant with the subject matter or my father's background and views. (For instance, one reporter asked me during the hearings, "What's the solicitor general?" another to explain federalism. Anyway, if the senators weren't able to master the constitutional debate—a greater percentage of whom had attended law school and who had vast staff resources—how could the press be expected to?) Because many, if not most of the reporters, did not have a basic understanding of the issues, they were susceptible to the propaganda of the special interests who during the hearings continued to generate an incredible amount of "analysis" attacking my father's every statement. And because the media was not knowledgeable about the legal issues, their coverage devolved to the politics of it, that is the fight. My father is not a politician, and for reasons of principle, he refused to try to become one. Under those rules of engagement that meant that he would lose in the media.

Also, I think—as Edward Jay Epstein has said in his excellent book *Between Fact and Fiction: The Problem of Journalism*—that it was because in the journalistic organization of Washington, the media depends on, indeed subsists on handouts from these sources within the counter-elite to challenge official information—in other words to create news. This would not work, however, unless reporters were predisposed to believe the disinformation they were being fed.

This brings us, finally, to the question of ideology. Like the groups that opposed my father, the media is, as Irving Kristol has written, "for the most part populated by members of [a] new class who believe—as the Left has always believed—it is government's responsibility to cure all the ills of the human condition, and who ridicule those politicians who deny the possibility (and therefore the propriety) of government doing any such ambitious thing."

Robert and Linda Lichter, and Stanley Rothman, authors of *The Media Elite,* concur: "Today's leading journalists are politically liberal and alienated from traditional norms and institutions . . . They differ most from the general public, however on the divisive social issues that have emerged since the 1960s—abortion, gay rights, affirmative action, et cetera. . . . Psychological tests show how their outlooks can unconsciously operate to shape their conceptions of the news."

Consequently, I believe that reporters were consciously or unconsciously motivated by the fear that by exposing the distortions they would be cut off by the sources on whom they depend and with whom they identify. In Washington, more than anywhere else, the journalist's morality becomes that of his sources; always cynical about authority and power, he or she accepts the judgments of those who seem most to challenge that authority and power and thus are most like themselves. This makes sense if for no other reason than in the case of my father's confirmation they were not interviewing anybody else as the statistics clearly show.

The great irony here is that my father was nominated principally because he opposed the growing "imperial" power of the Supreme Court in American life. Instead, he called for decisionmaking in the political/social arena to be returned to the legislature where it belongs. Stuart Taylor of the *New York Times* recognized this irony the week of my father's nomination. He wrote: "It is a measure of how deeply the institution of judicial review has taken root in America that elected senators are feeling so much pressure to reject a nominee whose philosophy rests on the premise that legislators should make laws." Perhaps it foretold the way the debate was to be reported when Taylor acknowledged this in the last paragraph of his first Sunday piece about the nomination after giving play to all the other spurious charges about the judge including his supposed support of discriminatory poll taxes.

Indeed, Taylor throughout his coverage showed a greater interest in allegations against my father than any information about the opposition's methods or tactics. One evening during the third week of hearings, Taylor and I shared a cab from the Russell Senate Office Building to downtown. During that ride I told him about how one of Senator Metzenbaum's staff had threatened a black law professor convincing him not to testify for my father. Taylor seemed intrigued and said that either he would look into it himself or would pass the information on to another reporter. He asked me for my phone numbers including the number of the war room. Weeks passed and I heard and read nothing of the matter. Finally, *Times* reporter Martin Tolchin and columnist William Safire broke the story. I learned subsequently that Taylor had not passed my tip to Tolchin or Safire.

Let me say, before I lose all my friends in the media, that I did see some good reporting toward the end by Ron Ostrow in the *Los Angeles Times* and Ethan Bronner in the *Boston Globe* about how the Left organized against my father. My question is, why didn't they do it earlier? The press, which was relentless in analyzing the White House motives and strategy to sell my father—quite incorrectly, I might add— never asked the corresponding question: What are the motives and strategy of the Left?

I thought that the generation of reporters after Woodward and Bernstein had traded in their stenopads for magnifying glasses. Indeed, I am part of that generation and believe as John Hohenberg, a professor of journalism at Columbia, has written that "skepticism is the hallmark of journalism." But from my own observations, I can testify that this is just not the case. Despite all protestations to the contrary, the overwhelming majority of journalists in Washington, D.C. simply took dictation from groups and individuals representing left/liberal philosophies and causes and printed it without critical analysis. The media— moved by disinformation attractively packaged and softpeddled to fit its political predispositions—became an unwitting accomplice in some cases and a willing ally in others of those special interests that did not want an honest debate. In that way the media itself contributed to the outcome.

Rx for the Media

What can or should be done?

Before Ted Kennedy whips up a general panic in the media about making reporters second-class citizens, rogue mediacops breaking into newsrooms in the middle of the night, and back-alley attitude-altering sessions, let me say that any worthwhile and effective solutions must be voluntary. Furthermore, I will subscribe here only to those very sensible and modest proposals made by David Cohen of the Advocacy Institute. The Advocacy Institute, a non-profit Washington outfit that advises leftwing special interest groups on how to pitch their causes, held a seminar on the use and abuse of symbolism in political debate three days after my father's defeat. Unfortunately, it was misreported as a post-mortem on the confirmation process, but it was far broader than that. Cohen offered three interesting recommendations.

First, Cohen said that expenditures by groups in the anti-Bork and pro-Bork campaigns should be disclosed, something that since his recommendation two years ago, no group has seen fit to do, at least not an audited accounting. It is surprising to me that the media never publicly demanded these figures. Certainly, since their newspapers and stations were the outlets for the ads, half the reporting was already done for them. When I asked one colleague about this at the hearings, he threw up the old excuse, "I would never talk to our sales department!" Of course, nobody was asking him to get in bed with his advertising people, just to ask them how many ads were booked and at what price. Hardly a gross violation of journalistic independence.

Second, Cohen said that the senators should be sent substantiation and documentatation for charges and claims made in advocacy advertising. I would expand the distribution list to include the media. However, when People for the American Way did submit a defense of its advertisements to the Senate Judiciary Committee, it was filled with as many lies and distortions as the original ads. This recommendation offers no guarantee of veracity on the part of the special interest groups. What is still needed is an aggressively skeptical media to keep the debate honest.

Third, Cohen suggested that the various media should commission an independent audit of their coverage. Its objective would be to look at "language debasement." By this Cohen was referring to the use of terms such as "special interest" and "lynchmob" by the Right. (One thing that would become immediately apparent from such review is, despite charges from the Left that this latter term was part of a right-wing smokescreen, the term was first used in my father's confirmation by the Washington *Post* editorial writers and David Broder.) It would certainly also apply to terms like "out of the mainstream" and "extremist" used by the Left to critcize my father. Not one to tell the media its business, Cohen called this proposal "the height of responsible participation." I would call it the barest minimum. Still, I agree with this suggestion wholeheartedly. I have been amazed at the media's silence about its coverage of my father's confirmation. Since the Senate vote, not one of the industry trades *(Washington Journalism Review, Columbia Journalism Review,* or *Editor & Publisher)* has printed an analysis of the media's reporting of what arguably could be the second or third most important story that year. (For the record, I would rank them, 1) Iran/Contra, 2) INF, and 3) the Bork nomination.) When I noted this in March 1988 at a panel on journalism ethics sponsored by the Center for Communication, New York *Times* media writer Alex Jones, agreed with me that this absence of self-analysis was shocking. And my subsequent query to Managing Editor Gloria Cooper of the *Columbia Journalism Review* about the article you are reading was rejected. Her arguments: I am too close to the subject, and it's "ancient history." (After a second letter outlining the same arguments for the story's importance and my qualifications to write it that I make at the top of this article, she still refused to commission the piece but agreed to look at a completed draft.)

Cohen's proposals all deal with the aftermath of the my father's confirmation fight. While eminently worthwhile, he should not have stopped there. To mitigate the effect of the same sort of distortion in future confirmations, or in any great public debate—be they from the Left or the Right—the media should adapt another of Cohen's recommendations to itself. "The advocacy community," he said, "has a Paul Revere role to play to alert people that there is an issue." I would argue the same role for the media—one that it shunned in my father's confirmation. Timothy Dyk, a First Amendment lawyer and a director of People For the American Way, said during a panel debate in which we both participated last April "I don't care whether the media coverage was fair or unfair. . . . The real question was whether the press involvement was desirable or undesirable." Of course, the answer has to be, yes. To pose it was either an argument for quantity over quality, or a display of monumental disingenuousness. Yes, we got news, but to paraphrase Jacques Barzun, is it too much to ask the media for both news and sense?

Let me conclude with a quotation from Mark Twain's *A Connecticut Yankee in King Arthur's Court*. It was given to me by a friend during my father's ordeal and more than anything I have read aptly sums up the media's failings in the Bork nomination:

> He spoke of me all the time in the blandest way, as "this prodigious giant," and "this horrible sky-towering monster," and "this tusked and taloned man-devouring ogre;" and everybody took in all this bosh in the naivest way and never smiled nor seemed to notice that there was any discrepancy between these watered statistics and me.

Appendix A

Mendacity Is No Defense:
An Analysis of Larry Tribe's
Testimony

—by Patrick B. McGuigan

I have deliberately not engaged, in this book, in many responses to
the varied distortions of Robert Bork's judicial philosophy offered
during the course of his confirmation hearings—except to report responses of my allies and myself which were offered at the time.

However, Professor Laurence Tribe's facile performance was particularly destructive for Judge Bork, as it gave serious intellectual patina
to the mounting opposition Bork faced at the time Tribe came before
the Committee. In addition, of course, there is the continued speculation that Tribe, a relatively young man, might be considered for the
Supreme Court in some future Administration. At the risk of being
tedious, I provide a partial catalogue of particulars in Tribe's mendacious performance.

This learned man's testimony was one of the low points of the
hearing. It consisted principally of half-truths and a few outright lies
about Judge Bork's views and innuendoes about his character, combined with earnest statements about Tribe's personal admiration and
respect for Judge Bork. The performance was particularly distasteful
because Tribe is a very smart man whose ability to make plausible

arguments for any position seems to have left him almost unable to tell truth from falsehood, and thus profoundly affected his intellectual integrity.

As to innuendo: In discussing what significance to attribute to Judge Bork's few shifts (over several years) in position, Tribe first noted that "Some of Judge Bork's most vocal conservative supporters in particular have been quite merciless in assessing this so-called 'confirmation conversion.'" Tribe went on to say, "I would not be so presumptuous as to cast aspersions on Judge Bork's motives" but that "even on the most charitable view, the noteworthy shifts in Judge Bork's positions subsequent to his nomination cannot escape attention" and that "each Senator must decide for himself what to make of those shifts." (Tribe's prepared statement, transcript, pp. 12–13) All this mealy-mouthed obfuscation was obviously an elaborate attempt to raise questions in the Senators' minds about Judge Bork's veracity without taking the responsibility for doing so by coming right out and saying so.

As for half truths: "Judge Bork has basically said that nothing in the Constitution authorizes judges to treat a married couple's intimacies in the bedroom any differently from a business enterprise's economic decisions in the boardroom," quoth Tribe. (Transcript, p. 6) What is this based on? The similarity that Bork has pointed to between the Court's method in its economic substantive due process decisions and its method in *Griswold* and *Roe*. As Tribe well knows, Bork is hardly the first, last or only person to have pointed out this similarity and to have questioned how critics of the first set of decisions can distinguish the second set. Justice Hugo Black, no less, made precisely that argument in his *Griswold* dissent. John Hart Ely, the former dean of Stanford and author of the leading book of the past decade on constitutional interpretation, made it in *Democracy and Distrust*. Gerald Gunther, the author of the leading constitutional law textbook, made it in connection with some Bicentennial celebration to a Los Angeles *Times* reporter. Indeed, discussion of whether the two lines of cases can be distinguished is a standard feature of first year constitutional law courses—something of which even many non-lawyers are fully aware. And Tribe, the author of the leading treatise on constitutional law, knows full well there is nothing scandalous about this comparison. But he is quite willing to suggest to a legally unsophisticated audience that it is a shocking position.

"[N]ot one of the 105 past and present Justices of the Supreme Court has ever taken a view at odds with [the] basic axiom" "that people retain unspecified fundamental rights that courts were supposed to discern and defend," says Tribe. (Transcript, pp. 6, 7) That is completely misleading: Justice Black, for example, opposed that view throughout his career. Although Black may have occasionally joined opinions that could not be squared with that position, Tribe knows full well that Black's *Griswold* dissent, precisely objecting to the creation of unspecified rights, represents his considered opinion, and that over the course of a long career, Justices—being men and women, not angels—sometimes join things that they do fully agree with for some tactical reasons. Bork might well have ended up doing the same thing. Tribe also knows full well that Justice Scalia, when he was on the Court of Appeals, joined Judge Bork's opinion attacking the unenumerated "fundamental" rights in *Dronenburg v. Zech.*

One other small point: Tribe cites Chief Justice Marshall's opinion in *Fletcher v. Peck* to show that Marshall believed in unenumerated "fundamental" rights—without noting that Marshall very carefully did *not* rest his decision on that ground and that there are *no* Marshall opinions that do! Instead, contrary to the concurrence of Justice Johnson, who wanted to rely on the argument from natural law, Marshall went on to demonstrate that the law at issue violated the contracts clause. The author of the leading treatise on constitutional law knows that there is *no* instance in which John Marshall held invalid *any* legislative act under the "unenumerated rights" theory.

In response to Senator Kennedy's question whether Judge Bork's "reasonable basis" equal protection test could invalidate race and sex discrimination, Tribe first stated that "I do not think there is any way to do it, Senator, in a manner that is intellectually honest." (Transcript, p. 47) Later on, however, Tribe states that "it is possible" to reach the same results under both Bork's and the Court's approach. (Transcript, p. 63) Finally, asked whether Stevens actually endorsed such a test, Tribe first says "I do not think so" but then goes on to say "Well, Justice Stevens occasionally uses the word 'reasonable,' but he makes it very clear that he is applying that standard from the perspective of what he calls an impartial law maker." (Transcript, p. 64) What would an uncharitable reader make of the inconsistencies in these statements, in the space of a single morning's testimony, one wonders? This uncharitable reader knows what he makes of them.

My personal favorite in this exchange, however, was the following. In response to a question from Senator DeConcini whether Bork's reasonableness standard would yield the same results in race cases as the Court's strict scrutiny approach, Tribe says, "It does not sound like it to me. His views of Shelly v. Kraemer [the racial covenants case] reinforce that view. That is, if he believes that it is consistent with the Fourteenth Amendment for courts to have enforced racially restrictive covenants, then he is certainly not applying the strictest scrutiny, and he is applying a version of reasonableness that will let various kinds of race discrimination as well. That is obviously a source of concern." (Transcript, p. 64) As Tribe well knows, however, Bork's qualms about *Shelley* had *nothing* to do with the equal protection standard. Instead, they were over whether court enforcement of private contracts was enough to make those contracts "state action" and thus covered by the equal protection clause's prohibition, which only applies to states, not to private actions. Tribe, who is an eminent authority on the equal protection clause and who has a lengthy discussion of *Shelley* in his treatise, cannot claim that he was personally confused on this point. Instead, his assertion that the standard has *anything* to do with Bork's views on the case is, in the Anglo-Saxon to which Tribe seems allergic, a lie—and one spoken under oath. It is not any less a lie because it is somewhat complicated to explain.

Less complicated, in fact quite straightforward, is one exchange with Senator Orrin Hatch, a discussion which speaks for itself:

SENATOR HATCH: You have been particularly critical of the Supreme Court with regard to the death penalty.

MR. TRIBE: Actually, I do not know that I have, Senator.

HATCH: Let me give you an illustration—and I am quoting out of your book *God Save This Honorable Court*. . . [There] you wrote, "No discussion of the Nixon Court would be complete without mention of its death penalty discussions. When Justice White parted company with the Nixon camp . . . the Court struck down all of the death penalty statutes then in effect on the ground that they gave juries too much leeway to select individuals for executi[ons] for prejudiced reasons, or for no reason at all. The four Nixon appointees. . . gained the upper hand in 1976 and formed the solid core of the majority that upheld rewritten death penalty laws . . . " Now I get the distinct impression as I read your writings that you think—

TRIBE: That is just a description—is not that an accurate description?

HATCH: Yes it is. But I get a distinct impression that you think the death penalty is never, or really rarely constitutional.

TRIBE: I have not decided that.

HATCH: Let me go on just a little bit. . . . You say that President Nixon picked these nominees for their "harsh commitment to law enforcement uber alles.'' And you conclude that, ''Ten years after Richard Nixon had been hounded from the White House, his nominees remained on the Supreme 'Court, exhibiting less interest in avoiding the death of possibly innocent people than in helping the Government keep the grim line of the condemned moving briskly to meet their appointments with the executioner.''

TRIBE: I was very distressed and I still am, Senator, with the notion that speed and efficiency here counts more than making sure that one never executes an innocent person.'' (Transcript, pp. 51–52)

One final point about Professor Tribe's testimony. His view on the role of a court of appeals judge—offered at Judge Bork's hearing—is remarkably different from that offered when the question was whether Professor Bernard Siegan should be confirmed as a judge on the Ninth Circuit.

Professor Tribe originally wrote a vicious letter in opposition to Siegan's confirmation to the Senate Judiciary Committee. After it was clear that Siegan would be defeated, he wrote a second letter greatly toning down his original attack, although still urging non-confirmation. Precisely what caused him to change his tone, other than the fact that the battle was won, is a fascinating question—one not remotely answered by anything he said in either of the two letters.

At Judge Bork's hearing, there were two questions to which the role of a court of appeals judge was relevant. The first was to what extent Judge Bork's unanimous confirmation for the D.C. Circuit and receipt of the highest rating the ABA assigns for such positions indicated that he was qualified for the Supreme Court. The second was to what extent was Bork's remarkable record of non-reversal on the Court of Appeals for the D.C. Circuit relevant in assessing whether he was within the mainstream of American legal thought, or how he would perform as a Supreme Court Justice. The politically opportune view to take in that context was that court of appeals judges are not really very important because they are so thoroughly constrained by Supreme Court precedent, and that is precisely the view taken by Professor Tribe in his prepared testimony:

Now, I had no objection to Judge Bork as a nominee to the Circuit Court. There, any major failure to follow Supreme Court precedent would rapidly be corrected by the Supreme Court itself. But as a Justice, Judge Bork would cast a vote that no higher court could correct. (Transcript, p. 5)

It is also the view he took in the course of questioning by Senators Gordon Humphrey and Alan Simpson. The Simpson colloquy adequately conveys the flavor:

> SENATOR SIMPSON: Five and a half years of writings of opinions on [the D.C. Circuit] and not one person yet has come in and said that any of those opinions are out of the mainstream. Is not that fascinating?. . . .
>
> MR. TRIBE: I do not think it is—with all respect, to be honest—I do not think it is that fascinating, because I have never doubted, nor has anyone else, Judge Bork's really fine intellect and his capacity to write fine opinions that will not be reversed by the Supreme Court.
>
> The fundamental difference between being on a Court of Appeals, where one is operating within a bound of precedent and being on the Supreme Court where one is making precedent is the reason that people. . . have looked to 20 years of prolific writing and speech making about the Supreme Court and about what it should do as a guide to what Judge Bork might do upon that Court. (Transcript, p. 60)

On the other hand, when the question was whether Professor Siegan should be confirmed for the Court of Appeals (and the opportune argument was that court of appeals judges have a lot of discretion and are very important) Professor Tribe's job description changed accordingly:

> I should add that I cannot credit Professor Siegan's suggestion, both in his testimony before this Committee and in his most recent written submission, that his philosophy is rendered largely irrelevant by the fact that he has been nominated only to a lower court. There is a great deal of room for the exercise of judgment in how federal appellate courts understand Supreme Court precedent, and it cannot be credibly maintained that the views of a nominee to a circuit court do not matter much. Indeed, Professor Siegan's testimony to that effect might justifiably give pause even to a Senator who was otherwise prepared to support his nomination. (Tribe letter to Senator Biden, April 19, 1988)

What should really give pause to a Senator impressed with Professor Tribe's intellect is the professor's willingness to take whatever view of the role of a court of appeals judge is required to win the particular fight being conducted, and his *hubris* in believing that somehow no one, even a non-lawyer from Oklahoma, will ever compare the two.

Appendix B

The Conservative Digest/Judicial Notice interview with Judge Robert H. Bork

—by Patrick B. McGuigan

(On September 5, 1985, Pat McGuigan conducted a lengthy interview with Judge Robert H. Bork in his chambers at the U.S. Court House in the District of Columbia. A little more than half of the interview appeared in the October 1985 issue of *Conservative Digest*. The following June, the Free Congress Foundation printed the entire text of the interview in its publication *Judicial Notice*.

In the interview, Bork discussed the "interpretivist" and "noninterpretivist" approaches to legal analysis, legal education and ideologies, criminal law, values in the law, the "privacy doctrine", limitation of court jurisdiction, libel law, standing, bureaucracies and liberty, and many other issues. In addition, he talked about his personal political philosophy, intellectual influences on his development as an attorney and writer, and the need for greater popular and intellectual understanding of this nation's founding documents. The text of the interview follows.)

Q: **I am going to try to cover several areas and I want to start out with a general discussion of judicial and legal policy, and your philosophy on some of those things. First question: What is the proper role of judges in a democratic society?**

A: The quick answer is: To try to discern the intent of the people who wrote the law they are applying, whether it is constitutional law or statutory law or precedential law.

Q: **In a speech three years ago to the Free Congress Foundation's Conference on Judicial Reform, you spoke of the difference between the "interpretivist" (or strict constructionist) school of constitutional and legal analysis and the "noninterpretivist" (or activist) school. Will you review that difference for our readers?**

A: There has recently grown up, in the law schools in particular, a school of constitutional philosophy which holds that judges are not properly bound by the intent of the framers of the Constitution, but may, indeed should, make new constitutional law, create new rights. And it is suggested that they may do so either because moral philosophy suggests inhibitions on legislative powers not found in the Constitution, or because judges think the legislative process is malfunctioning in some way that they themselves define.

Interpretivists believe the contrary. They think the job of a judge is to understand the principle that the framers were trying to protect, and apply that principle in today's circumstances, which the framers could not have foreseen. But the idea is always to protect the value or the freedom that the framers were trying to protect—and not some new freedom.

Q: **In that 1982 speech, you maintained that if the notion that judges can draw their constitutional rulings from outside the Constitution "achieves entire intellectual hegemony in law schools, as it is on the brink of doing, the results will be disastrous for the constitutional law of this nation." Why would that be disastrous?**

A: Because you would have a small group of unelected, unrepresentative judges making the basic law of the nation, quite irrespective of the desires of the electorate, and quite irrespective of the meaning of the Constitution. That would bring minority tyranny in spades.

Q: **In your Bicentennial speech to the American Philosophical Society back in 1976 you said something that struck me as especially profound. I want to quote just one sentence. Your words were these: "The case has been made, perhaps most effectively by Joseph Schumpeter, that the intellectual classes, given their typical desire to politicize all of society's processes, pose the greatest danger to the future of democratic government." You said something along the**

same line in your 1982 speech at the Free Congress conference, expressing concern about what you called the "gentrification" of the Constitution.

A: I was talking about the fact that if judges begin to create new personal freedoms on the theory that the times demand them or that it is the best moral view, or something of that sort, they will in fact enact as constitutional law the moral judgments of a particular socio-economic class to which they belong and to which they respond.

Judges are not representative of the population at large— either socially or economically or religiously or any other way. They tend to respond to law school faculties, to clerks coming out of those law schools, to journalists, to members of the writing intellectual class. Those are groups with a point of view which does not run the full spectrum of American opinion. If judges simply enforced their own morality, you would get as constitutional law those moral views of a particular class, and a morality that is not by any means generally shared in this country. That's what I meant by the gentrification of the Constitution.

As to the first quotation, I was talking about the fact that the intellectual classes—until very recently, when a significant counter-intellectual movement arose—really seemed to want to politicize, and hence regulate, a great many aspects of life, including markets. What I was talking about was that democratic government is endangered when you politicize everything because it is not possible for representative institutions like Congress to make all of the millions of regulations that are then essential.

So that power necessarily shifts from elected representatives to vast bureaucracies. When you have a democratic government, in the sense that elected representatives are making the decisions, you necessarily have a more or less limited government, because they can't handle everything at once.

Q: **In your speech on December 6, 1984, to the session at the American Enterprise Institute in which you were presented the Francis Boyer Award, you crafted what I thought was a powerful and succinct defense of the historically unique American political structure. Let me read that back to you. You said:**

> Our constitutional liberties arose out of historical experience, and out of political, moral, and religious sentiment. They do not rest upon any general theory. Attempts to frame a theory that removes from demo-

cratic control areas of life the framers intended to leave there can only succeed if abstractions are regarded as overriding the constitutional text and structure, judicial precedent and the history that gives our rights life, rootedness and meaning. It is no small matter to discredit the foundations upon which our constitutional freedoms have always been sustained, and substitute as a bulwark only abstractions of moral philosophy.

These are powerful words and it is a sentiment not necessarily shared in legal circles. Could you elaborate a little bit about what you were driving at there?

A: Yes. The effort to create individual rights out of a general, abstract, moral philosophy, I think, is doomed to failure from the beginning because I don't think there is any version of moral philosophy that can claim to be absolutely superior to all others. What I was saying in the passage you quote is that the rights we enjoy, which were handed down to us, arose out of particular circumstances and particular sentiments and religious beliefs. They are not connected by a general philosophy. And—

Q: In essence, were they a blending? A compromise, if you will?

A: Well, they are a compromise, but also, they were quite specific. The framers had known certain kinds of abuses by government, and they wanted to make sure those abuses did not recur in our national government.

They didn't sit down and work out a utilitarian philosophy or a contractarian philosophy or something of that sort. If the framers intended to leave large areas of life to the democratic process, and we say, "No the framers' intention doesn't count because we have a moral philosophy that says they shouldn't have," then that casts doubt upon the freedoms the framers did give us because they are not supported by that abstract moral philosophy.

I think that approach undercuts the legitimacy and the prestige of our historically rooted freedoms.

Q: Many of your comments on the present state of constitutional and legal interpretation seem to me to reflect implicit criticism of the prevailing mentality in our law schools. What ideology. . .

A: May I just stop and say it is not implicit. It is explicit.

Q: Quite all right. What ideology then, if any, animates the law schools?

A: I doubt that there is a single ideology that animates law schools today. Instead, there are a lot of competing ideologies ranging from the law and economics group to the Critical Legal Studies people.

Among many constitutional law professsors, there is a continual search for general philosophic principles about the nature of a just society which the professors would like judges to convert into constitutional law. This is a relatively new development and I can't say I understand all the reasons for it. Perhaps they just love playing with philosophy and find law too mundane and pedestrian. Or perhaps, in some cases, the professors have realized they are never going to get the electorate and their representatives to agree with them on sound social policy. A quick way, the only way, to the society they want is to get judges to make this society over.

The sin of wanting judges to do good things simply because the electorate won't do them is not confined to liberalism. Conservatives have been known to be infected with that desire, too. There are still a number of them around who want that.

Q. **How do we turn the situation around in the law schools? What is the agenda and what are some of the specific steps required to restore respect for judicial restraint in our law schools?**

A: When you say "an agenda", I don't know that I have an agenda. It seems to me that for the first time in quite a while there is a very sophisticated conservative intellectual movement taking place in law, economics, political science, and elsewhere. That is good because it provides a needed competition in the intellectual marketplace.

The thing to do is encourage young people of that sort to go into academic life and to engage in intellectual debate. We must trust that eventually the power of superior ideas will prevail.

Q: **You were a law professor for many years. Did you ever feel isolated in those days?**

A: Intellectually, not socially.

Q: **All right. Good answer! Turning for a moment to a specific area of the law flowing from what we have been talking about, how would the contending schools of interpretation—the interpretivists and the noninterpretivists—approach the constitutional legitimacy of, say, the death penalty? I am not necessarily asking for what the correct outcome is on the constitutionality (or lack thereof) of the death penalty, but how would an interpretivist approach the matter and noninterpretivist approach it?**

A: Well, I think for an interpretivist, the issue is almost concluded by the fact that the death penalty is specifically referred to, and assumed to be an available penalty, in the Constitution itself. In the Fifth Amendment and in the Fourteenth Amendment. It is a little hard to understand how a penalty that the framers explicitly assumed to be available, can somehow become unavailable because of the very Constitution the framers wrote.

I suppose the noninterpretivists would proceed, as some of them have, by saying, "Well, the standard, for example, of what is a cruel and unusual punishment under the Eighth Amendment is an evolving standard. It moves with the society's new consensus about what is consistent with human dignity, what is too cruel, etc., etc."

And then they say that evolving standard has now reached the death penalty, and eliminates it. But it is not made clear why the standard should evolve.

Q: **In the absence of a constitutional amendment?**

A: That's right. Furthermore, if we do look to what society's current standards are, it is quite clear from the statutes on the books that society's current consensus favors use of the death penalty.

I am not discussing whether the death penalty is a good or a bad idea but only the different constitutional approaches to it.

Q: **In the whole area of Fourth Amendment interpretation, namely the provisions protecting suspects from unreasonable searches and seizures, have the courts gone too far? Let me go on. In your opinion, in the case of *U.S. v. Mount* issued last March, you had a particularly succinct sentence, I thought:**

> **Where no deterrence of unconstitutional police behavior is possible, a decision to exclude probative evidence with the result that a criminal goes free to prey upon the public should shock the judicial conscience even more than admitting the evidence.**

That's pretty tough stuff, and my question is, is that view still a minority among the judiciary, or are things changing?

A: I think they may be changing, but I really can't speak for the judiciary because I don't know in general what most judges think. There appear to be two possible reasons for the exclusionary rule. One is to deter unconstitutional police behavior. It is still being debated whether or not the rule does do that.

The other reason sometimes given is that courts shouldn't soil their hands by allowing in unconstitutionally acquired evidence. I have never been convinced by that argument because it seems the conscience of the court ought to be at least equally shaken by the idea of turning a criminal loose upon society. The only good argument really rests on the deterrence rationale, and it's time we examine that with great care to see how much deterrence we are getting and at what cost.

Q: **In your 1976 speech entitled "Can Democratic Government Survive?" you contended that to many academics, "a sense of guilt had become as essential to good standing as proper manners used to be." Later in that speech you elaborated, "It takes confidence in your values to punish for crime, and yet punishment rates in the United States and all the western world declined even as crime rates soar. It takes assurance to enforce community standards of behavior, and though most of us do not like it, pornography in its ugliest form has become what a national magazine called a plague." In a powerful summation, after you sketched those things out with allusions to Alexis de Tocqueville, you asserted: "A people without energy and self-confidence runs a great risk of tyranny." True enough, but aren't things changing for the better?**

A: Yes, I think I have to qualify that somewhat. I am not so sure today that I see as many signs of guilt in the intellectual world as I did then. The late 1960s and early 1970s, with the student rebellions and turmoil, seemed to create a lot of intellectual guilt in their elders. There still may be some of that. But I don't think people flaunt their guilt quite as much as they did then. It got to the point where you couldn't go to a cocktail party without listening to at least one confession of guilt.

Q: **You also said, [paraphrasing] "It takes confidence to punish crime, to enforce community standards on things like pornography."**

A: Well, I think the electorate and the American people at large have begun to show that they don't suffer from this lack of confidence in their values, and that they want more punishment for crimes, they want high community standards. They want certain community standards enacted into law.

Q: **You said, "A people without energy and self-confidence runs a greater risk of tyranny." I found that a compelling sentence.**

A: Well, if a people does not have confidence in its values, and if it is not a vigorous people, then it's much easier for government or for a faction to get a hold of government and enforce its narrow values. An apathetic people or a people with a defeatist attitude would be easier to tyrannize than a people that stands up and resists because it has confidence in its values.

Q: Some analysts (political scientists and others) maintain that in essence the Equal Rights Amendment movement, the ERA movement, is dead. I am not so sure of that. In any case, ten years ago you observed, "The ERA represents less a revolution in sexual equality than it does a revolution in constitutional methods of government." What did you mean by that?

A: I no longer feel free to comment about ERA since I'm now a judge. But I do feel free to explain what I meant ten years ago, which was that the Amendment didn't say that Congress shall have power to provide for sexual equality in all cases, or something of that sort. What it said was, "Judges shall have power to decide what sexual equality is in all cases."

Now the role that men and women should play in society is a highly complex business, and it changes as our culture changes. What I was saying then was that it was a shift in constitutional methods of government to have judges deciding all of those enormously sensitive, highly political, highly cultural issues. If they are to be decided by government, the usual course would be to have them decided by a democratic process in which those questions are argued out.

Q: In your AEI lecture last year you maintained that "the institutions of law, in particular the schools, are becoming increasingly converted to an ideology of the Constitution that demands . . . an infusion of extra constitutional moral and political notions. A not untypical example of the first is the entry into the law of the First Amendment of the old and incorrect view that the only kinds of harm that a community is entitled to suppress are physical and economic injuries. Moral harms are not to be counted because to do so would interfere with the autonomy of the individual. That is an indefensible definition of what people are entitled to regard as harm."

Now you actually seemed to be saying there that lawmakers can act on moral impulses! Seriously, isn't that a self-evident proposition? And are there really serious consitutional scholars who disagree on this?

A: Oh, yes, I discussed a case which was, in fact, *Cohen v. California*, in which the Supreme Court was going to deny the community the right to say, "We find the use of that word in public immoral. . . "

Q: **The F—— word?**

A: Yes. You will find a long list of scholars who would say that. They've got the thing turned upside down. They would say the judges may have a view of morality which they may read into the Constitution and that this overrides any view of morality the legislature might have. So you wind up with judges instead of legislatures making public morality, which I think very odd where the Constitution doesn't speak to the question.

I could give you a long list of scholars who hold this odd view of judicial supremacy.

Q: **What is the rule or method of constitutional interpretation that led to the so-called "privacy doctrine" which has given us (through judicial interpretation) abortion on demand, constitutional protection of homosexual rights, and so forth?**

A: Well, the so-called right of privacy was born in the case of *Griswold v. Connecticut.* And again, but for the fact that I wrote this before I became a judge, I would be hesitant to say it, but I did write it before I became a judge.

I don't think there is a supportable method of constitutional reasoning underlying the *Griswold* decision. The majority opinion merely notes that there are a lot of guarantees in the Constitution which could be viewed as guarantees of aspects of privacy. As a matter of fact, that's a misnomer because a lot of them guarantee public action. But the opinion then says, since we have all these Amendments which can be viewed as guaranteeing particular rights of privacy, we can generalize and create a general right of privacy.

Of course, that right of privacy strikes without warning. It has no intellectual structure to it so you don't know in advance to what it applies.

Q: **Well, my next question is, I think you have already answered it—is this a legitimate expression of the intent of the framers?**

A: Well, as I said years ago, I thought the privacy notion had little to do with the intent of the framers.

Q: **I am now going to ask you a couple of questions about areas where some conservatives disagree with you. Many of us have pushed for "withdrawal" or significant restriction of federal court jurisdiction** over certain controversial social issues, including abortion and bus-ing, school prayer, and so forth. We have maintained that this power exists under Article III, Section 2, of the Constitution, which defines the Supreme Court's jurisdiction "with such Exceptions and under such Regulations as the Congress shall make." You have maintained, eloquently, that this power does not reach as far as many conserva-tives believe. Although none of the Court regulating measures appear likely to pass in the near future, the significance of the discussion and of the controversy is clear. Will you elaborate your views for our readers?

A: In the first place, I am quite clear that the Congress has the power to remove jurisdiction as it likes from district courts and courts of appeals. Those are courts that Congress need not have created, and I think it could remove all jurisdiction and leave us all sitting here until we died off. That would be constitutional. The problem really arises only with respect to the Supreme Court, which is created by the Constitution and given appellate jurisdiction by the Constitution.

Now, as to Article III, Section 2, which you point out has the exceptions clause. It says the courts shall have appellate jurisdic-tion with such exceptions and regulations as the Congress may make. The question then becomes whether that enables the Con-gress to remove entire categories of jurisdiction from the Supreme Court because it dislikes what the Court is doing. And I must confess, although I have given an answer to that in the past, it seems to me the answer is not entirely clear for the following reason: I am clear that the exceptions clause was never designed for a use like this. If you should only use a clause for the purposes for which it was designed, then you shouldn't use it for this purpose.

Q: For what purpose was it designed?

A: I think it was designed for administrative detail and convenience and so forth. The reason we know it was not designed for the purpose we are discussing is that if the framers had been trying to create a check against a runaway Supreme Court, that's the last check they would have devised, because in the most important classes of cases you can't use it.

For example, if a challenge to an all-male draft or registration came up on constitutional grounds, you could hardly take away the Supreme Court's jurisdiction. If you did, jurisdiction would remain in all the state court systems; and, under the supremacy clause which requires state judges to apply the Constitution, I don't think you can remove jurisdiction from state courts.

The result is that with respect to any policy that requires national uniformity you can't use the exceptions clause. The framers would never have designed a check on the Court that couldn't be used in very important cases.

The other reason is, if you were really devising a check to vindicate democracy against a runaway judiciary, you wouldn't devise a mechanism that puts the issue in a different set of judges. The framers would have devised a mechanism that put the issue back into Congress or state legislatures. But they didn't do that.

And that's what makes me think that they never intended the exceptions clause as a democratic check on the Supreme Court. They probably weren't even thinking about judicial review as a problem. In those days, nobody had ever seen judicial review. They didn't know what kind of a problem it could become.

Having said that, on the other side it must be said that Congress did not give the federal courts and indeed the Supreme Court certain kinds of jurisdiction for years and years and years after the Constitution was created. It's a little hard to say that Congress need not have given jurisdiction, but once having given it, may not take it away.

So I am a little bit in balance on this issue, and I would not want to have to decide it unless I heard arguments on both sides. On the one hand, the clause was not meant for this purpose; on the other hand, that isn't conclusive proof that it could not be used for this purpose.

Q: **Let me ask you about the *Ollman* libel-law case in which you filed a concurring opinion. The court had sided with the Evans and Novak columnist team in a dispute over a column they printed about a Marxist college professor. You expressed concern in your opinion about "a remarkable upsurge in libel actions accompanied by a startling inflation of damage awards."**

Mike McDonald, of the [Washington] Legal Foundation, has strongly criticized your opinion, saying "the old Bork would have frowned on the judicial identification of and attempt to solve perceived social problems caused by libel suits since such matters are quintessentially legislative tasks. The new Bork, though, rejects this separation of powers."

A: I don't think I have to defend myself. He's quite wrong about the old Bork. I mentioned the upsurge in libel actions, and there has been an enormous increase in such suits. It seems pretty clear that, along with the meritorious suits, there are a number that are filed not because anybody has been really damaged, but to punish columnists or somebody else who has written something the plaintiff does not like. It's not a question of judges assuming a general power to go out and solve social problems. Judges have no such power. But we do have a First Amendment. And the First Amendment enjoins judges to keep the process of political discussion open. If judges change the way libel law is applied, and they have, so that it begins to represent a threat to political discussion, then in an opinion like *Ollman* I don't think I am going out to solve a social problem. I think I am defending the central meaning of the First Amendment if I say, "Wait a minute. This particular lawsuit poses too much of a threat to political discussion and the freedom of the press." Not all libel suits pose such a threat, but some do.

Q: **Returning, almost, to some of the things we have talked about at the beginning of the interview. I think there is a very important matter in legal policy that is not understood by laymen, by nonlawyers, that I have come to understand from my work in the area. That is terribly important—and that is standing. What is standing, the term "standing"—explain it to the folks out there. First of all, what is it? And second, why has it become a problem in the modern judiciary?**

A: Standing is a requirement that courts have gotten out of Article III, the judiciary article of the Constitution. The issue of standing is jurisdictional. If a court concludes that a party lacks standing, the court may not proceed to decide the merits of the suit. Though it is sometimes said that standing raises the question whether the party is fit to litigate an issue, whether he has been injured directly so that he possesses "that concrete adverseness which sharpens the presentation of issues" (*Baker v. Carr*, 1962), it is clear that much more is involved. The standing requirement, at bottom, has to do with what kinds of interest courts will undertake to protect. As Justice Powell put it in *Warth v. Seldin* (1975):

> In essence the question of standing is whether the litigant is entitled to have the court decide the merits of the dispute or of particular issues. This inquiry involves both constitutional limitations on federal court jurisdiction and prudential limitations on its excercise. In both dimensions [standing] is founded in concern about the proper—and properly limited—role of the courts in a democratic society.

This should make it clear that the jurisdictional requirement of standing keeps courts out of areas that are not properly theirs.

It is thus an aspect of democratic theory. Questions of jurisdiction are questions of power, power not merely over the case at hand but power over issues and over other branches of government. Article III of the Constitution confers the "judicial Power of the United States" and limits that power in several ways. Among the most important limitations is that expressed in section 2 of article III, confining our jurisdiction to "Cases" and "Controversies." The meaning of those terms, however, is decided by federal courts. It follows that judges can determine the extent of their own power within American government by how they define cases and controversies. It is for this reason that the proper definition of those terms is crucial to the maintenance of the separation of powers that is central to our consitutional structure.

"Standing" is one of the concepts courts have evolved to limit their jurisdiction and hence to preserve the separation of powers. A critical aspect of the idea of standing is the definition of the interests that courts are willing to protect through adjudication. A person may have an interest in receiving money supposedly due him under law. Courts routinely regard an injury to that interest as conferring upon that person standing to litigate. Another person may have an equally intensely felt interest in the proper constitutional performance of the United States government. Courts have routinely regarded injury to that interest as not conferring standing to litigate. The difference between the two situations is not the reality or intensity of the injuries felt but a perception that according standing in the latter case would so enhance the power of the courts as to make them the dominant branch of government. There would be no issue of governance that could not at once be brought into the federal courts for conclusive disposition. Every time a court expands the definition of standing, the definition of the interests it is willing to protect through adjudication, the area of judicial dominance grows and the area of democratic rule contracts.

Q: **Back in that 1976 speech you observed that recently there has occurred a shift in opinion about "the omniscience of government." You continued: "Detailed bureaucratic government may be benevolent in intention, but it is often perceived by its beneficiaries as officious intermeddling." The subsequent election seemed to show**

that you perceived a political trend that was just beginning. Is this shift in mood good? And what is the proper role of government?

A: I think the shift in mood is good. I think we were and still are an overregulated people, and the regulation, in many cases, really doesn't accomplish any identifiable good result. That is a pragmatic judgment and has nothing to do with my job as a judge. In this court we deal with a lot of governmental regulation and I try to apply it as was intended.

I don't think I can define the role of government in abstract terms. This is kind of a parallel to my feeling that you can't define the rights of the individual by abstract general philosophy.

In discussing the role of government, we really ought to have something in the back of our head, a kind of an idea about a budget of regulation. There is just so much regulation we can handle as a society and do so effectively. We must not overregulate people so that they begin to lose their vigor and their innovativeness and so forth.

What the government should do is identify those areas where it can make a real contribution at a relatively low cost to free social processes. And I can't define those for you. It seems to be a pragmatic judgment in each case.

Q: **It might vary from era to era.**

A: Sure. And I can't define it in philosophical terms.

Q: **In that same 1976 speech, you said: "The enormous profusion of regulations is incompatible with the democratic process. Democratic government is limited government for the simple reason that there are economies of scale in government institutions, as in all others." Is that the point you are making?**

A: Yes, that's right. That's a point I think I made, well, earlier in this interview, that you can't have ten Congresses all working at once. You have one Congress. We can only handle so much information. When you try to regulate too many things, the innumerable decisions simply can no longer be made democratically. They are going to be made by bureaucracies and by so many bureaucracies that even congressional oversight may be ineffective. That's what I meant by the tendency to get away from democratic government.

Q: **What—I want to ask you a few personal questions, just things about your philosophy, as it were. One, is why are you a lawyer? Why is Bob Bork a lawyer? What things started you down that path?**

A: Well, I think the major thing was that Columbia School of Journalism wouldn't send me an application. So I went to law school instead.

Q: **Really?**

A: Yes. I like words, I like writing, I like argument, I like thinking about problems of public affairs which seemed to me to mean either journalism or law. When I got out of college I thought, quite wrongly, that in order to be a journalist I should go to a graduate school of journalism.

It turns out that was not necessary at all but I didn't know that. I didn't know any journalists, so I sent off to Columbia and asked for an application, and they wrote back and said, "We see you have a degree from the University of Chicago." That was the old Hutchins degree, which was a bit weird. They said, "We don't recognize it. So if you will go some place else for two years, we will then send you an application form." That infuriated me, so I went to law school.

Q: **That's great! That's a great story. I would be remiss if I didn't ask the obvious question to handle however you wish. Judge Bork, you are frequently mentioned as being among the top five from whom President Reagan might select his next Supreme Court nominee. I realize this is really a tough question for you, but how does that make you feel, and do you think it is really in the cards?**

A: I know no more than what the newspapers say, so I have no idea whether it might be in the cards. And, it has been going on for a number of years now, so it doesn't really make me feel any particular way. I have gotten inured to it.

Q: **What is your personal political philosophy, broadly defined?**

A: Well, I suppose it is generally known so there is no harm in speaking about it. In matters of economics, I belong in general to the Free Market school. On the other hand, I am not a libertarian in social matters. Most people would probably say I am a conservative. But political outlook has little to do with judicial philosophy. As you pointed out, there are conservatives who favor judicial activism, and I know political liberals who favor judicial restraint.

Q: **I sense an increasing attention and concern among average Americans about the role of the judiciary in a democratic society. What book or books would you recommend from the past or present for** the intelligent layman to read if he wants to comment on or criticize ongoing legal policy, legal decisions? In essence, what I mean by this is what should the average guy who gets interested in these issues read to become better informed on the theory and reality of American law?

A: That's an impossible question. I taught a seminar on constitutional theory using books and articles for three semesters, as the course materials, and I didn't find any work that I regarded as adequate.

I hope to write that book myself, but I am sure lots of people won't think it adequate either.

Q: **What four or five books most powerfully influenced your political philosophy?**

A: It was more a long series of conversations at the University of Chicago and at Yale than it was any particular book. But I suppose back then *The Road to Serfdom* influenced me. Perhaps the *Federalist Papers*, *The Possessed* by Dostoevski, *Witness* by Whittaker Chambers, *Darkness at Noon* by Arthur Koestler. It would take me days to recall all of the books you would have me mention.

One difficulty is that a lot of books influenced my philosophy because I disagreed with them. Often our ideas are formed and refined as much by those with whom we disagree as by those with whom we agree.

You see, I think political philosophy is more a matter of practical wisdom than of abstract speculation. What's consistent with freedom in this case? How much is it going to cost us? Not in terms of money alone, but also in terms of freedom and social cohesions.

These are matters of understanding the world in a very practical sense and making judgments both about values and costs and benefits. The *Federalist Papers* perceived of political philosophy that way.

Q: **What four or five books most powerfully influenced your judicial/ legal philosophy?**

A: What influenced it primarily was a seminar I taught with Alex Bickel in which we argued about these matters all the time. We taught it for seven years, and I finally worked out a philosophy which is expressed pretty much in that 1971 *Indiana Law Journal* piece which you have probably seen—"Neutral Principles And Some First Amendment Problems." I have read a lot of books that influenced me. But I never read one that came to me as a revelation.

Q: **No, but the ones that you played off and disagreed with?**

A: Oh, that. I can give you the names of those. *The Least Dangerous Branch*, by Alex Bickel, which was the best of the ones I disagreed with. *Democracy and Distrust*, by John Ely. Ronald Dworkin's writing. Harry Wellington's articles. There are a lot more. I could go through the reading list for my seminar. I think I disagreed in some respects with everybody that I gave to the students to read. I couldn't find much to give them to read of what I believed.

Q: **In essence, we are inventing the system? We are inventing the philosophy all over again, reempowering . . . ?**

A: Bickel made this point years ago. The judiciary had sort of a tradition. There wasn't much theory. It was tradition. Judges do this; they don't do that. The last thirty years shattered that tradition and now the theories justify judicial activism. These are the theories I referred to earlier as noninterpretivist. And there is the interpretivist counter theorizing beginning to pick up. We can't rely upon tradition any more. Now we need theory.

Q: **The question is, what are the theoretical constructs? What are the practical rules of legal procedure to reempower the intent of the framers in 1986?**

A: Well, I have given five or six speeches that seem to me to contain most of the pieces. Now, I've got to sit down and put them together in a short book, as soon as I find the time.

Q: **A few years ago I remember talking at length with a man I came to admire more and more with the passage of time. He is Professor Raoul Berger, an old-line FDR liberal Democrat whose intellectual honesty has led him, in essence, to be a defender of conservative critics of the modern judiciary, and one of your more articulate and forceful admirers.**

   Berger made the point, in his speech at the 1982 Conference on Judicial Reform, that he did not think there were many grounds for optimism. He counseled the audience against "facile optimism" for resolving the difficult problems, and for getting the courts back on track, and winning the intellectual battles and so forth. What is your perspective on that?

A: Well, there is obviously no room for "facile optimism". There never is. But there is reason for some optimism.

   There was a time, when I first started writing about antitrust and teaching it, that the situation seemed hopeless. Many of the rules created by the courts make little economic sense and were doing consumers more harm than good. But only a few people thought that. It seemed the weight of the political and the intellectual traditions of antitrust were too heavily against the free market for reform ever to take place. Most people in the field regarded what a few of us were saying as eccentric if not ridiculous, so far out of the mainstream as to be mostly irrelevant. But look now. Gradually those ideas have become the dominant ideas in antitrust scholarship. And they have significantly affected the enforcement policies of the Department of Justice and the Federal Trade Commission, a result I would have thought absolutely impossible twenty years ago.

I am not at all sure that the debate over the proper role of the courts is an intellectual argument we can't win similarly.

Q: One step at a time?

A: Yes. I find a lot of young people today who are quite responsive to the way I argue about constitutional law. That was not so true twenty years ago.

Q: Might it not be a good idea, getting back to our earlier discussion of legal education, for constitutional law courses, for example, to spend the whole semester on the Constitution, *The Federalist Papers*, and perhaps Joseph Story's *Commentaries*, rather than a week on those things and the remaining eleven weeks on case law?

A: As a matter of fact, usually there are fourteen weeks, and few professors spend even a week on Story, or The *Federalist Papers*, or the original Constitution. I know I didn't. I think you have put your finger on something. Walter Berns has made the point that nobody in law school is teaching the Constitution. They are teaching Supreme Court opinions. If we are going to have a well-rounded legal profession that understands the philosophy as well as the latest precedent, we really ought to have a full semester at least on the history, The *Federalist Papers*, Story, and so forth.

Most law students today read primarily cases of the last twenty years or so because the older cases get weeded out of the case book. They have no idea that some constitutional subjects have undergone a revolution, because they don't know any prior history. They sometimes think that some decision is really essential to our freedom, and if it were overruled, all kinds of terrible things would happen, without realizing that this country went on for a century and three quarters without that decision. Maybe it's a good decision or a bad decision—but it is not, as students tend to suppose, an inevitable decision.

I would like to see a course built of that sort you describe. Indeed, I would like to teach it for my own education.

Appendix C

Larry Tribe's America

(Uninvited, one day, this came in over the transom. No doubt a better job could be done to summarize Professor Tribe's creative jurisprudence—but this will have to do for now.)

In Larry Tribe's America, there is, as he argued to the Supreme Court, a constitutional right to privacy protecting homosexual sodomy.

In Larry Tribe's America, there is a constitutional right to take drugs.

In Larry Tribe's America, the taxpayers are required by the Constitution to pay for abortions.

In Larry Tribe's America, we the people cannot in any way restrict obscene words, pictures, movies or magazines.

In Larry Tribe's America, motorcyclists have a constitutional right to ride helmetless, because their choice to do so is an "expressive" activity.

In Larry Tribe's America, students, policemen, firemen, teachers and military personnel all have a constitutional right to wear their hair at any length they choose, otherwise society is imposing on them a "falsification of self."

In Larry Tribe's America, unelected federal judges would decide the type of housing to which he says every American is constitutionally entitled.

In Larry Tribe's America, unelected federal judges would decide the level of education to which he says every American is constitutionally entitled.

In Larry Tribe's America, unelected federal judges govern, as one commentator stated, "almost any aspect of human conduct," such as "aid to parochial schools, almost any aspect of the political process, school dress codes, ombudsman, psychiatric treatment, motorcycle helmets, the distribution of wealth, sexual preferences, beer-drinking, hair length, dying, family life—the list is virtually endless."

In Larry Tribe's America, the people do not rule. Judges do.

Biographical Notes

Patrick B. McGuigan is Editor of the *Family, Law and Democracy Report*, a monthly newsletter monitoring national, state and local policy developments on issues of the family, legal policy and direct democracy. He is also Senior Scholar at the Free Congress Foundation's Center for Law and Democracy. From 1980–87, he was Director of the Foundation's Judicial Reform Project, and from 1983–87 he served as legal affairs analyst at Coalitions for America. McGuigan is the author of *The Politics of Direct Democracy: Case Studies in Popular Decision Making* (1985), and the editor of six books on legal policy issues, including *Crime and Punishment in Modern America* (1986) and *The Judges War* (1987).

Dawn M. Weyrich is a reporter for the Washington *Times*. A graduate of Virginia Commonwealth University in Richmond, she is a former correspondent for American Press International. In spring of 1988, she worked as a Research Associate at the Free Congress Foundation, and later as press secretary/issues director for U.S. Senate candidate Steve King in Wisconsin.

R. H. Bork, Jr. is a speech writer for Senator Gordon Humphrey (R-NH). He wrote the essay in this book while the visiting fellow in journalism at the Heritage Foundation in Washington, D.C. A former Associate Editor at *U.S. News and World Report*, he has also worked at *Forbes* magazine.

Index

ABC, 7, 59, 99, 102, 149, 171, 194, 245, 260, 269–270.
Abraham, E. Spence, 86.
Abrams, Floyd, 21.
Access to Justice, 66.
Ad Hoc Committee in Defense of Life, 33.
Adams, Brock, 16, 90, 178, 242.
Advocacy Institute, 38, 276.
Albuquerque Journal, 115.
AFL-CIO, 23, 74, 98, 175, 211, 249, 250.
Aiken, George, 95.
Alabama Democratic Conference, 124.
Alabama New South Coalition, 124.
Allentown (PA) Morning Call, 252.
Alliance for Justice, 8, 18, 23, 32, 39, 60, 89, 137, 148, 208, 249, 250.
Alsop, Joseph, 272.
Alsop, Stewart, 272.
American Association of University Women, 94.
American Bar Association (ABA), 12, 43, 59, 60, 87–89, 140, 142, 152, 163, 192, 216, 224, 227, 236, 267, 283.
American Civil Liberties Union (ACLU), xvi, 32, 38, 39, 70, 74, 75, 137, 148, 149, 153, 162,

168, 173, 174, 195, 250, 252, 256, 261, 268.
American Conservative Union, x, xvii, xix, 3, 29, 31, 44, 51, 56, 57, 71, 76, 80, 101, 123, 124, 125, 130, 136, 149, 150, 160, 164, 173, 174, 187, 203, 252.
American Enterprise Institute, 287.
American Farm Bureau Federation, 73.
American Federation of State, County and Municipal Employees (AFSCME), 211, 250.
American Legislative Exchange Council, 67, 234–235.
American Political Science Association, 207.
American Philosophical Society, 286.
American Press International, (the reporting of Dawn M. Weyrich, 227–243).
American University, 7, 65,249.
Americans for Bork, 177, (October 9 rally, 183–187), 192.
Americans for Robertson, 173.
Americans for Tax Reform, 173.
Americans United for Separation of Church and State, 137, 139, 165.
Anderson, Carl, 124.

Anderson, Curt, 123, 125, 150, 173, 174.
Antosh, Cindy, 95.
Aponte, Maria Carmen, 41.
Arizona, University of, 144, 154.
Arizona Republic, 81, 154, 239.
Armstrong, William, 16, 90, 242.
Aron, Nan, 8, 18–19, 32, 39, 60, 89, 148, 228, 249.
Arsht, Leslye, 99.
Associated Press (AP), 124, 127.
Atlanta Journal and Constitution, 167.

Babbitt, Bruce, 5, 24.
Babcock, Barbara, 268.
Baer, Steve, 70, 91, 124, 133.
Baker, John T., 197–199.
Baker, Howard, 11, 24, 47, 50, 80, 99, 142, 157, 161, 162, 167, 171, 176, 188, 193, 194, 219–220, 253, 254.
Bakst, Charles, 62.
Baldwin, Donald, xvii, xxi, 28, 82, 123, 145–146, 150, 164, 173, 201.
Ball, Will, 47, 51, 106, 138, 216, 219–220, 224, 253, 254.
Baltimore Sun, 20, 57, 127, 229, 269.
Barnes, John, 151.
Barone, Michael, 21.
Baryshnikov, Mikail, 76.
Barzun, Jacques, 257, 258, 278.
Bass III, Kenneth, 21, 22.
Baucus, Max, 16, 30, 90, 169, 230, 242.
Bauer, Gary, 43, 47.
Baum, Gerry, 62.
Beards for Bork, 31–32, 174, 204–205.
Beckwith, David, 28, 115, 247.
Bellizzi, John, 146.
Benchmark, 82.

Bell, Griffin, 102, 158.
Bell, March, 173.
Bennett, William, xix, 47, 221.
Bentsen, Lloyd, 16, 90, 125, 167, 202, 242.
Berger, Raoul, 33, 239, 301.
Berman, Jerry, 148, 250.
Berns, Walter, 302.
Bernstein, Carl, 275.
Between Fact and Fiction: The Problem of Journalism, 274.
Bickel, Alexander, 137, 252, 300, 301.
Biden, Joseph, 4, 5, 6, 7, 8, 11, 16, 19, 20, 21, 22, 23, 28, 29, 33, 36, 37, 40, 41, 43, 44, 46, 48, 56, 58, 59, 60, 61, 62, 64, 69, 70, 74, 76, 88, 89, 90, 94, 95, 96–98, 108–131, 132, 137, 138, 139, 142, 146, 147, 153, 158, 161, 163, 166, 178, 188, 196, 197, 198, 203, 210, 211, 212, 213, 215, 227–228, 242, 250, 259–60, 262–263, 268, 272, 284. (expressions of support for Bork, 19–20)
Bierbower, James, 88.
Billings, Jo, 173, 177, 180, 183–185, 201.
Bingaman, Bob, 39.
Bingaman, Jeff, 16, 90, 115, 169, 192, 202, 242.
Bismark Tribune, 229.
Bittick, L. Cary, 146.
Black, Charles, 114.
Black, Justice Hugo, 54, 71, 88, 113, 255, 280, 281.
Blackmun, Justice Harry, 64.
Blackwell, Kenneth, 133.
Blackwell, Morton, 173, 185, 186–187, 189, 201.
Blair, Kristin, 67.
Bloom, Allan, 197.
Blumenthal, Jackie, 101.

B'nai B'rith, 70.
Bole, William, 232.
Bolton, John, 136, 142.
Bond, Christopher (Kit), 16, 90, 242.
Boone, Pastor Wellington, 183, 185.
Boren, David, 16, 90, 125, 168, 169, 202, 240, 242.
bork, to (definition), 213.
Bork, Charles (son), 107, 172, 205.
Bork, Claire (Davidson, first wife, deceased), 13, 121.
Bork, Ellen (daughter), 107, 172, 205.
Bork, Mary Ellen (second wife), 61, 107, 165, 172, 179, 201, 205, 270.
Bork, Judge Robert H.,
   abortion issue and nomination of (c.f. National Abortion Rights Action League, Kate Michelman), 9, 14, 18–19, 23, 25, 27, 33, 39, 42, 62, 63, 69, 84, 86–87, 93, 100, 109, 111, 142, 143, 148, 172, 222–223.
   "agnostic" charge and, 28, 114–116, 247.
   attacks on sensitivity, honesty, integrity and ethics of (c.f. James Gordon; c.f. Bork, Watergate and), 10, 14, 19, 24, 25, 26, 37–38, 40, 42, 56, 58, 59, 63, 64, 65, 70–71, 75, 76, 83, 99–100, 107, 111, 114, 118, 119, 121, 122–123, 126, 127–129, 138,139, 141, 142–143,144,153, 159, 160–161, 162, 163, 172, 189, 202–203, 209, 211–212, 214, 218–219, 221, 223, 225, 231, 232, 235, 247–248, 255–256, 261, 262, 268–269, 270–271.
   background of, 13, 59, 92–93.

Communist Party, U.S.A. opposition to, 62.
conservative "movement" support for nomination and confirmation of, 2–6, 8, 15–18, 22, 27–30, 50–51, 57–58, 62–65, 66–67, 67–70, 71, 73–75, 77–78, 78–80, 86, 89–92, 94, 95–96, 101–103, 115, 123–127, 133, 139, 150–152, 154–156, 164–166, 173–174, 175, 176–177, 179–182, 183–187, 189–190, 191–192, 195–196, 198, 199, 201–202, (analysis of) 207–226, 234, 236, 252–254.
delay in hearings of, 40–41, 68–69, 191.
immediate reaction to nomination of, 13–15.
judicial philosophy of (see also all of Chapter Five), 109, 119, 285–303.
law enforcement issues/organizations and, 28, 49, 61–62, 65–66, 124–125, 145–146, 182, 184, 231.
liberal/Left opposition to nomination and confirmation of, 3, 6, 7–8, 9–10, 14–15, 20–24, 42–44, 48, 53, 56–58, 62–65, 66, 70–71, 74, 75–76, 77–78, 81, 84–86, 94, 98–99, 100–103, 105–107, 124, 165–166, (analysis of) 207–226, 234, 235, 236, 239, 249–252.
liberal support for, 32–35, 103, 113–114, 147, 152–153, 166, 231.
National Rifle Association decision to remain neutral and nomination of, 78–80.
polls on the nomination and confirmation of, 47, 50, 59,

127, 149–150, 158, 167, 194, 270, 271, 272.
Watergate and, 26, 54, 58, 64, 99, 108, 114, 160–161, 229–230, 259, 265–266.
White House "strategy" in support of nomination and confirmation of, 8–9, 11–13, 24–25, 47, 50–51, 53–56, 82, 92–94, 105–107, 142, 157–158, 160, 162, 166–167, 169, 170, 175–176, 186–187, 188–189, 216–217, 219–220, 224, 253–254.
Bork, Jr., Robert H. (son), 107, 171–172, 201, 205, 245–278, 307.
Born, Gary, 144.
Boschwitz, Rudy, 16, 90, 242.
Boston Globe, 168, 230, 241, 275.
Boston Herald, 151.
Bott Broadcasting, 167.
Boulet, James (Jim), 123, 173.
Bradley, Tom, 88.
Bradley, William (Bill), 16, 90, 162, 242.
Bradbury, Dieter, 151.
Brandeis, Justice Louis, 88, 221.
Breaux, John, 16, 90, 125, 138, 149, 167, 169, 177, 178, 179, 202, 222, 242.
Brennan, Justice William J., 3, 20, 64.
British Broadcasting Corporation, 98.
Broder, David, 277.
Broadcast, 101.
Broff, Nancy, 137.
Bronner, Ethan, 243, 275.
Brown, Chris, 168.
Brownstein, Ronald, 93.
Brubaker, Stanley C., 243.
Buchanan, John, 252.
Buchanan, Patrick, 218, 254.
Buckley, Jr., William F., 223.

Bumpers, Dale, 16, 90, 182, 242.
Burdick, Quentin, 16, 90, 242.
Burger, Chief Justice Warren, 19, 60, 62, 89, 136, 146, 174, 267.
Burns, Conrad, 222.
Bush, George, xiv, 43, 44, 176, 207–208, 214, 215, 222, 246.
Bushmill (c.f. Irish Whiskey), 204–205.
Byrd, Robert, 8, 11, 16, 26, 36, 49, 90, 92, 125, 130, 133, 159, 161–162, 169, 171, 191, 198, 236, 242, 260–261.

Cable News Network (CNN), 136, 192, 252.
Cahill, Gordon & Reindel, 21.
Calgary, University of, 207.
California at Davis, University of, 273.
California at Los Angeles, University of (UCLA), 21.
California Bar Association, 88.
Canisius College (Buffalo), 128.
Cannon, Carl, 257.
Carlucci, Frank, 9.
Carmen, Gerald (Gerry), 195.
Carper, Judy, 4, 203.
Carrington, Frank, 137, 146.
Carroll, Daniel, xv.
Carter, Jimmy, 21, 32, 88, 147, 152, 158, 163, 191, 216, 224, 265.
Casanova, Jose Mănuel, 41.
Case Western Reserve University, 99.
Casey, Daniel (Dan), ix, x, xvii, xix, xxi, 3, 16, 27, 28, 29, 39–40, 44, 45, 56, 57, 72, 76, 80, 99, 100, 101, 112, 114, 123, 124, 125, 130–133, 136, 138–39, 149, 150, 160, 161–162, 163, 164–165, 169, 173, 177, 182, 183–185, 187, 188, 194, 195–196, 201, 203, 204–205, 209, 222, 252.

Catholic League for Religious and
Civil Rights, 133.
CBN University, 67.
CBS, 6, 70, 71, 74, 139, 168, 247,
260, 272.
Center for Communication, 277.
Center for Judicial Studies, 30, 173,
176, 198, 253.
Center for Peace and Freedom, 173.
Center for Media Studies, 271.
Chafee, John, 16, 62, 90, 125, 151,
169, 171, 192, 202, 222, 242.
Chambers, Whittaker, 300.
Chappaquiddick, 138, 199.
Chicago, University of, 13, 21, 34,
56, 144, 159, 197, 299, 300.
Chiles, Lawton, 16, 90, 125, 149,
169, 177, 178, 192, 194, 202,
242.
Christian Legal Defense & Educa-
tion Foundation, 173–174.
Christian Science Monitor Radio,
168.
Christian Voice, 86, 175.
Christic Institute, 38, 232.
Chwast, Seymour, 257.
Ciarrocchi, Guy, 156.
Citizens for America, 154, 172, 195.
Citizens for Reagan, 133.
City Paper, 111, 247.
Claybrook, Joan, 32.
Clayton, Jack, 173–174, 195.
Cleaver, Beaver, xvii.
Cleveland Plain Dealer, 236, 239.
Clifford, Clark, 21.
Clifford & Warnke, 21.
Coalition for Lesbian & Gay
Rights, 195.
Coalitions for America, x, xix, 2, 3,
4, 27, 28, 29, 30, 42, 44, 50,
51, 57, 63, 67, 71, 72, 73, 78,
86, 105, 112, 123, 125, 150, 167,
173, 174, 176, 177, 189, 202,
213, 214, 230–231, 233, 234,

252. [Kingston, 177]; [Library
Court, 2, 177]; [721 Group, 3,4,
27, 28, 50, 63, 73, 78, 176–177,
189, 213.]
Cochran, Thad, 16, 90, 125, 242.
Cohen, David, 38, 276–278.
Cohen, Richard, 214.
Cohen, William, 16, 90, 125, 151,
169, 177, 182, 202, 240, 242.
Coleman, William, 140.
College Republicans, 156.
Collins, Carrie, 19.
Columbia Journalism Review, 277.
Columbia Law Review, 98.
Columbia magazine (Knights of
Columbus), 218.
Columbia University, 240, 271, 275,
299.
Commentaries on the Constitution,
302.
Commentary, 243.
Common Cause, 32, 38, 39, 53, 74.
Communist Party U.S.A., 62.
Concerned Citizens for Democracy,
41.
Concerned Women for America,
xvii, 27, 28, 31, 58, 63, 72, 74,
123, 124, 125, 152, 154–156,
163, 173, 252.
*Conflict of Visions: Ideological
Origins of Political Struggles*,
252.
Congress of Racial Equality, 8, 162.
Connover, Dave, 78.
Conrad, Kent, 16, 26, 90, 179, 242.
Conservative Caucus, 30, 184, 195,
201.
Conservative Digest, 4, 82, 225,
236, 285–303 (Bork interview).
Conservative Leadership Political
Action Commiitte, 189, 201.
Contact America, 64, 167, 168, 174.
Cooper, Charles (Chuck), 2.
Cooper, Gloria, 277.

Cox, Archibald, 13, 26, 38, 99, 114, 126, 160, 229–230, 265, 266.
Council for National Policy, 82.
Cranston, Alan, 7, 16, 44, 60, 90, 161, 163, 171, 178, 179, 193–194, 242.
Craver, Roger, 86, 250.
Cribb, T. Kenneth (Ken), xviii, 124, 195.
Criminals Against Bork (c.f. Eugene Delgaudio), 199.
Critical Legal Studies, 289.
Csorba, Les, 66, 77, 139, 165–166.
C-SPAN (Cable Satellite Public Affairs Network), 18–19, 124, 136, 145, 228, 271.
Cuban Women for Human Rights, 124.
Culvahouse, Arthur B. (A.B.), 11, 53.
Cuomo, Mario, 24, 48, 57, 95.
Cutler, Lloyd, 32, 33, 102, 113, 126, 147, 166.

D'Amato, Alfonse, 16, 90, 192, 202, 242.
Dallas Morning News, 234, 236, 241.
D'Ermo, Phyllis, 107.
Danforth, John (Jack), 16, 90, 126–127, 192, 225, 242.
Darkness at Noon, 300.
Daschle, Thomas, 16, 90, 170, 242.
Dean, Rev. Kenneth, 159.
Deaver, Michael, 220.
DeConcini, Dennis, 16, 30, 35, 39, 49, 53, 58, 80, 81–82, 90, 95, 99, 100, 116–117, 120, 124, 125, 130, 139, 153–154, 154–156, 158, 162, 169, 171, 180, 190, 202, 231, 242, 266–267, 281–282.
DeConcini, Susan, 81.
Delaware, University of, 130.
Delgaudio, Eugene, 199.

del Junco, Tirso, 41.
Dellinger III, Walter, 21, 22, 147.
Democracy and Distrust, 280, 301.
Dennelly, Thomas, 14.
Denniston, Lyle, 269.
Denton, James, 77.
Denton, Jeremiah, 77.
Denver Post, 233.
Dershowitz, Alan, xv, 30.
Detroit Free Press, 238.
Detroit News, 37, 231.
Deukmejian, George, 30.
Diamon, Al, 151.
Dickstein, Shapiro & Morin (D.C. firm), 195.
District Lawyer, 128–129.
Dixon, Alan, 16, 90, 125, 169, 177, 178, 192, 202, 242.
Dobson, James (Jim), 124, 189.
Dodd, Christopher, 16, 90, 178, 242.
Dole, Robert, 11, 16, 26, 27, 37, 40, 46, 48, 58, 61, 90, 94, 108, 164–165, 179, 184, 191, 242.
Dolphin Group (We the People), 30.
Domenici, Pete, 16, 90, 242.
Donaldson, Sam, 171.
Dornan, Robert (Bob), 182, 184.
Dorsen, Norman, 70, 75.
Dostoevski, Feodor, 300.
Douglas, William O., xx, 248.
Dowd, Ann Reilly, 223, 243.
Dowd, Maureen, 165.
Dubbert, Carole, 96.
Duberstein, Ken, 169, 254.
Duffy, John, 146.
Dunn, James, 77–78, 165–166.
Dukakis, Michael, 165, 207–208, 214, 215, 222.
Duke University, 21, 76, 147.
du Pont, Pete, xvii, xix, 82, 135, 150–152, 184.
Durenberger, David, 16, 90, 125, 163, 242.

Dworkin, Ronald, 301.
Dyk, Timothy, 277–278.

Eagle Forum, 27.
Eagleton, Thomas F. (Tom), 159.
Eastland, Terry, 29, 76, 89, 213, 243, 253.
Eastwood, Clint, 253.
Editor & Publisher, 277.
Edwards, Harry, 256.
Edwards, Michael, 25, 84, 235.
Eisenach, Jeffrey (Jeff), 150.
Eisenhowever, Dwight David, 191.
Eldredge, Mary, 95.
Ellingwood, Herb, 208.
Ely, John Hart, 280, 301.
Epstein, Edward Jay, 274.
Escape of the Guilty, 60.
Evans, Daniel, 16, 39, 62, 90, 125, 169, 177, 192, 194, 202, 240, 242.
Evans, Rowland, 166, 295.
Exon, James, 16, 90, 125, 149, 169, 177, 178, 192, 242.

Fahrenkopf, Frank, 112.
Federal Criminal Investigators Association, 146.
The Federalist Papers, 300, 302.
Federalist Society, 15, 128.
Federation of Women Lawyers, 35, 60.
Fein, Bruce, 2, 56, 67, 137.
Feminist Men's Alliance, 196, 252.
Field, Ted, 227.
Fine, Ralph Adam, 60, 234.
Finn, Tom, 66.
Fischer, Aaron, 249.
Fish, Hamilton, xvii-xviii, xxi.
Fiss, Owen, 137.
Fitzwater, Marlin, 12, 36, 66, 83, 159, 160.
Fitzwater, Sidney, 67, 208, 249.
Flaherty, Peter, 133.
Focus on the Family, 124, 189.

Ford, Gerald, 30, 107, 114, 143, 209, 257.
Ford, Wendell, 16, 90, 125, 149, 169, 177, 178, 202, 242.
Fortas, Justice Abe, 6, 19, 119.
Fortune magazine, 223, 243.
Fowler, Wyche, 16, 58, 90, 125, 167, 178, 242.
Fox (television) network, 101, 193.
Frampton, Jr., George T., 160.
Frank, John, 81.
Franklin, Benjamin, 118.
Franklin, John Hope, 147.
Frankfurter, Justice Felix, 54, 56, 88.
Fraternal Order of Police (FOP), 61, 62, 65, 70, 125, 145, 231.
Free Congress Foundation, x, 1, 2, 4, 67, 96, 98, 120, 135, 167–168, 186, 214, (227–243, reference material), 285, 286, 287.
Free the Court! (c.f. United Republicans of Illinois), 50, 70, 124, 133.
Friends of the Earth, 148.
Fritts, Deborah, 77.
Fuesel, Robert R., 146.

Gannon, Paul, x.
Gardiner, Richard, 78.
Garment, Leonard, 195.
Garment, Suzanne, 195.
Garn, Jake, 16, 90, 242.
George III, King, 159.
George Mason University School of Law (VA), 86.
George Washington University, 149.
Georgetown Law Weekly, 237.
Georgetown University Law Center, 101–103, 107, 163.
Gephardt, Richard, 24, 63.
Gest, Ted, 272–273.
Gibbon, Edward, 221.

Gibson, Charles, 270.
Gingrich, Newt, 14, 190–191, 193.
Ginsburg, Douglas, xviii–xx, 203.
Ginsburg, Ruth Bader, 256.
Gipper, 9, 243.
Glasser, Ira, 70.
Glenn, John, 16, 90, 242.
God Save This Honorable Court, 282.
Goldberger, David, 153.
Goldman, Sheldon, 215.
Goldstein, Joseph, 152–153.
Goldwater, Barry, xi, 86, 174.
Gordon, James F., 83, 99, 111.
Gore, Jr., Albert (Al), 15, 16, 17, 24, 90, 95, 125, 169, 177, 179, 202, 242.
Graham, Robert (Bob), 16, 90, 125, 149, 169, 177, 178, 192, 194, 202, 242.
Graglia, Lino, 249.
Gramm, Phil, 17, 90, 175, 179, 242.
Grant, Cary, 111.
Grassley, Charles (Chuck), 17, 35, 90, 118–119, 175, 242.
Green, Charles, 167.
Greene, Linda, 197–199.
Greenhouse, Linda, 6, 262.
Greenpeace, 148.
Griffin, Stephen M., 243.
Grimm, Angela, 96.
Griscom, Tom, 254.
Gunther, Gerald, 280.

Hagelin, Rebecca, 27, 63, 123.
Haig, Alexander, 114.
Hall, Gus, 62.
Hall, Joan, 88.
Halperin, Morton, 250.
Harkin, Thomas (Tom), 17, 90, 182, 242.
Harlan, John Marhsall, 54, 113.
Harris, Leslie, 250.
Harris, Louis, 158.

Hart, Benjamin, xx.
Harvard Journal of Law and Public Policy, 86.
Harvard (Kennedy School of Government), 248.
Harvard University Law School, xv, 22, 30, 33, 142, 268.
Hatch, Orrin, xix, 4, 8, 9, 17, 35, 36, 87, 90, 100, 109, 110–111, 140, 143, 146, 170, 192, 198, 201, 225, 242, 282–283.
Hatfield, Mark, 17, 62, 90, 169, 177, 179, 202, 240, 242.
Hecht, Chic, 17, 90, 242.
Hedges, Michael, 232.
Hefley, James Carl, 78, 165–166, 234, 235, 238, 240.
Heflin, Howell, 8, 13, 16, 30, 35, 39, 53, 58, 78, 90, 115, 118, 119, 125, 130, 149, 169, 170, 177, 178, 188, 192, 202, 242, 247, 248.
Heinz, H. John, 17, 90, 125, 192, 242.
Helena (MT) Independent Record, 201.
Hell's Angels, xvi.
Helms, Jesse, 17, 33, 90, 242.
Heritage Foundation, xx, 2, 56, 69, 123, 124, 137, 217, 253.
Herrod, Kathy (c.f. Concerned Women for America), 155–156.
Heston, Charlton, 253.
Hills, Carla, 143.
Hirshkoff, Helen, 38.
Hispanic Economic Council, 41.
Hiss, Alger, 225.
Hodel, Donald P., 93, 236.
Hoffman, Paul, 38.
Hohenberg, John, 271, 275.
Hollings, Ernest, 16, 90, 125, 182, 202, 242.
Holmes, Oliver Wendell, 89, 100.
Holzer, Henry Mark, 174.

Hooks, Benjamin, 14, 23.
Horowitz, Michael, 249.
Hosenball, Mark, 232.
House, Toni, 146.
Houston Chronicle, 236.
Howard University, 198.
Hufstedler, Shirley, 152, 268.
Hughes, Charles Evans, 31.
Hughes, Johnny, 145–146.
Human Rights Campaign Fund, 84.
Hume, Brit, 102.
Humphrey, Gordon, 8, 17, 35, 36, 40, 41, 90, 117, 121, 156, 158, 175, 176, 192, 198, 202, 225, 242, 268, 284.
Humphrey, Hubert, 97.

Ignatieff, Michael, 269.
Indiana Law Journal, 300.
Indiana University Law School, 198.
Innis, Roy, 8, 162.
Inouye, Daniel, 17, 90, 182, 242.
Inter-American Bank, 41.
International Association of Chiefs of Police, 65, 66, 125, 146.
International Narcotics Enforcement Officers Association, 65, 125, 146.
Iowans for Life, 95.
Irish Whiskey, 204–205.

Jackson, Andrew, 190–191.
Jackson, Jesse, 149, 175, 188.
Jackson, Justice Robert, 56.
James, Kay, 123.
Jameson (c.f. Irish Whiskey), 204–205.
Jarmin, Gary, 175.
Jaworski, Leon, 229.
Jefferson, Mildred, 184.
Jimenez, Martha, 168.
Johnson, Douglas (Doug), 123, 164.
John, Justice William, 281.

Johnson, Lyndon, 6, 141, 224, 254–255.
Johnston, J. Bennett, 16, 90, 125, 149, 166, 202, 211, 242, 247.
Jones, Alex, 277.
Jones, Gordon, 123.
Jordan, Barbara, 140–141.
Joseph Story Society (c.f. Story, Joseph), 204–205.
Journal of Law & Politics, 243.
The Judges War, ix, 1, 5, 67–69, 72, 84, 190, 207, 209, 214, 227, 232, 236.
Judicial Notice, 4, 12, 22, 98, (227–243), 285–303 (Bork interview).
Judicial Selection Project (c.f. Alliance for Justice), 65, 249.

Kai, Lisa, 202.
Kamen, Al, 247, 261.
Kamenar, Paul D., 67, 101–103, 173, 236.
Kamisar, Yale, 7.
Kansas City Times, 127.
Karnes, David, 17, 90, 242.
Kassebaum, Nancy Landon, 16, 90, 96, 171, 242.
Kasten, Robert W. (Bob), 17, 90, 242.
Kaufman, Robert, 152.
Katzenbach, Nicholas, 141.
Keen, Lisa, 84.
Keene, Linda, 62.
Keiper, Claudia A., 231, 239.
Keisler, Peter, 2.
Kemp, Jack, 64, 95, 135, 182, 183, 189.
Kennedy, Justice Anthony, xiii–xviii, xx-xxi, 207, 246, 272–273.
Kennedy, Gregory, xvii.
Kennedy, Justin, xvii.
Kennedy, Kristin, xvii.
Kennedy, Mary (Davis), xvii.

Kennedy, Edward M. (Ted), 7, 13, 14, 17, 30, 33, 35, 36, 39, 43, 47, 54, 58, 68, 84, 85, 90, 101–103, 108, 109–10, 113, 128–130, 138, 151, 153, 175, 180, 188, 196, 199, 201, 203, 209, 210–211, 214, 215, 223, 231, 242, 251, 259, 263–266, 276, 281. ("Robert Bork's America", 14.)

Kennedy, John Fitzgerald, xii, 97, 130.

Kennedy, Robert Francis, 97, 130.

Kepley, Elizabeth, xvii-xviii, xxi, 28, 63, 74, 99, 152, 154–156, 164–165, 201.

Kerrison, Ray, 14.

Kerry, John, 17, 90, 242.

King, Coretta Scott, 24.

King, Karen, 30.

King, Martin Luther, 24, 34, 43, 130.

King, James Lawrence, 232.

Kinnock, Neil, 96–97, 98.

Kirkland & Ellis (Chicago law firm), 13.

Kirkland, Lane, 23.

Kleckner, Dean, 73.

Klein, Joe, 210–211, 243, 266.

Kling, William (Bill), 112–113, 150, 174, 233.

Knight-Ridder Newspapers, 257.

Knights of Columbus, 73, 74, 218.

Koestler, Arthur, 300.

Kopkind, Andrew, 227–228.

Koppel, Ted, 260.

Kornhauser, Anne, 88.

Korologos, Tom, 49, 94, 105–107, 123, 154, 178.

Kozinski, Alex, xiv, 67, 208, 249.

Kramer, Michael, 273.

Krauthammer, Charles, 214.

Kristol, Irving, 274.

Kropp, Arthur (Art), 15, 23, 26, 57, 86, 98, 227, 250, 251.

Ku Klux Klan, 71, 232.

Kuralt, Charles, 260.

Kurland, Philip, 21, 22, 56, 159.

Kwapis, John, 173.

Lacovara, Philip A., 161.

Lacayo, Richard, 256–257.

LaFontant, Jewell, 158–159.

LaHaye, Beverly, 27, 72, 155–156, 163.

LaJeunesse, Ray, 173.

Lane, John D., 88.

LaPierre, Wayne, 79–80.

Larkin, Paul J., 83.

Latin Liturgy Association, 5–6.

Lautenberg, Frank, 17, 90, 242.

Lawyers Committee for Civil Rights Under Law, 32, 88, 103.

Laxalt, Paul, 133.

Leadership Conference on Civil Rights (LCCR), 9, 10, 14, 15, 20, 22, 55, 80, 84, 105, 122–123, 211, 212, 249–250, 252.

Leadership Institute, 173.

Leahy, Patrick, 17, 35, 90, 99, 118, 121, 138, 163, 242.

Lear, Norman, 15, 29, 215, 223, 227, 250.

The Least Dangerous Branch, 301.

Legal Assistance Foundation (Chicago), 88.

Legal Times, xv, 88, 139, 213, (227–243), 250.

Lee, Rex, 26.

Leuchtenburg, William, 147.

Levi, Edward. 141.

Levick, Marsha, 3.

Levin, Carl, 17, 90, 242.

Levine, Jan, 168.

Levy, Paul, 168.

Lewis, Mary, 186.

Lewis & Rocca (Phoenix), 81.

Liberman, Lee, 86.
Lichter, Robert and Linda, 274.
Lieberman, Joseph, 223.
Lincoln, Abraham, xii, 106, 180, 253.
Lippman, Jr., Theo, 127.
Los Angeles Times, 93, 210, 235, 236, 275, 280.
Lucas, Rev. George, 164.
Lugar, Richard, 17, 90, 163, 242.

MacCrate, Robert, 88.
MacIntyre, Kevin, 107.
Madison, James, xv.
Maddoux, Marlin, (c.f. USA Radio), 179–182, 185, 209, 213.
Mahe, Eddie, 85.
Major City Chiefs Association, 125.
Manchester *Union Leader*, 45, 151.
Mangone, Joe, 64.
Manion, Daniel, xiv, 1, 22, 27, 38, 42, 68, 208, 233, 249, 254.
Manne, Neal, 80.
Marcus, Paul, 154.
Marine Corps, 13, 185–186.
Marshall, Burke, 141.
Marshall, Chief Justice John, xxi, 281.
Marshall, Justice Thurgood, 20, 64, 260.
Marshall, William, 99.
Marshner, Connaught (Connie), 2, 189.
Marttila & Kiley, 211, 250, 252.
Maryland Hispanic Chamber of Commerce, 41.
Maryland State Police, 145.
Maseng, Mari, 184.
Matsunaga, Spark, 17, 90, 242.
Mauro, Tony, xv.
McCain, John, 17, 90, 242.
McCarthy, John, 197.
McClellan, James, 30, 176.
McClure, James, 17, 79, 90, 202, 225, 242.

McConnell, Michael, 144.
McConnell, Mitch, 17, 90, 242.
McCorvey, Norma, 87.
McDonald, Michael (Mike), 295.
McDowell, Gary, 198.
McEntee, Gerald, 211.
McFadden, Monica, 94.
McLaughlin, John, 146.
McGeorge Law School, 273.
McGrory, Mary, 259.
McGuigan, Andrew Patrick, xi, 5, 42.
McGuigan, Bonnie F., xx, 196–197.
McGuigan, Bruce F., xx, 130, 196–197.
McGuigan, Erin Kathleen, xi, 5, 42.
McGuigan, Josef Bruce, xi, 5, 42.
McGuigan, Pamela, v,xi, 5, 32, 42, 67, 187.
McGuigan, Stefan Aleksandr, xi, 5, 42.
Media Elite, The, 274.
Media General, 127.
Media Monitor, 149–150.
Meeker, Suzanne E., 63.
Meese III, Edwin (Ed), 2, 9, 11, 28, 38, 40, 47, 53, 166, 208, 215–216, 220, 267.
Melcher, John, 17, 90, 169, 177, 192, 201, 202, 222, 242.
Mendez, Mike, 41.
Mental Health Law Project, 148.
Meserve, Robert, 152.
Metzenbaum, Howard, 17, 31, 36, 90, 99, 114, 122, 127, 138, 141, 153, 155, 167, 196, 215, 231, 242, 259, 261–262, 275.
Mexican-American Foundation, 124.
Mexican-American Legal Defense Fund, 88, 168.
Meyerson, Adam, 221.
Miami Herald, 167, 240.
Michelman, Kate, 10, 39, 123.

Michigan, University of, 7.
Mikva, Judge Abner, 6, 14, 256.
Milkulski, Barbara, 17, 90, 94, 242.
Milone, Michael, 37.
Mintz, Richard, 23, 84.
Mitchell, George, 17, 90, 125, 150, 169, 177, 182, 242.
Moesser, Alba, 41.
Monahan, Father David, 196–197.
Mondale, Walter, 44.
Moore, Cleatis, x.
Montgomery (AL) Advertiser, 252.
Moral Majority, 42, 123, 124, 173.
Moran, Terence, 139.
Moritz, Amy, 217, 219, 243.
Morton, Frederick L., 207, 243.
Moses, 253.
Moshenberg, Sammie, 85.
Moynihan, Daniel Patrick (Pat), 16, 17, 90, 240, 242.
Ms. magazine, 148, 239.
Murkowski, Frank, 17, 90, 192, 202, 242.
Myers, William, x, 235.

Nader, Ralph, 32, 56, 255.
The Nation, 227–228.
Nation Institute, 252.
National Abortion Rights Action League (NARAL), 10, 21, 23, 39, 84, 94, 100, 123, 124, 137, 168, 195, 250, 252.
National Association of Evangelicals, 27, 77.
National Association for the Advancement of Colored People (NAACP), 14, 20, 23–25, 48, 85, 124, 133, 137, 153, 213, 249. 250, 260.
National Association of Police Organizations, 125.
National Center for Hispanic Women, 41.
National Council of Jewish Women, 85.

National Conference of State Legislatures, 48.
National Conservative Political Action Committee (NCPAC), 30.
National District Attorneys Association, 65, 125.
National Education Association (NEA), 25, 84–85, 235, 250.
National Federation of Business and Profession Women's Clubs, 94.
National Forum Foundation, 77.
National Gay Task Force, 84.
National Hispanic Bar Association, 41.
National Institute for Women of Color, 94.
National Jewish Coalition, 124.
National Law Enforcement Council, xvii, 28, 49, 65, 123, 145, 164.
National Law Journal, 50, 233, 235.
National Lawyers Guild, 196.
National Legal Aid & Defender Association, 75, 88, 235.
National Organization for Women (NOW), 3, 23, 42, 80, 94, 124, 155, 173, 196, 213.
National Public Radio (NPR), 247.
National Press Club, 67, 82.
National Review, 215, 220, 234, 243.
National Rifle Association, 78–80, 253.
National Right to Life Committee, 28, 31, 80, 123, 150, 164, 184.
National Right to Work Committee, 23, 27, 28, 31, 80, 123, 150, 173, 195.
National Sheriffs Association, 65, 66, 125, 146.
National Troopers Coalition, 65, 125, 145.

National Women's Law Center, 63, 98.
National Women's Political Caucus, 22, 63, 70.
Natividad, Irene, 22.
NBC, 99, 112–113, 187, 260.
Neas, Ralph, 10, 14, 15, 22, 55, 80, 81, 84, 105, 112–113, 132–133, 212, 249, 252.
Nelson, Frederick D., 86.
Nelson, Lars Eric, 126.
New York Bar Association, 152.
New York Daily News, 78, 126.
New York magazine, 210, 214, 266.
New York Post, 14, 34, 231, 233.
New York Times, 6, 7, 31, 32, 47, 49, 84, 96, 98, 113, 114, 116, 126, 152, 165, 193, 210, (227–243, primarily the reporting of Stuart Taylor and Linda Greenhouse), 252, 262, 275, 277.
New York University, 268.
New Yorkers for Bork ad, 114.
Newsweek, 213, 229, 237.
Nickles, Don, 17, 90, 164, 242.
Nixon, Richard, 3, 13, 42, 86, 114, 126, 143, 224, 229–230, 257, 265, 282, 283.
Noble, Kenneth, 126.
Noonan, Peggy, 223.
Norquist, Grover, 173.
North, Oliver, 94, 217, 258.
North Carolina, University of, 147.
Notre Dame Law School, 2.
Novak, Robert, 166, 295.
Nunn, Sam, 16, 35, 89, 90, 92, 125, 149, 169, 177, 191, 202, 242.

Oakley, John, 273.
O'Brien, Tim, 245.
O'Chester, Shannon, 123, 173.
O'Connell, Jeffrey, 67.
O'Connor, Justice Sandra Day, 5, 12, 220, 248.

Ohio State University, 153.
Oklahoma State University, 18, 201.
Order of the Sons of Italy in America, 124.
O'Steen, Dave, 123, 164.
Ostrow, Ron, 275.

Packing the Courts, 211, 243, 249, 260.
Packwood, Robert (Bob), 17, 29, 39, 62, 70, 90, 125, 142, 242.
Pacifica Radio, 133, 168.
Padilla, Hernan, 41.
Parents of Murdered Children, 157.
Patrick, Robert M., 33.
Paul, St. 225.
PBS, 70, 271.
Peck, Gregory, 101, 106, 180, 253.
Peck, Jeffrey, 76.
Pell, Claiborne, 16, 90, 169, 177, 242.
Pendleton, Clarence, xvi.
Pennsylvania, University of, 156.
People for the American Way [*sic*], 4, 15, 23, 26, 29–30, 55, 57, 84, 85, 86, 98, 100, 101, 107, 124, 137, 149, 168, 174, 176, 196, 200, 208, 210, 211, 214, 215, 223, 227, 228, 230, 235, 249, 250, 251, 252, 253, 254, 255, 261, 267, 276, 277.
Perez, Carlos, 41.
Petersen, Henry E., 161.
Peterson, Dan, 67, 173.
Philadelphia Daily News, 268.
Philadelphia Inquirer, 228, 235, 236.
Phillips, Howard, (Howie), 29, 115, 182, 184, 195–196, 201.
Piser, Jenny, 168.
Pitofksy, Dean Robert, 101, 102, 163.
Planned Parenthood, 100, 137, 149, 153, 196, 252, 255, 261.

Podesta, Anthony (Tony), 4, 15, 211.
Policy Review, 217, 221, 243.
Popeo, Daniel J., 3, 5, 94, 236.
Porter, Kenneth, 249.
Portland (OR) Oregonian, 168.
Portland (ME) Press Herald, Evening Express and *Sunday Telegram,* 151.
The Possessed, 300.
Povich, Maury, 193.
Powell, Justice Lewis, x, xiv, xv, 1, 2, 3, 5, 7, 8, 9, 11, 15, 25, 28, 49, 54, 56, 62, 89, 108, 113, 137, 148, 207, 210, 215, 218, 296.
Powell III, Lewis, 1
Prager, Susan, 21.
Presidential Commission on Broadcasting to Cuba, 41.
Presidential Scholars Commission, 41.
Presser, Jackie, 147.
Pressler, Larry, 17, 90, 242.
Progressive Baptist Convention, 165.
Providence (RI) Journal-Bulletin, 62.
Proxmire, William, 16, 69, 90, 168–169, 177, 192, 202, 242.
Pryor, David, 16, 90, 149, 166, 242.
Public Citizen, 32, 56, 98, 136, 168, 255–256.
Public Policy Education Fund, 70.

Quayle, J. Danforth (Dan), xiv, 17, 90, 222, 242.
Queral, Luis, 41.

Raleigh (NC) News Observer, 25, 229.
Randolph, Raymond A., 34.
Range, Rebecca, 50, 124, 125, 186, 195.

Rasky, Larry, 98.
Raspberry, William, 126.
Rauch, Gerry, 225.
Rauschenberg, Robert, 144–145.
Reagan, Nancy, xix, 176, 186.
Reagan, Ronald Wilson, x, xiv, xviii, xix, xx, 1, 3, 4, 5, 8, 9, 10, 11, 12, 13, 25, 28, 30, 31, 34, 40, 43, 44, 49, 59, 60, 61, 64, 65, 76, 77, 88, 95, 105–107, 108, 131, 138, 141, 142, 146, 152, 163–164, 166, 169–170, 171, 172, 174, 175, 176, 178, 182, 183, 184, 185–187, 190, 192, 193, 197, 200, 202, 203, 205, 208, 219, 220, 224, 228, 240, 248, 254, 265, 267, 272, 299.
Rees, III, Grover Joseph, 243.
Regan, Donald, 254.
Rehnquist, Chief Justice William H., xiv, xxi, 1, 5, 6, 19, 20, 22, 25, 27, 35, 38, 39, 68, 100, 208, 249.
Reid, Harry, 16, 17, 95, 169, 177, 191, 192, 202, 242.
Renaissance Women, 124.
Republican National Committee, 112, 175, 219.
Revere, Paul, 277.
Reynolds, William Bradford (Brad), 2, 80, 82, 208.
Richards, A.J., 268.
Richardson, Elliott, 160, 229–230, 247.
Richardson, John, 2.
Richmond Times-Dispatch, 7, 228.
Riegle, Donald (Don), 17, 90, 242.
Riggs, Betty, 122.
Riker, Walt, 58.
The Road to Serfdom, 300.
Robb, Roger, 83.
Roberts, Bill, 64.
Roberts, Clayton, 23, 27.

Roberts, Kimberly, 173.
Roberts, Steven, 31.
Robertson, Pat, 47, 95, 157–158, 184.
Rockefeller, IV, John D., 17, 90, 125, 133, 242.
Rogers, Estelle, 35.
Rogers, William, 141.
Roosevelt, Franklin, 264, 301.
Roth, William, 17, 90, 192, 242.
Rothman, Stanley, 274.
Rowan, Carl, 86.
Rubens, Peter Paul, 76.
Rubenstein, Leonard, 148.
Ruckelshaus, William D., 229–230, 247.
Rudman, Warren, 17, 45, 90, 150, 164–165, 192, 242.
Russakopf, Dale, 257.
Ruth, Henry S., 160.
Rutkus, Denis Steven, 40.
Rymer, Harold, x.

Sabato, Larry, 120, 153.
Safire, William, 275.
St. John's Law School, 48.
Saint Petersburg (FL) Times, 25, 229.
San Diego Union, 62.
San Francisco Chronicle, 235.
San Gabriel (CA) Valley Tribune, 37, 231.
Sanford, Terry, 16, 58, 90, 166, 167, 202, 242.
Sarbannes, Paul, 17, 90, 94, 182, 242.
Sasser, Jim, 16, 17, 125, 169, 177, 178, 242.
Sasso, John, 165.
Saxbe, William, 141.
Scalia, Justice Antonin, xv, xxi, 5, 12, 15, 20, 157, 220, 262, 281.
Schaber, Gordon, 273.
Schlafly, Phyllis, 27.

Schultz, William B., 98, 136.
Schneiders, Greg, 5.
Schroeder, Christopher, 76.
Schumpeter, J.A., 252, 286.
Schwartz, Herman, xv, 7, 65, 211, 212, 213, 243, 249, 260.
Seattle Times and Post-Intelligencer, 62.
Service Employees Union, 249.
Sessions, III, Jefferson B, 249.
Shaddix, Doug, 184.
Shaw, Russell, 218.
Shakespeare, William, 76.
Sheehan, Daniel, 37, 232.
Shelby, Richard, 16, 90, 125, 167, 169, 177, 178, 192, 202, 242.
Shestack, Jerome J., 88.
Shortley, Maiselle, 195.
Shultz, George, 197.
Siegan, Bernard, 69, 246, 283–284.
Sierra Club Legal Defense Fund, 148.
Simmons, Althea, 24, 85.
Simon, Paul, 7, 17, 33, 36, 46, 70, 90, 96, 121, 162, 242.
Simpson, Alan, 17, 35, 46, 90, 111, 115–116, 131, 140, 161, 178, 192, 225, 242, 284.
Singlaub, John, 232.
Smeal, Eleanor, 9, 23, 228.
Smith, Chesterfield, 152.
Smith, George, 202.
Smith, Peter, 41.
Smith, William French, 141, 209, 232.
Society of Former Special Agents of the FBI, 125.
The Sooner Catholic, 196.
Sophie's Choice, 144.
Southern Baptist Convention, Public Affairs Committee, 66, 67, 74, 77–78, 139, 165–166.
Sowell, Thomas, 152, 252.
Sparks, John, 70.

Specter, Arlen, 16, 35, 39, 58, 70,
71, 80–81, 82, 90, 100, 112,
118, 121, 122, 124, 125, 130,
131, 138, 152, 155, 156–157,
163, 166, 193, 198, 236, 242,
263.
Specter, Joan, 156.
Stafford, Robert, 17, 90, 95, 96,
125, 150, 169, 177, 178, 192,
202, 242.
Stanford University, 197, 251, 268,
280.
Stanley, Scott, ("the editor of
Conservative Digest") 225,
236.
States News Service, 62.
Stennis, John C., 16, 90, 125, 169,
177, 192, 202, 242.
Stern, Carl, 260.
Stern, Jane, 25.
Stern, Phillip, 249.
Stevens, Justice John Paul, 49–50,
102, 113, 174, 248, 281.
Stevens, Ted, 17, 90, 182, 242.
Stewart, Justice Potter, 113.
Stokes, Dewey, 145–146, 231.
Stone, Geoffrey, 34.
Story, Justice Joseph (c.f. The
Joseph Story Society), 302.
Stratton, Hal, 115.
Strauss, Peter, 240.
Strickland, Phil, 139.
Stuart, John, x.
Stuart, Reginald, 268–269.
Styron, William, 144–145.
Sunny Von Bulow National Victim
Advocacy Center (c.f. Frank
Carrington), 137, 146.
Sunstein, Cass, 159.
Supreme Court Watch, 208.
Swartz, Arlene, 39.
Symms, Steve, 17, 90, 242.
Syracuse University Law School,
120, 130.
Syren, Les, 2.

Tate, Doris, 157.
Tate, Sharon, 157.
Taylor, Stuart, 275.
Taylor, William, 249.
Teamsters, 147, 239.
Texas Christian Life Commission,
139.
Thompson, James (Jim), 65, 147.
Thornburgh, Richard, 158.
Thurmond, Strom, 5, 6, 11, 17, 35,
68, 91, 96, 110, 120, 140, 166,
192, 242.
Tille, David, 150–151.
Time magazine, 28, 115, 228, 230,
234, 247, 256–257.
Tolchin, Martin, 275.
Toqueville, Alexis de, 249, 291.
Totenberg, Nina, 247.
Tower, John, 224.
Tribe, Laurence, x, xv, 22, 142–
143, 209, 212, 219, 238, 243,
268, 279–284, 305–306 ("Larry
Tribe's America").
Trible, Paul, 17, 91, 242.
Troutt, Jeffery D., xi, 4, 67, 111,
120, 167, 242.
Tuck, John, 161.
Tully, Paul, 165.
Tuttle, Holmes, 30.
Twain, Mark, 278.
Tyler Jr., Harold R., 87, 141–142,
192.

United Auto Workers, 64, 234, 249.
United Church of Christ, 58, 67.
United Food and Commercial
Workers, 249.
United Methodist Church, 67.
United Press International (UPI),
124, 233.
United Republican Fund of Illinois
(c.f. Free the Court!). 91
University of California at Davis,
273.

University of California at Los
Angeles (UCLA), 21.
U.S. News & World Report, 272–
273.
USA Radio (c.f. Marlin Madoux),
167.
USA Today, xv, 76, 168, 173, 182,
227–243 (primarily the reporting of Tony Mauro).

Vaughan, Jerry, 66, 146.
Venable, Baetjer, Howard & Civi-
letti, 21.
Verveer, Melanne, 55.
Victims Assistance Legal Organiza-
tion, (VALOR,c.f. Frank Car-
rington), 125.
Viguerie, Richard, 93, 149, 175,
187–188, 195.
Ville Platte (LA) Gazette, 179, 241.
Virginia, University of, 153.
Volz, Joseph, 126.

Wade, Lawrence, 34.
Wald, Patricia, 256.
Waldron, Peter, 64.
Walker, Robert, 6, 157.
Wall Street Journal, 57, 71, 137,
138, 168, 169, 224, (227–243),
263.
Wallace, George, 43.
Wallace, Judge J. Clifford, 4, 8, 9.
Wallop, Malcolm, 17, 91, 222, 242.
Walsh, Edward, 261.
Walters, Barbara, 270.
Warden, Dick, 64.
Warner, John, 17, 91, 192, 202, 203,
204–205, 242.
Warren, Chief Justice Earl, 3.
Washington Blade, 84, 235.
Washington Council of Lawyers,
46.
Washington Journalism Review,
277.

Washington Inquirer, 232, 234.
Washington Legal Foundation, 4,
94, 102, 173, 295.
Washington Post, 21, 35, 45, 57, 59,
68, 105, 114, 149, 150, 172, 194,
197, 214, 227–243, (the report-
ing of Al Kamen, Ruth Marcus
and others), 247, 248, 252, 257,
259–262, 267, 269, 270, 271–
272, 277.
Washington Times, 43, 112, 168,
227–243 (primarily the report-
ing of Gene Grabowski).
WBBM radio (Chicago), 70.
WBEZ radio (Chicago), 70.
Webber, Mildred, 124.
We the People (c.f. Dolphin
Group), 30, 64, 106, 107, 182.
Weddington, Sarah, 87.
Weicker, Lowell, 16, 39, 90, 125,
149, 169, 171, 202, 223, 242.
Wellington, Harry, 301.
Wells, Melissa, 9.
West, Jade, 198.
West, Mat, 89.
Weyrich, Dawn M. (co-author), x,
307.
Weyrich, Paul, xi,xix, 1, 2, 4, 6, 41–
42, 45, 69, 79, 80, 89, 168–169,
199–200, 202, 203, 233.
WFYR radio (Chicago), 70.
White, Justice Byron, 5, 113, 146.
Wilkinson, J. Harvie, 208.
Will, George, 223, 257.
Williams, Sam, 88.
Williams, Scott, 30.
Wilmer, Cutler & Pickering, 32.
Wilson, Pete, 17, 62, 91, 125, 242.
Wilson, William, 30.
Wilson, Woodrow, xii.
Wirth, Timothy, 17, 90, 242.
Witness, 300.
WLS radio (Chicago), 70.
WMAL-AM radio (Washington,
D.C.), 173.

WNTR radio (Silver Spring, MD), 173.
Women for Bork, 133, 180, 182.
Women's Legal Defense and Education Fund, 20, 249.
Woodward, Robert (Bob), 275.
Woodward, Joanne, 250.
WPOR AM-FM radio (Portland, ME), 151.

WRQX-FM (Silver Spring, MD), 173.
Yale Law School, 13, 37, 46, 126, 137–138, 141, 153, 300.
Yard, Molly, 42, 80, 233.
Young, Andrew, 140.
Zaelke, Durwood, 148.
Zaccarro family, 199.